MAGA-TSUKI vol. 3

HOSHINO TAGUCHI

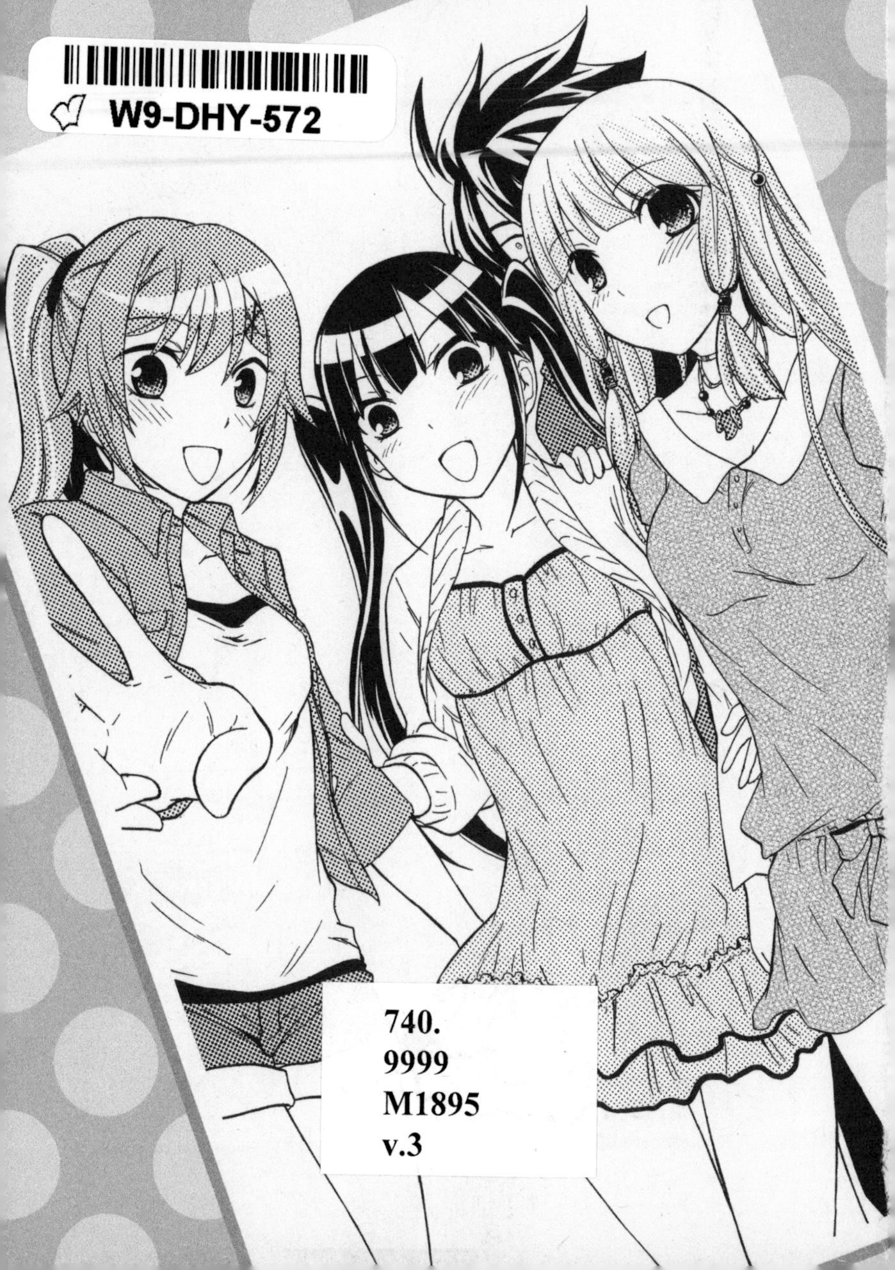

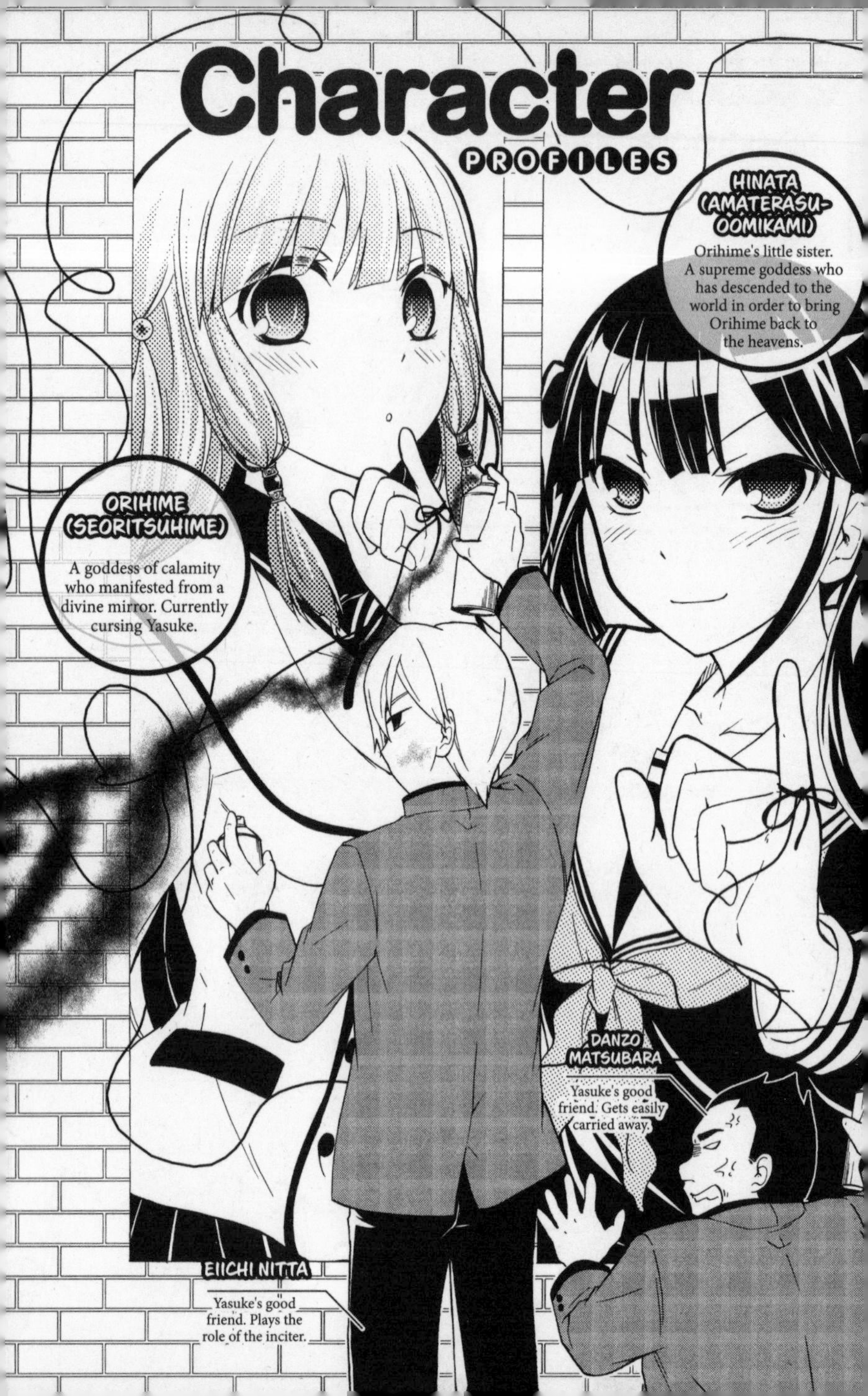
Character
PROFILES
HINATA (AMATERASU-OOMIKAMI)
Orihime's little sister. A supreme goddess who has descended to the world in order to bring Orihime back to the heavens.
ORIHIME (SEORITSUHIME)
A goddess of calamity who manifested from a divine mirror. Currently cursing Yasuke.
DANZO MATSUBARA
Yasuke's good friend. Gets easily carried away.
EIICHI NITTA
Yasuke's good friend. Plays the role of the inciter.

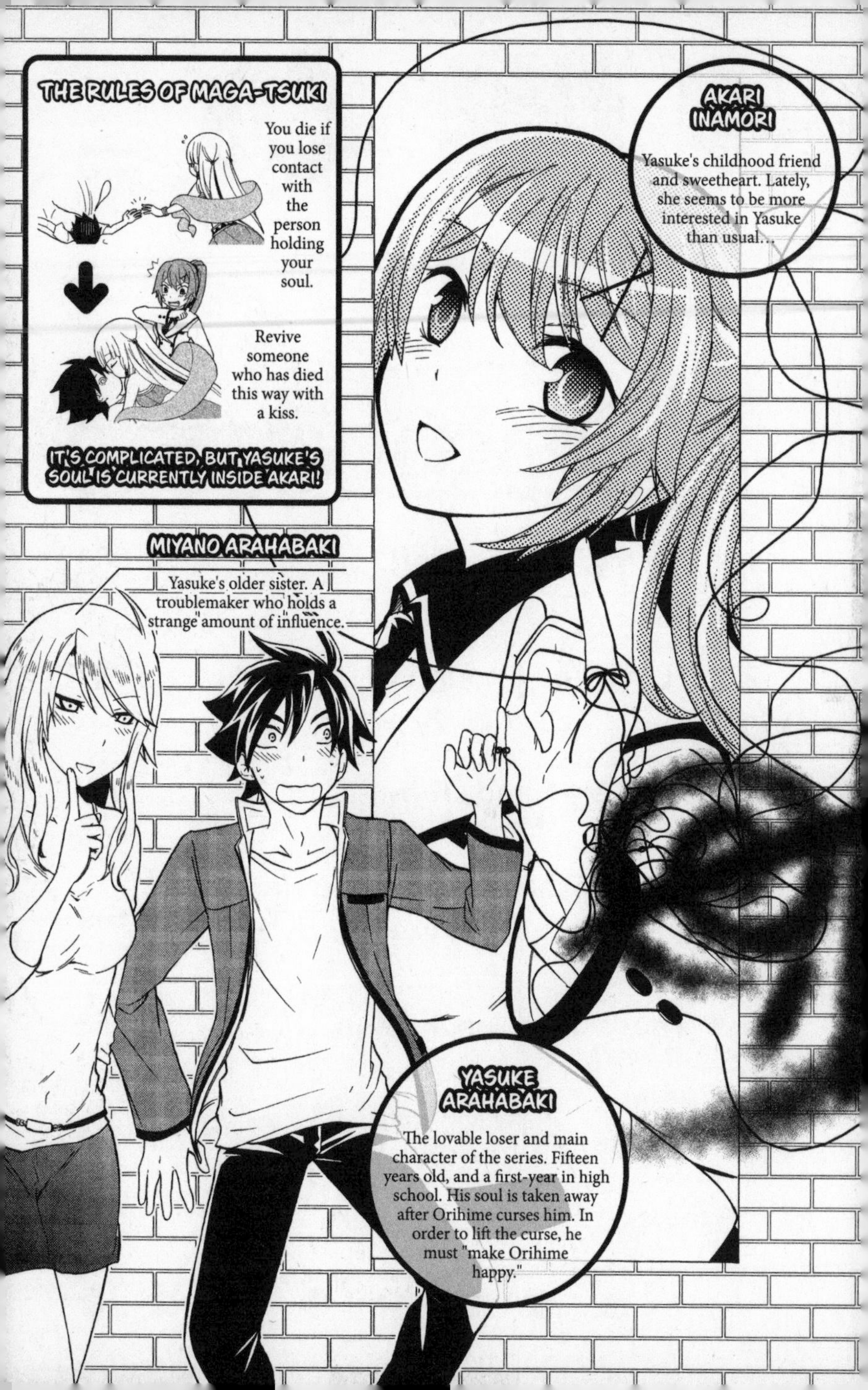

AKARI INAMORI
Yasuke's childhood friend and sweetheart. Lately, she seems to be more interested in Yasuke than usual...
THE RULES OF MAGA-TSUKI
You die if you lose contact with the person holding your soul.
Revive someone who has died this way with a kiss.
IT'S COMPLICATED, BUT YASUKE'S SOUL IS CURRENTLY INSIDE AKARI!
MIYANO ARAHABAKI
Yasuke's older sister. A troublemaker who holds a strange amount of influence.
YASUKE ARAHABAKI
The lovable loser and main character of the series. Fifteen years old, and a first-year in high school. His soul is taken away after Orihime curses him. In order to lift the curse, he must "make Orihime happy."

TEE-HEE!
うふん

MAGA-TSUKI

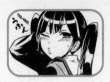

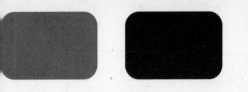

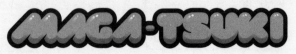

CONTENTS

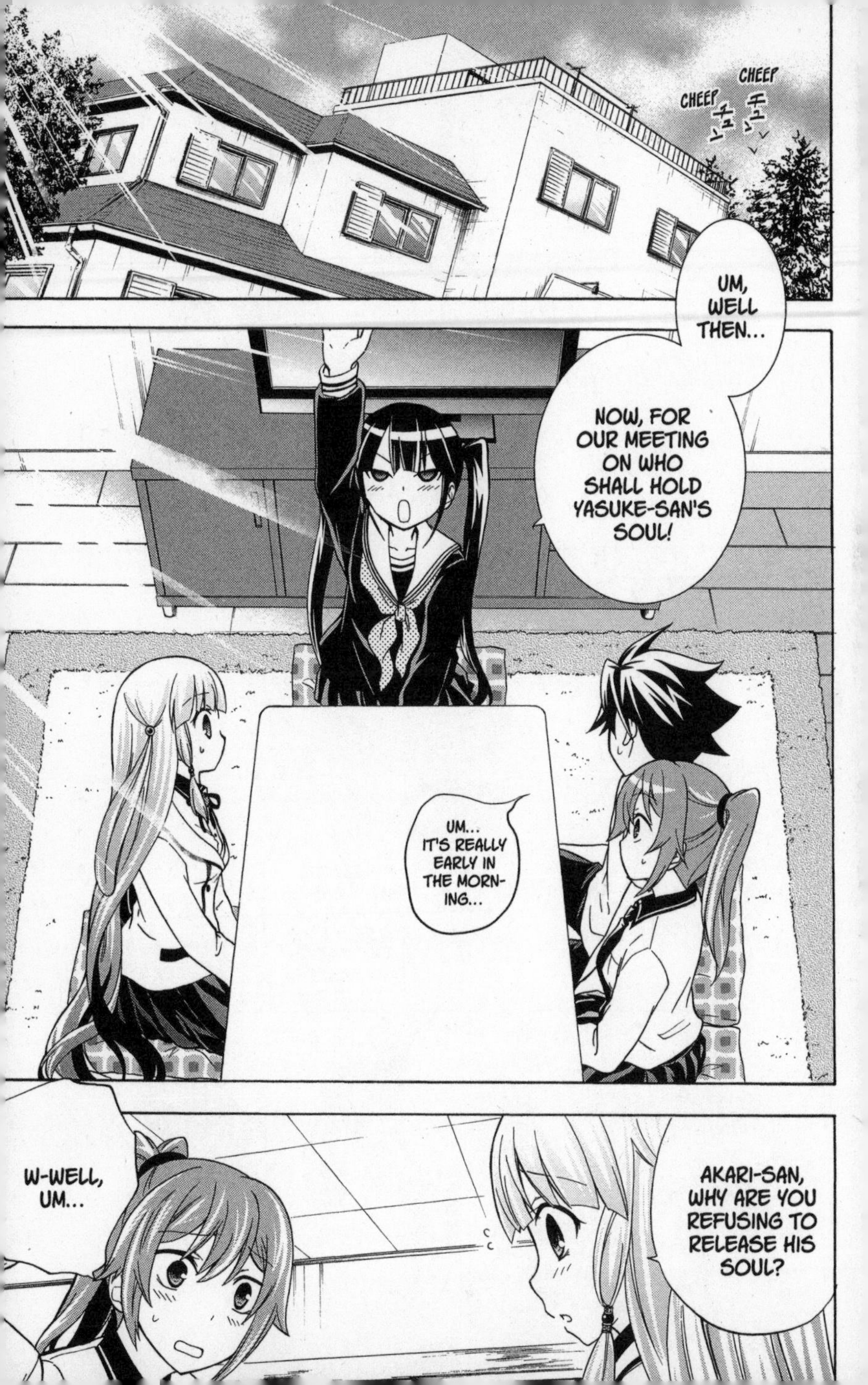
CHEEP
CHEEP
UM, WELL THEN...
NOW, FOR OUR MEETING ON WHO SHALL HOLD YASUKE-SAN'S SOUL!
UM... IT'S REALLY EARLY IN THE MORN-ING...
AKARI-SAN, WHY ARE YOU REFUSING TO RELEASE HIS SOUL?
W-WELL, UM...

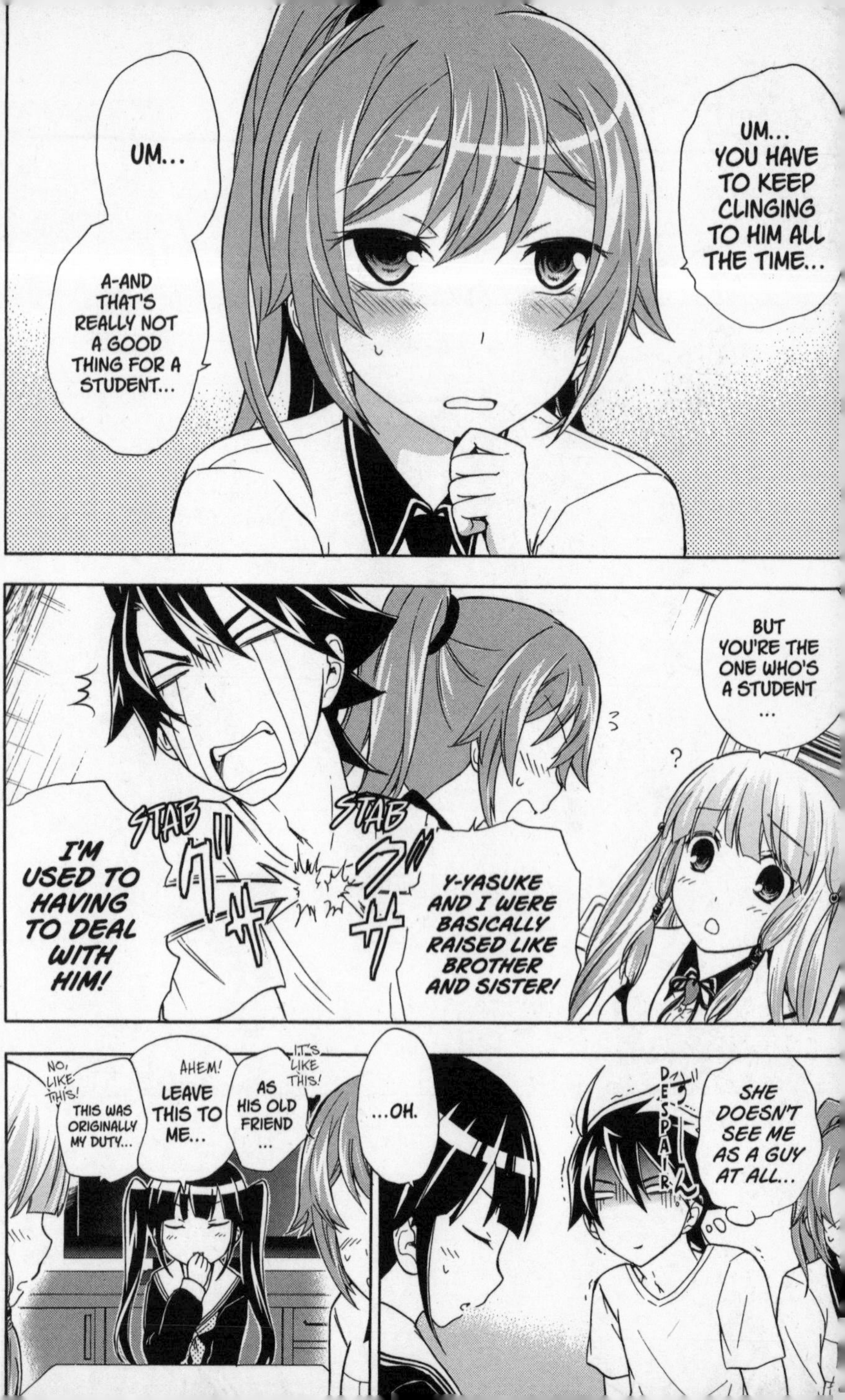
UM... YOU HAVE TO KEEP CLINGING TO HIM ALL THE TIME...
UM...
A-AND THAT'S REALLY NOT A GOOD THING FOR A STUDENT...
BUT YOU'RE THE ONE WHO'S A STUDENT ...
Y-YASUKE AND I WERE BASICALLY RAISED LIKE BROTHER AND SISTER!
STAB
STAB
I'M USED TO HAVING TO DEAL WITH HIM!
SHE DOESN'T SEE ME AS A GUY AT ALL...
DESPAIR
...OH.
IT'S LIKE THIS!
AS HIS OLD FRIEND ...
AHEM!
LEAVE THIS TO ME...
NO, LIKE THIS!
THIS WAS ORIGINALLY MY DUTY...

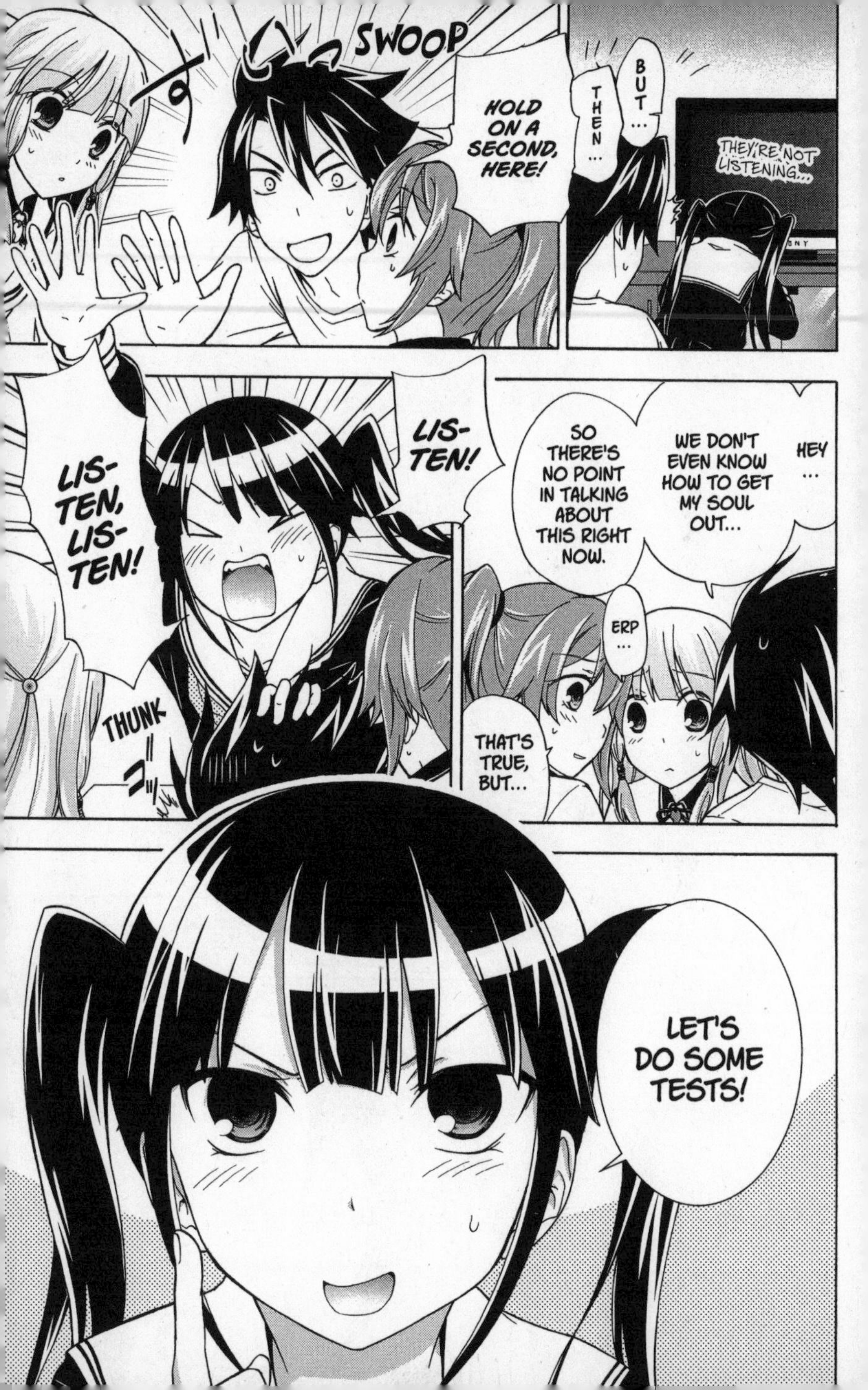

BUT...
THEN...
THEY'RE NOT LISTENING...
SWOOP
HOLD ON A SECOND, HERE!
HEY...
WE DON'T EVEN KNOW HOW TO GET MY SOUL OUT...
SO THERE'S NO POINT IN TALKING ABOUT THIS RIGHT NOW.
ERP...
THAT'S TRUE, BUT...
LIS-TEN!
LIS-TEN, LIS-TEN!
THUNK
LET'S DO SOME TESTS!

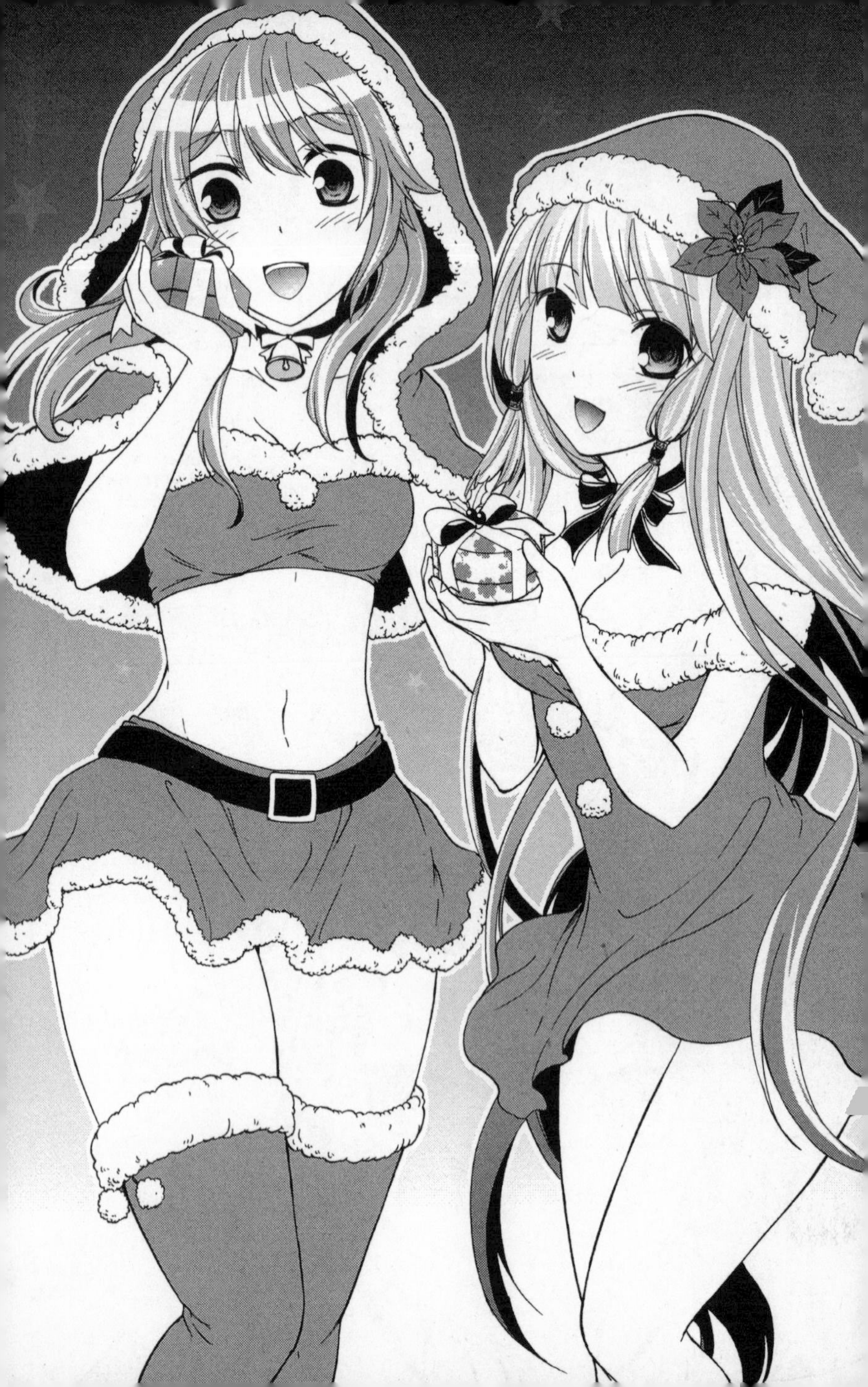

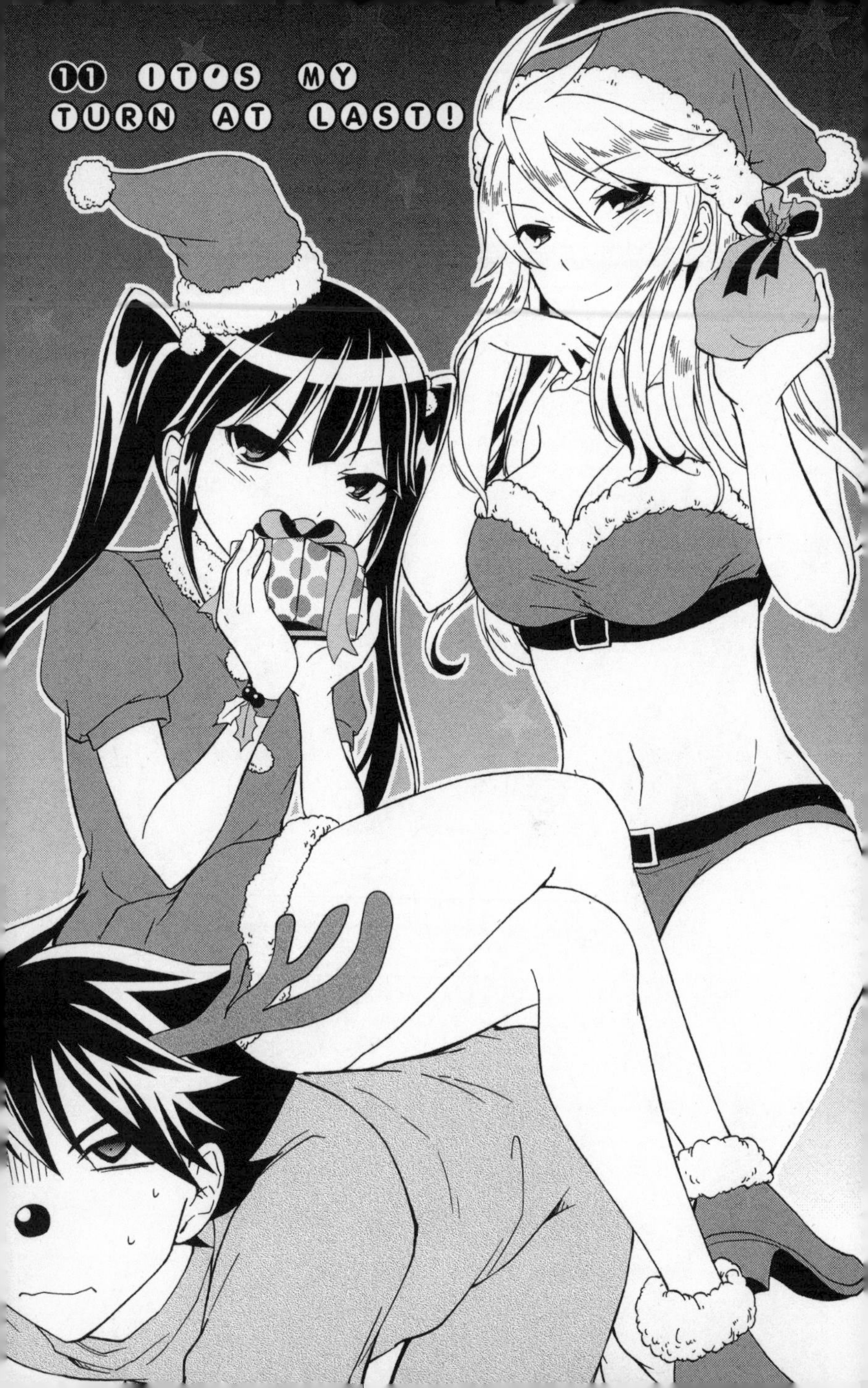
11 IT'S MY TURN AT LAST!

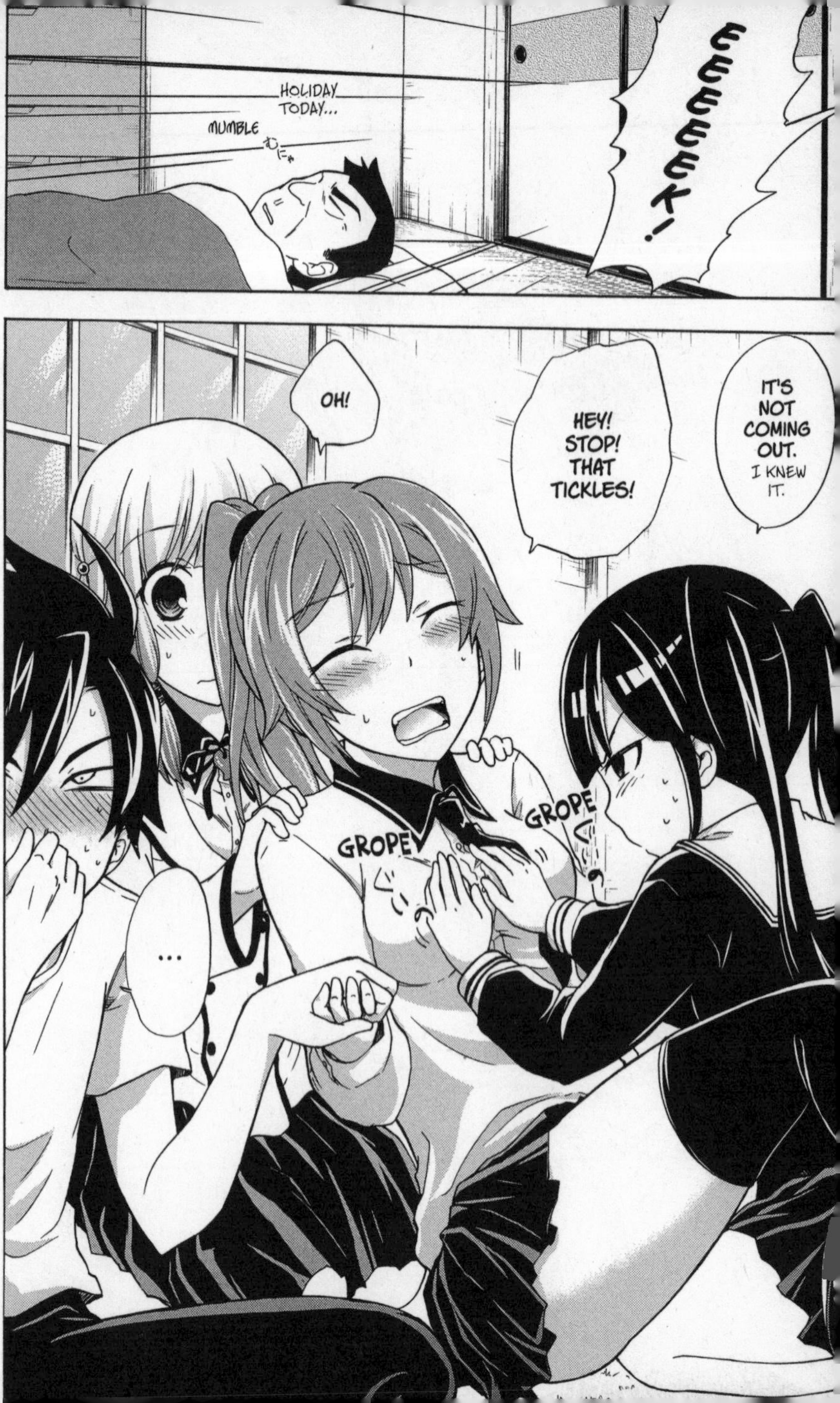
EEEEEEK!
HOLIDAY TODAY...
MUMBLE
むにゃ
IT'S NOT COMING OUT.
I KNEW IT.
HEY! STOP! THAT TICKLES!
OH!
GROPE
GROPE
...

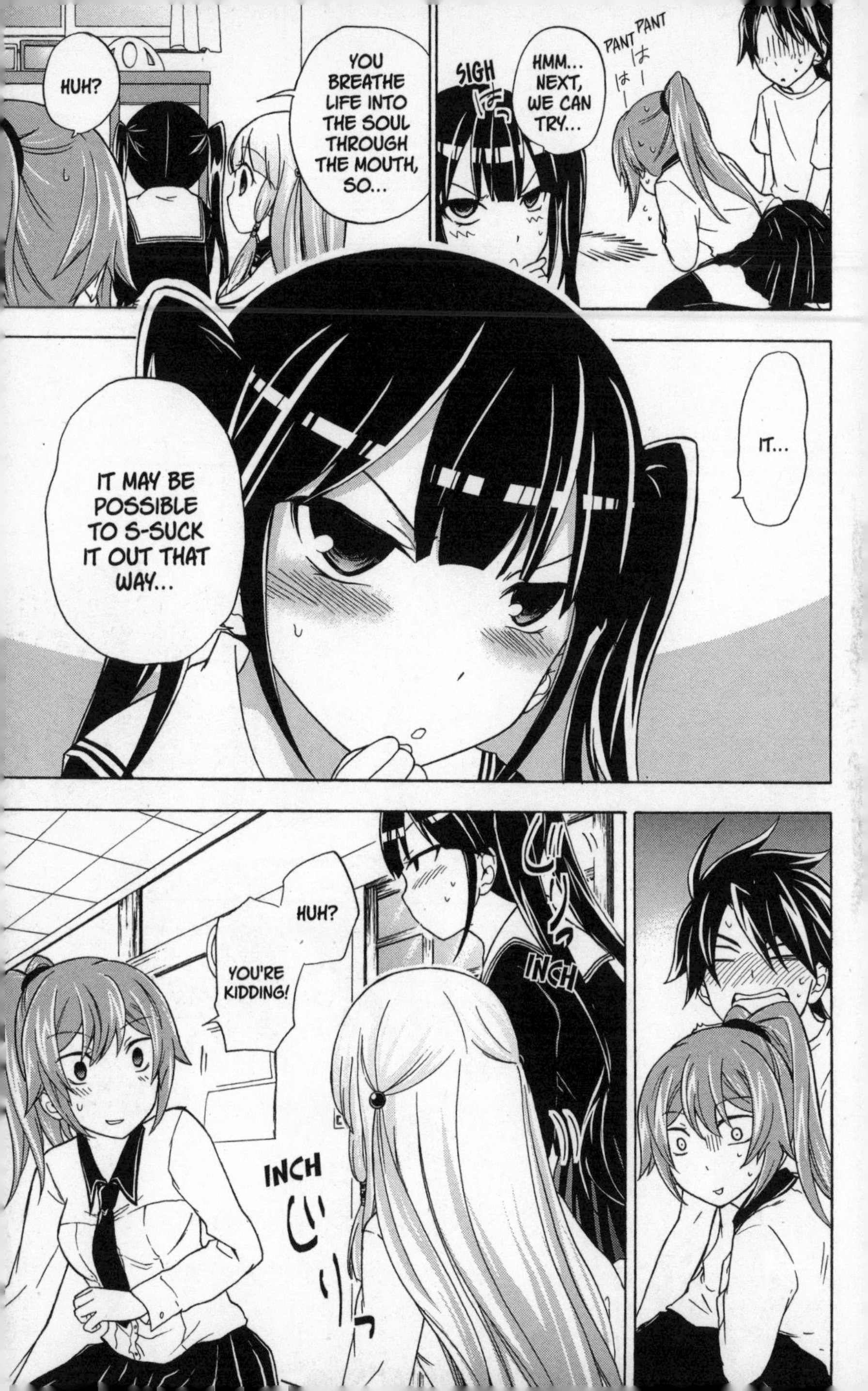
PANT PANT
HMM... NEXT, WE CAN TRY...
SIGH
YOU BREATHE LIFE INTO THE SOUL THROUGH THE MOUTH, SO...
HUH?
IT...
IT MAY BE POSSIBLE TO S-SUCK IT OUT THAT WAY...
INCH
HUH?
YOU'RE KIDDING!
INCH

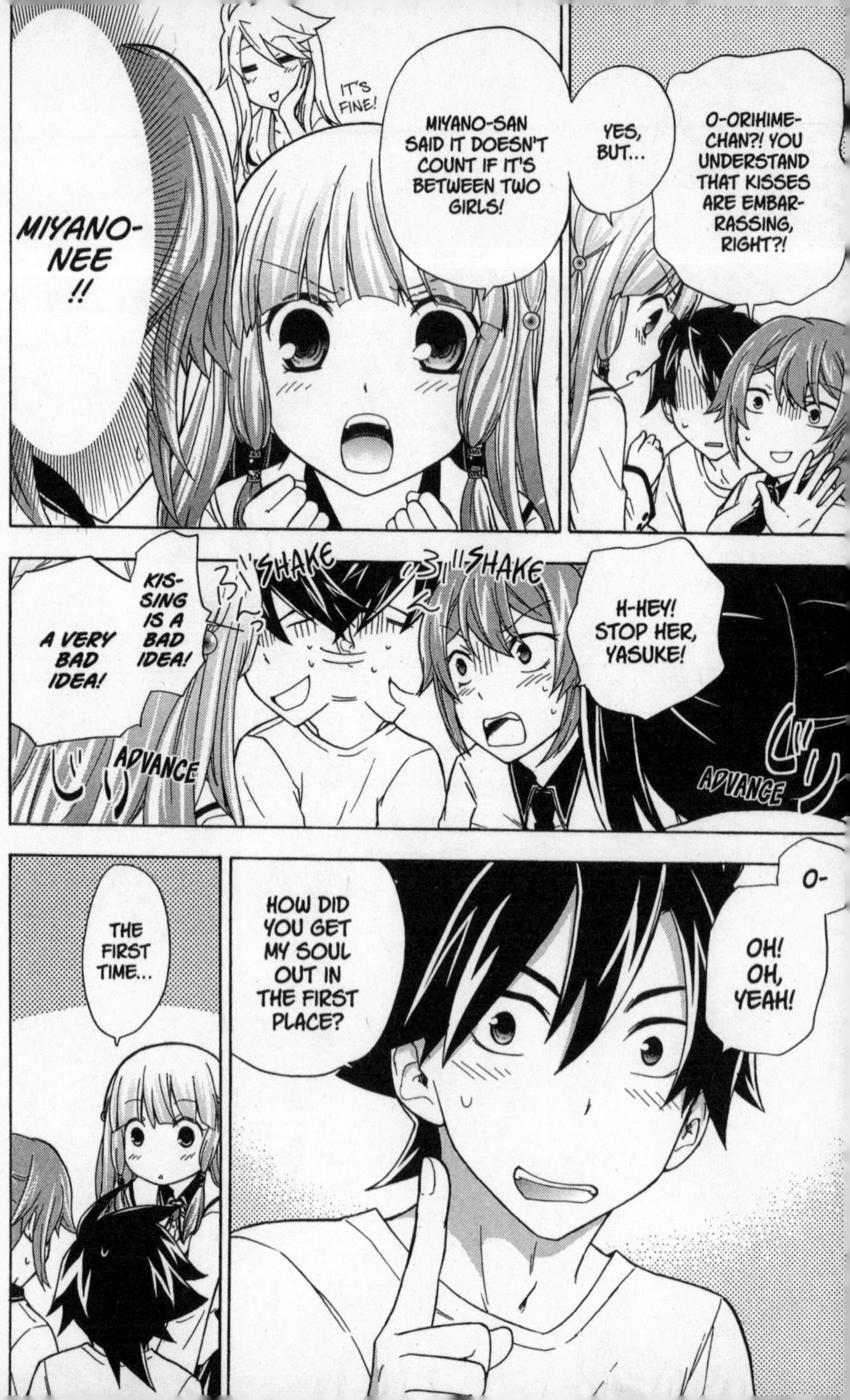
O-ORIHIME-CHAN?! YOU UNDERSTAND THAT KISSES ARE EMBAR-RASSING, RIGHT?!
YES, BUT...
MIYANO-SAN SAID IT DOESN'T COUNT IF IT'S BETWEEN TWO GIRLS!
IT'S FINE!
MIYANO-NEE!!
H-HEY! STOP HER, YASUKE!
ADVANCE
SHAKE
SHAKE
KIS-SING IS A BAD IDEA!
A VERY BAD IDEA!
ADVANCE
O-
OH! OH, YEAH!
HOW DID YOU GET MY SOUL OUT IN THE FIRST PLACE?
THE FIRST TIME...

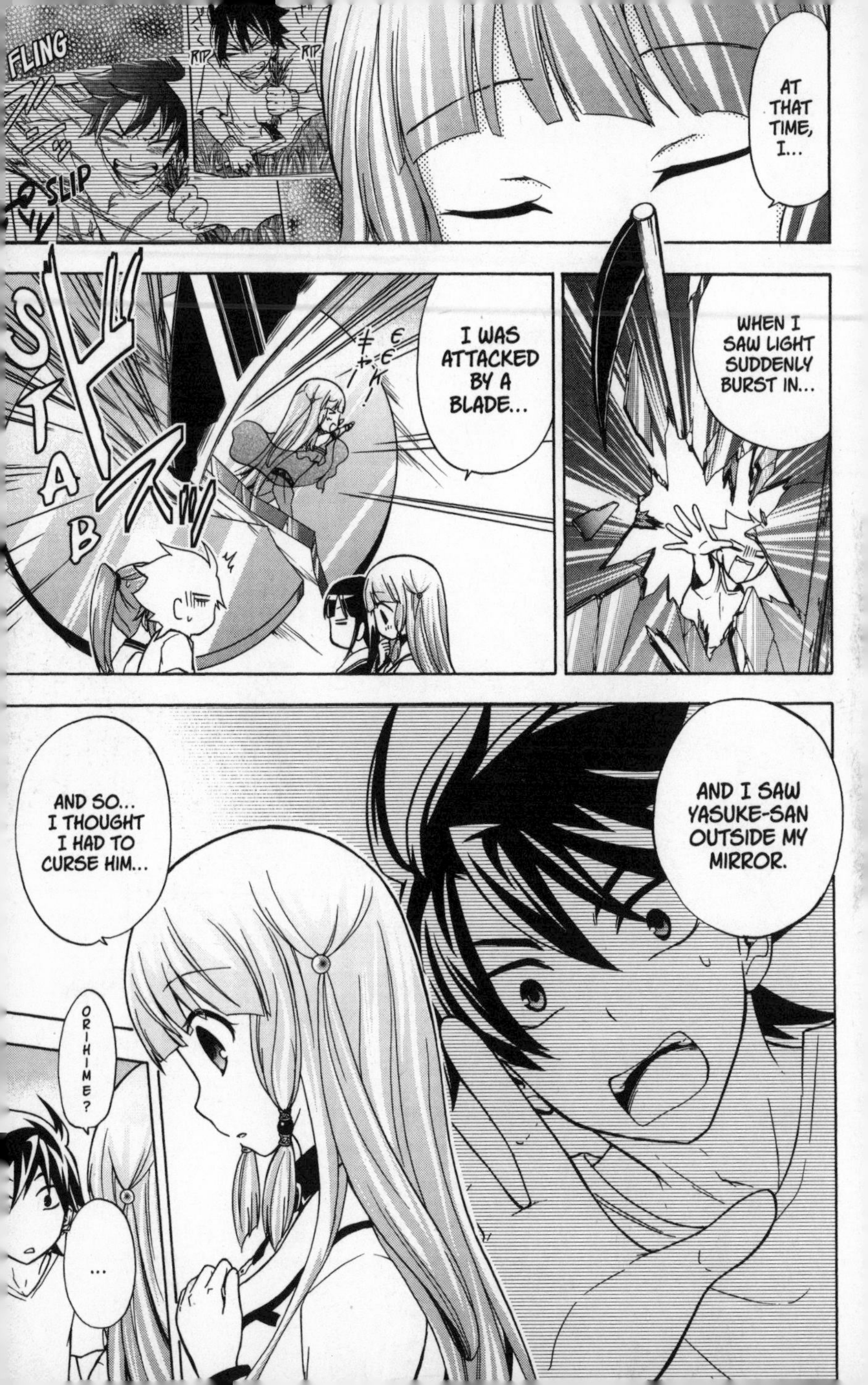
AT THAT TIME, I...
FLING
RIP
RIP
SLIP
WHEN I SAW LIGHT SUDDENLY BURST IN...
I WAS ATTACKED BY A BLADE...
EEK
STAB
AND I SAW YASUKE-SAN OUTSIDE MY MIRROR.
AND SO... I THOUGHT I HAD TO CURSE HIM...
ORIHIME?
...

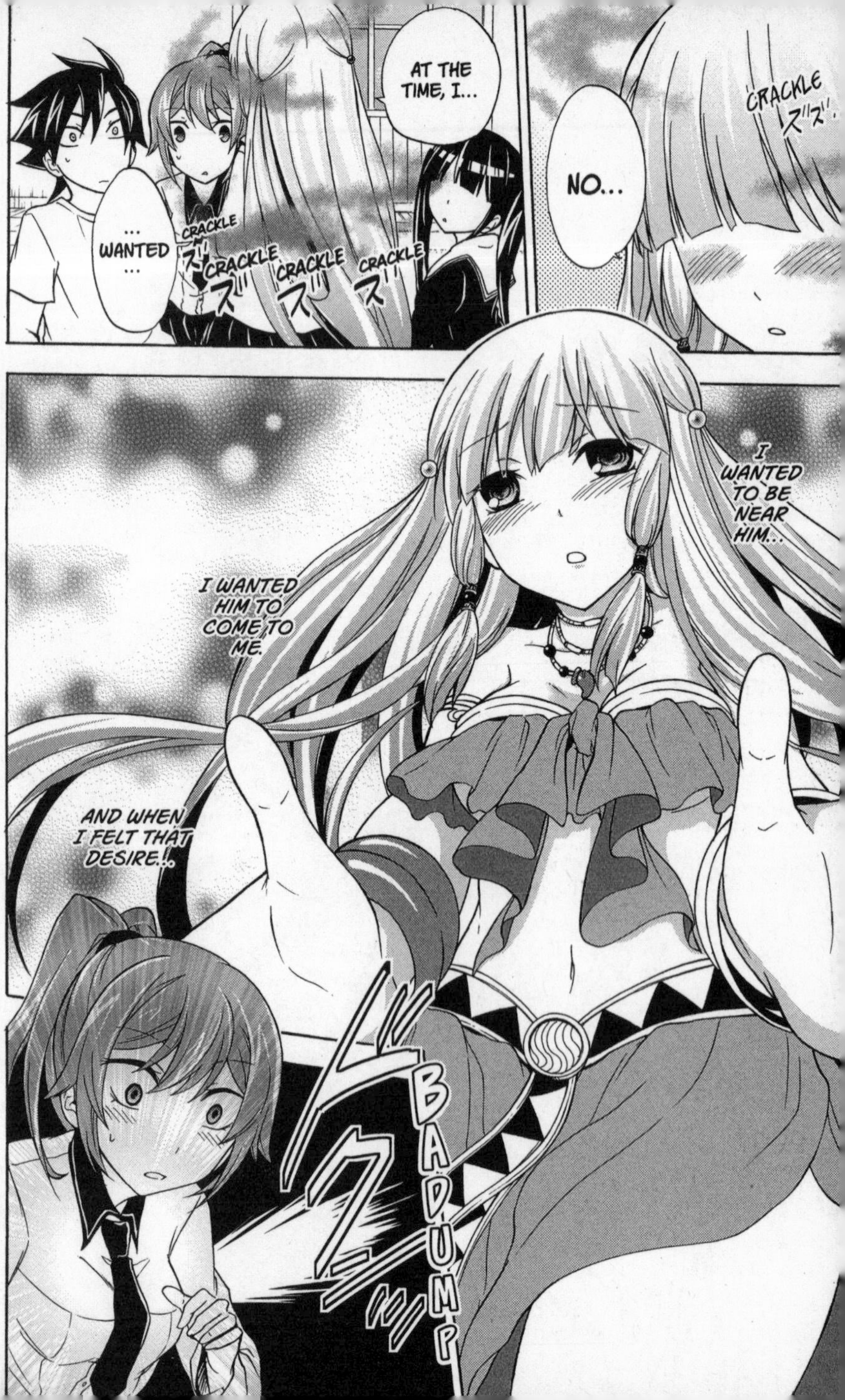
CRACKLE ズズ
NO...
AT THE TIME, I...
... WANTED ...
CRACKLE ズ
CRACKLE ズ
CRACKLE ズ
CRACKLE ズ
I WANTED TO BE NEAR HIM...
I WANTED HIM TO COME TO ME.
AND WHEN I FELT THAT DESIRE...
BADUMP

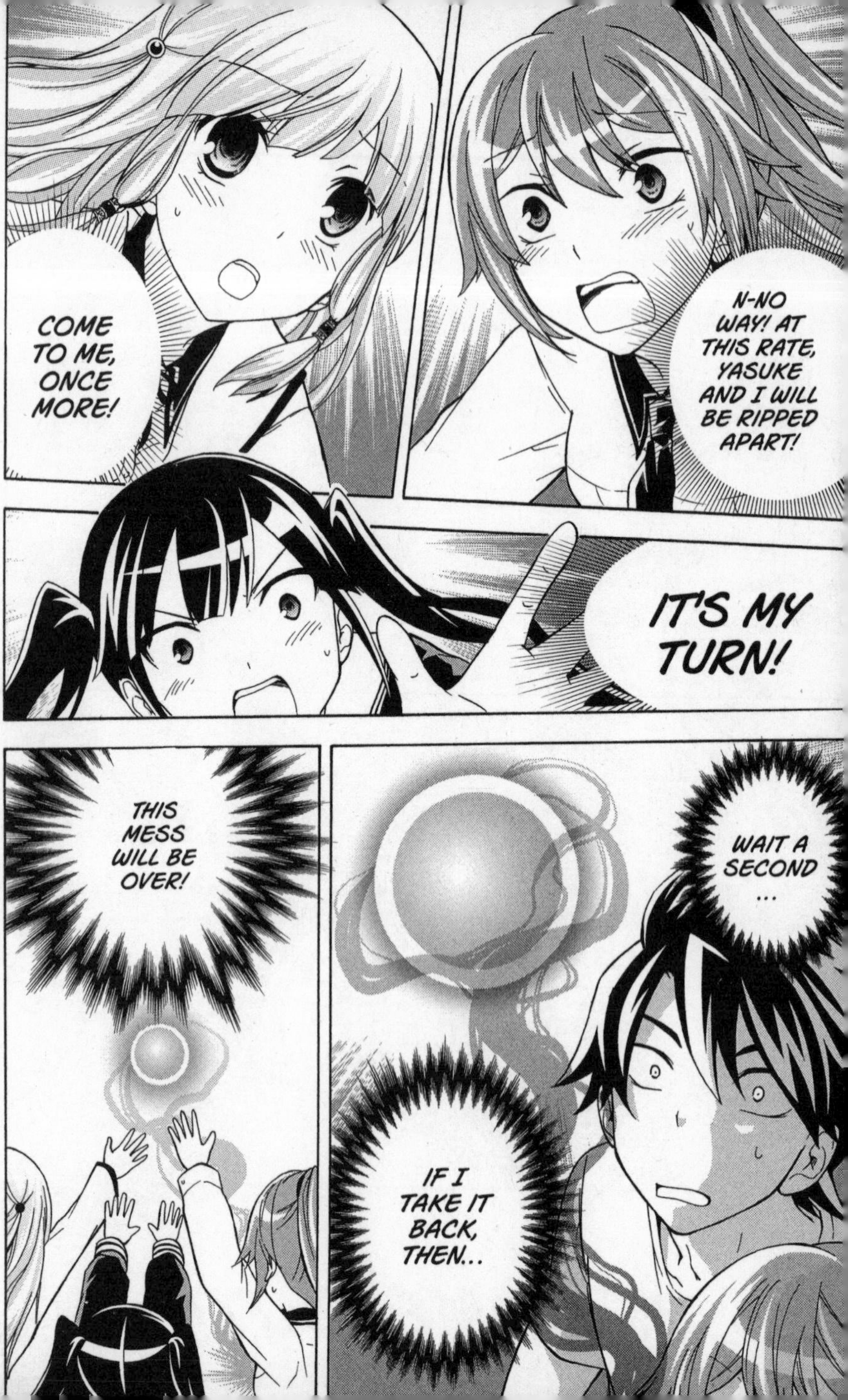
N-NO WAY! AT THIS RATE, YASUKE AND I WILL BE RIPPED APART!
COME TO ME, ONCE MORE!
IT'S MY TURN!
WAIT A SECOND ...
IF I TAKE IT BACK, THEN...
THIS MESS WILL BE OVER!

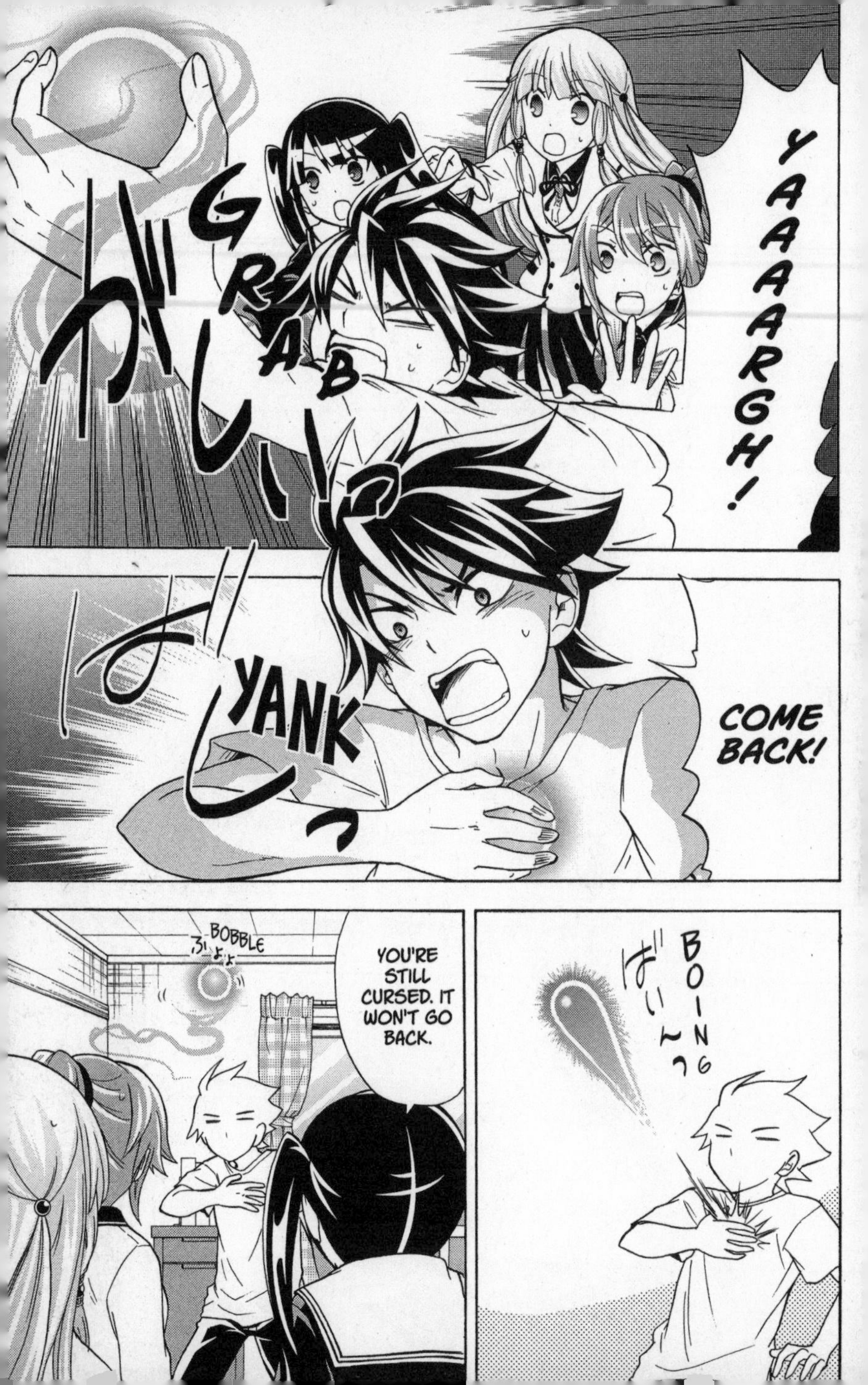
YAAAARGH!
GRAB
がしいっ
COME BACK!
YANK
BOING
ばいん〜っ
YOU'RE STILL CURSED. IT WON'T GO BACK.
BOBBLE
ぷよ

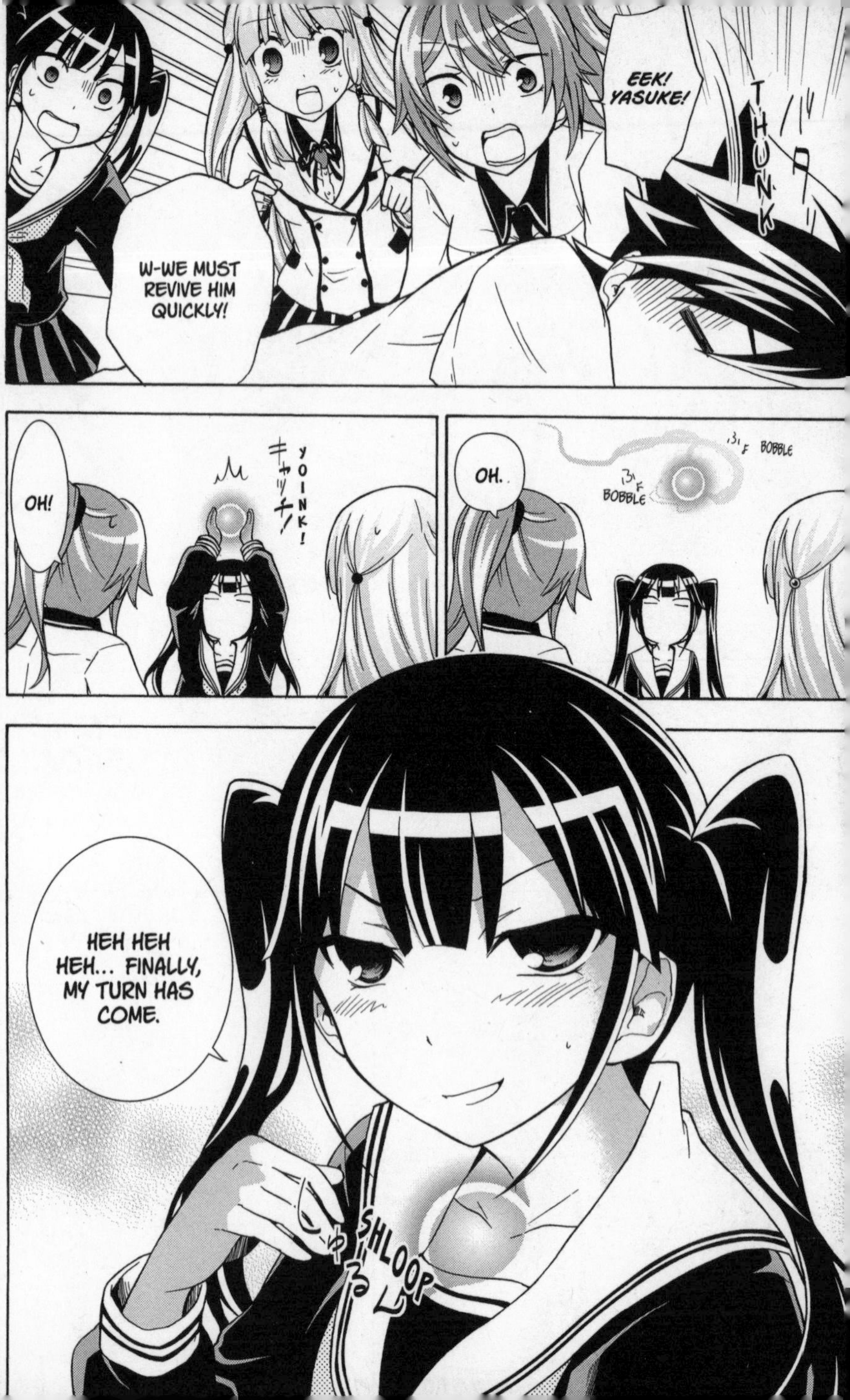
EEK! YASUKE!
THUNK
W-WE MUST REVIVE HIM QUICKLY!
OH..
BOBBLE
BOBBLE
キャッチ!
YOINK!
OH!
HEH HEH HEH... FINALLY, MY TURN HAS COME.
SHLOOP

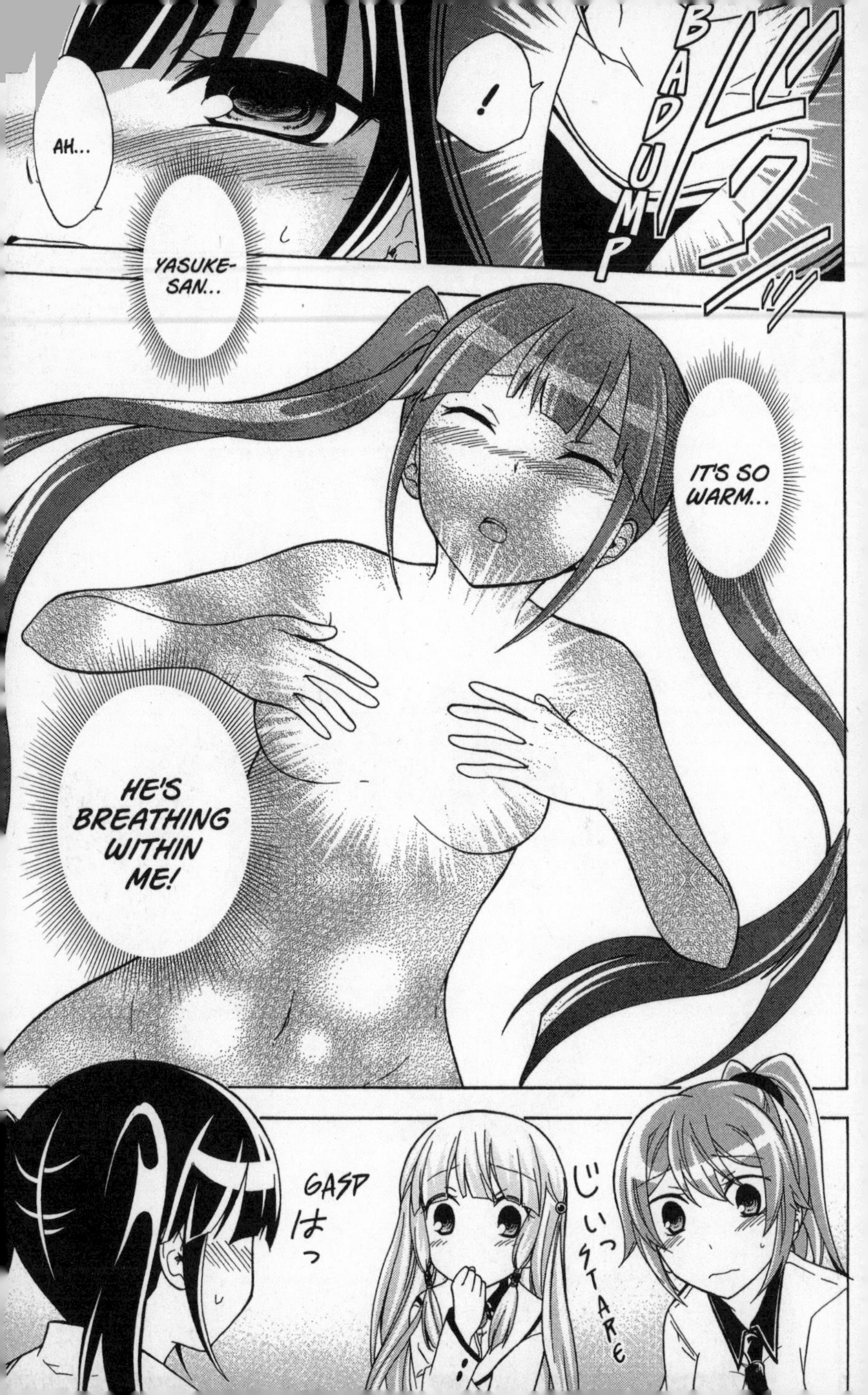
ドクン
BADUMP
!
AH...
YASUKE-SAN...
IT'S SO WARM...
HE'S BREATHING WITHIN ME!
じいっ
STARE
GASP
はっ

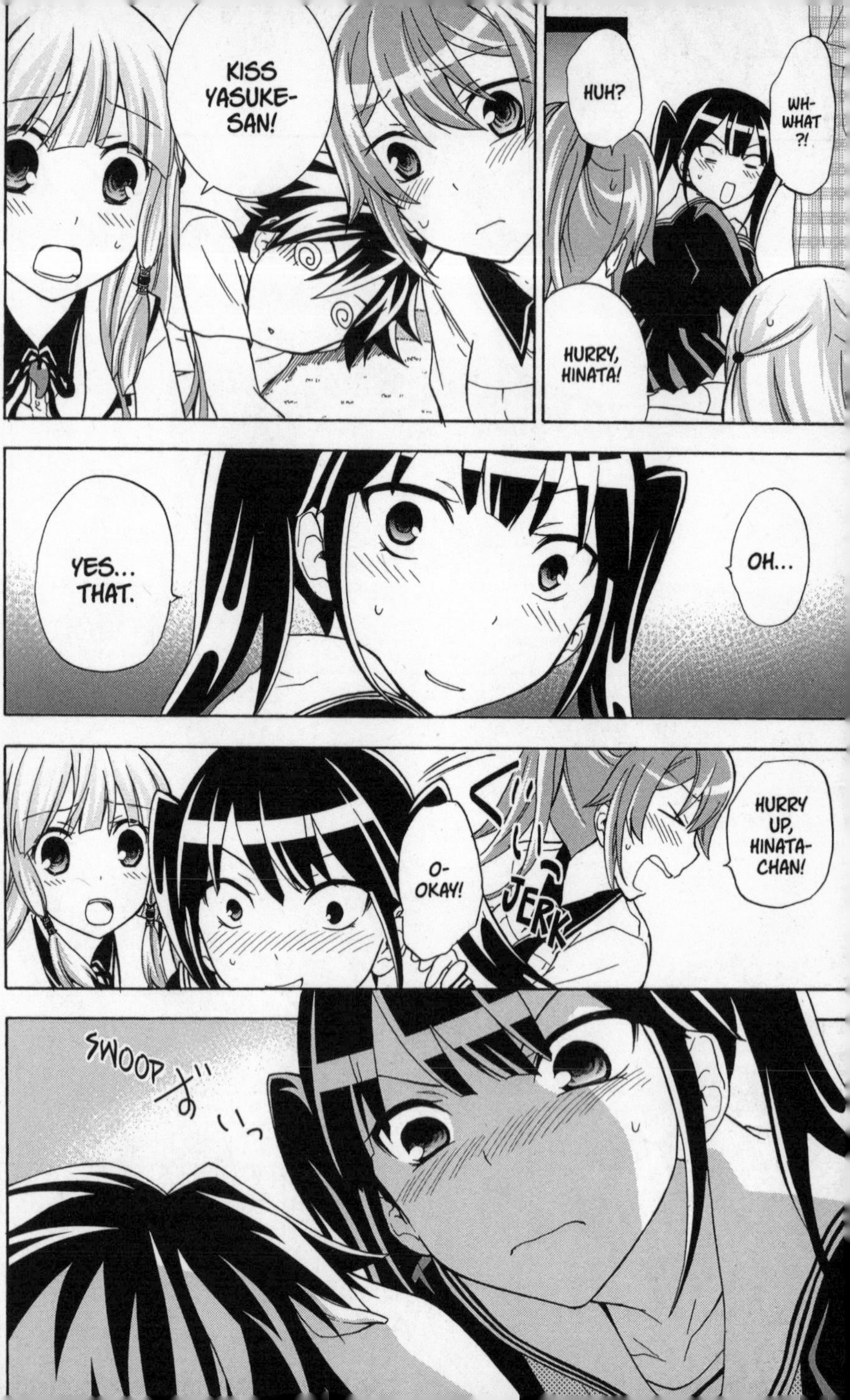
WH-WHAT?!
HUH?
HURRY, HINATA!
KISS YASUKE-SAN!
OH...
YES... THAT.
HURRY UP, HINATA-CHAN!
JERK
O-OKAY!
SWOOP

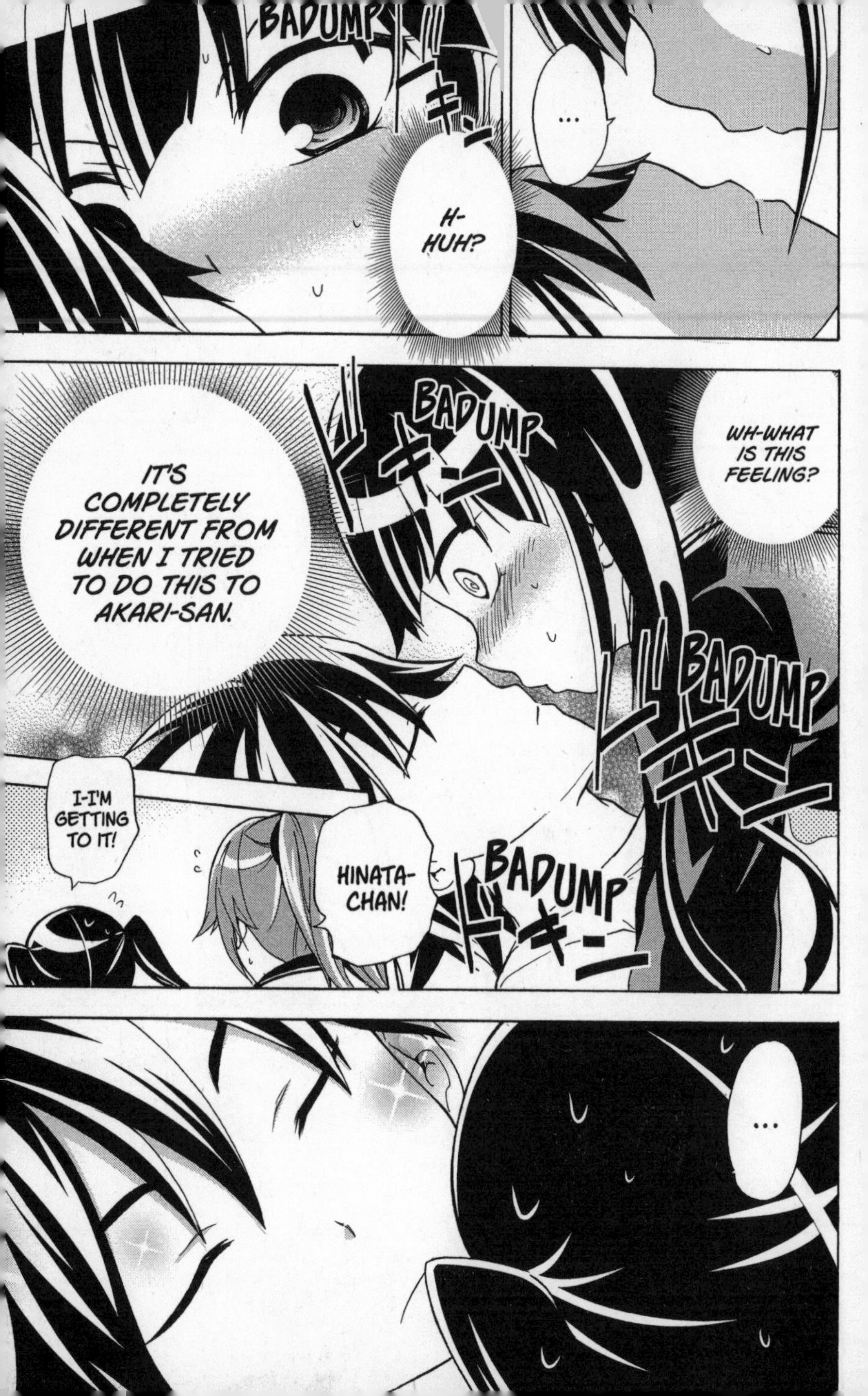
...
BADUMP
H-HUH?
WH-WHAT IS THIS FEELING?
BADUMP
IT'S COMPLETELY DIFFERENT FROM WHEN I TRIED TO DO THIS TO AKARI-SAN.
BADUMP
BADUMP
HINATA-CHAN!
I-I'M GETTING TO IT!
...

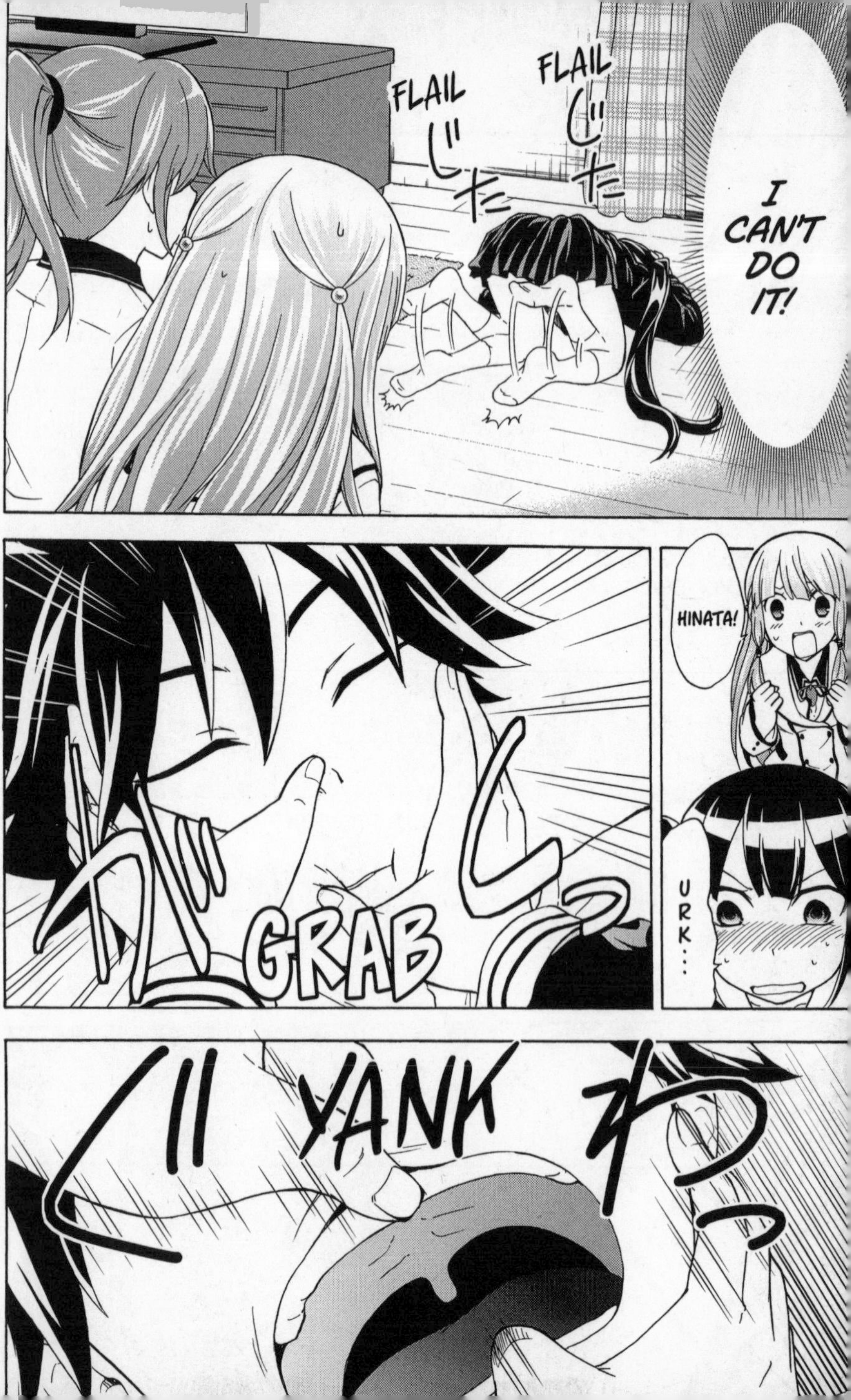
I CAN'T DO IT!
FLAIL
FLAIL
HINATA!
URK...
GRAB
YANK

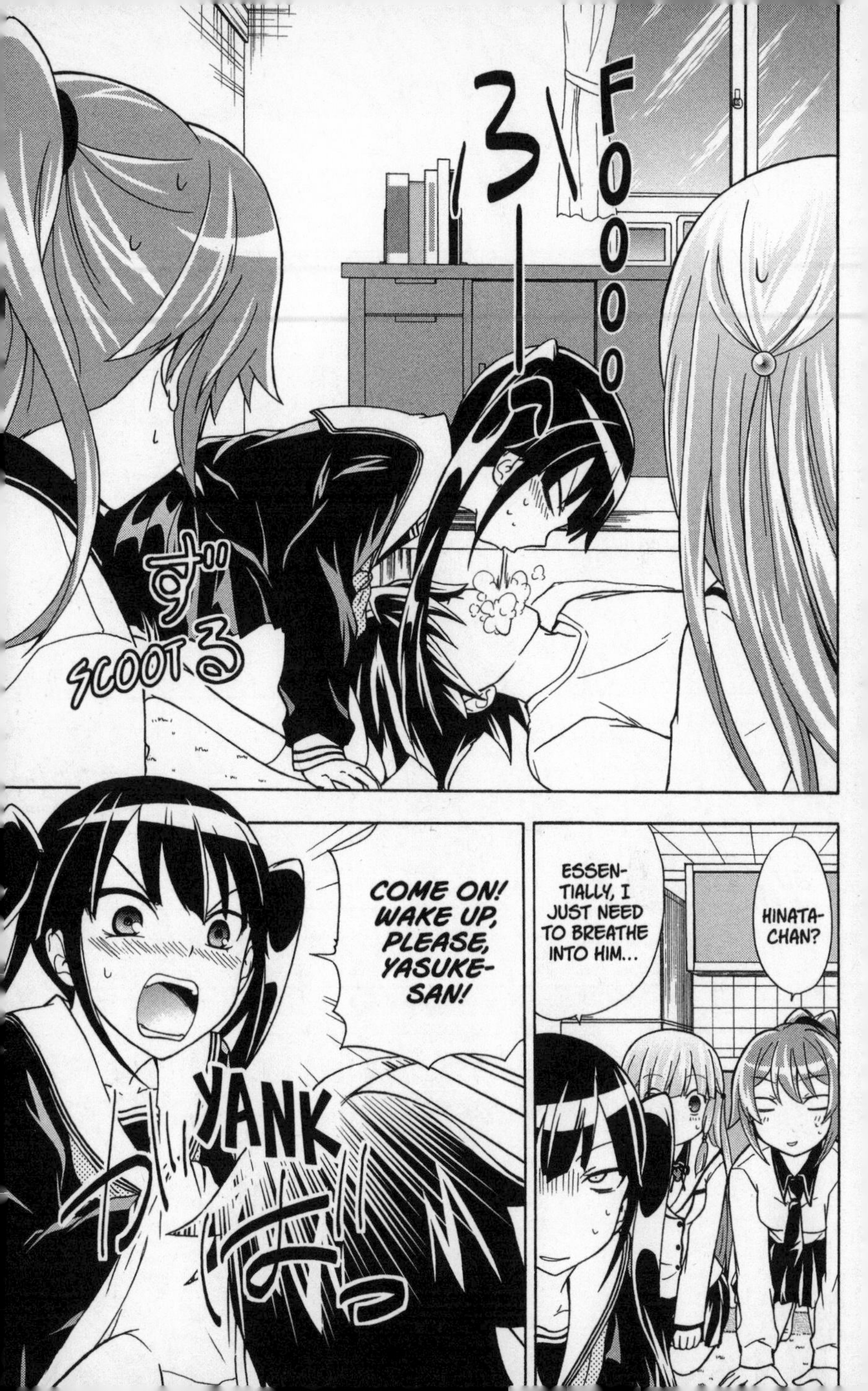

FOOOO
すずる
SCOOT
HINATA-CHAN?
ESSEN-TIALLY, I JUST NEED TO BREATHE INTO HIM...
COME ON! WAKE UP, PLEASE, YASUKE-SAN!
YANK

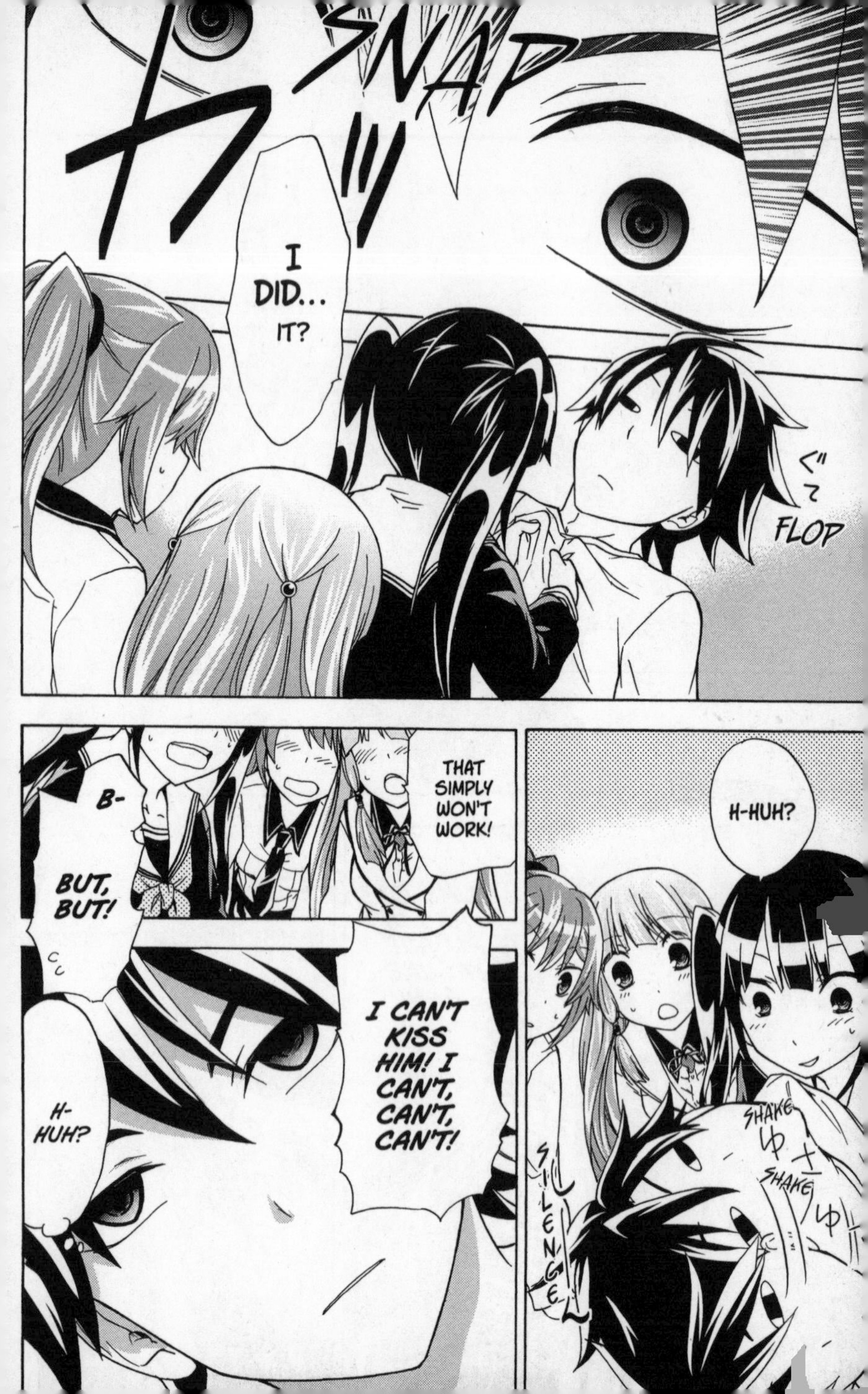
SNAP
I DID... IT?
FLOP
H-HUH?
SHAKE
SHAKE
SILENCE
THAT SIMPLY WON'T WORK!
B- BUT, BUT!
I CAN'T KISS HIM! I CAN'T, CAN'T, CAN'T!
H-HUH?

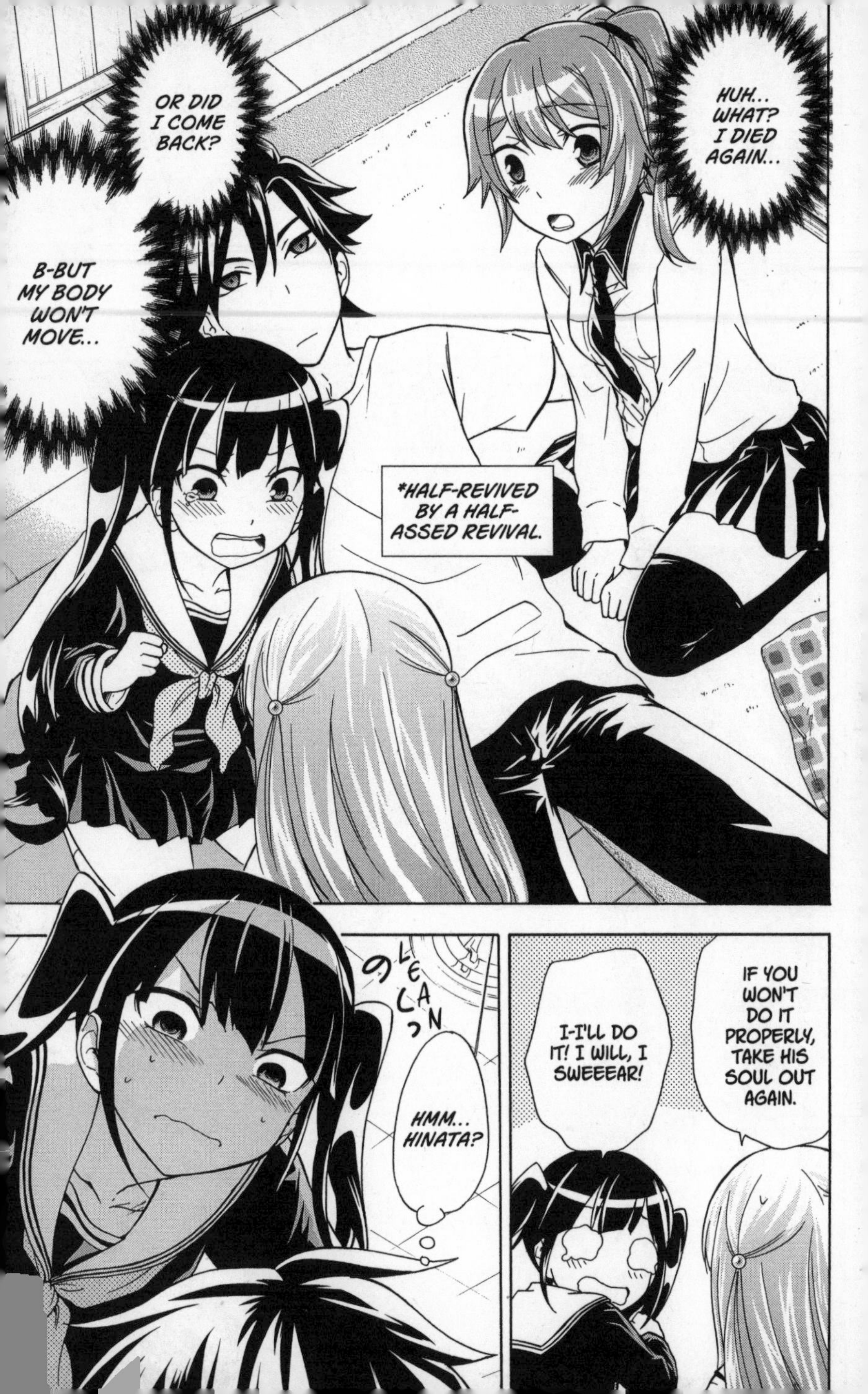
HUH... WHAT? I DIED AGAIN...
OR DID I COME BACK?
B-BUT MY BODY WON'T MOVE...
*HALF-REVIVED BY A HALF-ASSED REVIVAL.
IF YOU WON'T DO IT PROPERLY, TAKE HIS SOUL OUT AGAIN.
I-I'LL DO IT! I WILL, I SWEEEAR!
HMM... HINATA?

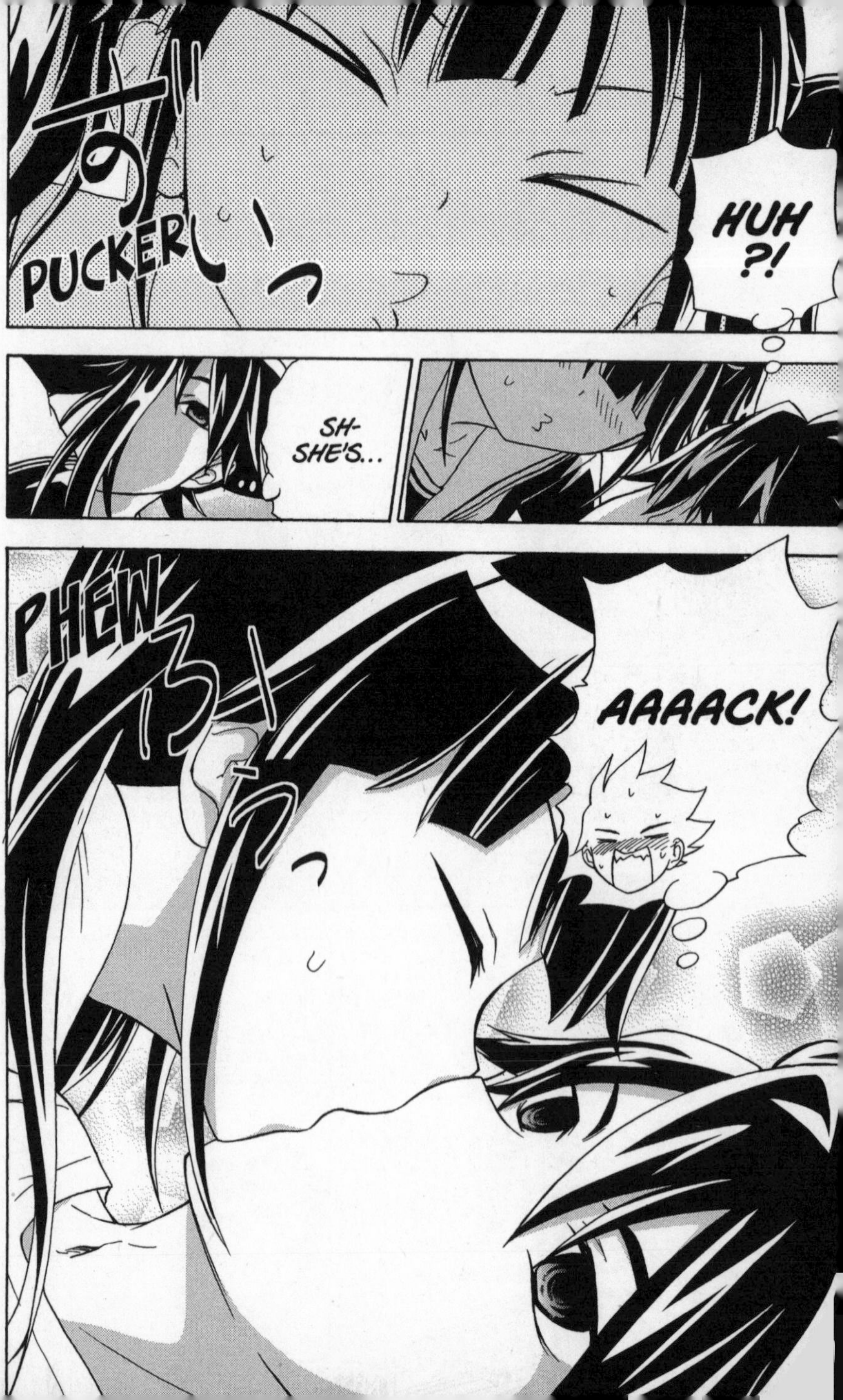
HUH ?!
PUCKER
SH- SHE'S...
PHEW
AAAACK!

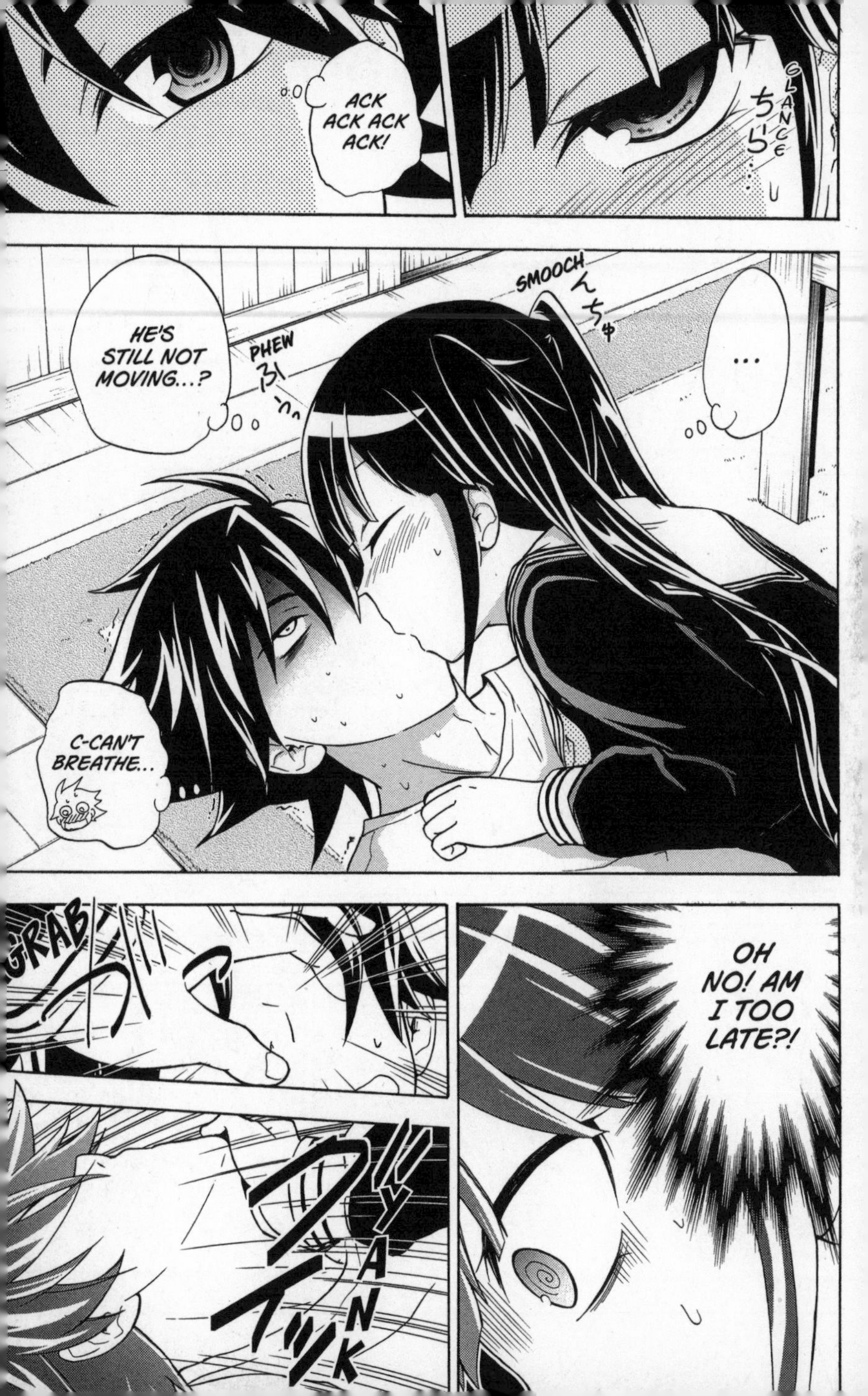
GLANCE
ACK ACK ACK ACK!
...
SMOOCH
PHEW
HE'S STILL NOT MOVING...?
C-CAN'T BREATHE...
OH NO! AM I TOO LATE?!
GRAB
YANK

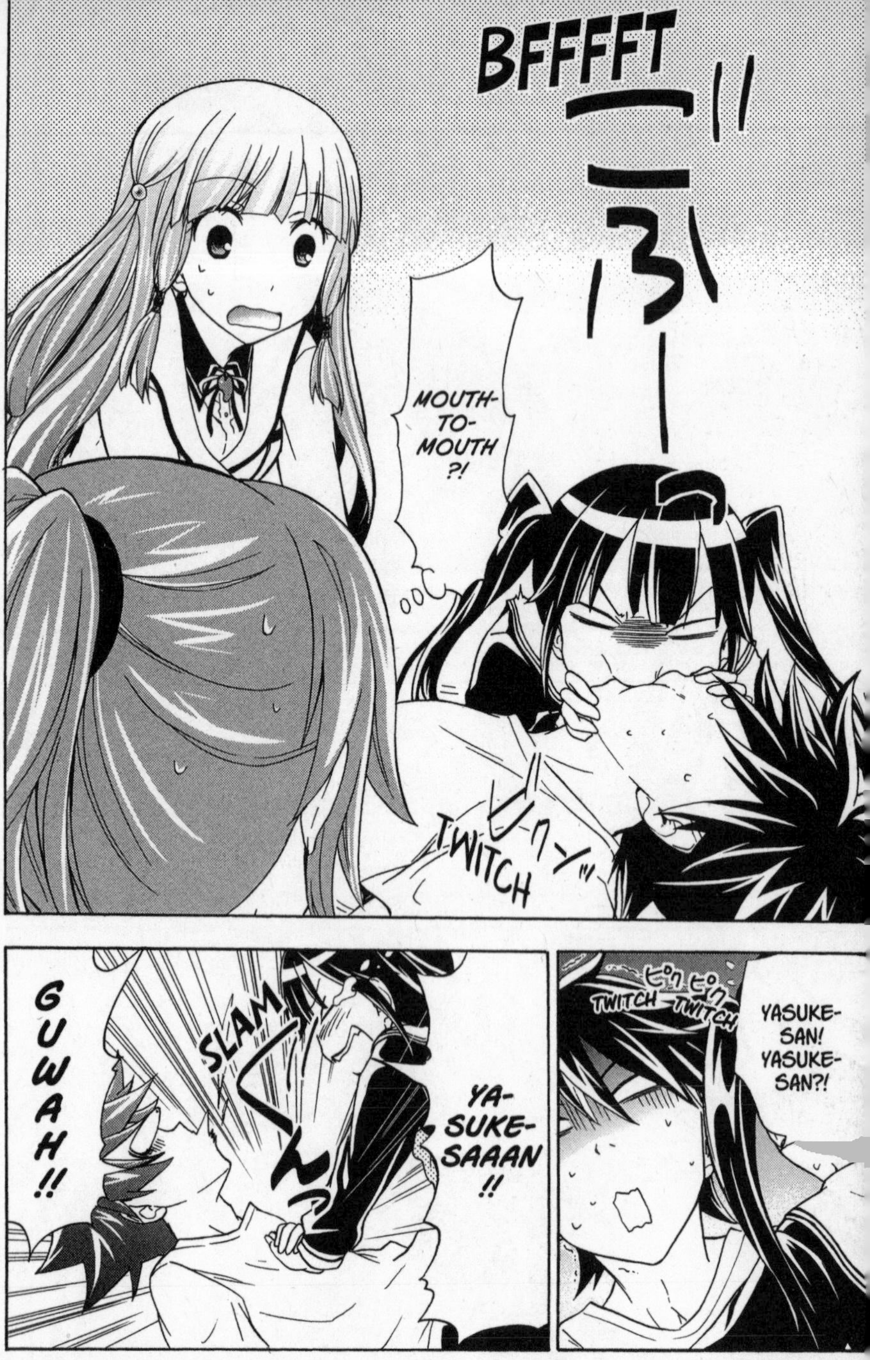
BFFFFT
MOUTH-TO-MOUTH?!
TWITCH
TWITCH TWITCH
YASUKE-SAN! YASUKE-SAN?!
SLAM
YA-SUKE-SAAAN!!
GUWAH!!

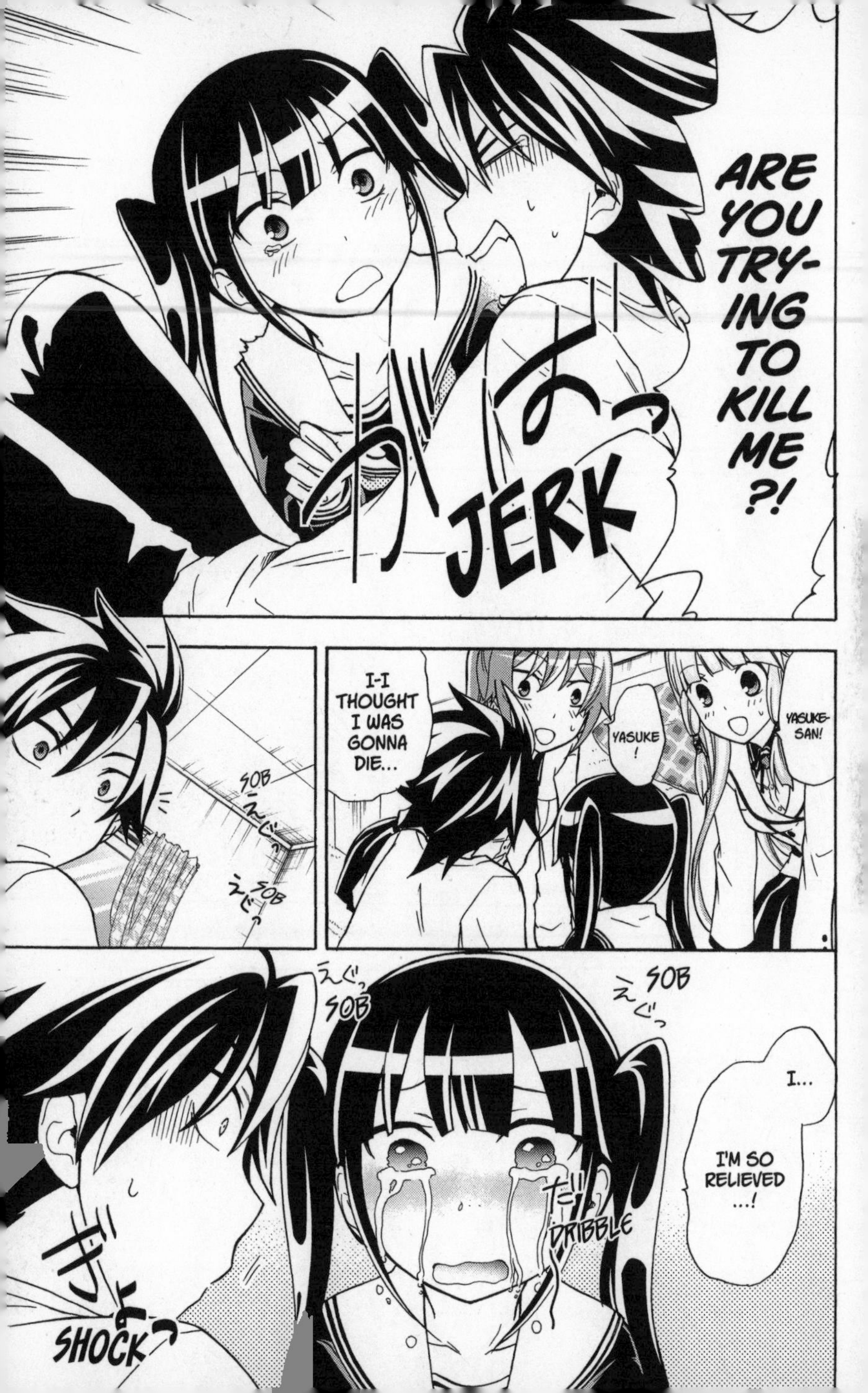
ARE YOU TRY-ING TO KILL ME?!
JERK
YASUKE-SAN!
YASUKE!
I-I THOUGHT I WAS GONNA DIE...
SOB
えぐっ
SOB
えぐっ
SOB
えぐっ
SOB
えぐっ
I...
I'M SO RELIEVED...!
DRIBBLE
SHOCK

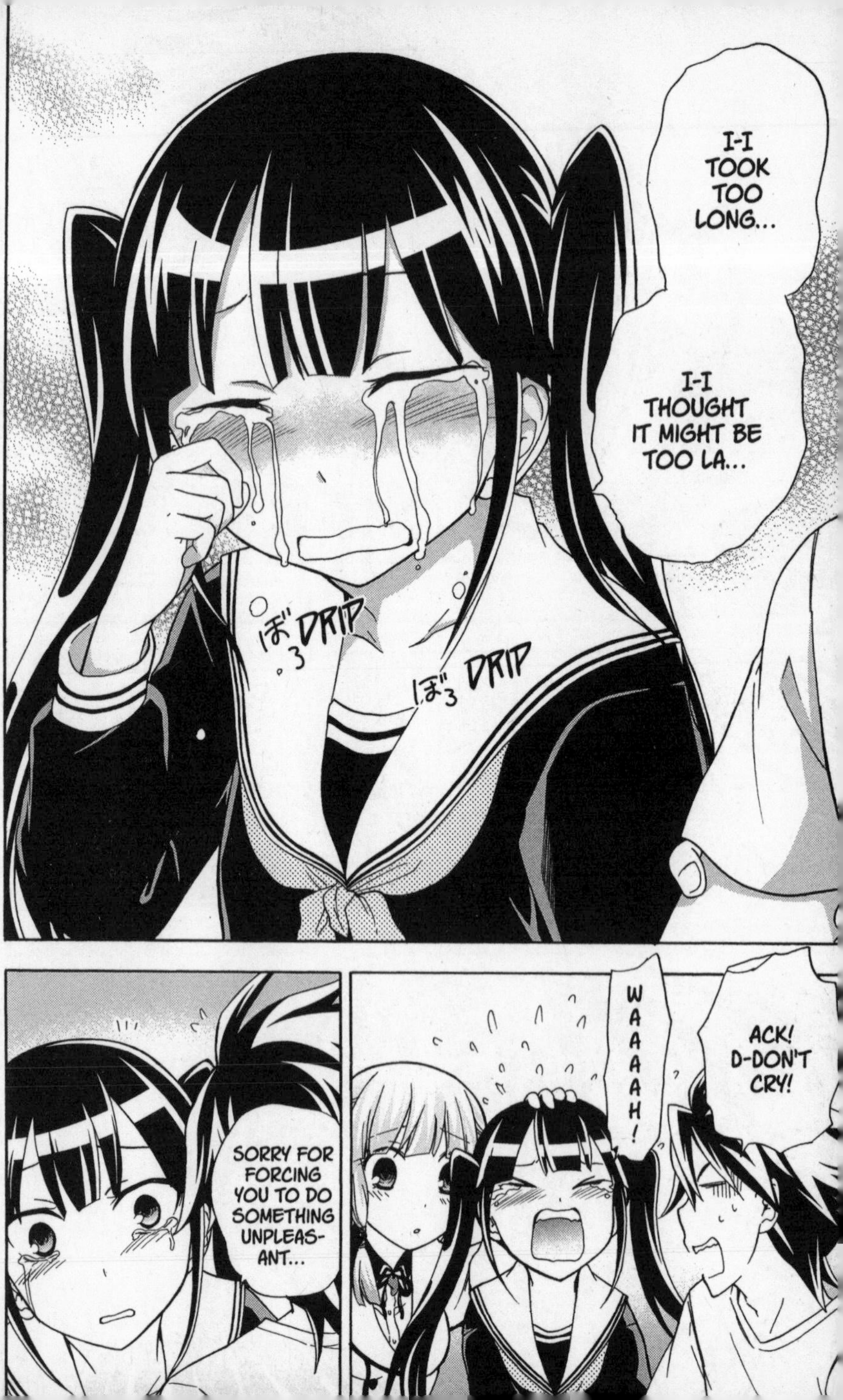
I-I TOOK TOO LONG...
I-I THOUGHT IT MIGHT BE TOO LA...
ぼろ DRIP
ぼろ DRIP
ACK! D-DON'T CRY!
WAAAAAH!
SORRY FOR FORCING YOU TO DO SOMETHING UNPLEAS-ANT...

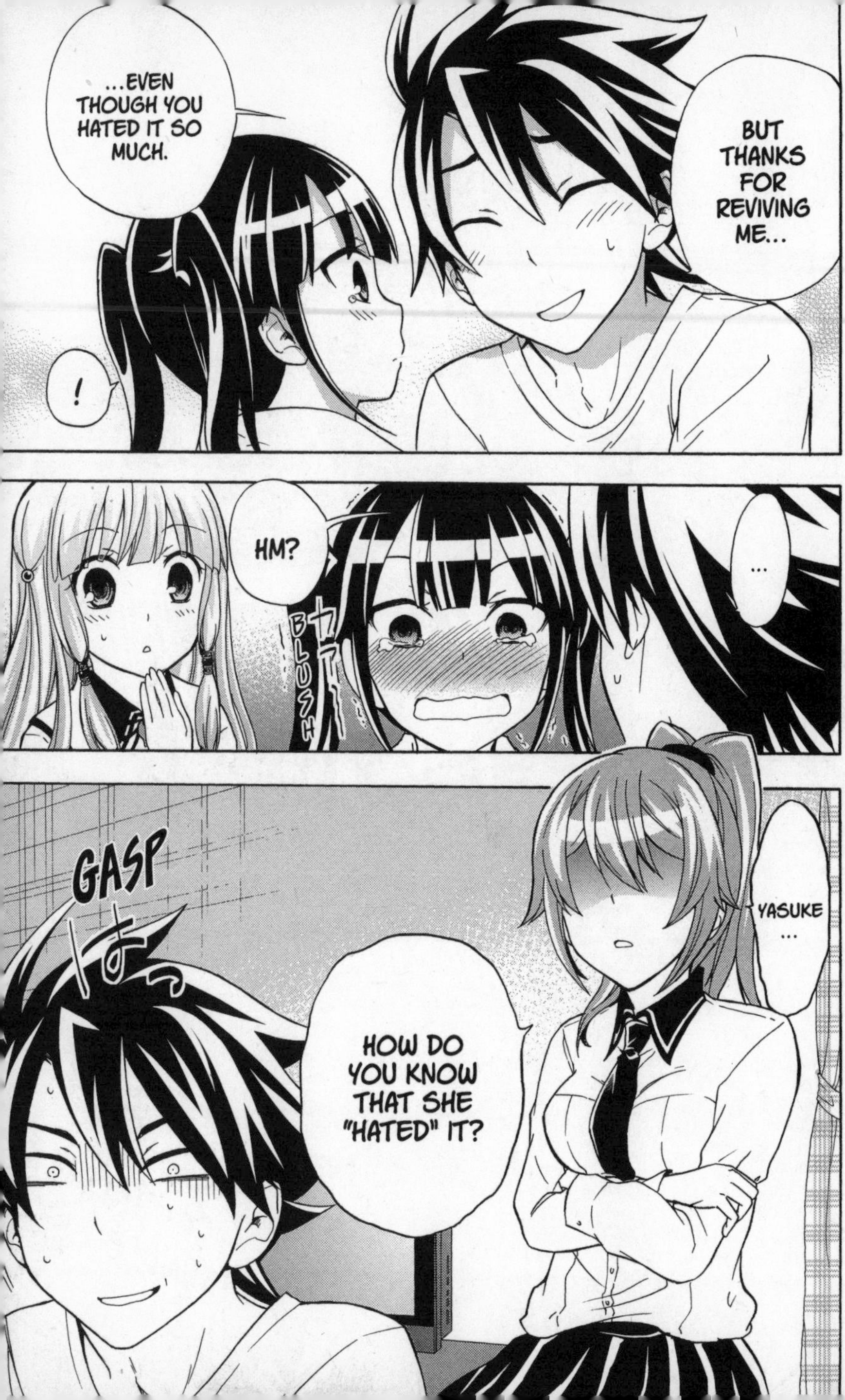
BUT THANKS FOR REVIVING ME...
...EVEN THOUGH YOU HATED IT SO MUCH.
!
...
HM?
BLUSH
YASUKE ...
GASP
HOW DO YOU KNOW THAT SHE "HATED" IT?

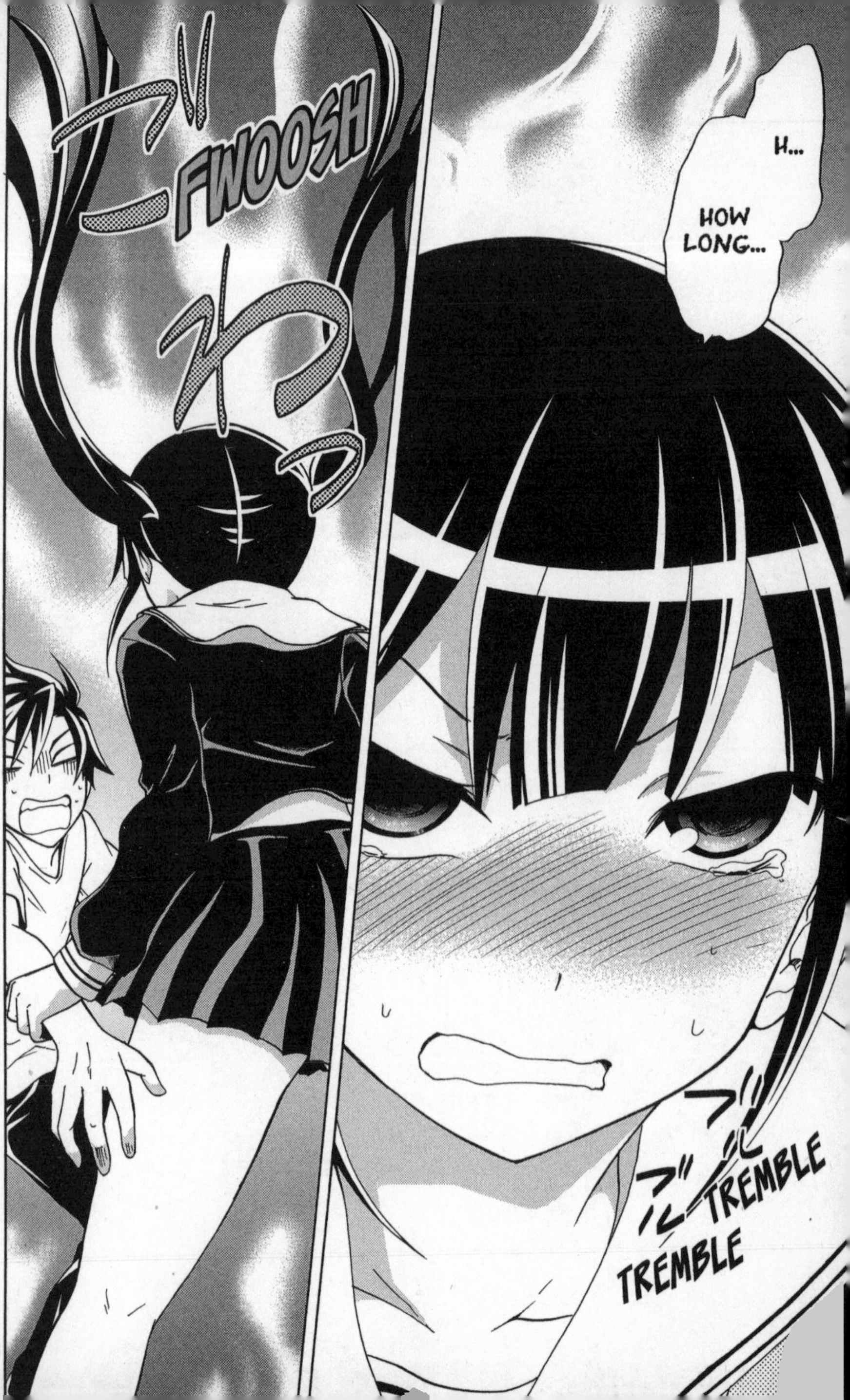

H...
HOW LONG...
TREMBLE
TREMBLE
FWOOSH

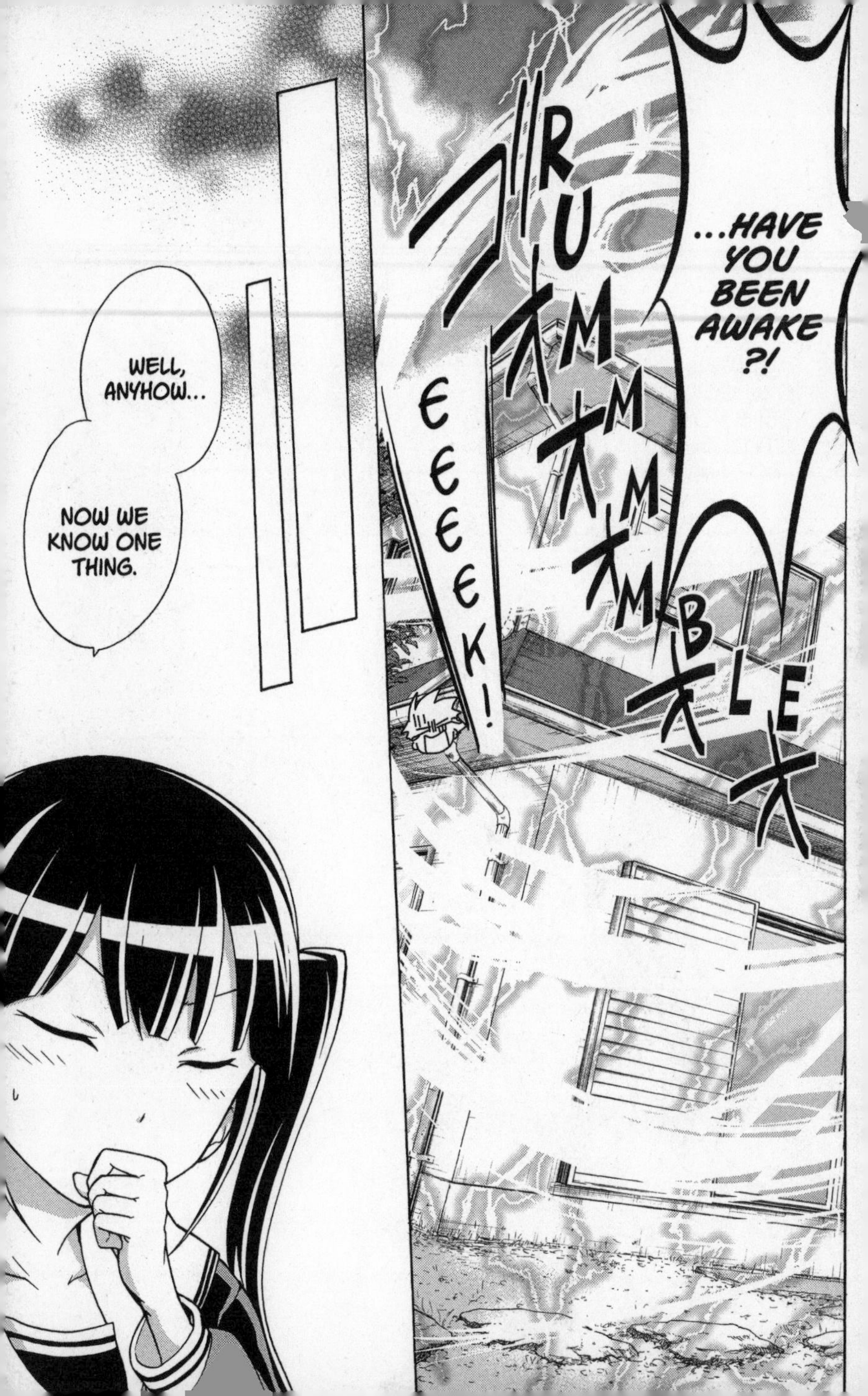
...HAVE YOU BEEN AWAKE ?!
RUMMMMBLE
EEEEEK!
WELL, ANYHOW...
NOW WE KNOW ONE THING.

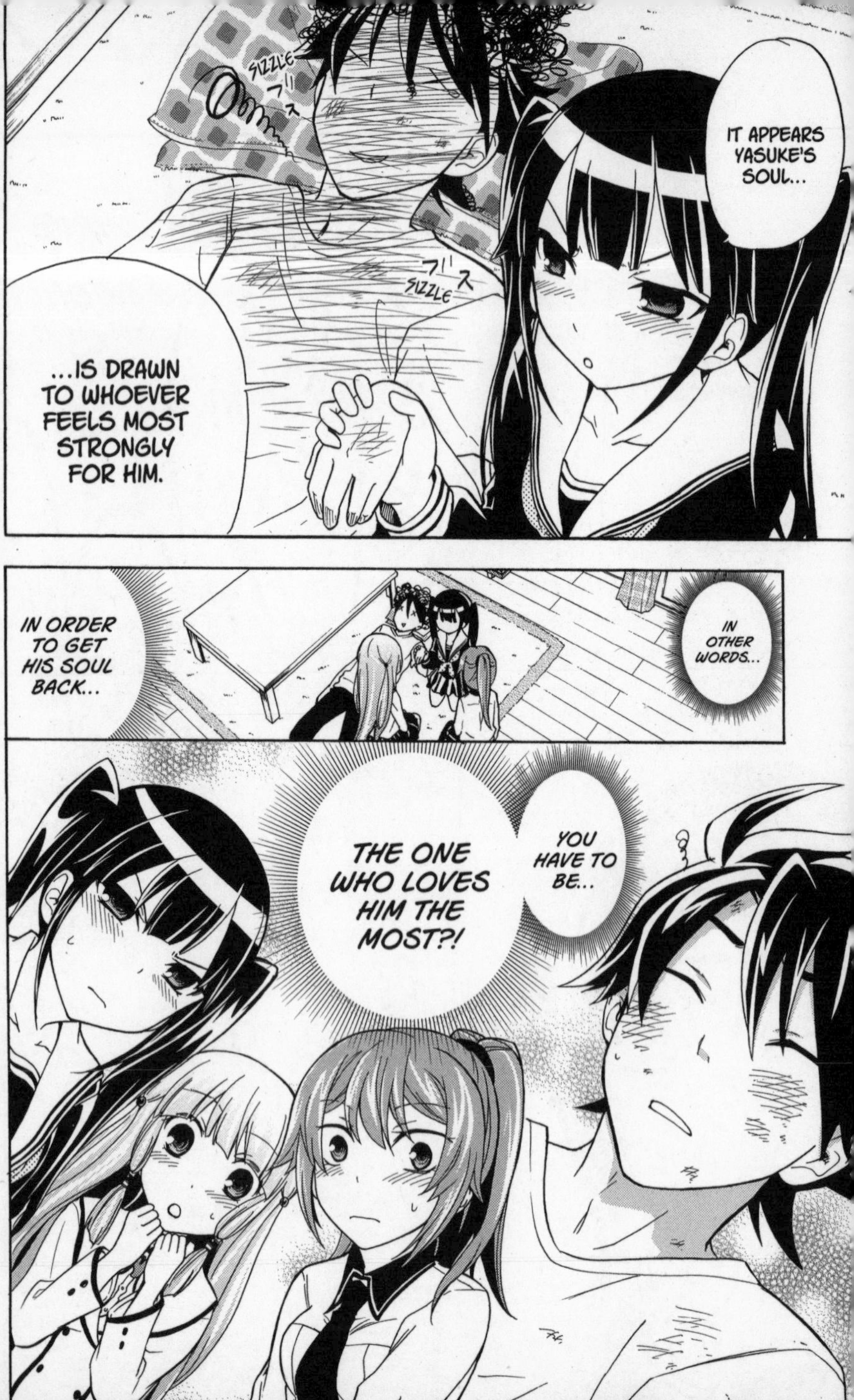
IT APPEARS YASUKE'S SOUL...
SIZZLE
SIZZLE
...IS DRAWN TO WHOEVER FEELS MOST STRONGLY FOR HIM.
IN OTHER WORDS...
IN ORDER TO GET HIS SOUL BACK...
YOU HAVE TO BE...
THE ONE WHO LOVES HIM THE MOST?!

Maga-Tsuki
Presented by Hoshino Taguchi

COLLATERAL DAMAGE
ごお〜
GAAH
POSITIVE ENERGY

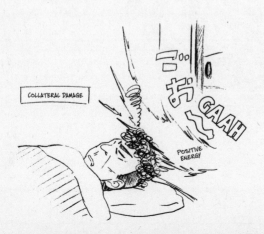

まがつき

Maga-Tsuki
Presented by Hoshino Taguchi

Maga-Tsuki Taguchi Hoshino

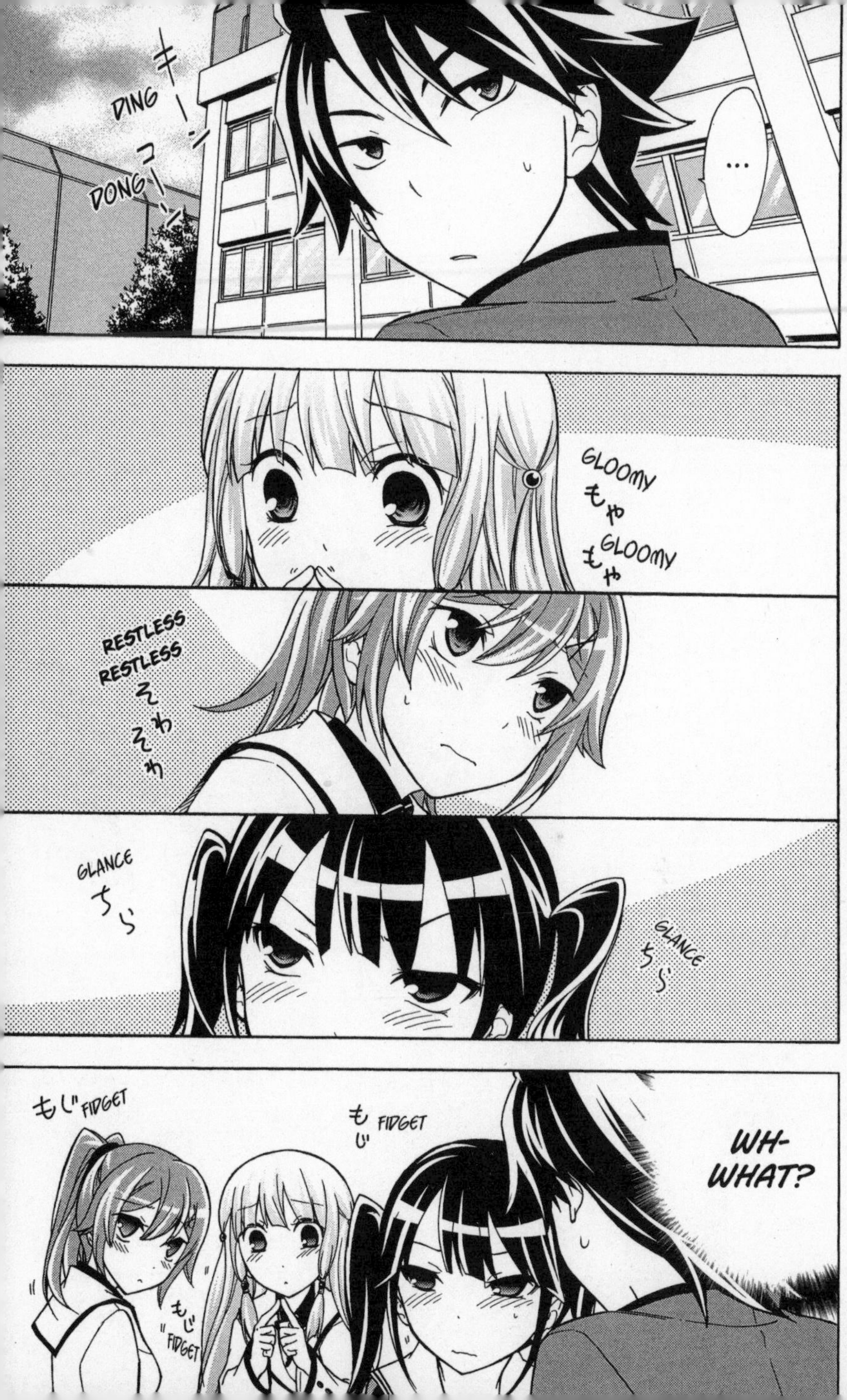
...
キーン
DING
コーン
DONG
もや
GLOOMY
もや
GLOOMY
RESTLESS
RESTLESS
そわそわ
ちら
GLANCE
ちら
GLANCE
WH- WHAT?
もじ
FIDGET
もじ
FIDGET
もじ
FIDGET

12 I LOVE YOU ENOUGH TO DO THIS!

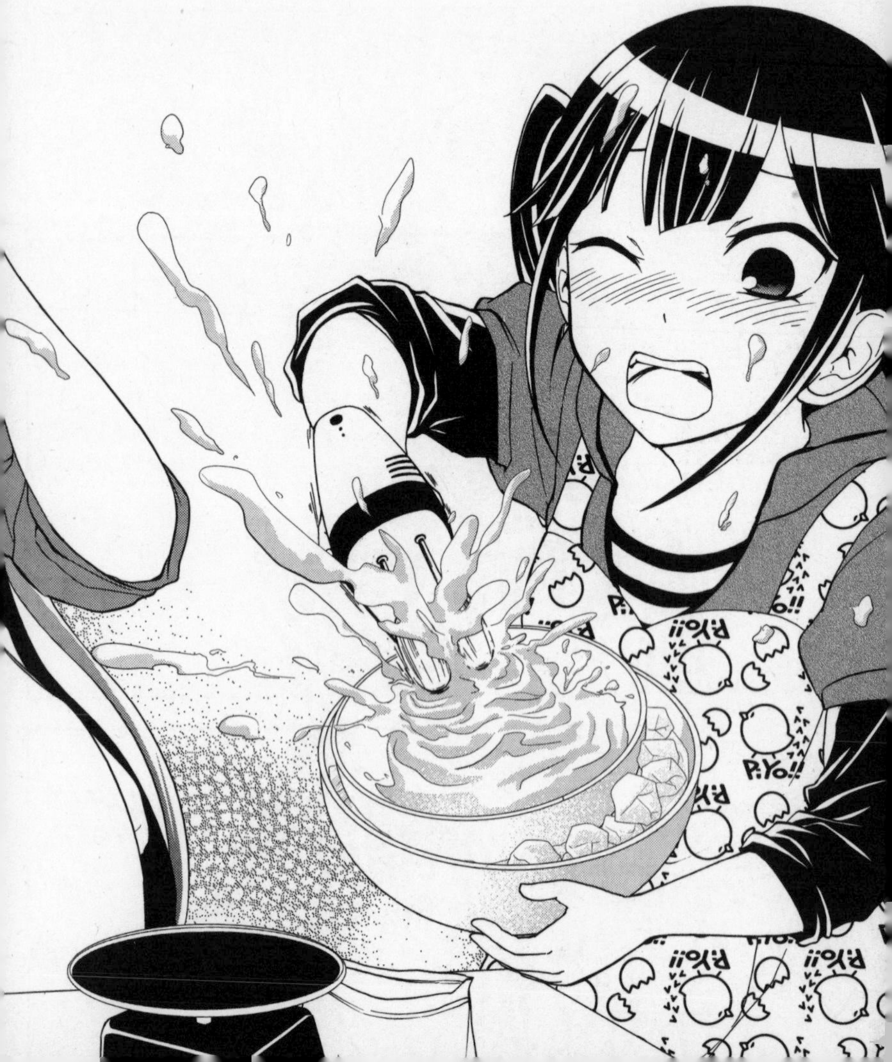
P.Yo!!

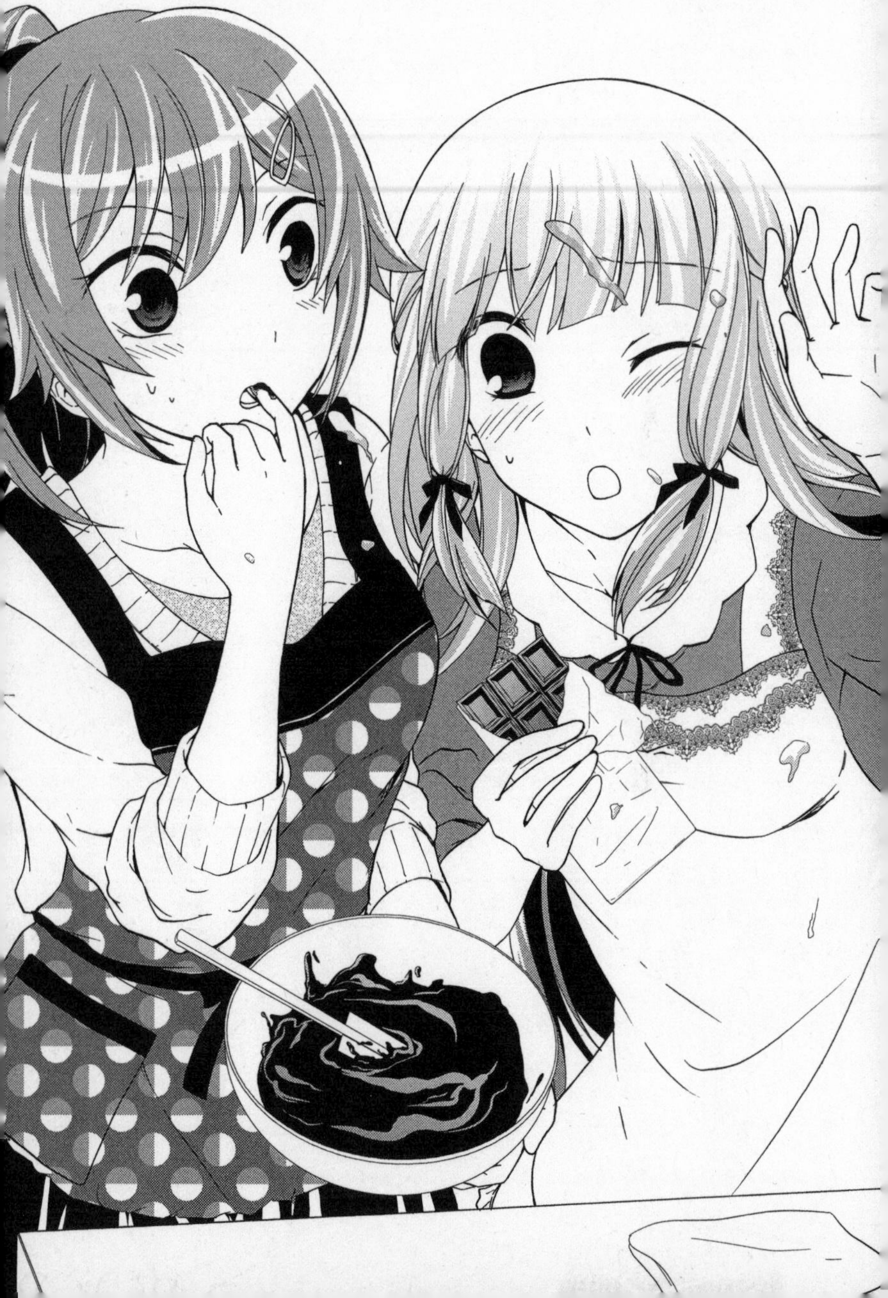

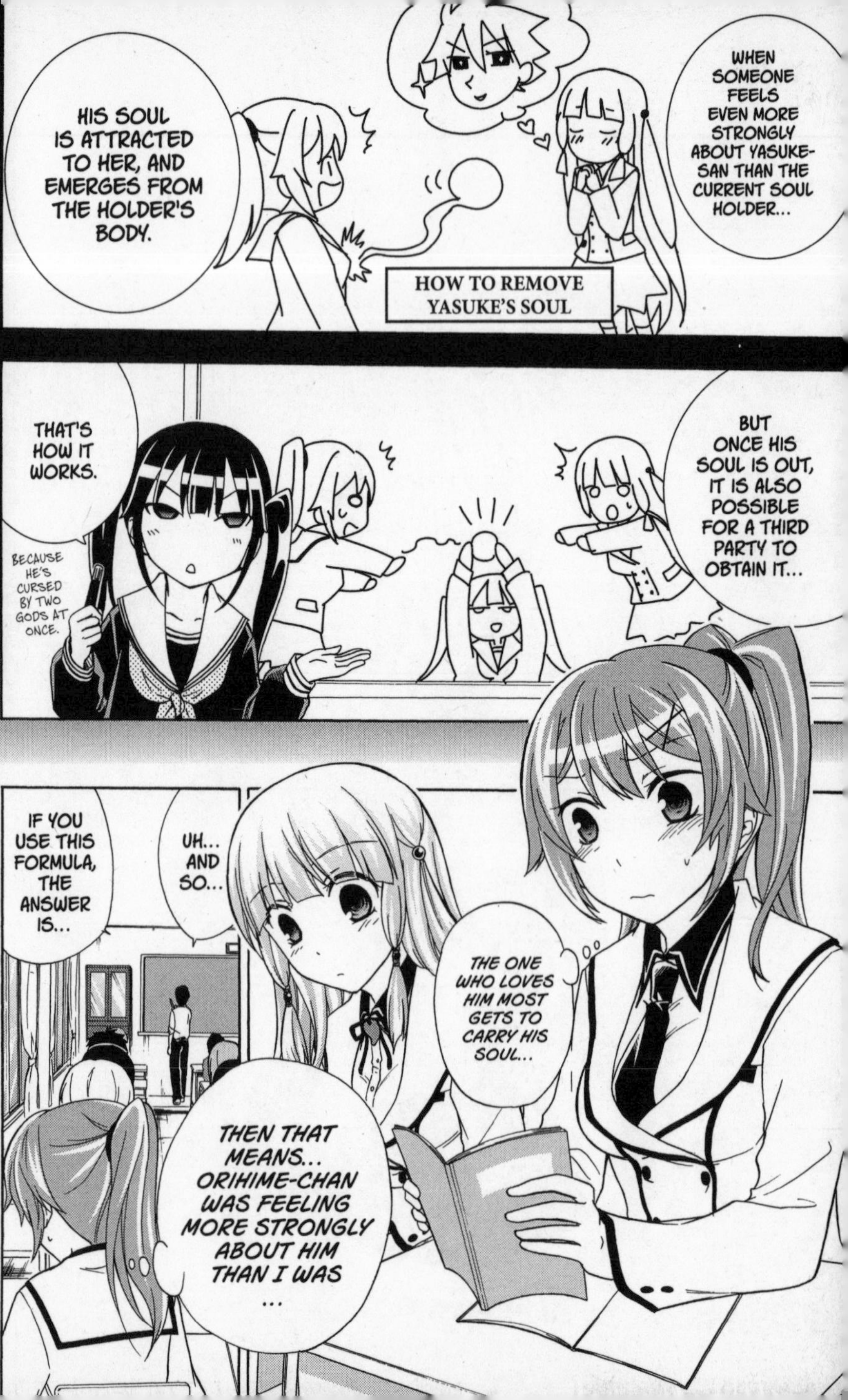
WHEN SOMEONE FEELS EVEN MORE STRONGLY ABOUT YASUKE-SAN THAN THE CURRENT SOUL HOLDER...
HIS SOUL IS ATTRACTED TO HER, AND EMERGES FROM THE HOLDER'S BODY.
HOW TO REMOVE YASUKE'S SOUL
BUT ONCE HIS SOUL IS OUT, IT IS ALSO POSSIBLE FOR A THIRD PARTY TO OBTAIN IT...
THAT'S HOW IT WORKS.
BECAUSE HE'S CURSED BY TWO GODS AT ONCE.
THE ONE WHO LOVES HIM MOST GETS TO CARRY HIS SOUL...
UH... AND SO...
IF YOU USE THIS FORMULA, THE ANSWER IS...
THEN THAT MEANS... ORIHIME-CHAN WAS FEELING MORE STRONGLY ABOUT HIM THAN I WAS ...

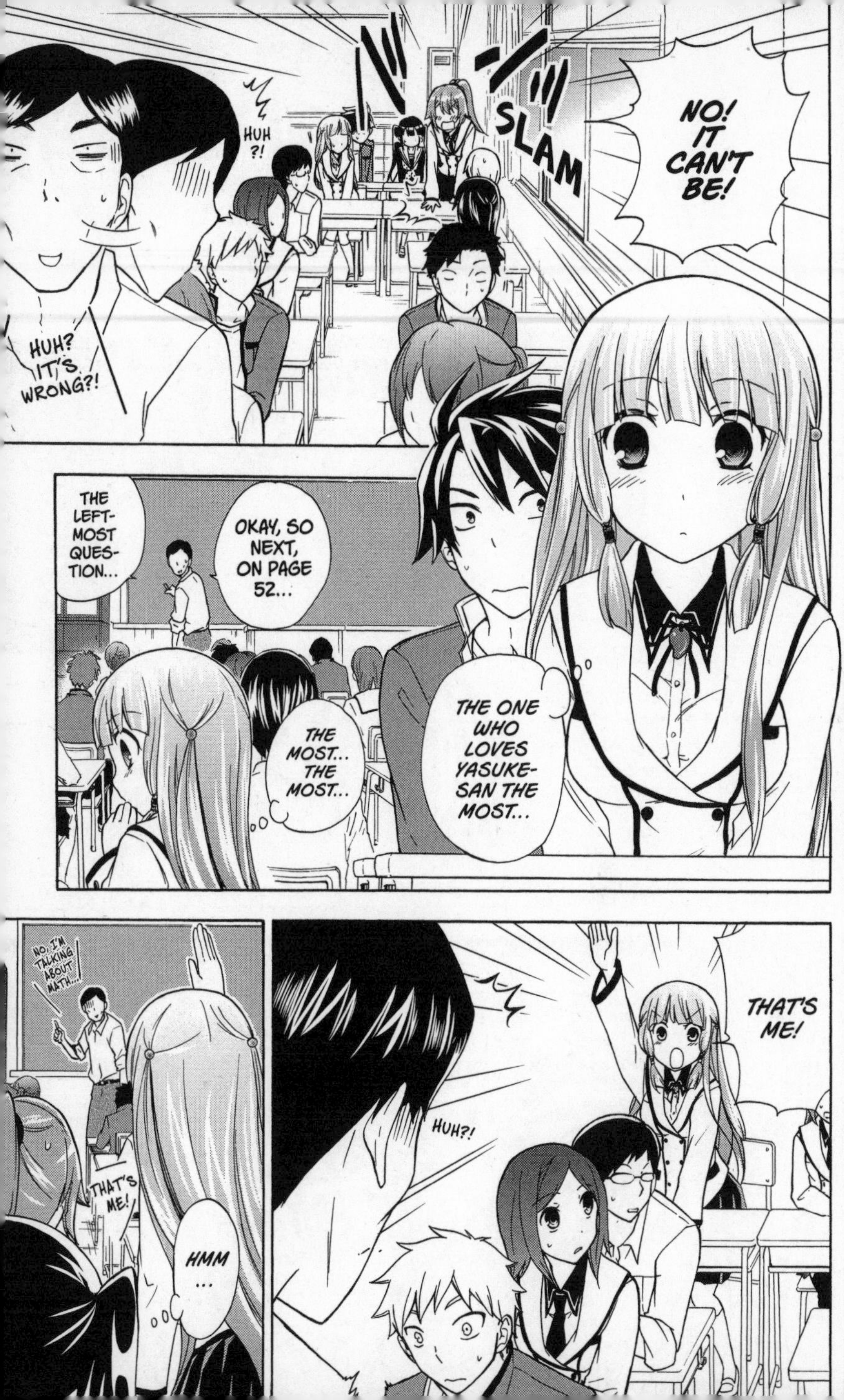
NO! IT CAN'T BE!
SLAM
HUH ?!
HUH? IT'S WRONG?!
OKAY, SO NEXT, ON PAGE 52...
THE LEFT-MOST QUES-TION...
THE ONE WHO LOVES YASUKE-SAN THE MOST...
THE MOST... THE MOST...
THAT'S ME!
HUH?!
NO, I'M TALKING ABOUT MATH...!
THAT'S ME!
HMM ...

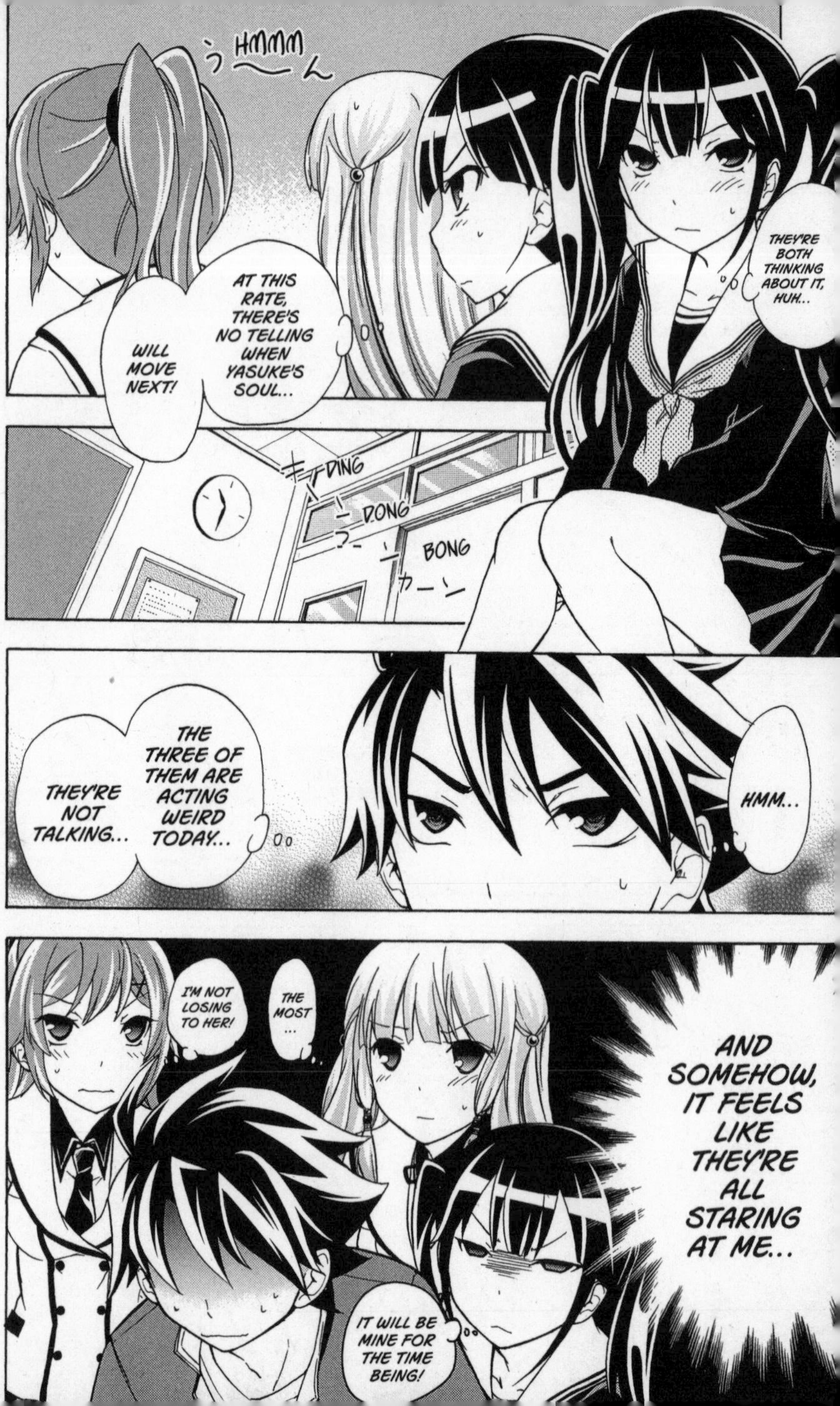
HMMMM
う〜ん
THEY'RE BOTH THINKING ABOUT IT, HUH...
AT THIS RATE, THERE'S NO TELLING WHEN YASUKE'S SOUL...
WILL MOVE NEXT!
DING
DONG
BONG
カーン
HMM...
THE THREE OF THEM ARE ACTING WEIRD TODAY...
THEY'RE NOT TALKING...
AND SOMEHOW, IT FEELS LIKE THEY'RE ALL STARING AT ME...
THE MOST...
I'M NOT LOSING TO HER!
IT WILL BE MINE FOR THE TIME BEING!

ハニ
ツイッ
チョ？！

WHAT
?!
....IS
IT?

UM
....

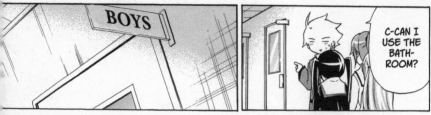

BOYS

C-CAN I
USE THE
BATH-
ROOM?

FRETTING TO
OURSELVES
IS NOT GOING
TO GET US
ANYWHERE...

SO LET'S
BE OUT
WITH IT!

WHISPER

WHISPER

OKAY!

ERM
....

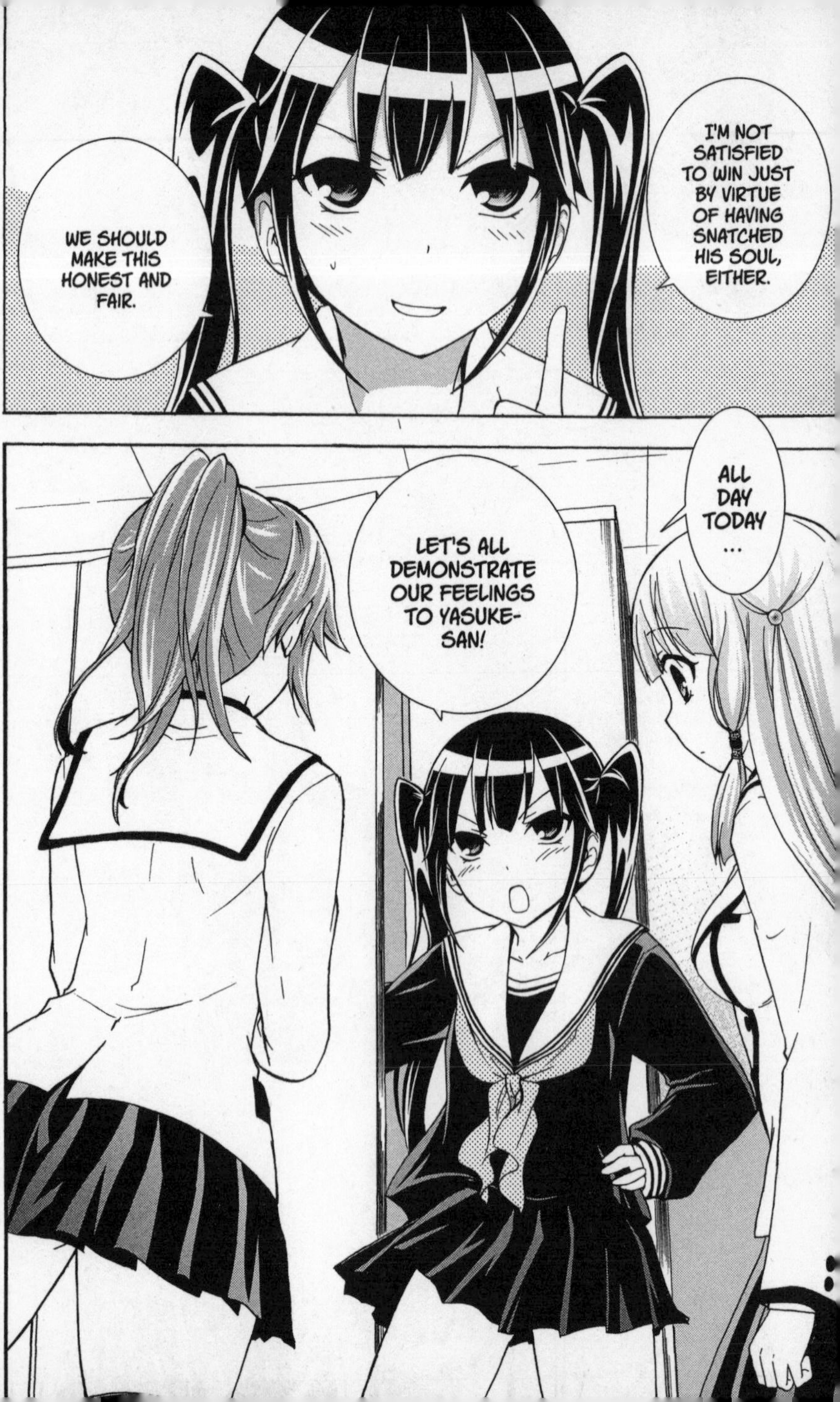
I'M NOT SATISFIED TO WIN JUST BY VIRTUE OF HAVING SNATCHED HIS SOUL, EITHER.
WE SHOULD MAKE THIS HONEST AND FAIR.
ALL DAY TODAY ...
LET'S ALL DEMONSTRATE OUR FEELINGS TO YASUKE-SAN!

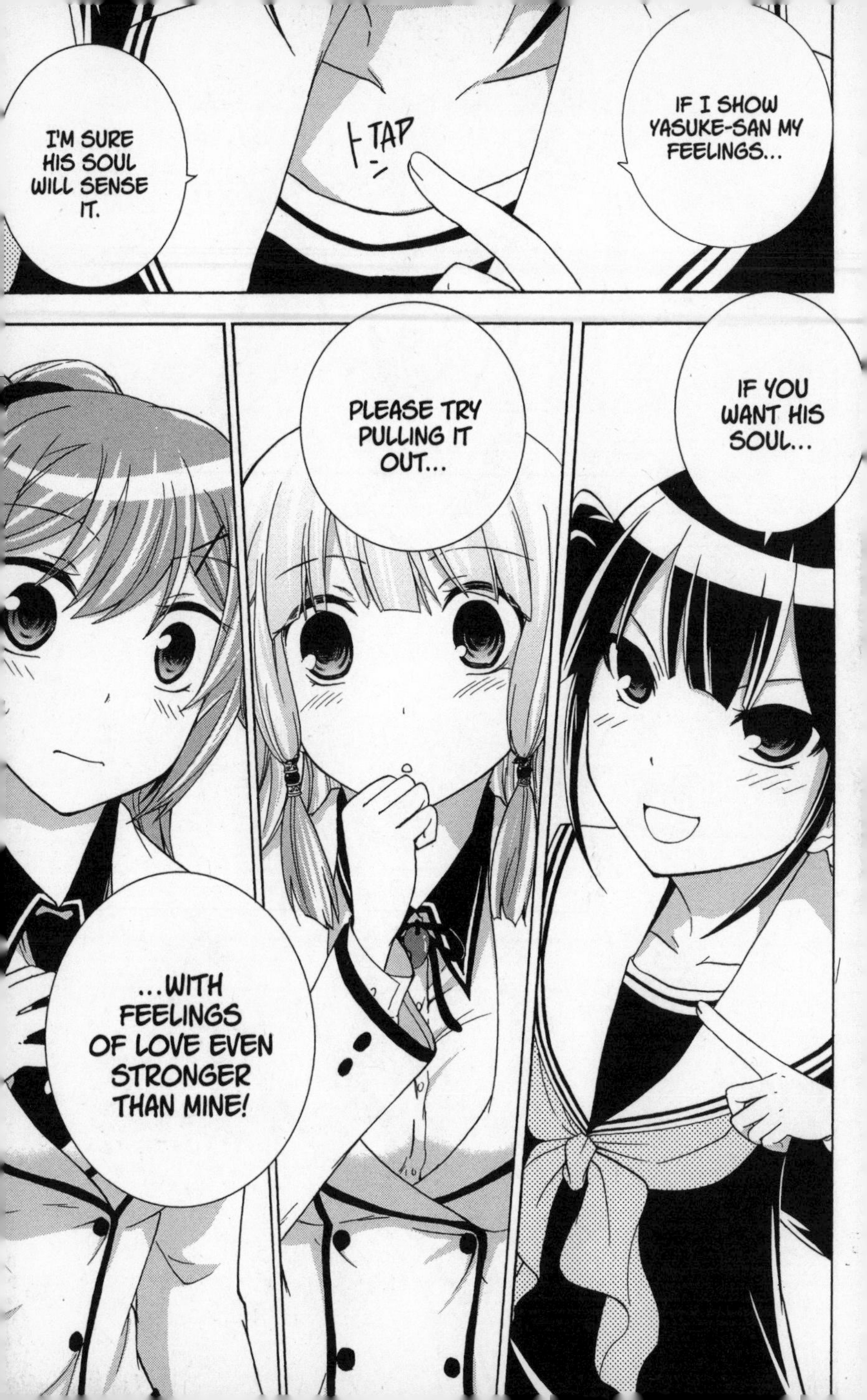
IF I SHOW YASUKE-SAN MY FEELINGS...
TAP
I'M SURE HIS SOUL WILL SENSE IT.
IF YOU WANT HIS SOUL...
PLEASE TRY PULLING IT OUT...
...WITH FEELINGS OF LOVE EVEN STRONGER THAN MINE!

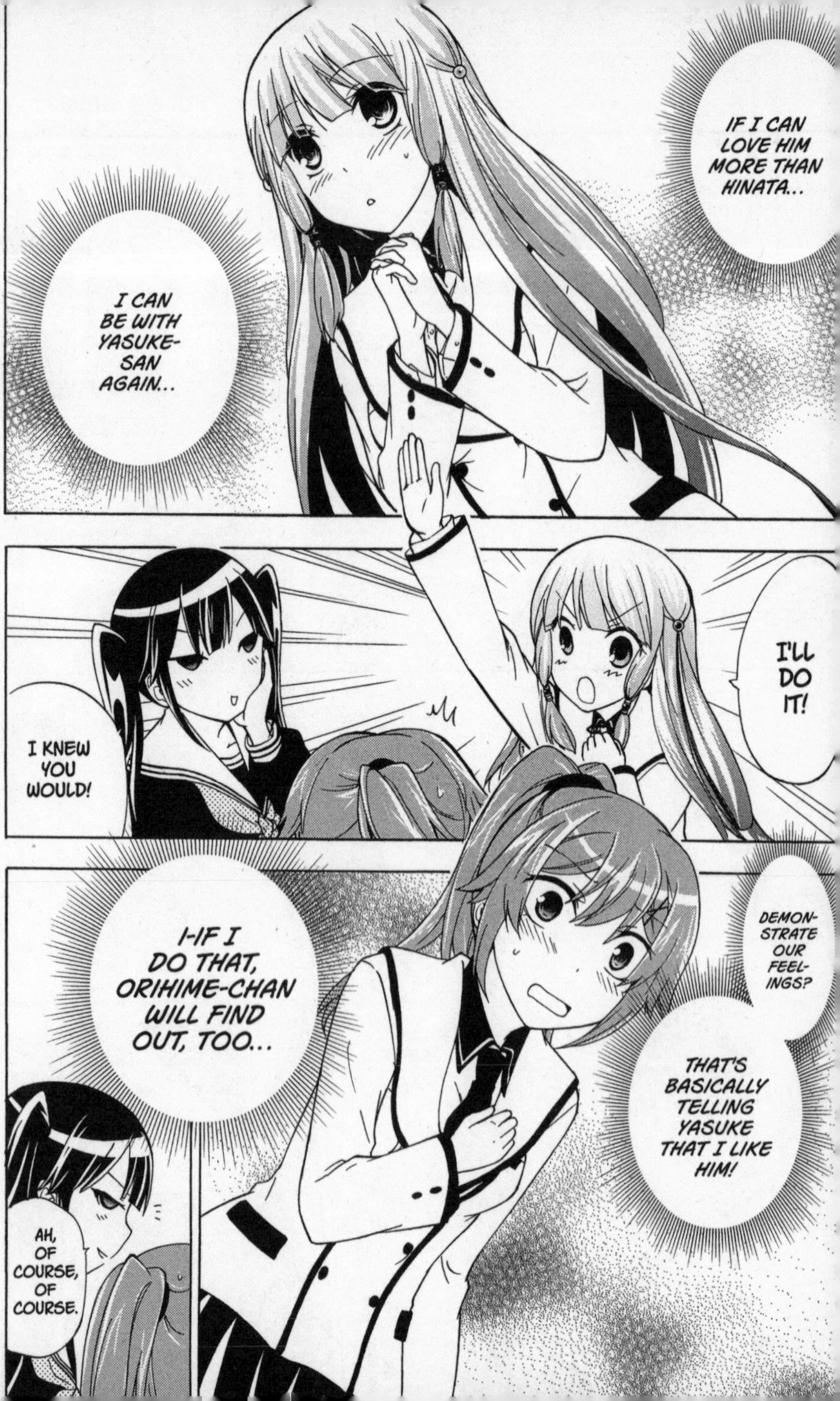
IF I CAN LOVE HIM MORE THAN HINATA...
I CAN BE WITH YASUKE-SAN AGAIN...
I'LL DO IT!
I KNEW YOU WOULD!
DEMONSTRATE OUR FEELINGS?
THAT'S BASICALLY TELLING YASUKE THAT I LIKE HIM!
I-IF I DO THAT, ORIHIME-CHAN WILL FIND OUT, TOO...
AH, OF COURSE, OF COURSE.

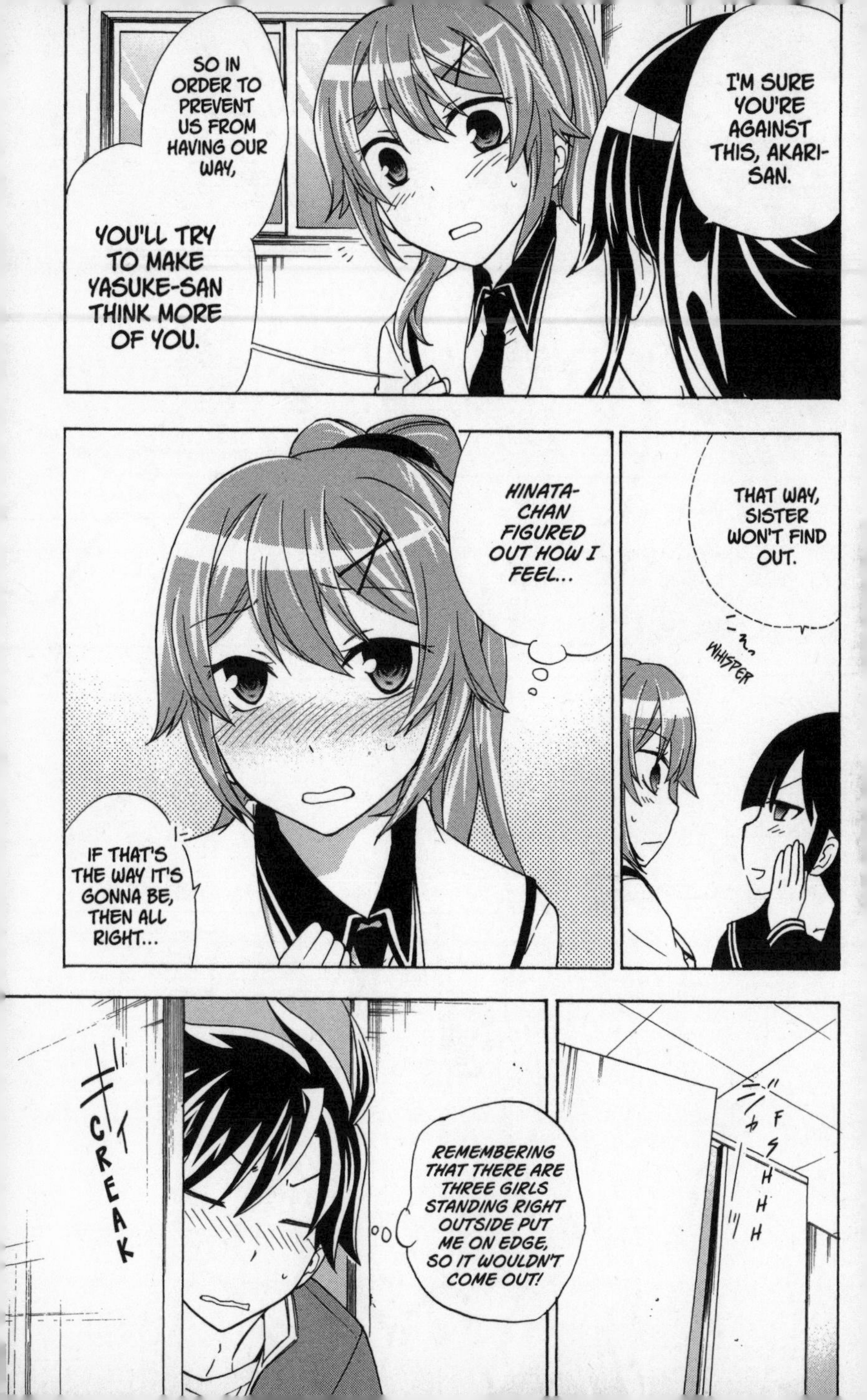
I'M SURE YOU'RE AGAINST THIS, AKARI-SAN.
SO IN ORDER TO PREVENT US FROM HAVING OUR WAY,
YOU'LL TRY TO MAKE YASUKE-SAN THINK MORE OF YOU.
THAT WAY, SISTER WON'T FIND OUT.
WHISPER
HINATA-CHAN FIGURED OUT HOW I FEEL...
IF THAT'S THE WAY IT'S GONNA BE, THEN ALL RIGHT...
FSHHHH
REMEMBERING THAT THERE ARE THREE GIRLS STANDING RIGHT OUTSIDE PUT ME ON EDGE, SO IT WOULDN'T COME OUT!
CREAK

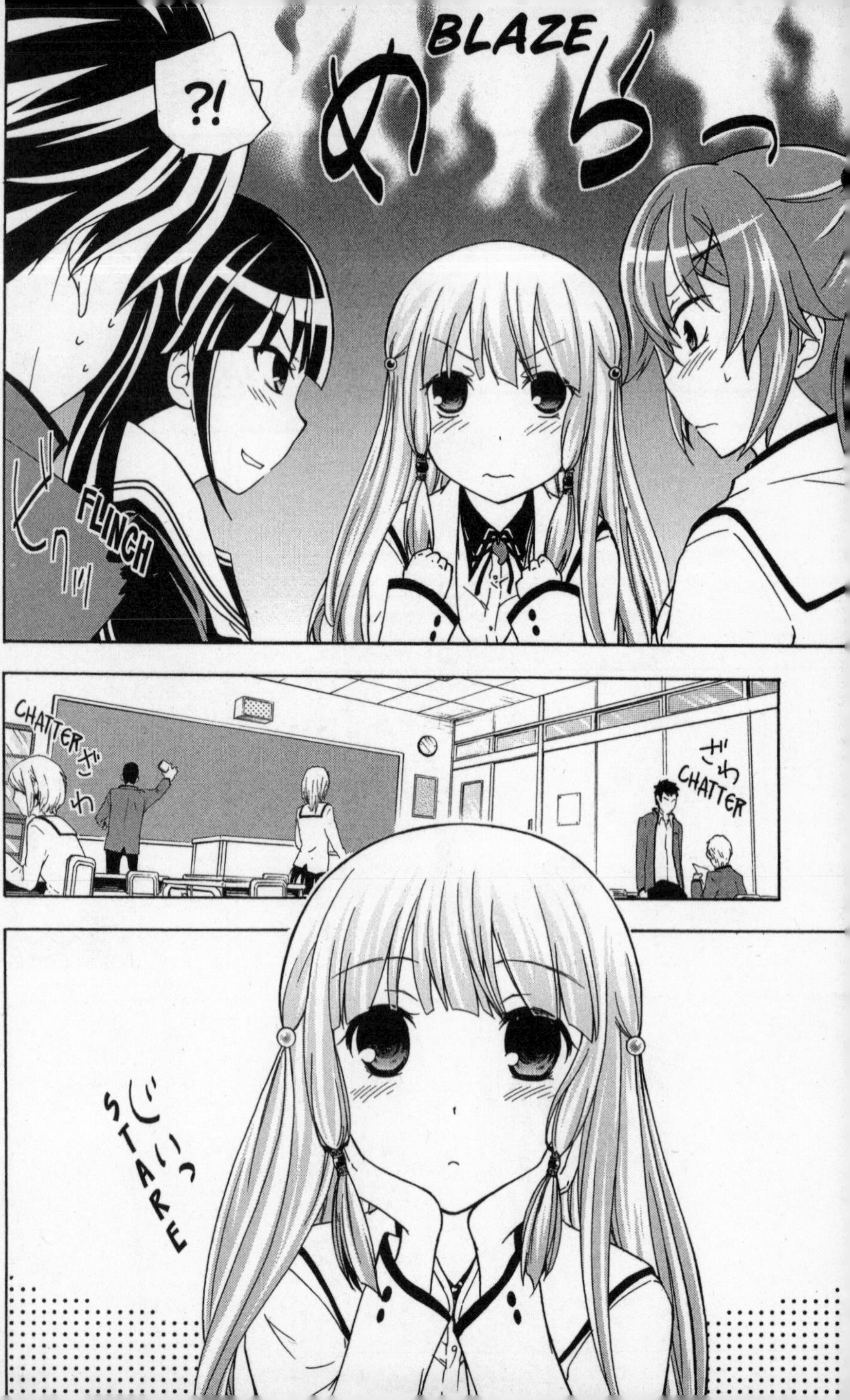
BLAZE
めらーっ
?!
FLINCH
ざわ
CHATTER
CHATTER
ざわ
じいっ
STARE

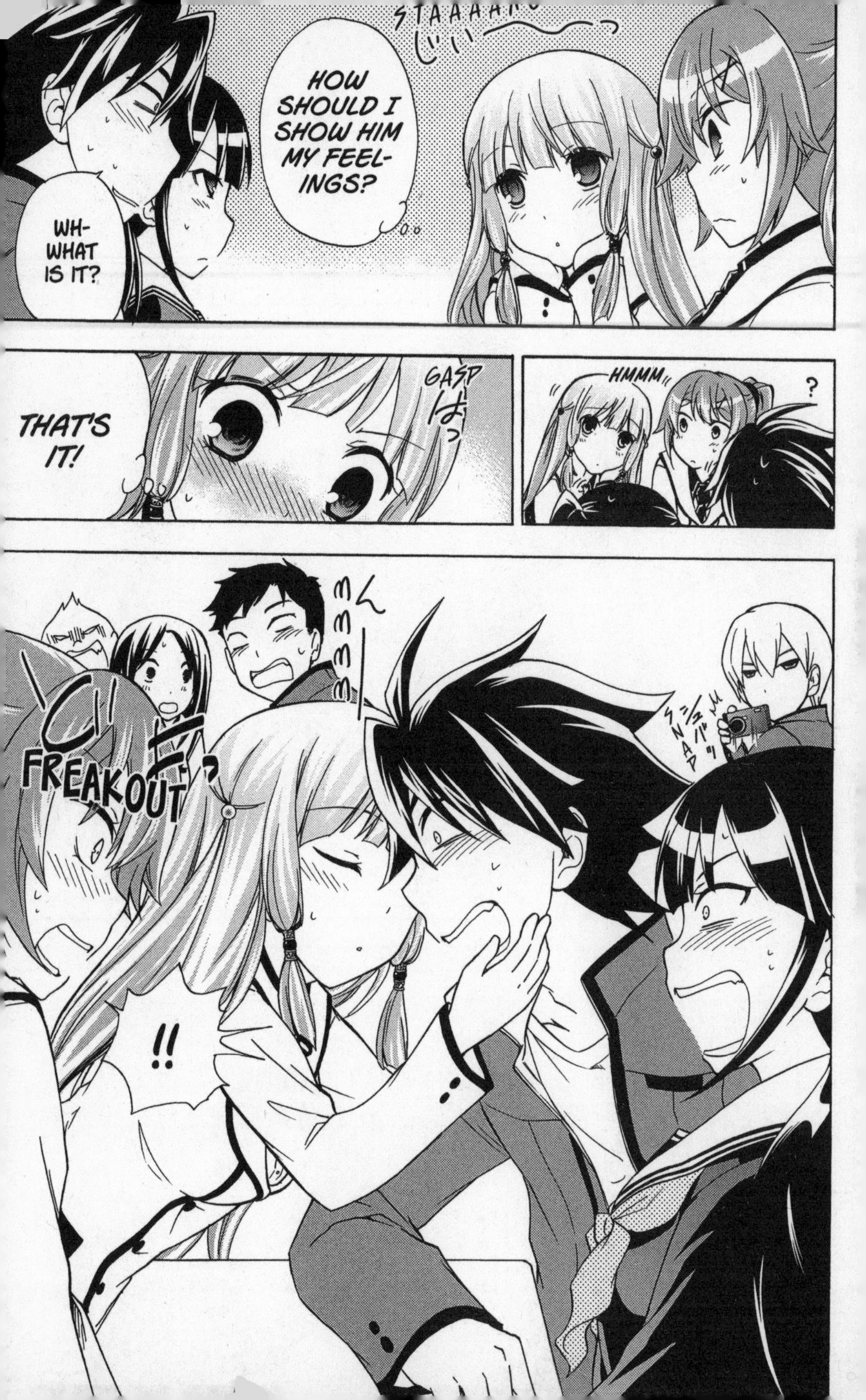
STAAAAR
HOW SHOULD I SHOW HIM MY FEEL-INGS?
WH- WHAT IS IT?
HMMM
?
GASP
THAT'S IT!
MMMMMM
SNAP
FREAKOUT
!!

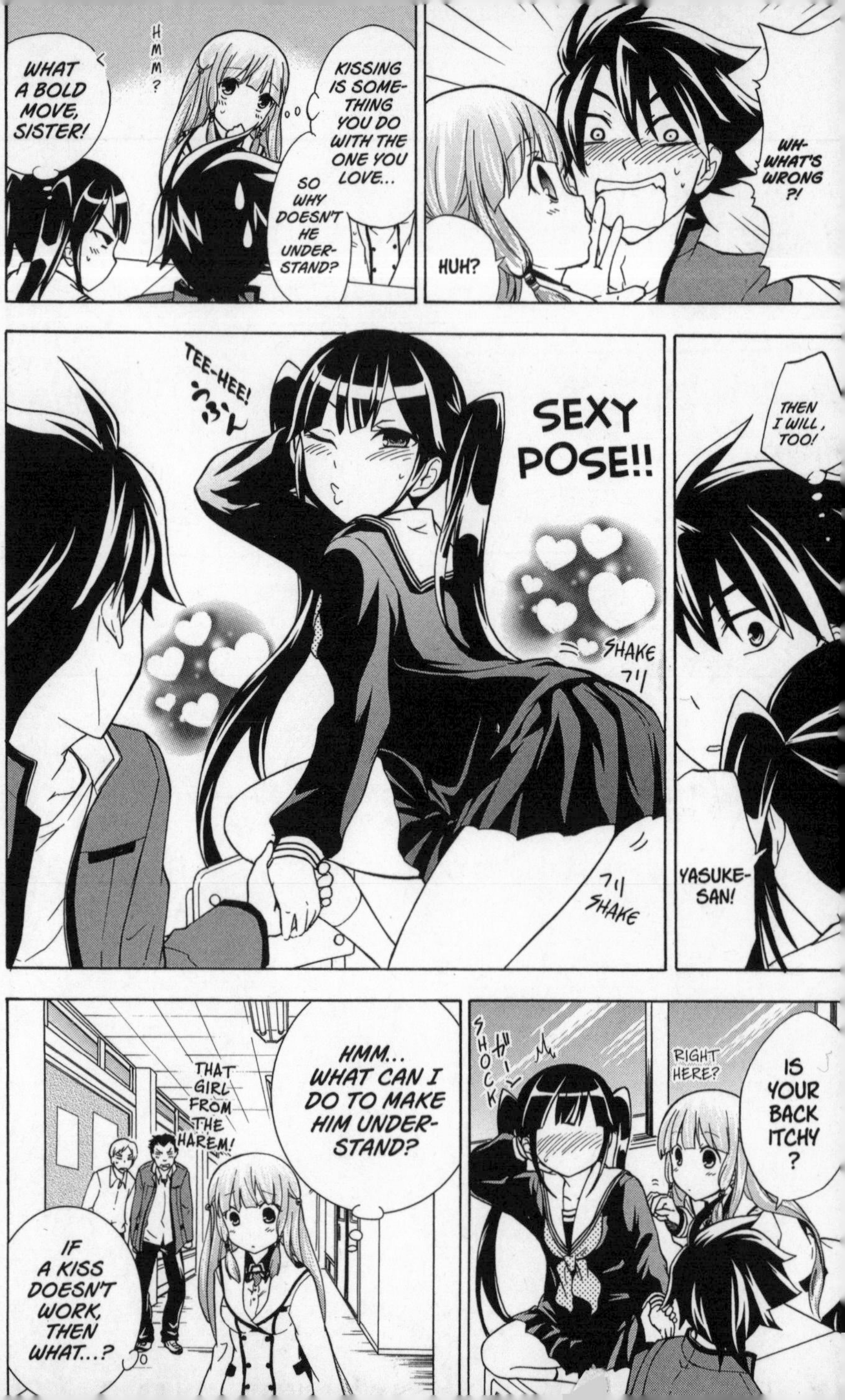
WH-WHAT'S WRONG?!
HUH?
KISSING IS SOME-THING YOU DO WITH THE ONE YOU LOVE...
SO WHY DOESN'T HE UNDER-STAND?
HMM?
WHAT A BOLD MOVE, SISTER!
THEN I WILL, TOO!
YASUKE-SAN!
SEXY POSE!!
TEE-HEE!
SHAKE フリ
フリ SHAKE
IS YOUR BACK ITCHY?
RIGHT HERE?
SHOCK
HMM... WHAT CAN I DO TO MAKE HIM UNDER-STAND?
THAT GIRL FROM THE HAREM!
IF A KISS DOESN'T WORK, THEN WHAT...?

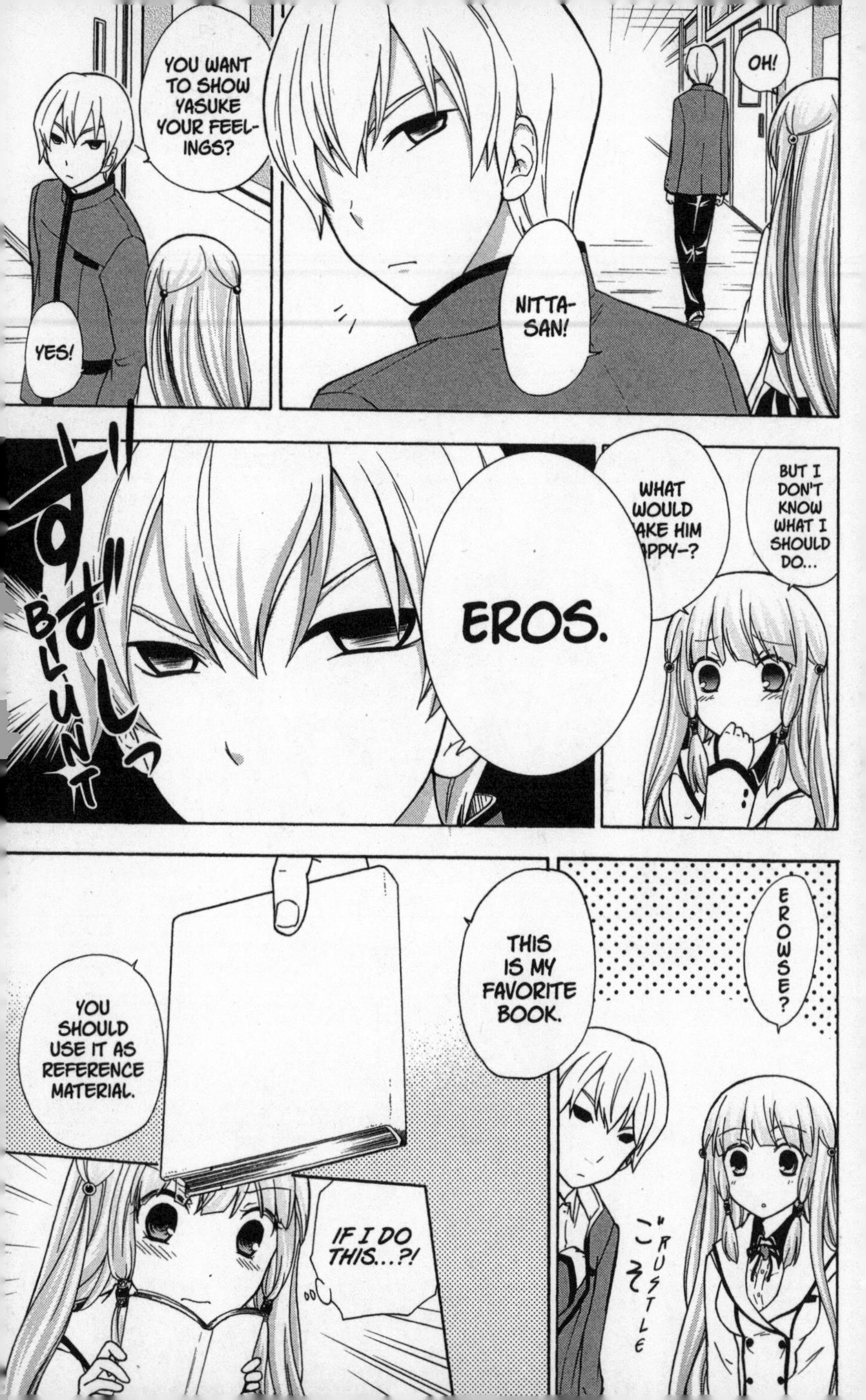
OH!
NITTA-SAN!
YOU WANT TO SHOW YASUKE YOUR FEELINGS?
YES!
BUT I DON'T KNOW WHAT I SHOULD DO...
WHAT WOULD AKE HIM APPY–?
EROS.
BLUNT
EROWSE?
THIS IS MY FAVORITE BOOK.
RUSTLE
YOU SHOULD USE IT AS REFERENCE MATERIAL.
IF I DO THIS...?!

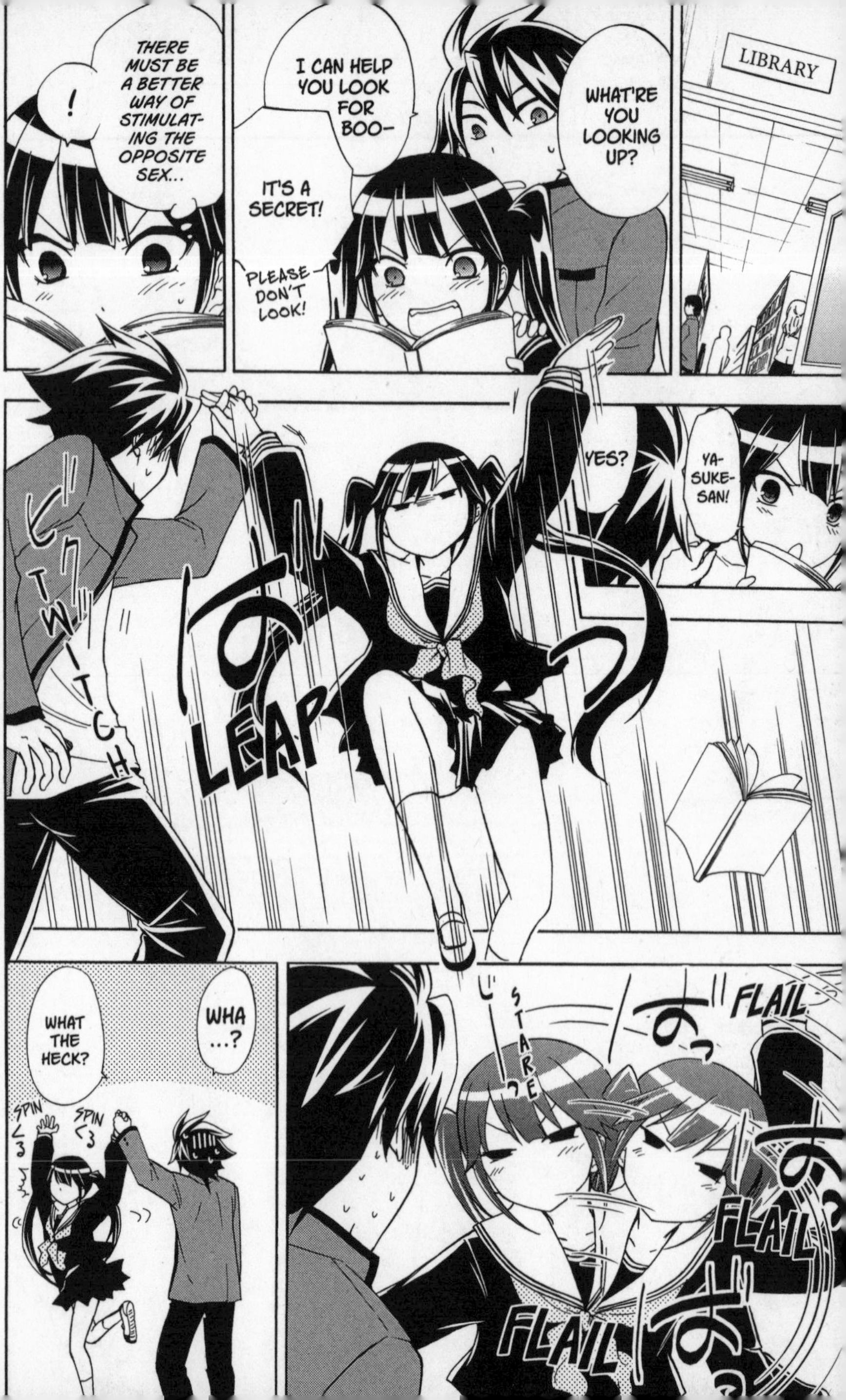
LIBRARY
WHAT'RE YOU LOOKING UP?
I CAN HELP YOU LOOK FOR BOO–
IT'S A SECRET!
PLEASE DON'T LOOK!
THERE MUST BE A BETTER WAY OF STIMULATING THE OPPOSITE SEX...
!
YA-SUKE-SAN!
YES?
TWITCH
LEAP
STARE
FLAIL
FLAIL
FLAIL
WHA ...?
WHAT THE HECK?
SPIN <3
SPIN <3

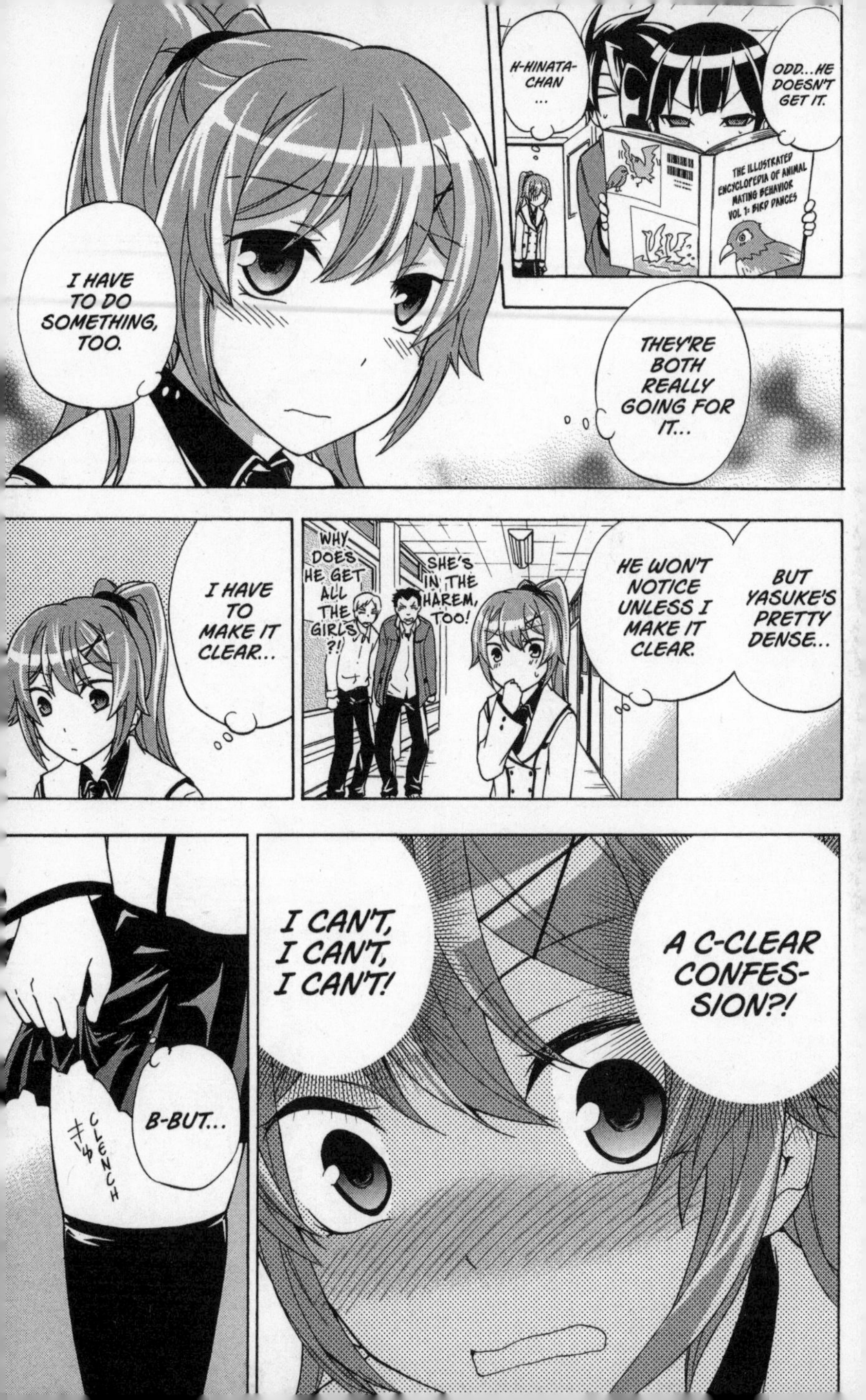
ODD...HE DOESN'T GET IT.
H-HINATA-CHAN ...
THE ILLUSTRATED ENCYCLOPEDIA OF ANIMAL MATING BEHAVIOR VOL 1: BIRD DANCES
THEY'RE BOTH REALLY GOING FOR IT...
I HAVE TO DO SOMETHING, TOO.
BUT YASUKE'S PRETTY DENSE...
HE WON'T NOTICE UNLESS I MAKE IT CLEAR.
SHE'S IN THE HAREM, TOO!
WHY DOES HE GET ALL THE GIRLS?!
I HAVE TO MAKE IT CLEAR...
A C-CLEAR CONFESSION?!
I CAN'T, I CAN'T, I CAN'T!
B-BUT...
CLENCH

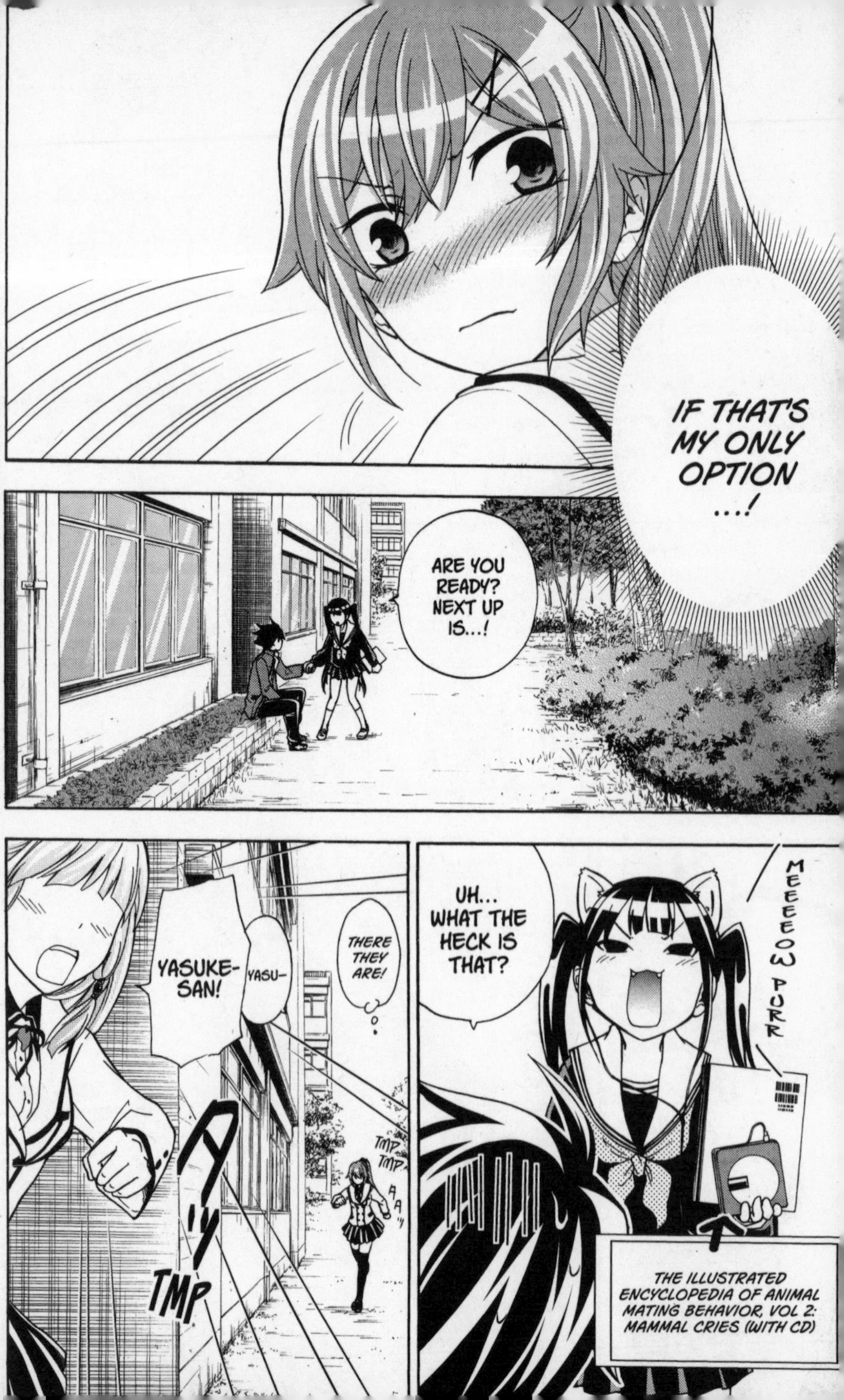
IF THAT'S MY ONLY OPTION ...!
ARE YOU READY? NEXT UP IS...!
MEEEEOW PURR
UH... WHAT THE HECK IS THAT?
THE ILLUSTRATED ENCYCLOPEDIA OF ANIMAL MATING BEHAVIOR, VOL 2: MAMMAL CRIES (WITH CD)
THERE THEY ARE!
YASU-
YASUKE-SAN!
TMP TMP
TMP

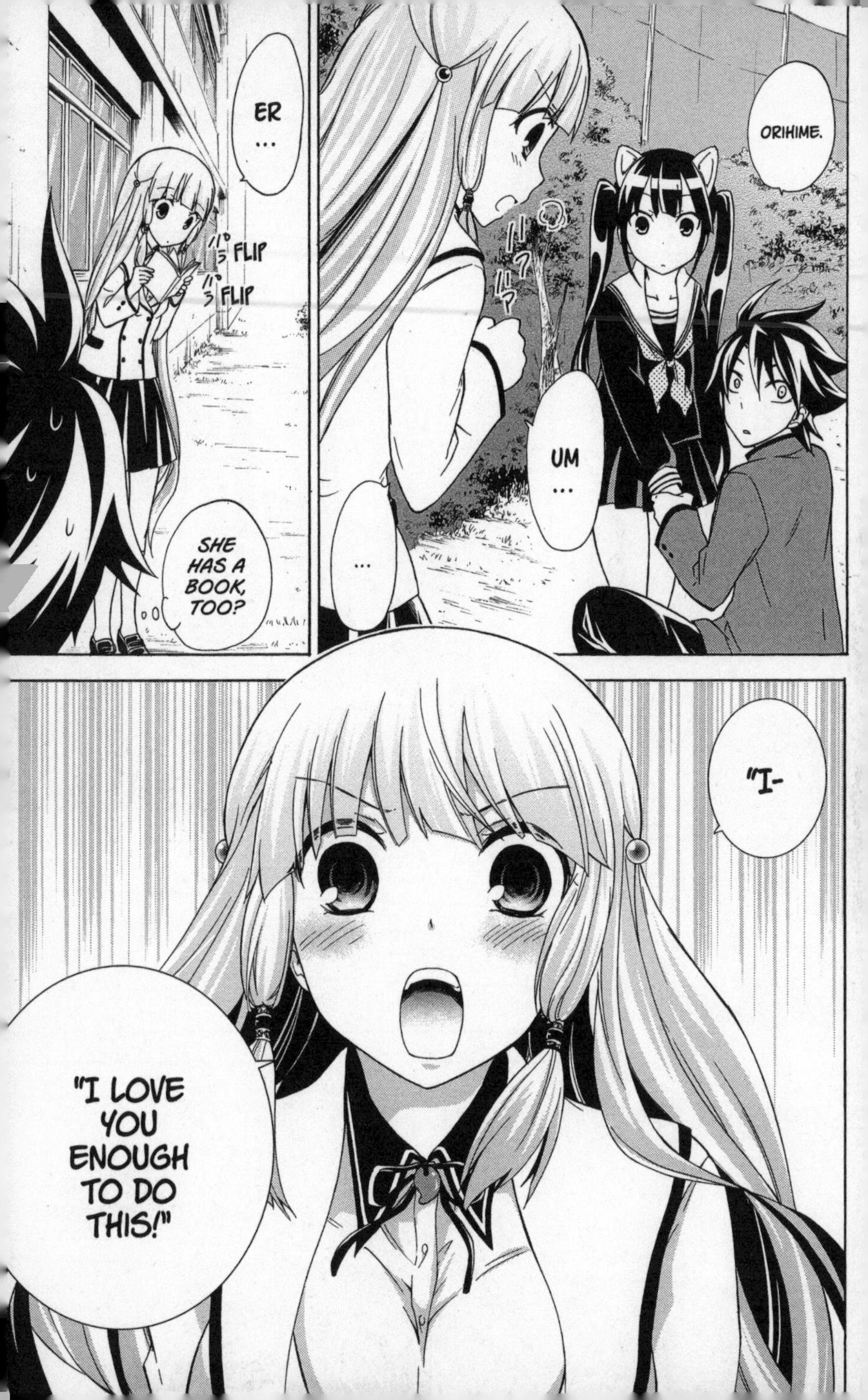
ORIHIME.
UM ...
...
ER ...
FLIP
FLIP
SHE HAS A BOOK, TOO?
"I-
"I LOVE YOU ENOUGH TO DO THIS!"

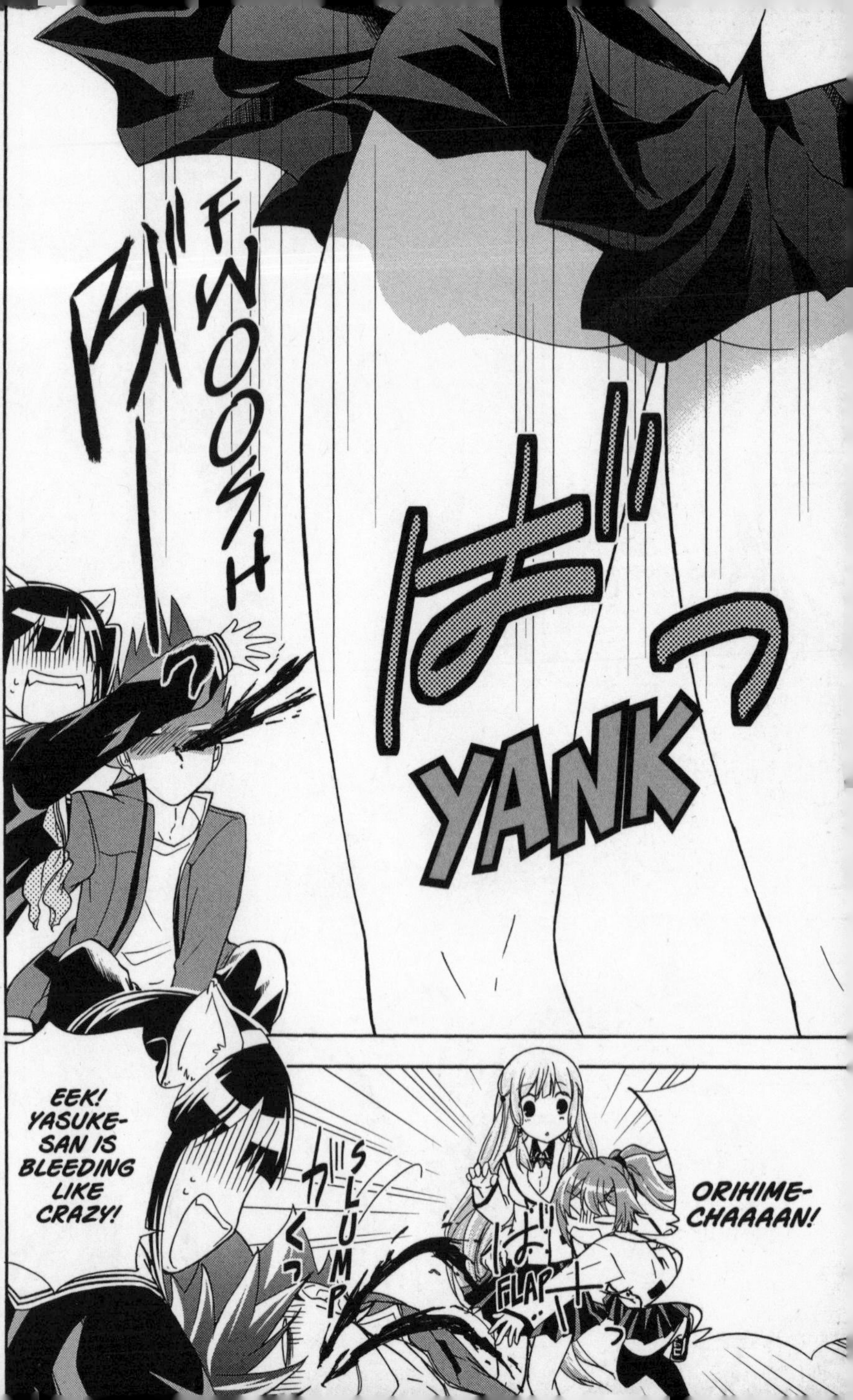
ばっ
YANK
ばー
FWOOSH
ORIHIME-CHAAAAN!
ばっ
FLAP
EEK! YASUKE-SAN IS BLEEDING LIKE CRAZY!
がくっ
SLUMP!

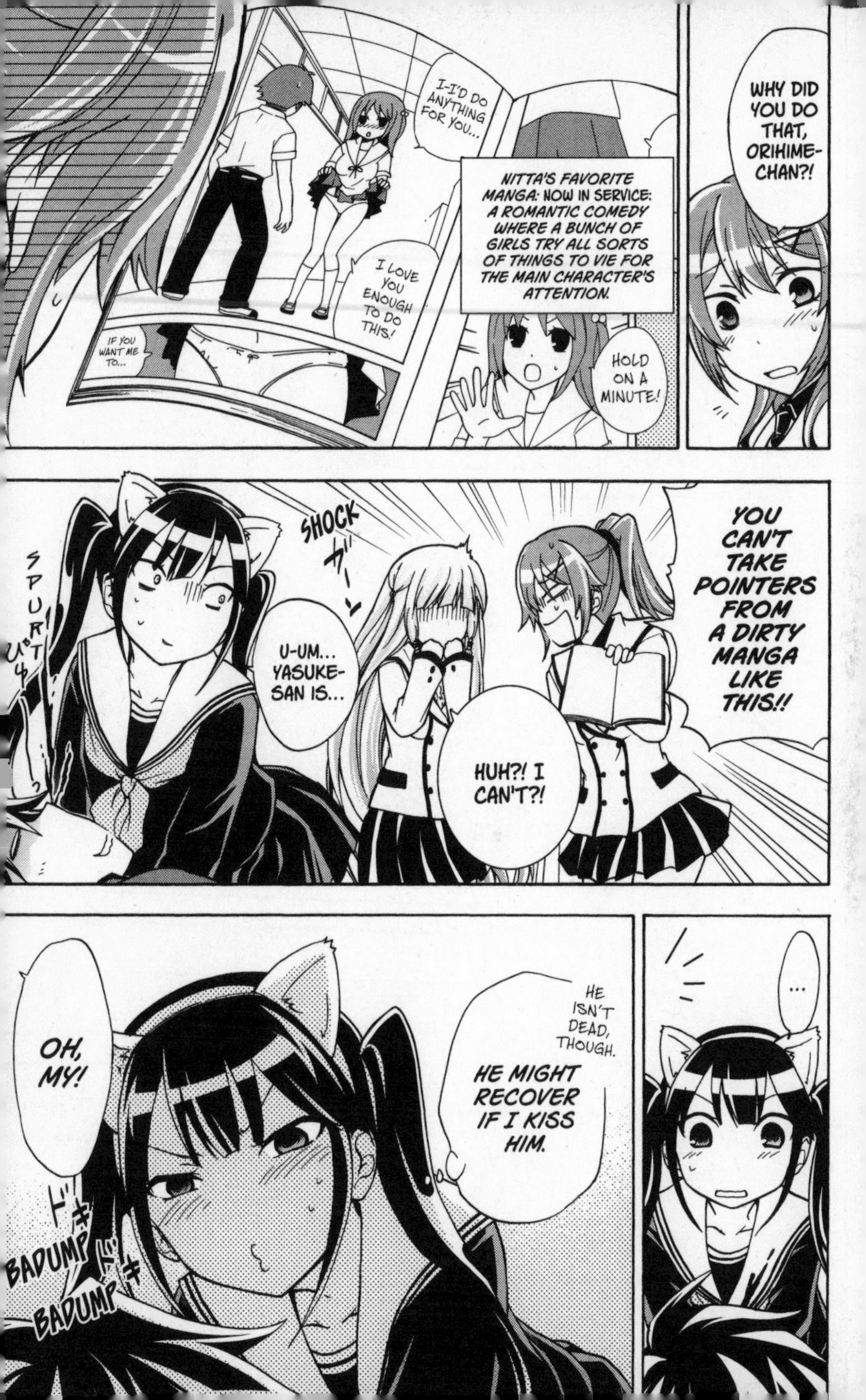
WHY DID YOU DO THAT, ORIHIME-CHAN?!
NITTA'S FAVORITE MANGA: NOW IN SERVICE: A ROMANTIC COMEDY WHERE A BUNCH OF GIRLS TRY ALL SORTS OF THINGS TO VIE FOR THE MAIN CHARACTER'S ATTENTION.
I-I'D DO ANYTHING FOR YOU...
HOLD ON A MINUTE!
I LOVE YOU ENOUGH TO DO THIS!
IF YOU WANT ME TO...
YOU CAN'T TAKE POINTERS FROM A DIRTY MANGA LIKE THIS!!
SHOCK
HUH?! I CAN'T?!
U-UM... YASUKE-SAN IS...
SPURT
...
HE ISN'T DEAD, THOUGH.
HE MIGHT RECOVER IF I KISS HIM.
OH, MY!
BADUMP
BADUMP

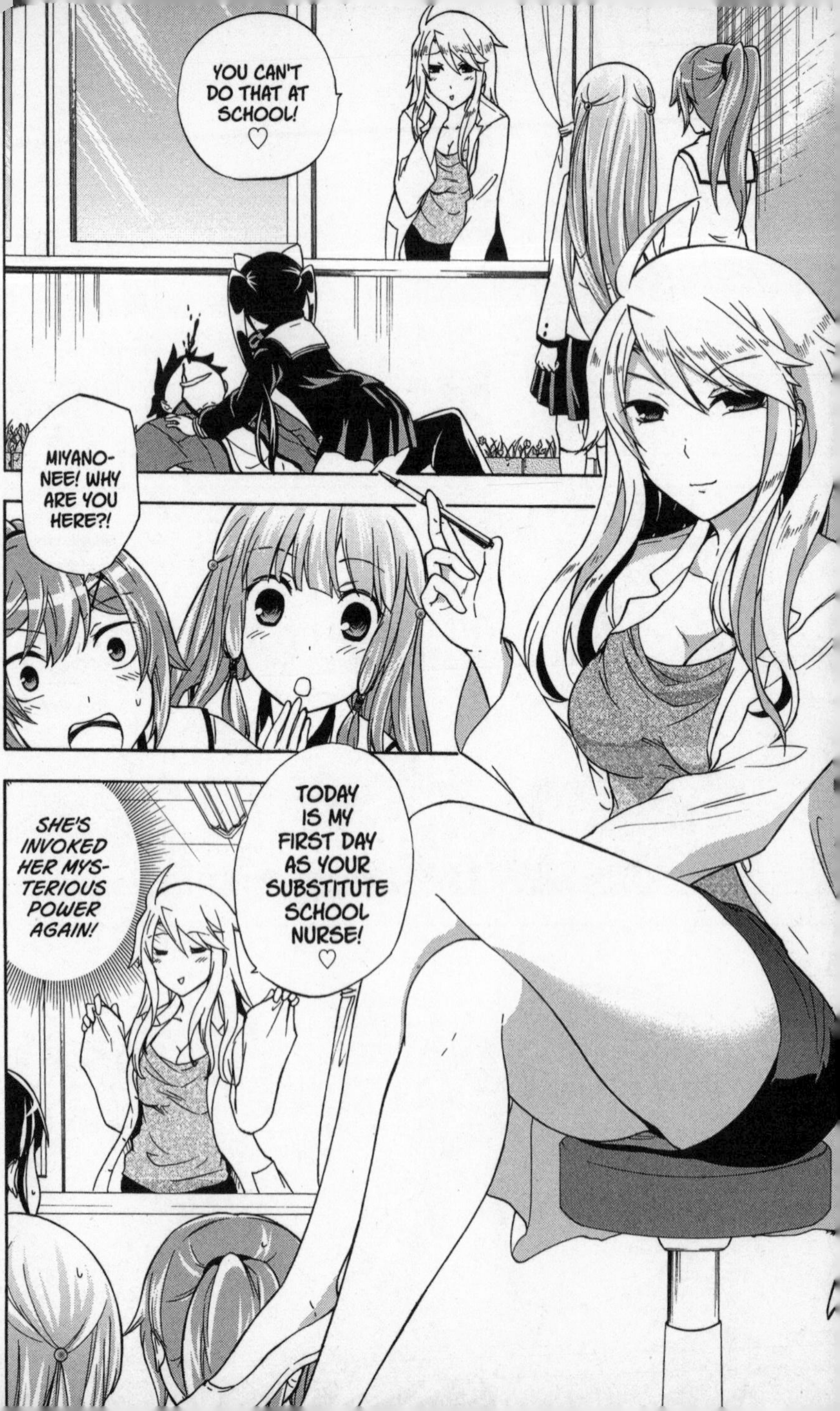
YOU CAN'T DO THAT AT SCHOOL! ♡
MIYANO-NEE! WHY ARE YOU HERE?!
TODAY IS MY FIRST DAY AS YOUR SUBSTITUTE SCHOOL NURSE! ♡
SHE'S INVOKED HER MYS-TERIOUS POWER AGAIN!

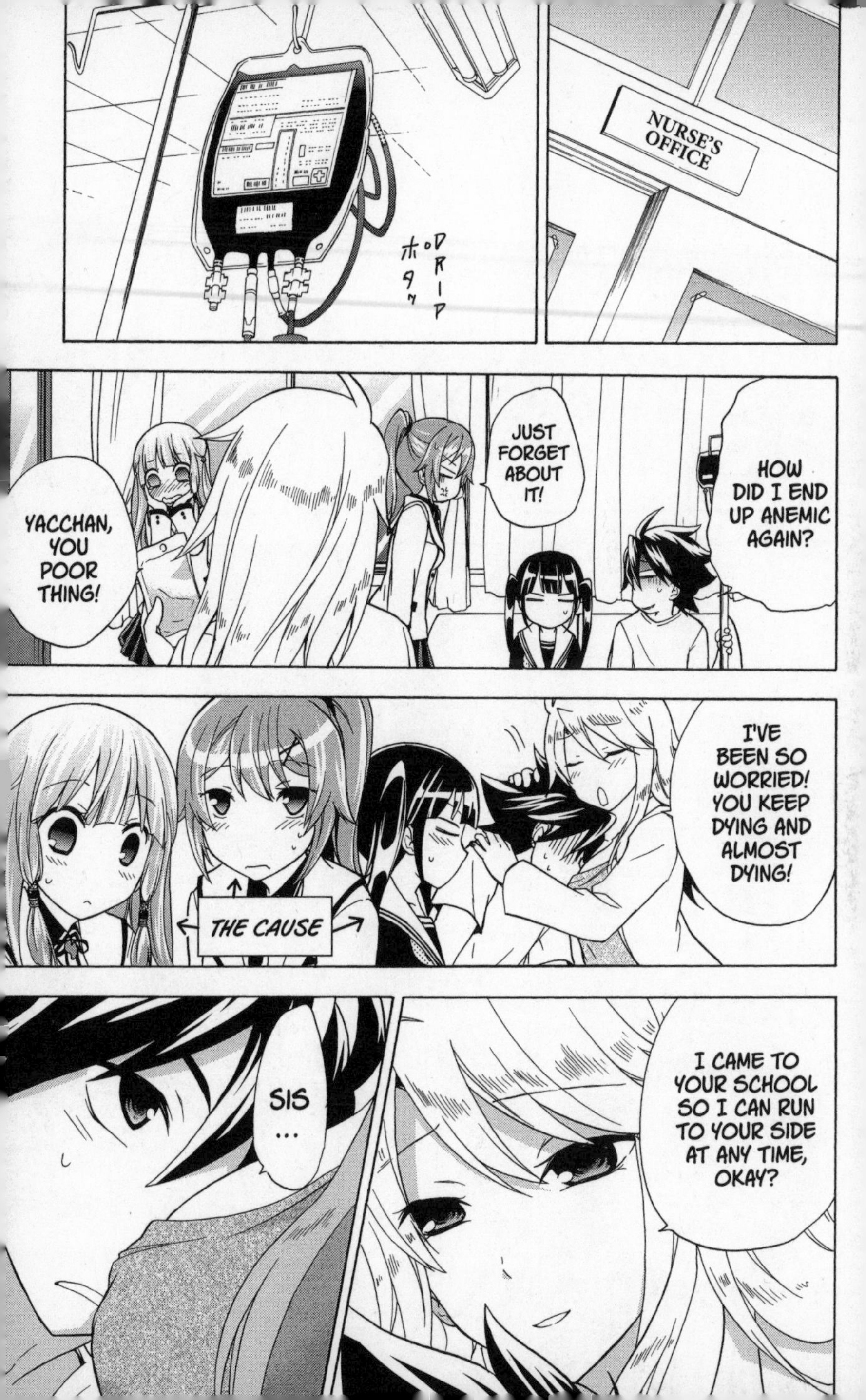
NURSE'S OFFICE
DRIP
ポタッ
HOW DID I END UP ANEMIC AGAIN?
JUST FORGET ABOUT IT!
YACCHAN, YOU POOR THING!
I'VE BEEN SO WORRIED! YOU KEEP DYING AND ALMOST DYING!
THE CAUSE
I CAME TO YOUR SCHOOL SO I CAN RUN TO YOUR SIDE AT ANY TIME, OKAY?
SIS ...

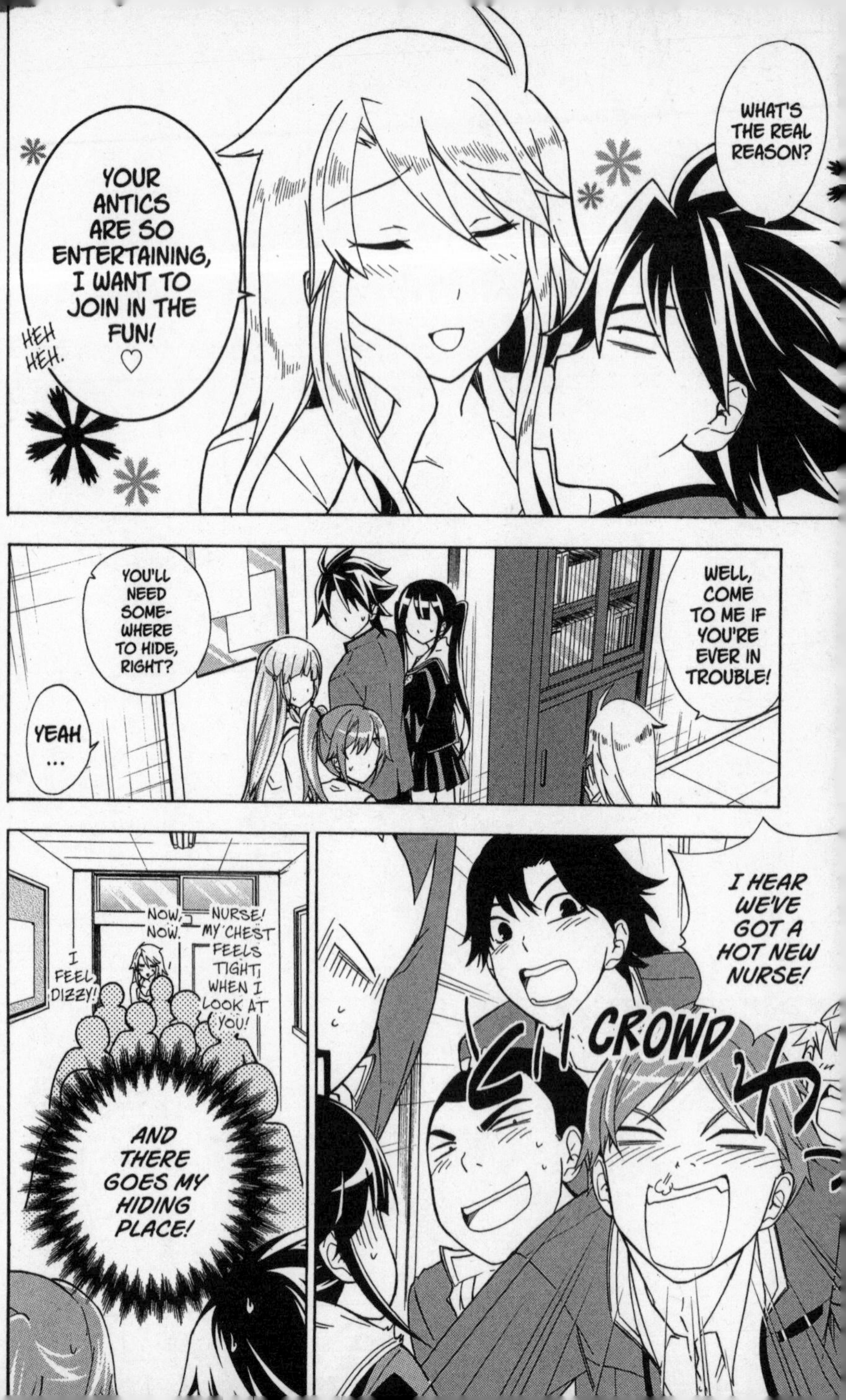
WHAT'S THE REAL REASON?
YOUR ANTICS ARE SO ENTERTAINING, I WANT TO JOIN IN THE FUN! ♡
HEH HEH.
WELL, COME TO ME IF YOU'RE EVER IN TROUBLE!
YOU'LL NEED SOME-WHERE TO HIDE, RIGHT?
YEAH ...
I HEAR WE'VE GOT A HOT NEW NURSE!
CROWD
NURSE! MY CHEST FEELS TIGHT, WHEN I LOOK AT YOU!
NOW, NOW.
I FEEL DIZZY!
AND THERE GOES MY HIDING PLACE!

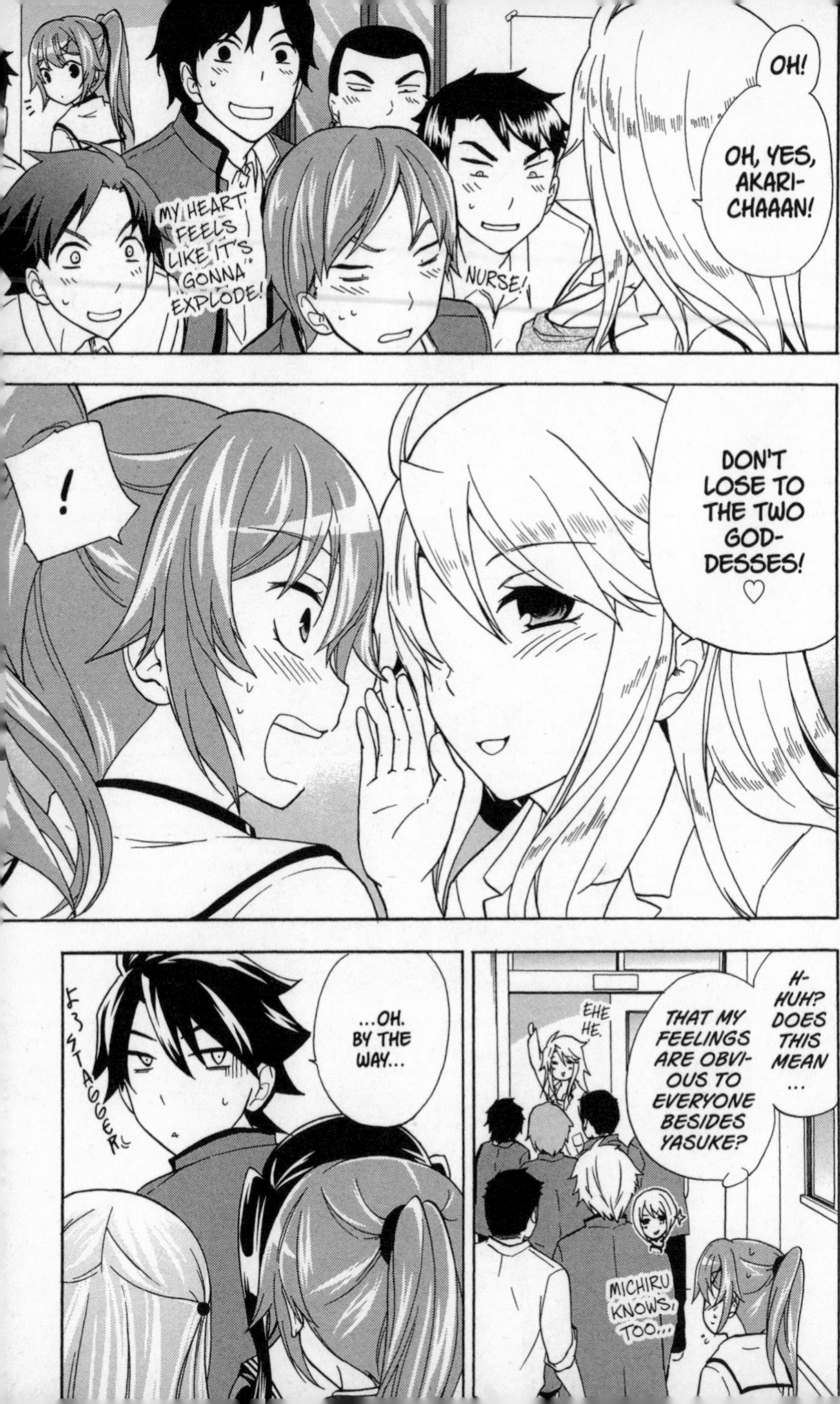
OH!
OH, YES, AKARI-CHAAAN!
NURSE!
MY HEART FEELS LIKE IT'S "GONNA" EXPLODE!
DON'T LOSE TO THE TWO GOD-DESSES! ♡
!
H-HUH? DOES THIS MEAN ...
THAT MY FEELINGS ARE OBVI-OUS TO EVERYONE BESIDES YASUKE?
EHE HE.
MICHIRU KNOWS, TOO...
...OH. BY THE WAY...
よろ STAGGER

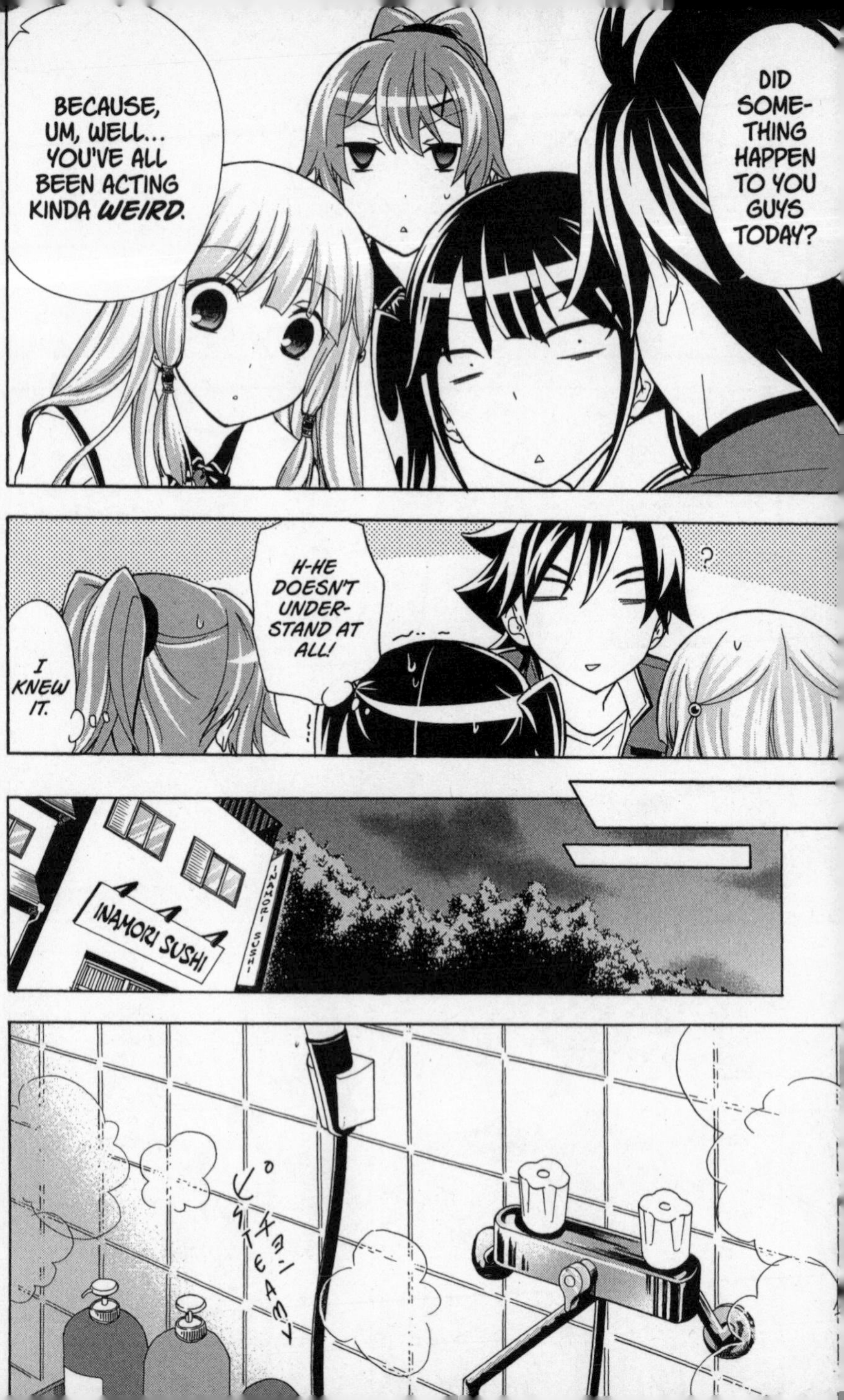
DID SOMETHING HAPPEN TO YOU GUYS TODAY?
BECAUSE, UM, WELL... YOU'VE ALL BEEN ACTING KINDA WEIRD.
?
H-HE DOESN'T UNDERSTAND AT ALL!
I KNEW IT.
INAMORI SUSHI
INAMORI SUSHI
STEAM

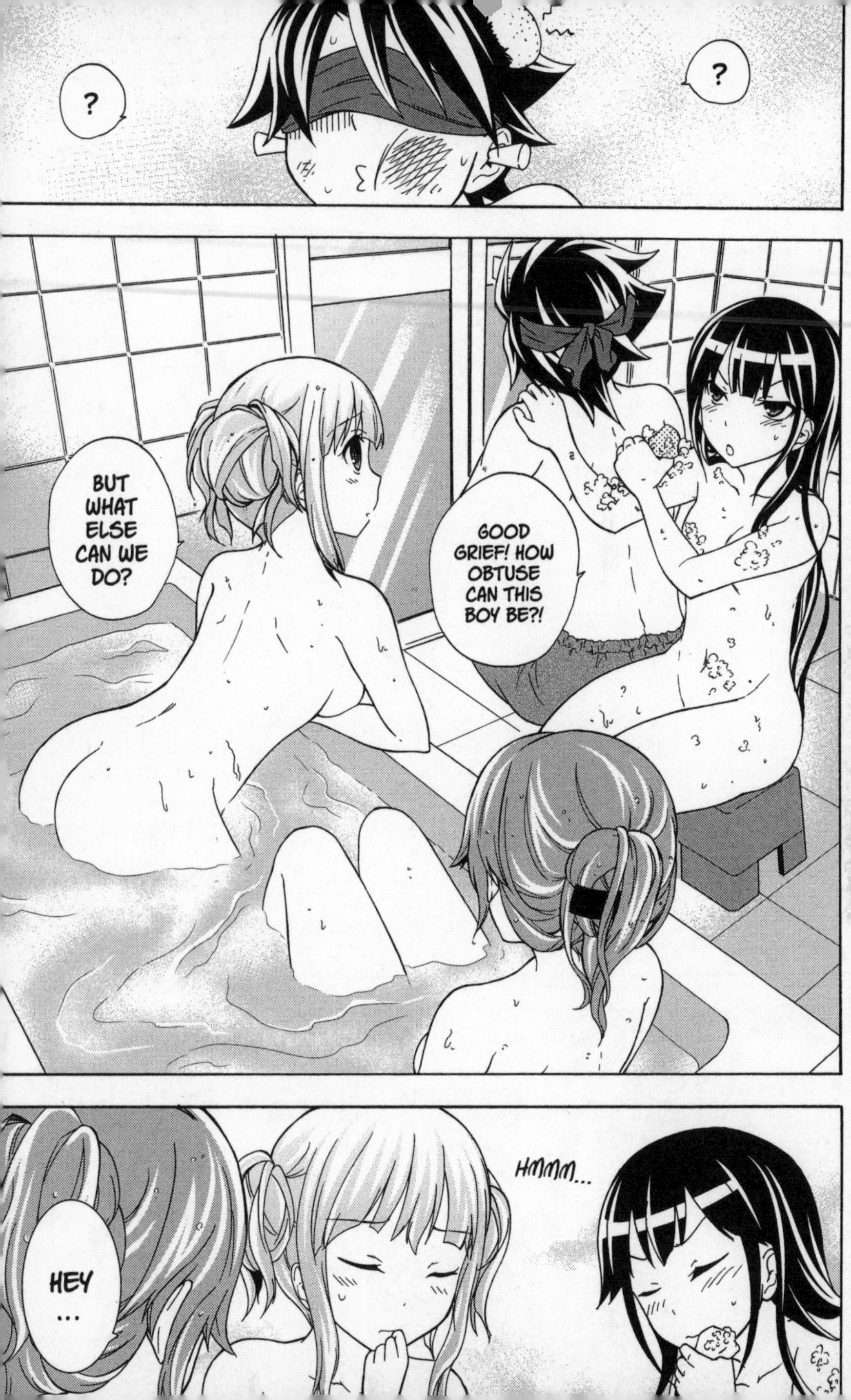
?
?
GOOD GRIEF! HOW OBTUSE CAN THIS BOY BE?!
BUT WHAT ELSE CAN WE DO?
HMMM...
HEY ...

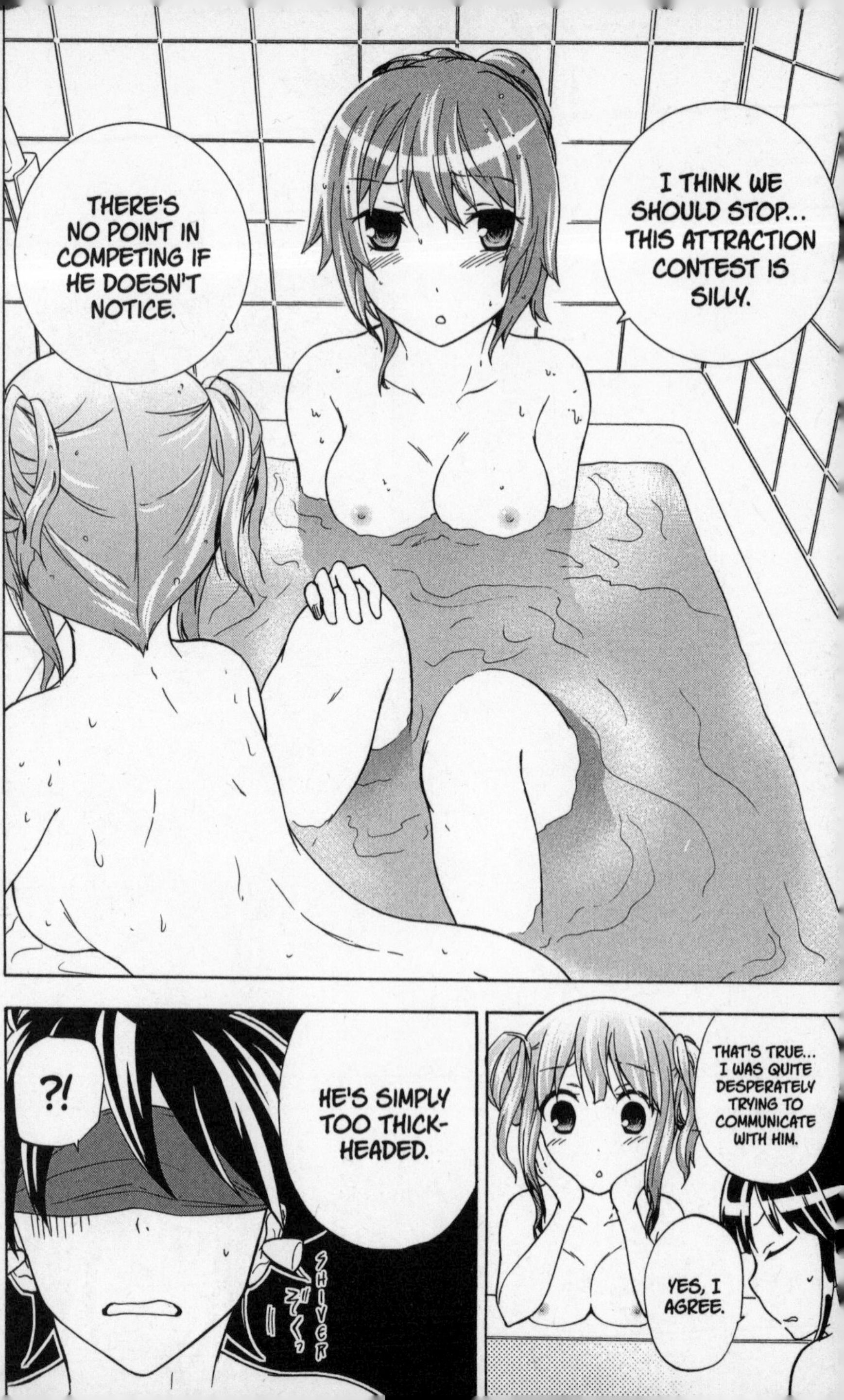
I THINK WE SHOULD STOP... THIS ATTRACTION CONTEST IS SILLY.
THERE'S NO POINT IN COMPETING IF HE DOESN'T NOTICE.
THAT'S TRUE... I WAS QUITE DESPERATELY TRYING TO COMMUNICATE WITH HIM.
YES, I AGREE.
HE'S SIMPLY TOO THICK-HEADED.
?!
SHIVER

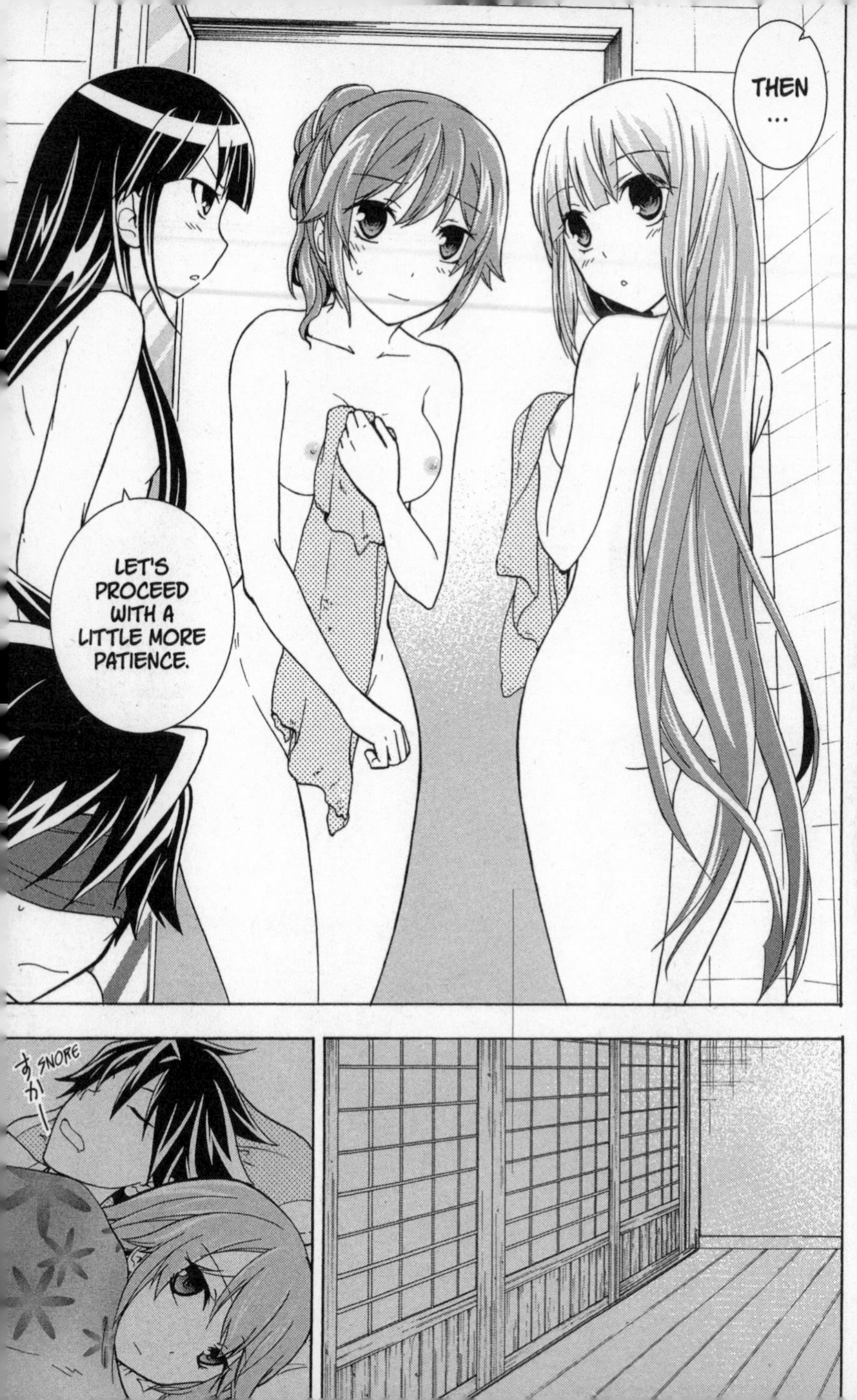
THEN ...
LET'S PROCEED WITH A LITTLE MORE PATIENCE.
すかー SNORE

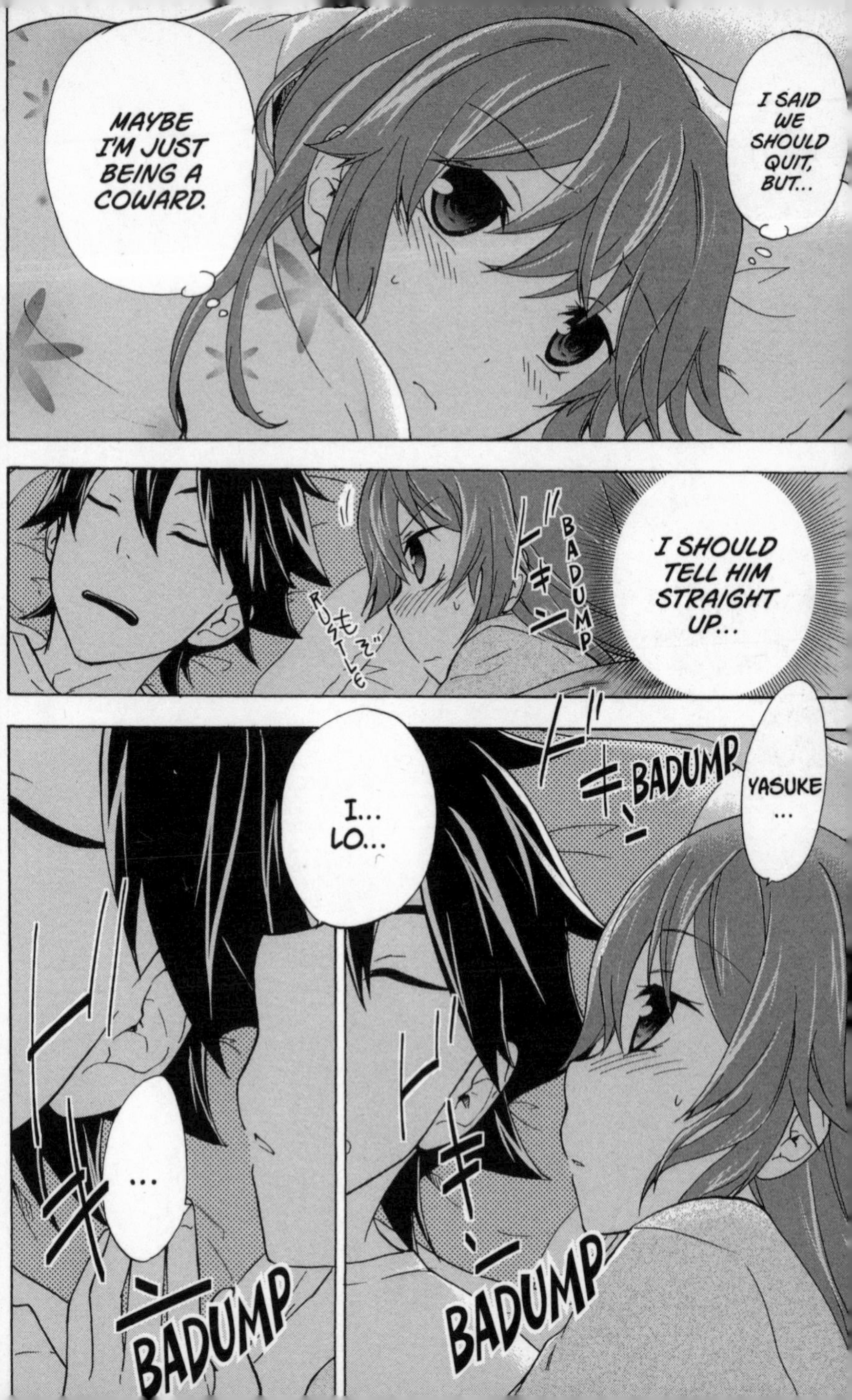
I SAID WE SHOULD QUIT, BUT...
MAYBE I'M JUST BEING A COWARD.
I SHOULD TELL HIM STRAIGHT UP...
BADUMP
RUSTLE
BADUMP
YASUKE...
I... LO...
BADUMP
...
BADUMP

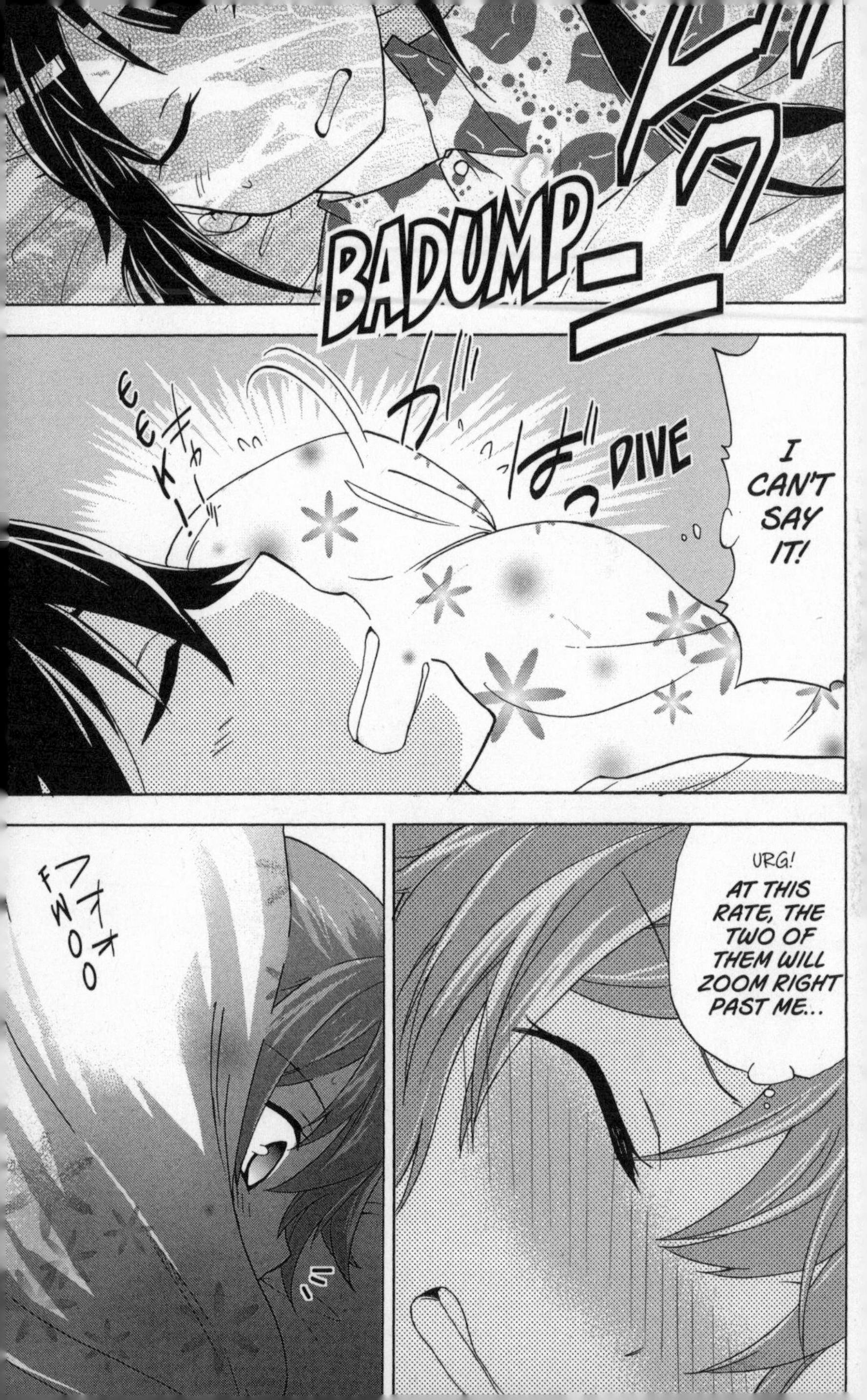
BADUMP
I CAN'T SAY IT!
DIVE
EEK!
URG!
AT THIS RATE, THE TWO OF THEM WILL ZOOM RIGHT PAST ME...
FWOO

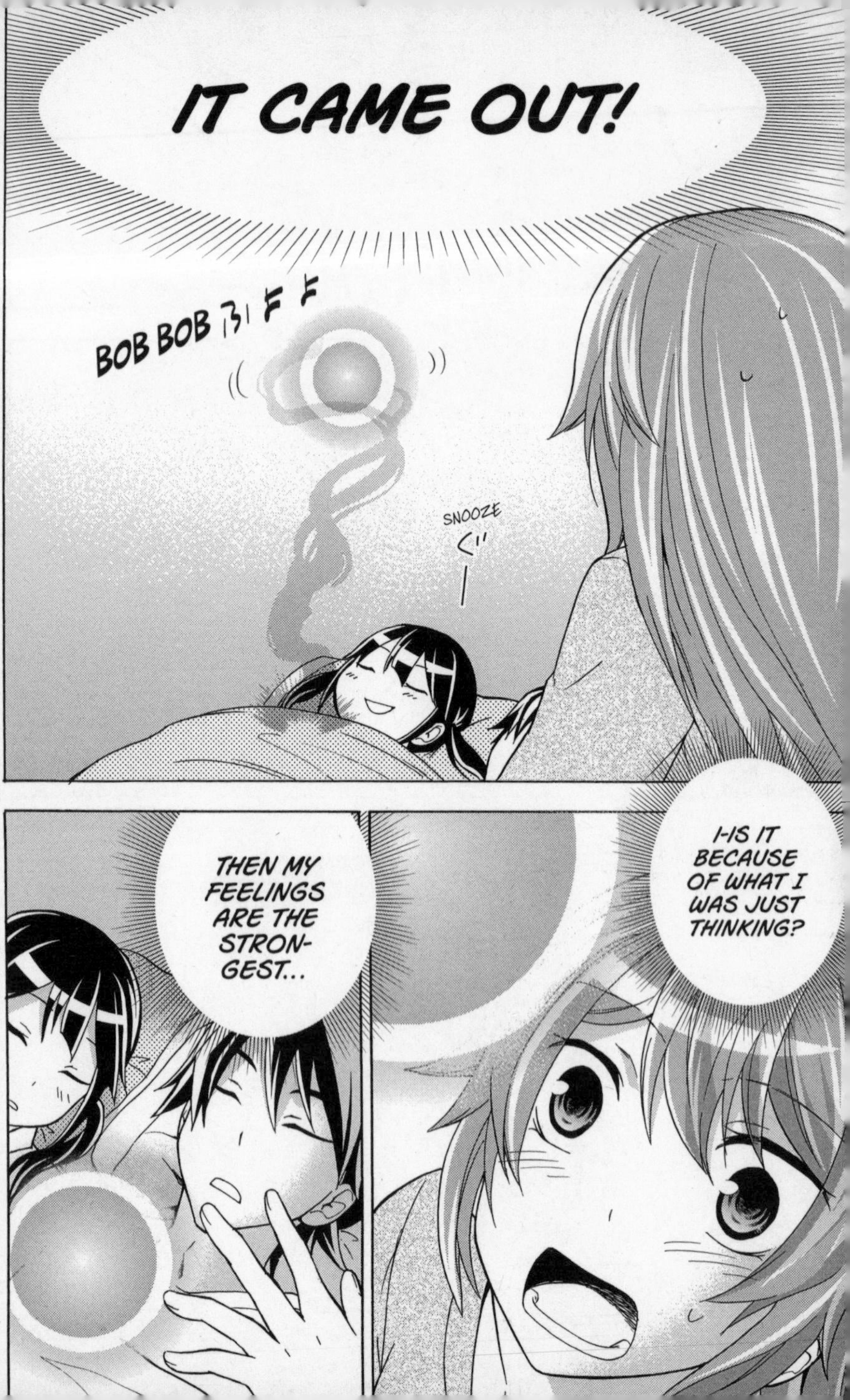
IT CAME OUT!
BOB BOB ふよ
SNOOZE ぐー
I-IS IT BECAUSE OF WHAT I WAS JUST THINKING?
THEN MY FEELINGS ARE THE STRON-GEST...

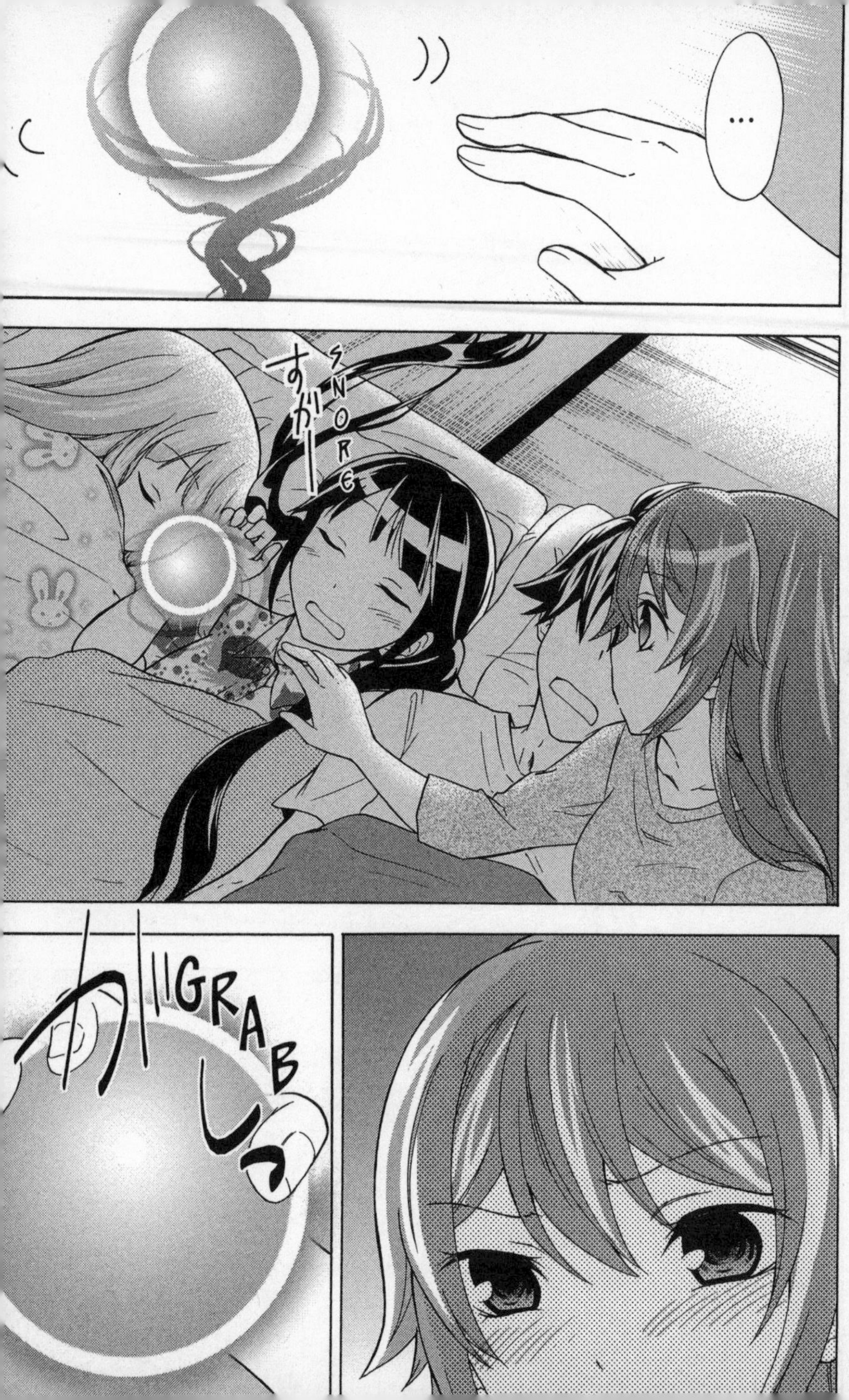
...
すかー
SNORE
がしっ
GRAB

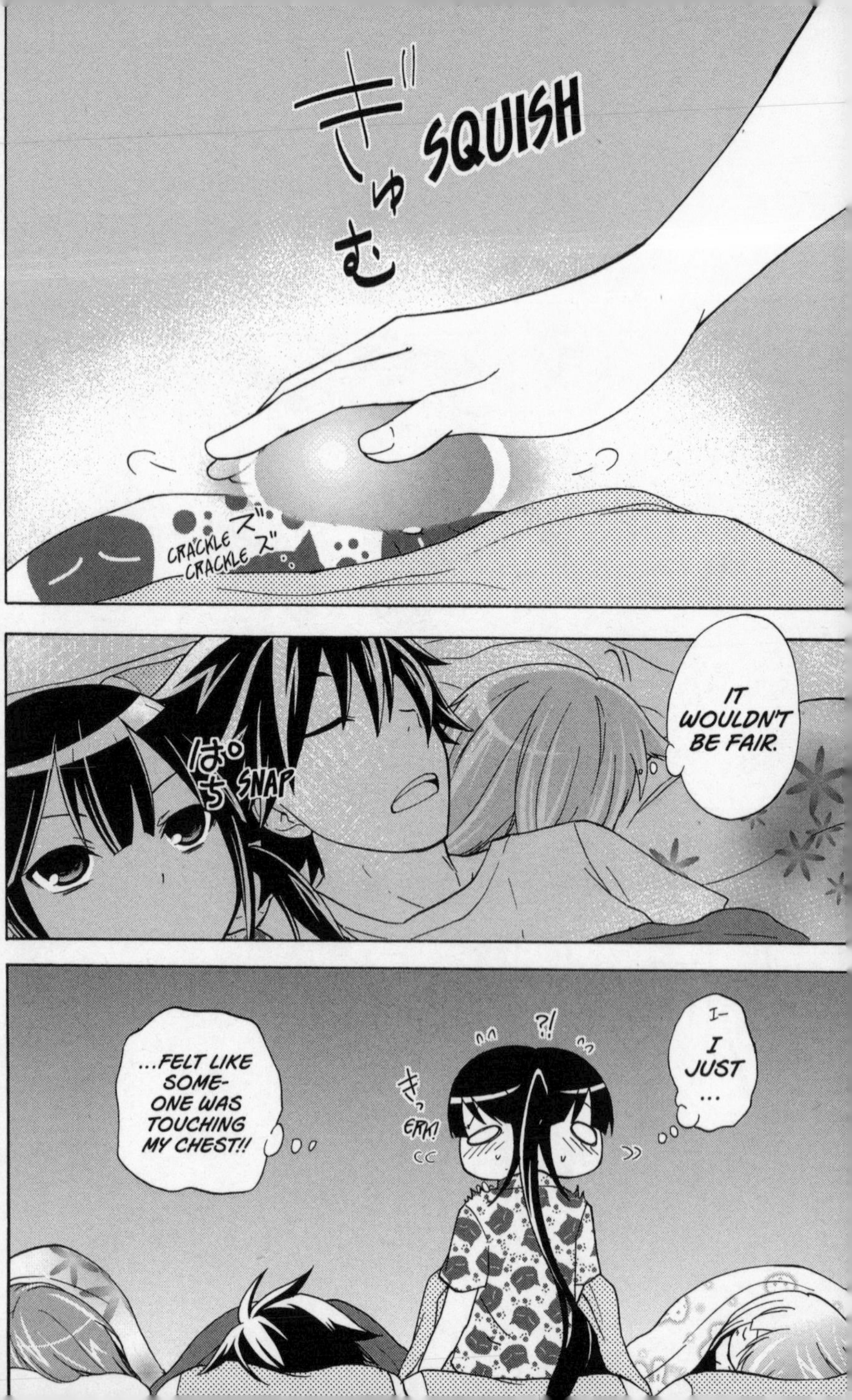

ぎゅむ
SQUISH
ズズ
CRACKLE
CRACKLE
IT WOULDN'T BE FAIR.
ぱち
SNAP
I- I JUST ...
?!
きっ
ERK!
...FELT LIKE SOME- ONE WAS TOUCHING MY CHEST!!

Maga-Tsuki
Presented by Hoshino Taguchi

DANCE OF THE RIFLEBIRD. FROM
"AN ILLUSTRATED GUIDE TO
ANIMAL COURTSHIP BEHAVIORS:
VOLUME I, BIRD DANCES."

まがつき

Maga-Tsuki
Presented by Hoshino Taguchi

Maga-Tsuki Taguchi Hoshino

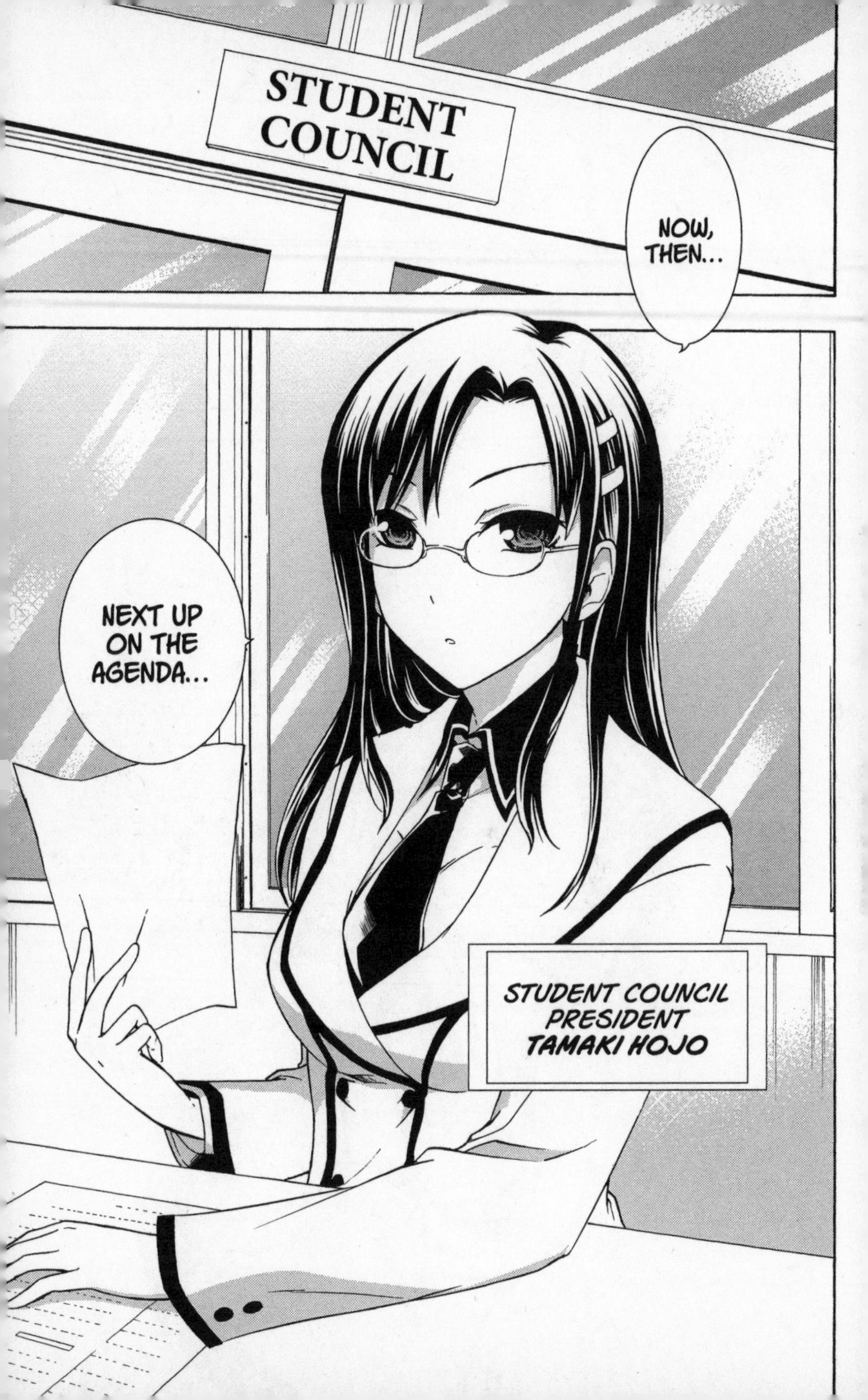
STUDENT COUNCIL
NOW, THEN...
NEXT UP ON THE AGENDA...
STUDENT COUNCIL PRESIDENT TAMAKI HOJO

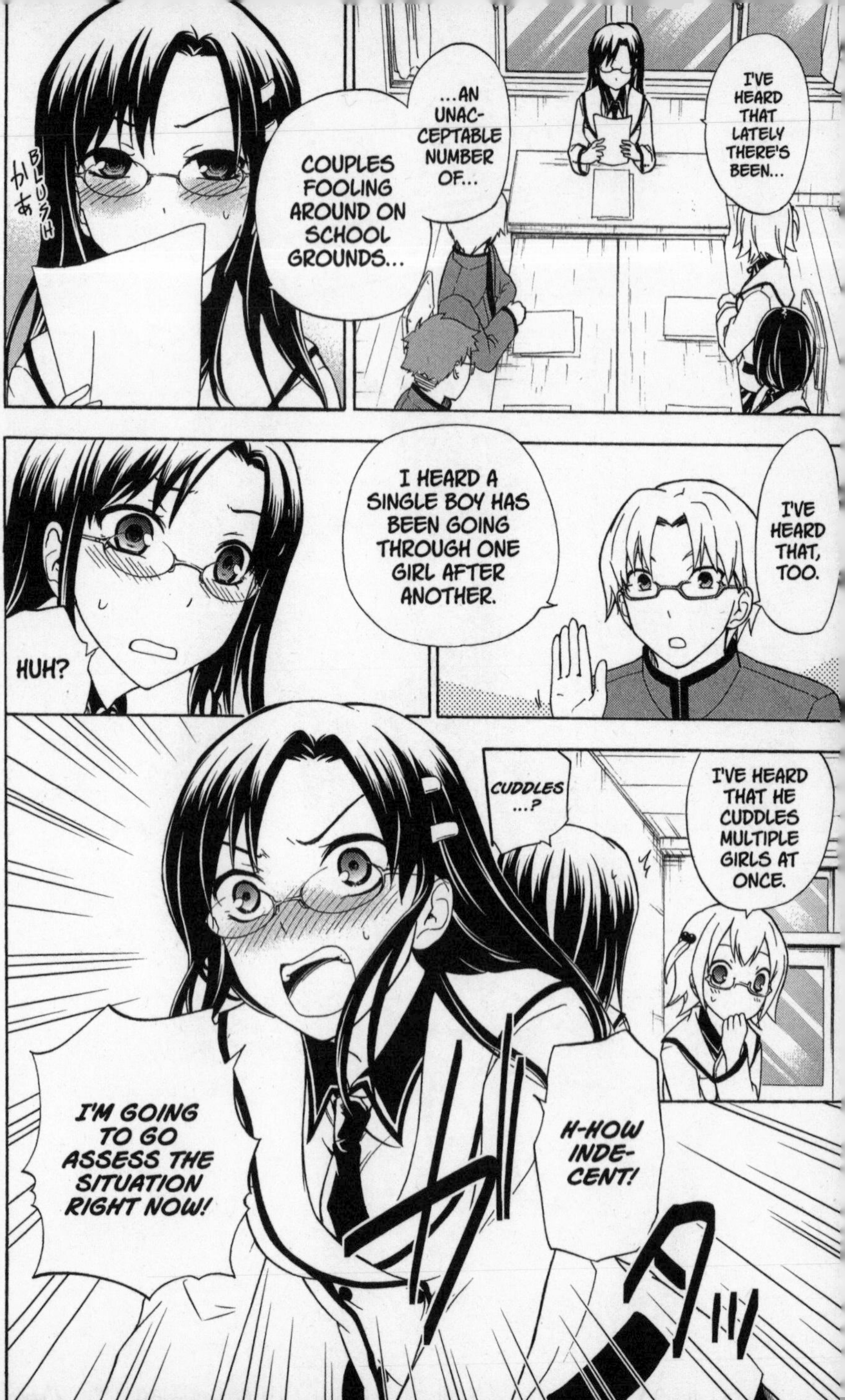
I'VE HEARD THAT LATELY THERE'S BEEN...
...AN UNAC-CEPTABLE NUMBER OF...
COUPLES FOOLING AROUND ON SCHOOL GROUNDS...
BLUSH
かあ
I'VE HEARD THAT, TOO.
I HEARD A SINGLE BOY HAS BEEN GOING THROUGH ONE GIRL AFTER ANOTHER.
HUH?
I'VE HEARD THAT HE CUDDLES MULTIPLE GIRLS AT ONCE.
CUDDLES ...?
H-HOW INDE-CENT!
I'M GOING TO GO ASSESS THE SITUATION RIGHT NOW!

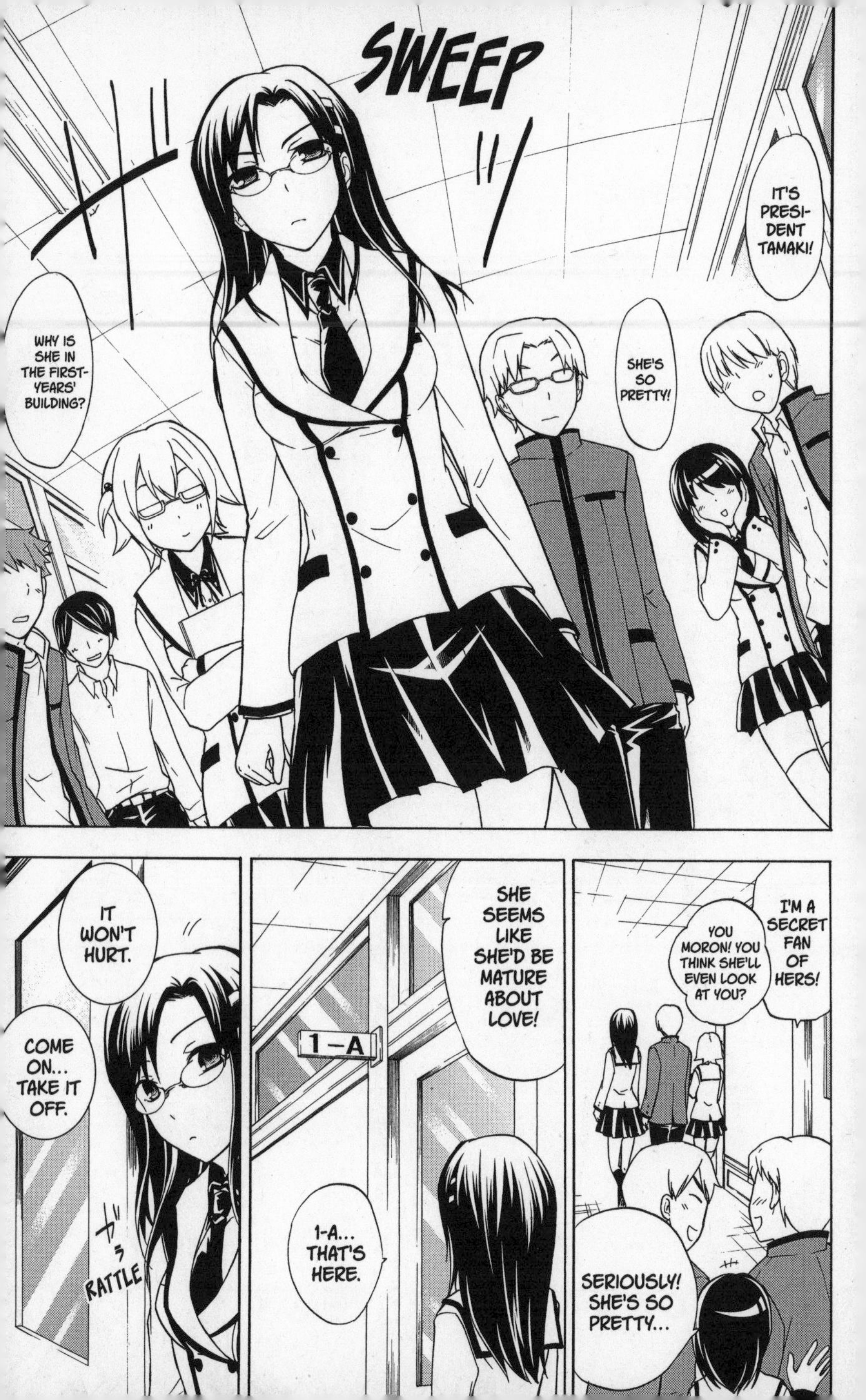
SWEEP
IT'S PRESIDENT TAMAKI!
SHE'S SO PRETTY!
WHY IS SHE IN THE FIRST-YEARS' BUILDING?
I'M A SECRET FAN OF HERS!
YOU MORON! YOU THINK SHE'LL EVEN LOOK AT YOU?
SERIOUSLY! SHE'S SO PRETTY...
SHE SEEMS LIKE SHE'D BE MATURE ABOUT LOVE!
1-A
1-A... THAT'S HERE.
IT WON'T HURT.
COME ON... TAKE IT OFF.
ガラ
RATTLE

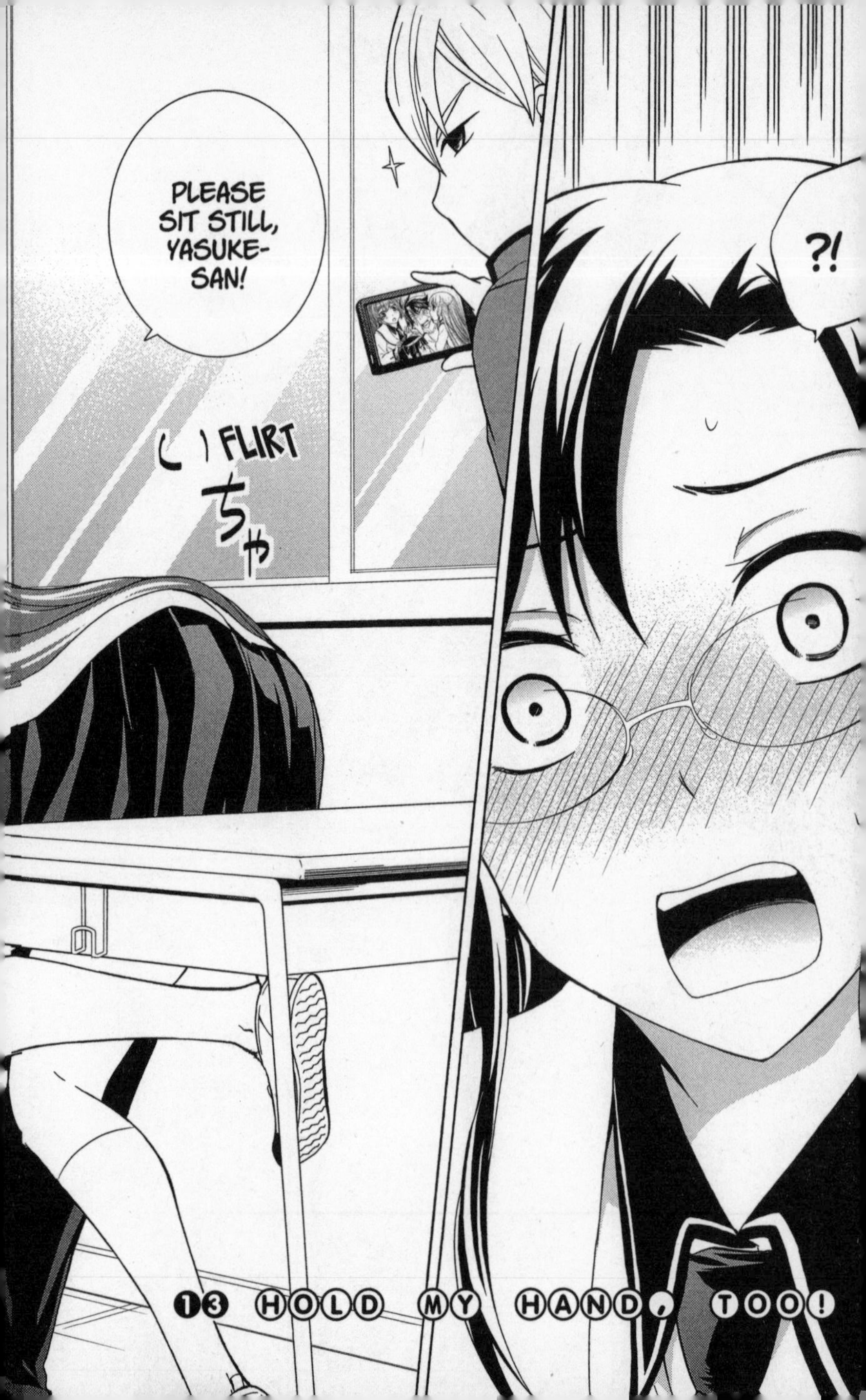
?!
PLEASE SIT STILL, YASUKE-SAN!
FLIRT
ちゃ
13 HOLD MY HAND, TOO!

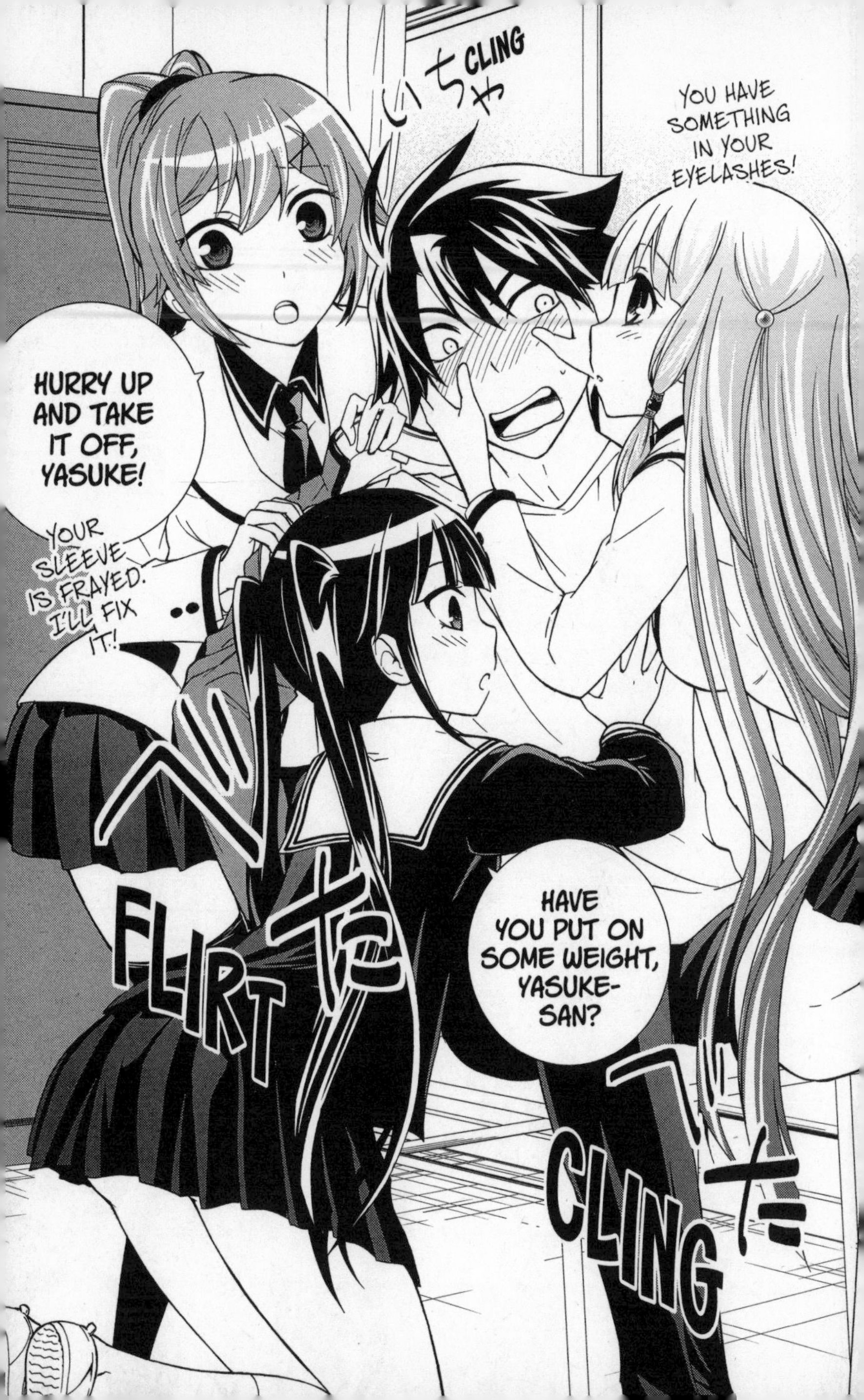
いちゃ CLING
YOU HAVE SOMETHING IN YOUR EYELASHES!
HURRY UP AND TAKE IT OFF, YASUKE!
YOUR SLEEVE IS FRAYED. I'LL FIX IT!
..
HAVE YOU PUT ON SOME WEIGHT, YASUKE-SAN?
CLING
FLIRT

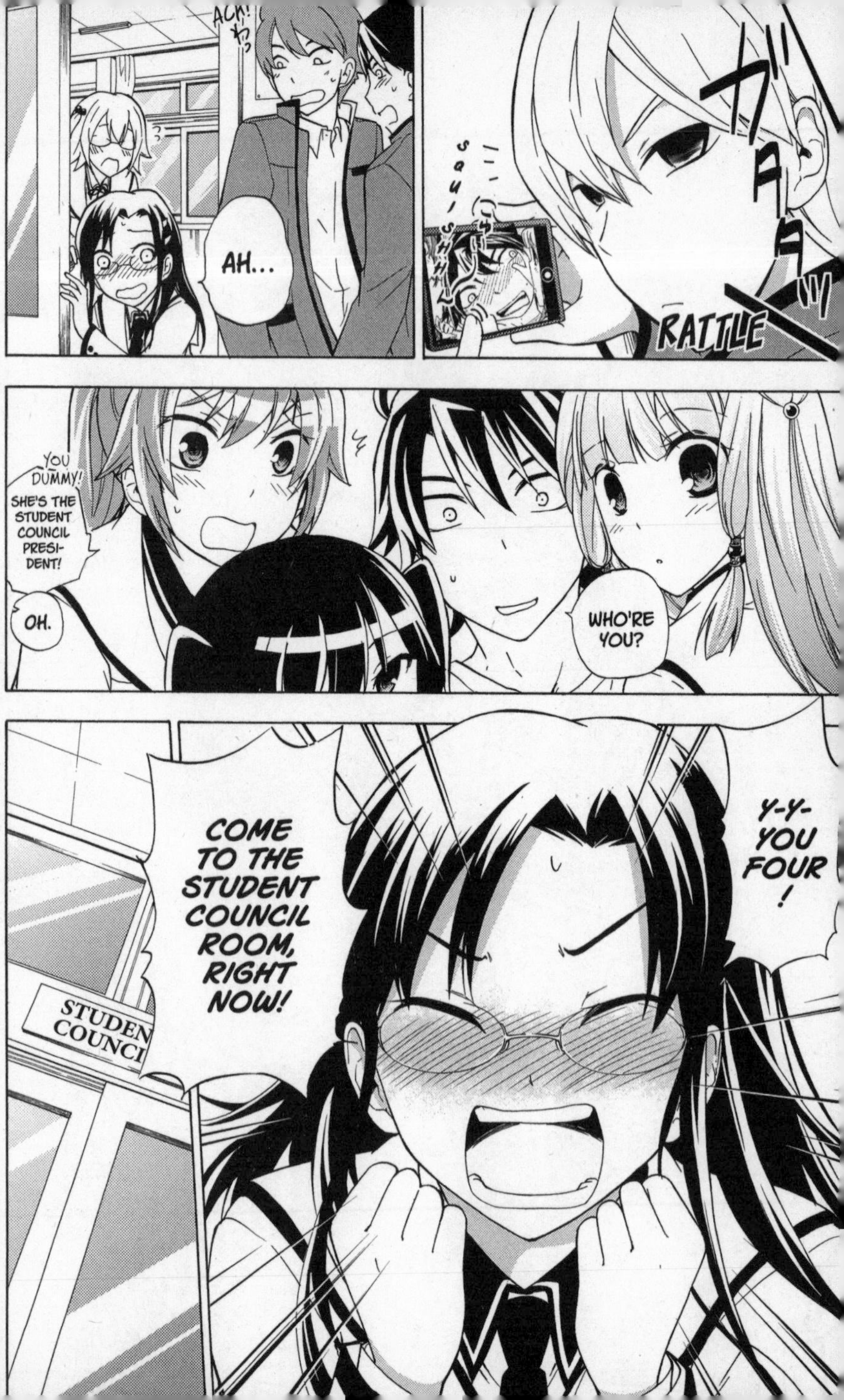
RATTLE
SQUI-SHHH
ACK!
AH...
WHO'RE YOU?
YOU DUMMY!
SHE'S THE STUDENT COUNCIL PRESI-DENT!
OH.
Y-Y-YOU FOUR!
COME TO THE STUDENT COUNCIL ROOM, RIGHT NOW!
STUDEN
COUNCI

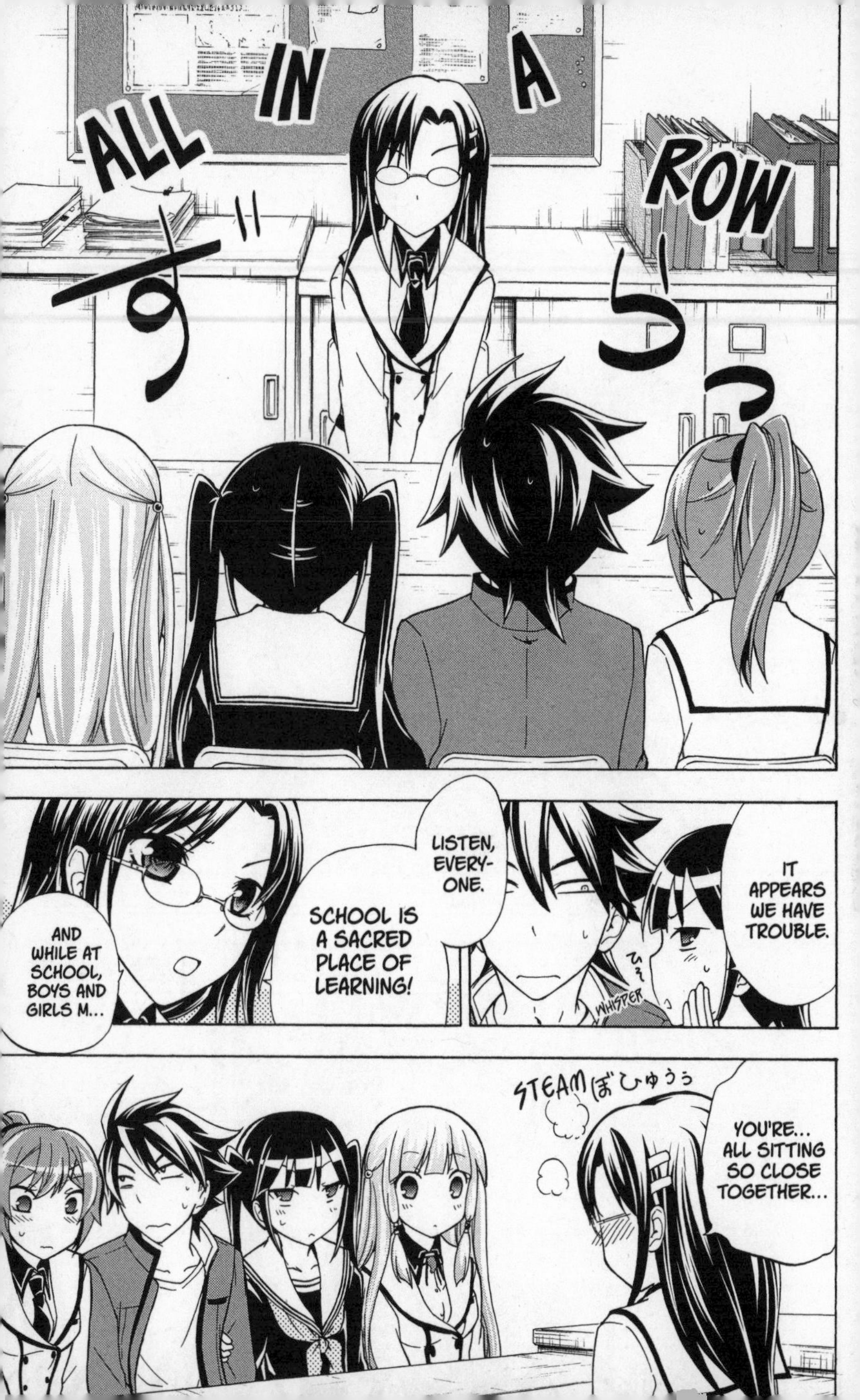
ALL IN A ROW
ずらっ
IT APPEARS WE HAVE TROUBLE.
ひそ
WHISPER
LISTEN, EVERY-ONE.
SCHOOL IS A SACRED PLACE OF LEARNING!
AND WHILE AT SCHOOL, BOYS AND GIRLS M...
STEAM ぼひゅうぅ
YOU'RE... ALL SITTING SO CLOSE TOGETHER...

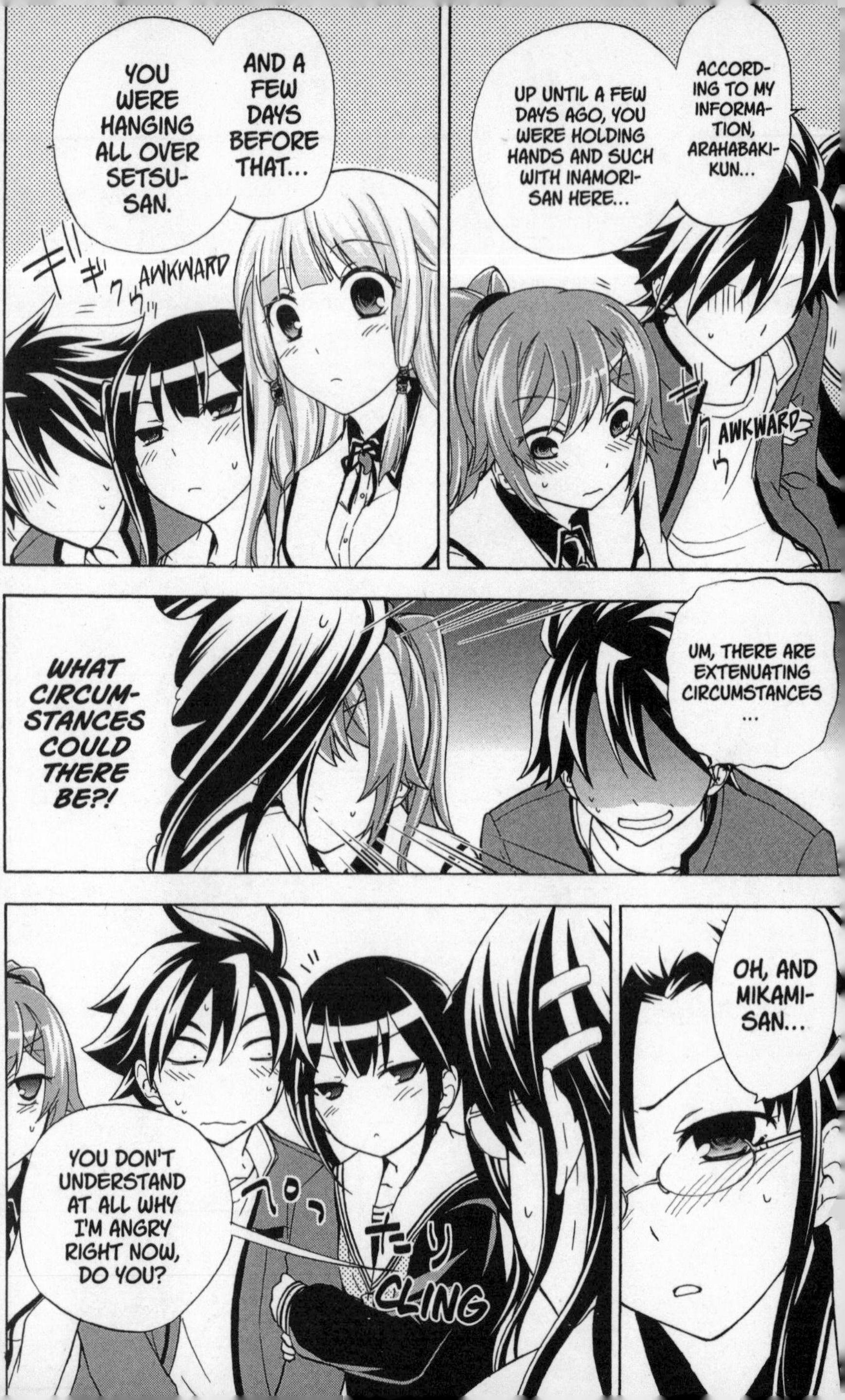
ACCORDING TO MY INFORMATION, ARAHABAKI-KUN...
UP UNTIL A FEW DAYS AGO, YOU WERE HOLDING HANDS AND SUCH WITH INAMORI-SAN HERE...
AWKWARD
AND A FEW DAYS BEFORE THAT...
YOU WERE HANGING ALL OVER SETSU-SAN.
AWKWARD
UM, THERE ARE EXTENUATING CIRCUMSTANCES...
WHAT CIRCUMSTANCES COULD THERE BE?!
OH, AND MIKAMI-SAN...
YOU DON'T UNDERSTAND AT ALL WHY I'M ANGRY RIGHT NOW, DO YOU?
CLING

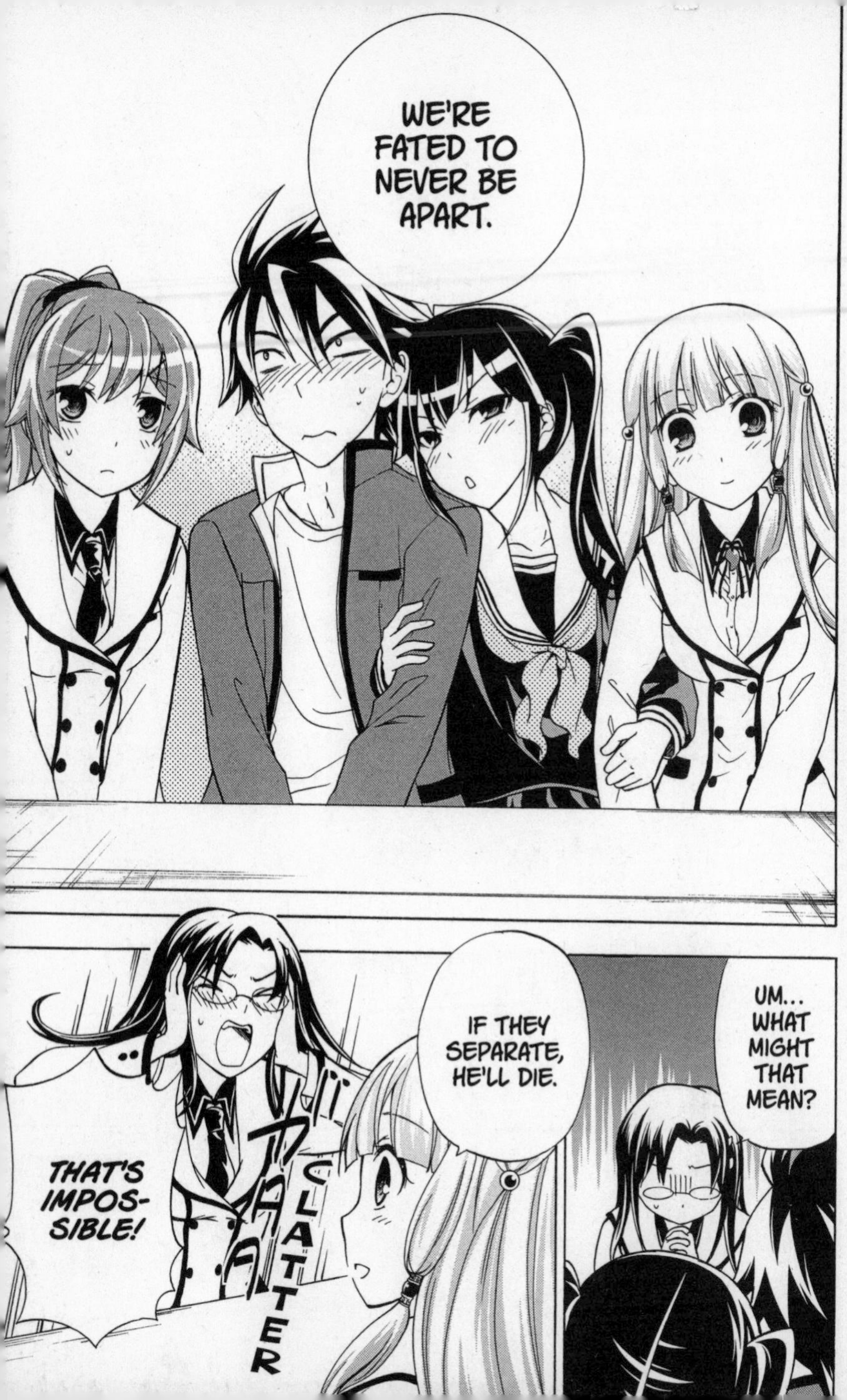
WE'RE FATED TO NEVER BE APART.
UM... WHAT MIGHT THAT MEAN?
IF THEY SEPARATE, HE'LL DIE.
CLATTER
THAT'S IMPOSSIBLE!

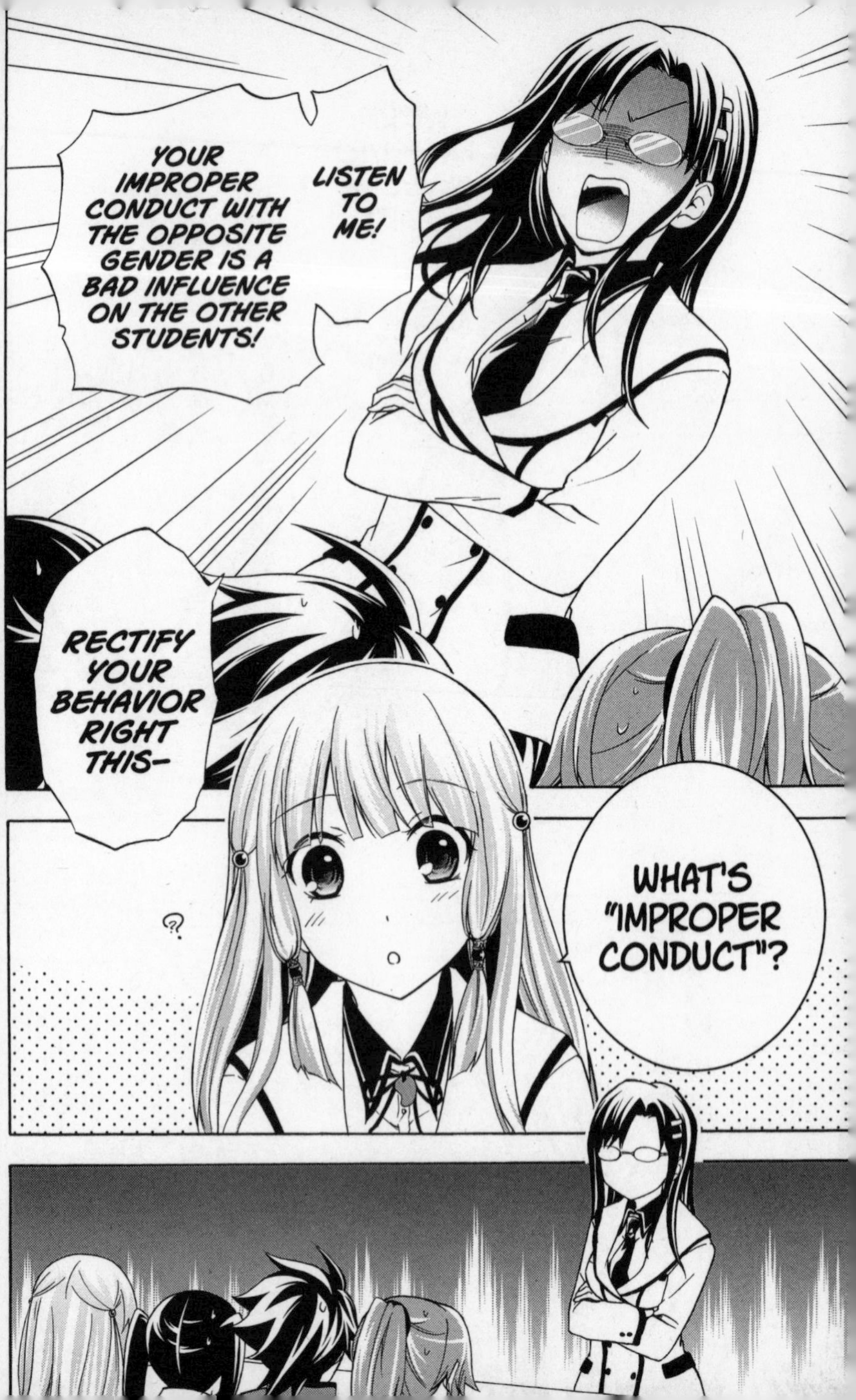
LISTEN TO ME!
YOUR IMPROPER CONDUCT WITH THE OPPOSITE GENDER IS A BAD INFLUENCE ON THE OTHER STUDENTS!
RECTIFY YOUR BEHAVIOR RIGHT THIS-
WHAT'S "IMPROPER CONDUCT"?

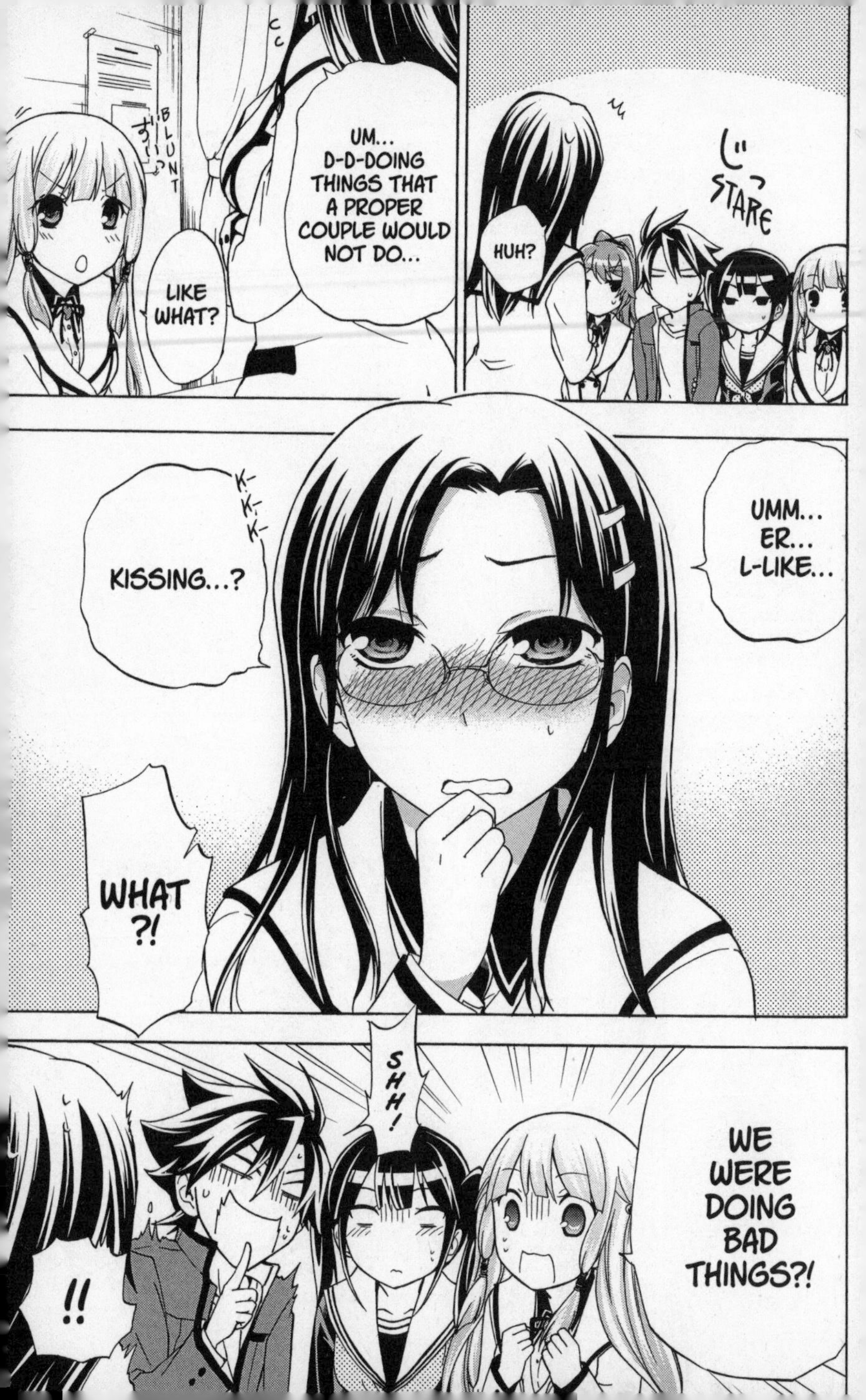

STARE
HUH?
UM... D-D-DOING THINGS THAT A PROPER COUPLE WOULD NOT DO...
BLUNT
LIKE WHAT?
UMM... ER... L-LIKE...
K-K-K-KISSING...?
WHAT?!
WE WERE DOING BAD THINGS?!
SHH!
!!

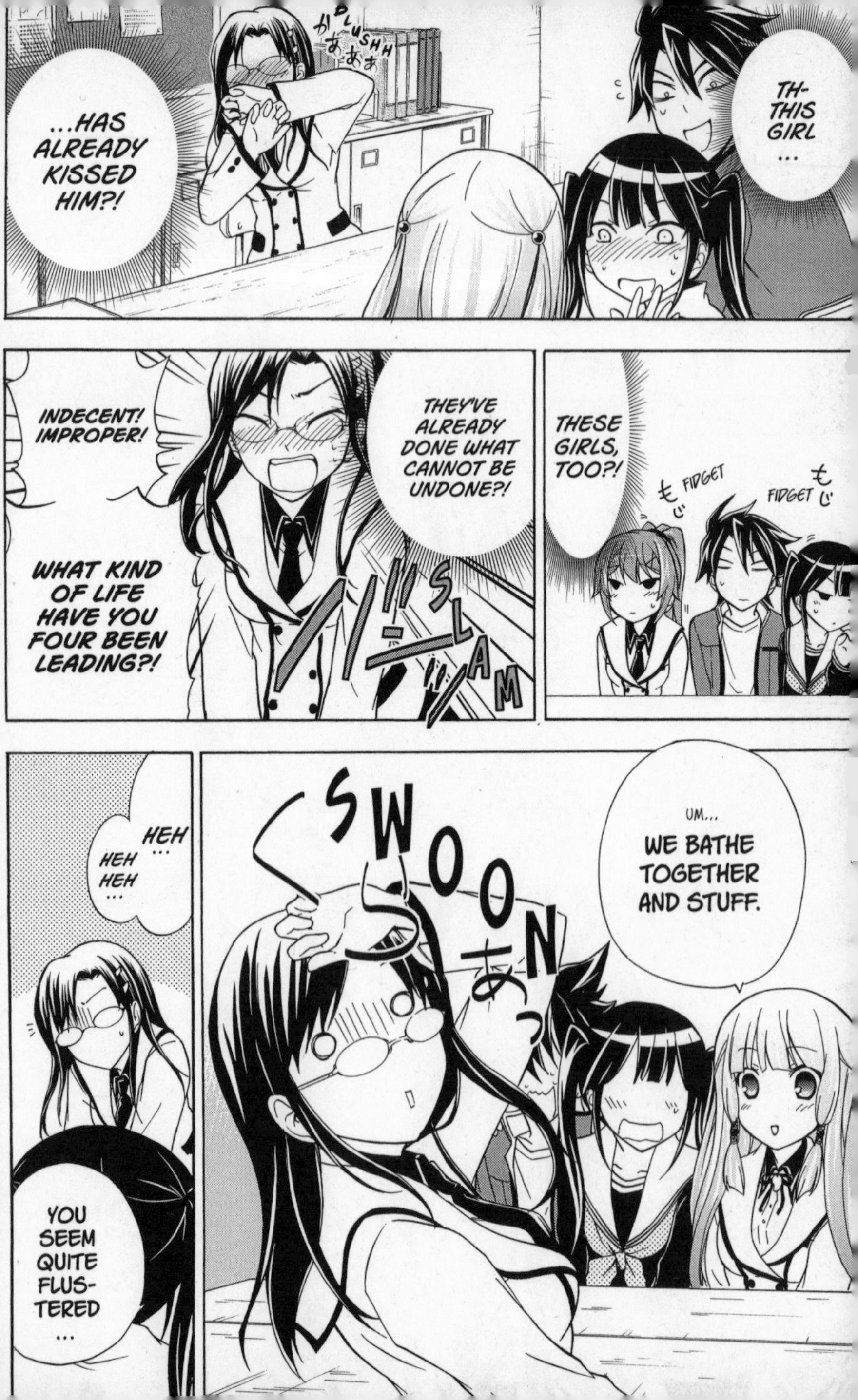
TH- THIS GIRL ...
...HAS ALREADY KISSED HIM?!
PLUSHH
THESE GIRLS, TOO?!
FIDGET
FIDGET
THEY'VE ALREADY DONE WHAT CANNOT BE UNDONE?!
INDECENT! IMPROPER!
SLAM
WHAT KIND OF LIFE HAVE YOU FOUR BEEN LEADING?!
UM...
WE BATHE TOGETHER AND STUFF.
SWOON
HEH ...
HEH HEH ...
YOU SEEM QUITE FLUS-TERED ...

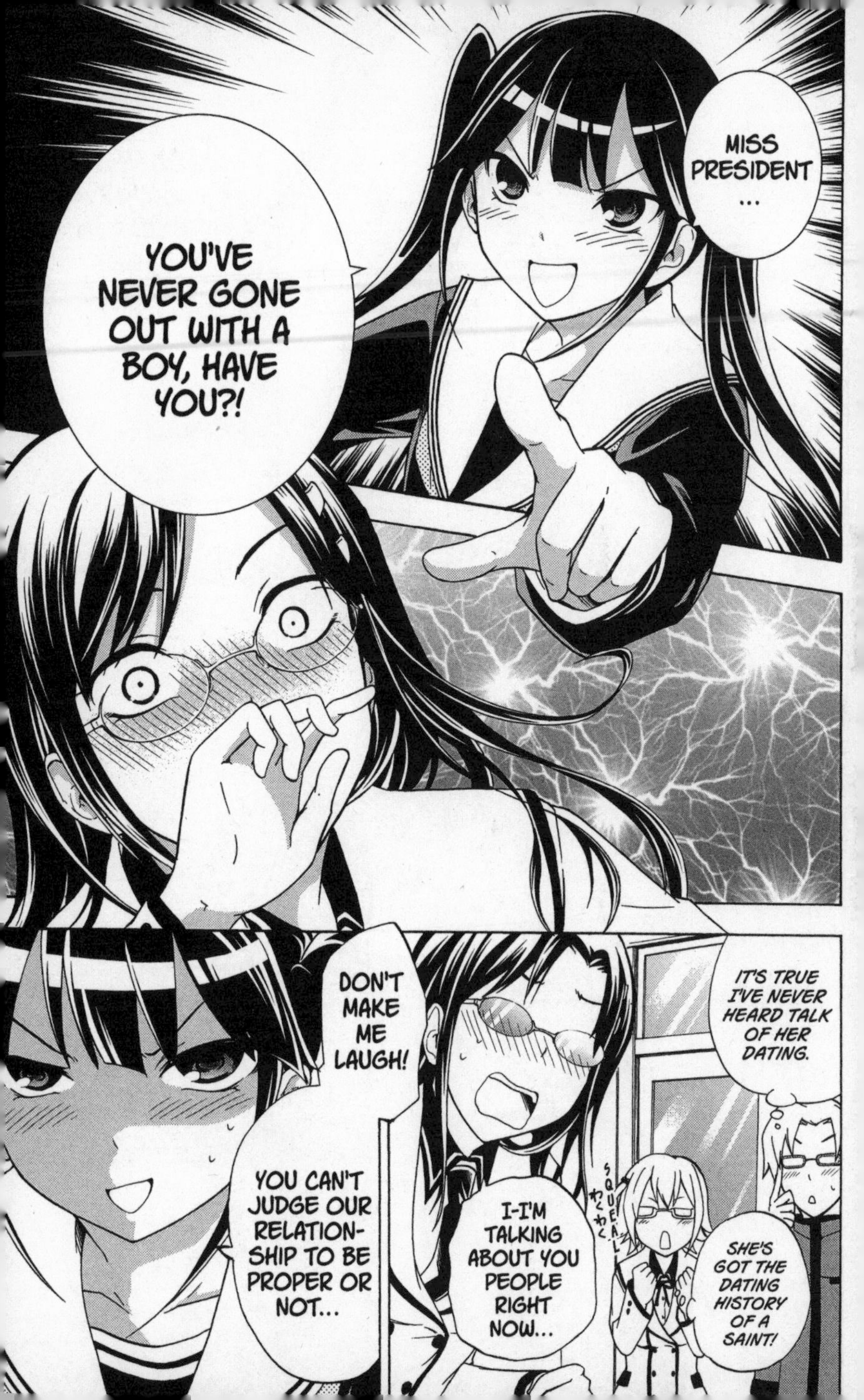
MISS PRESIDENT ...
YOU'VE NEVER GONE OUT WITH A BOY, HAVE YOU?!
IT'S TRUE I'VE NEVER HEARD TALK OF HER DATING.
SQUEAL
わくわく
SHE'S GOT THE DATING HISTORY OF A SAINT!
DON'T MAKE ME LAUGH!
I-I'M TALKING ABOUT YOU PEOPLE RIGHT NOW...
YOU CAN'T JUDGE OUR RELATION-SHIP TO BE PROPER OR NOT...

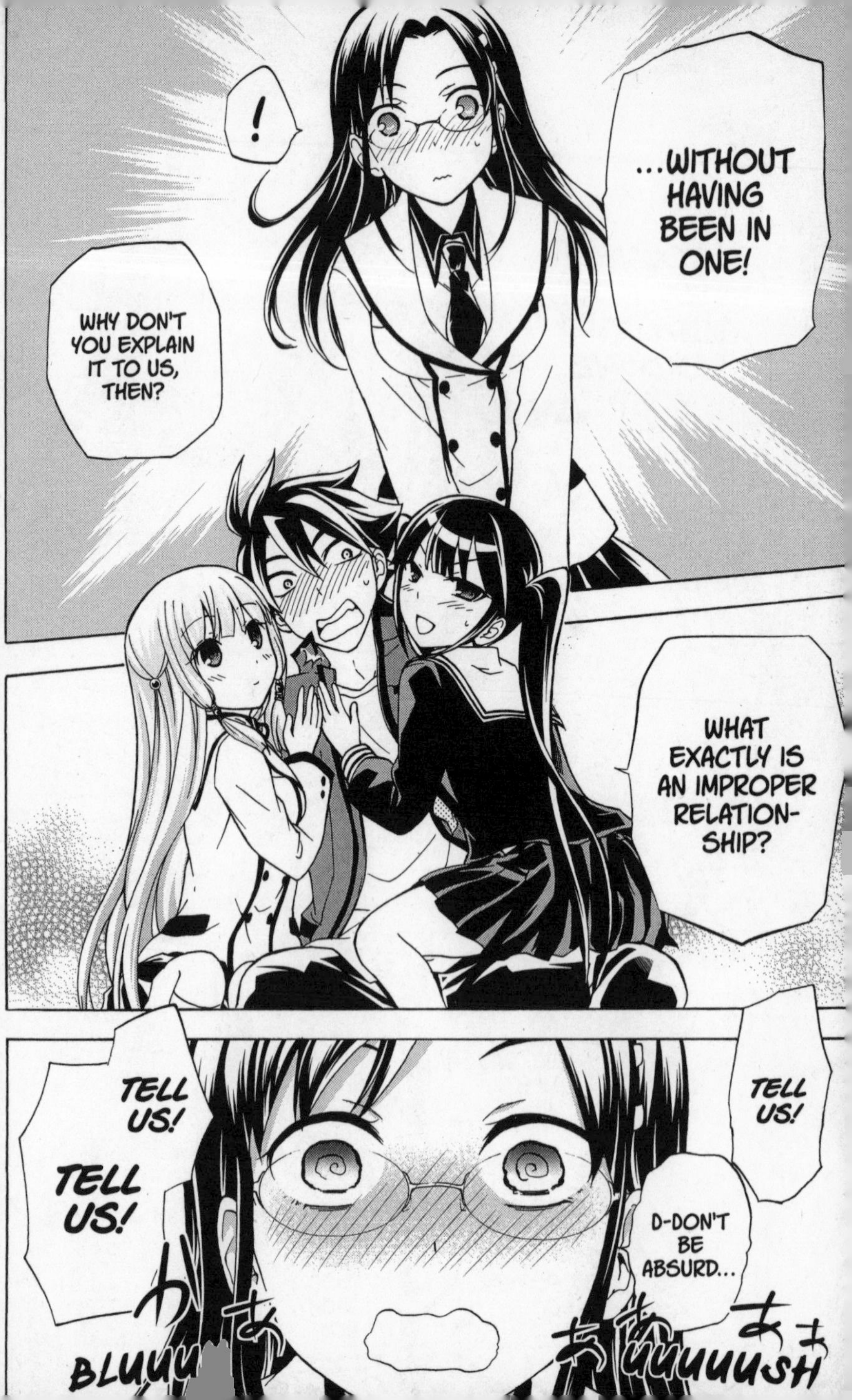
...WITHOUT HAVING BEEN IN ONE!
!
WHY DON'T YOU EXPLAIN IT TO US, THEN?
WHAT EXACTLY IS AN IMPROPER RELATION-SHIP?
TELL US!
D-DON'T BE ABSURD...
TELL US!
TELL US!
UUUUUUSH
BLUUU

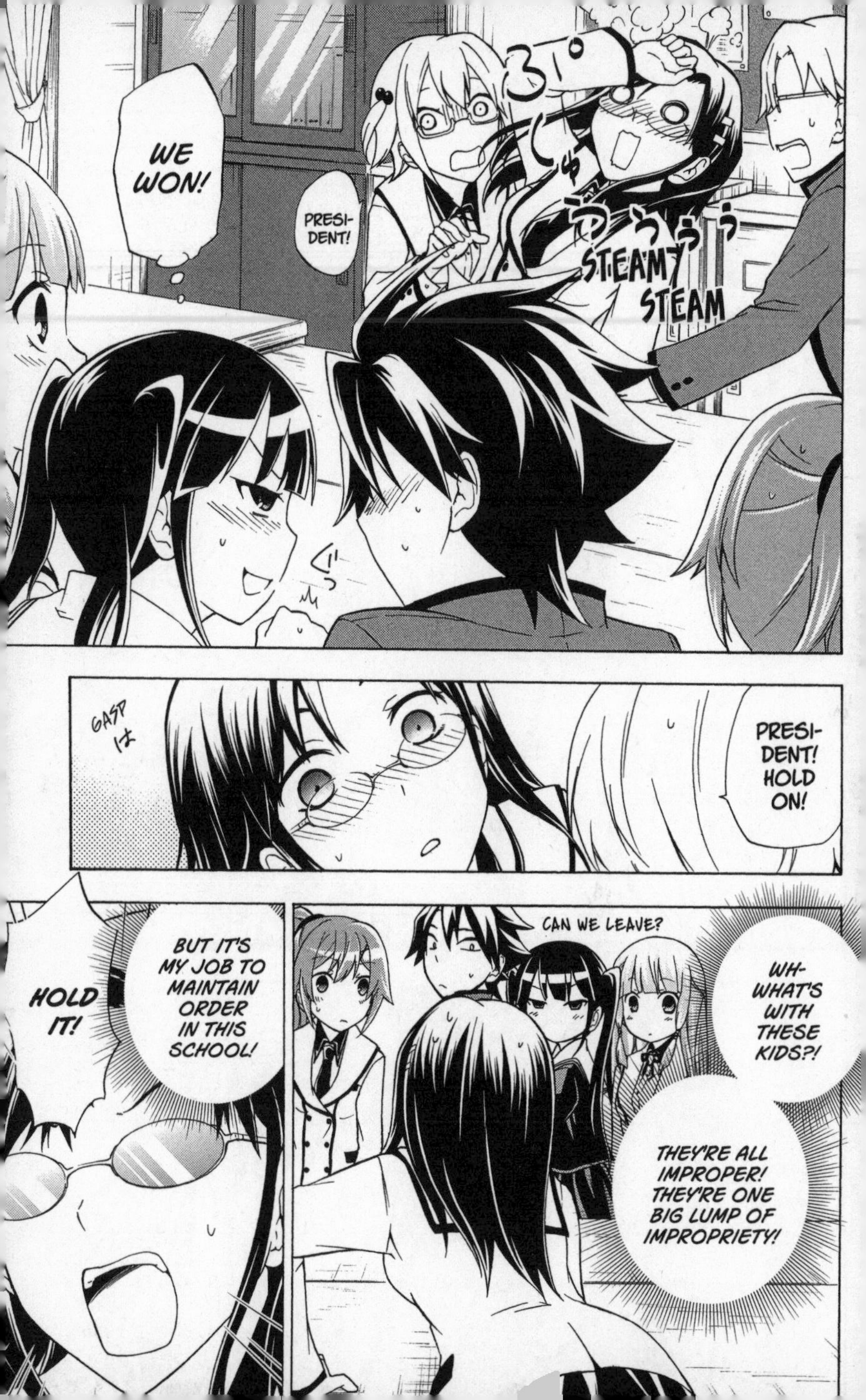
STEAM STEAM
PRESI-DENT!
WE WON!
PRESI-DENT! HOLD ON!
GASP は
WH-WHAT'S WITH THESE KIDS?!
CAN WE LEAVE?
THEY'RE ALL IMPROPER! THEY'RE ONE BIG LUMP OF IMPROPRIETY!
BUT IT'S MY JOB TO MAINTAIN ORDER IN THIS SCHOOL!
HOLD IT!

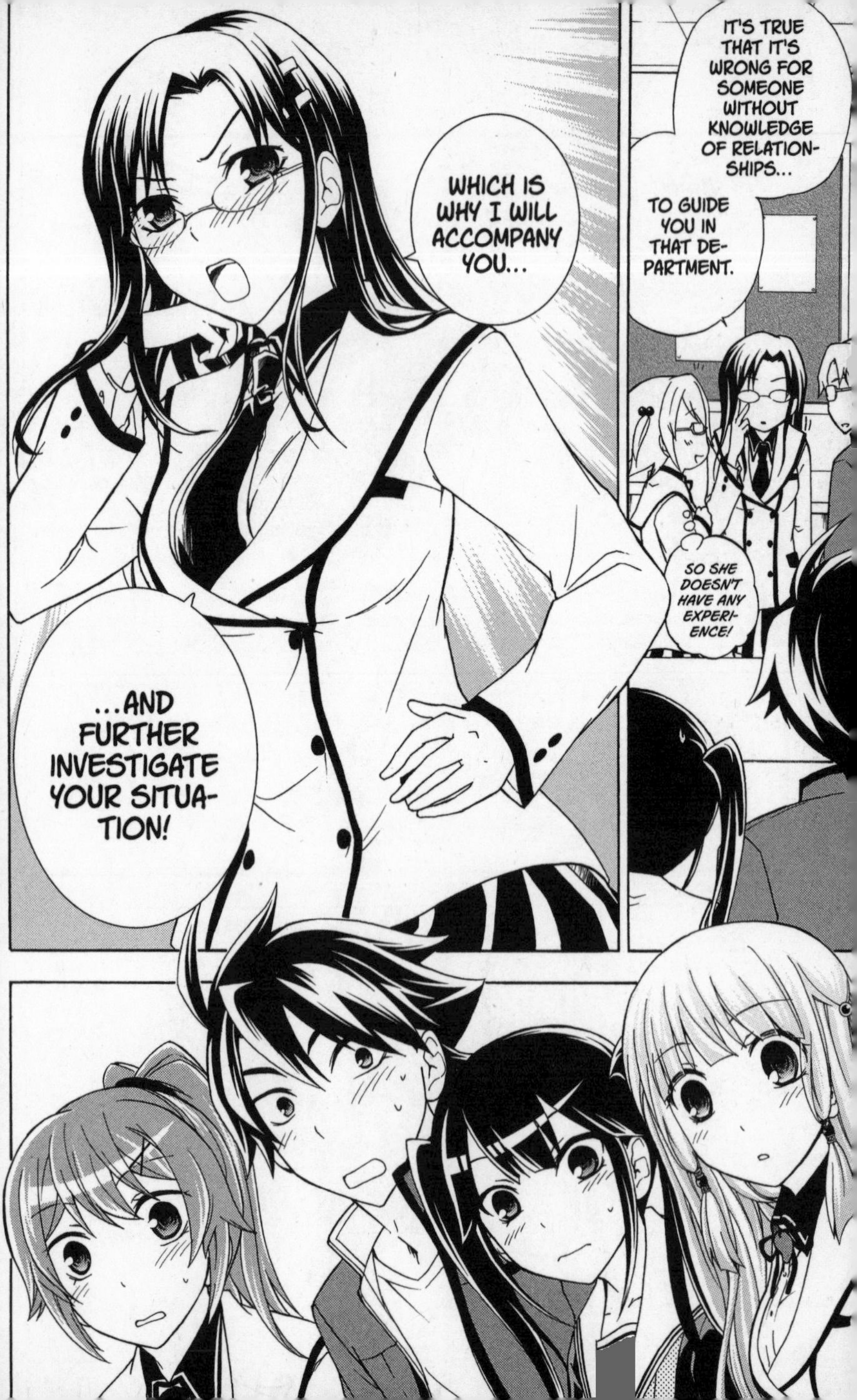
IT'S TRUE THAT IT'S WRONG FOR SOMEONE WITHOUT KNOWLEDGE OF RELATION-SHIPS...
TO GUIDE YOU IN THAT DE-PARTMENT.
SO SHE DOESN'T HAVE ANY EXPERI-ENCE!
WHICH IS WHY I WILL ACCOMPANY YOU...
...AND FURTHER INVESTIGATE YOUR SITUA-TION!

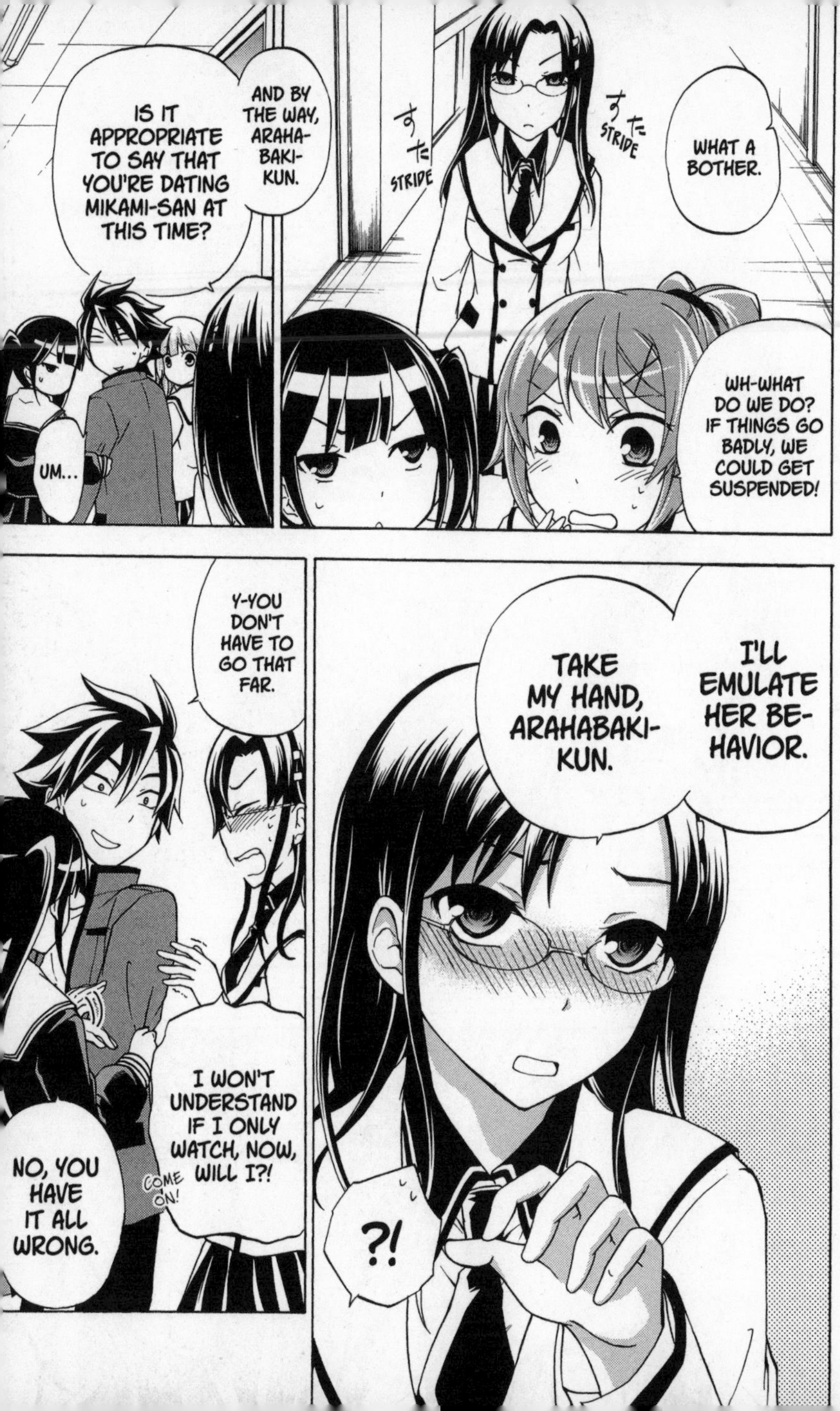
WHAT A BOTHER.
すた STRIDE
すた STRIDE
WH-WHAT DO WE DO? IF THINGS GO BADLY, WE COULD GET SUSPENDED!
AND BY THE WAY, ARAHABAKI-KUN.
IS IT APPROPRIATE TO SAY THAT YOU'RE DATING MIKAMI-SAN AT THIS TIME?
UM...
I'LL EMULATE HER BE-HAVIOR.
TAKE MY HAND, ARAHABAKI-KUN.
?!
Y-YOU DON'T HAVE TO GO THAT FAR.
I WON'T UNDERSTAND IF I ONLY WATCH, NOW, WILL I?!
COME ON!
NO, YOU HAVE IT ALL WRONG.

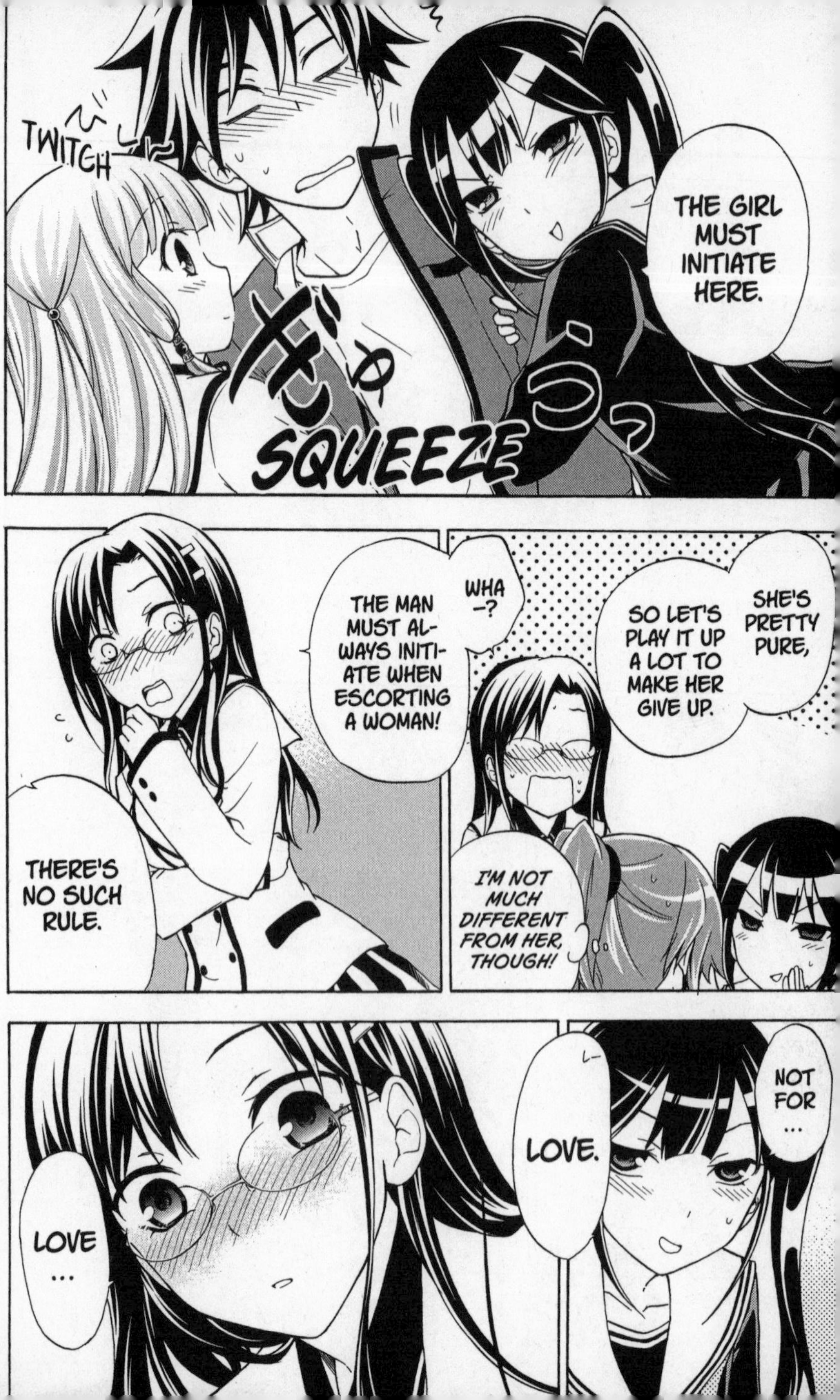
THE GIRL MUST INITIATE HERE.
SQUEEZE
TWITCH
SHE'S PRETTY PURE,
SO LET'S PLAY IT UP A LOT TO MAKE HER GIVE UP.
WHA—?
I'M NOT MUCH DIFFERENT FROM HER, THOUGH!
THE MAN MUST AL-WAYS INITI-ATE WHEN ESCORTING A WOMAN!
THERE'S NO SUCH RULE.
NOT FOR...
LOVE.
LOVE...

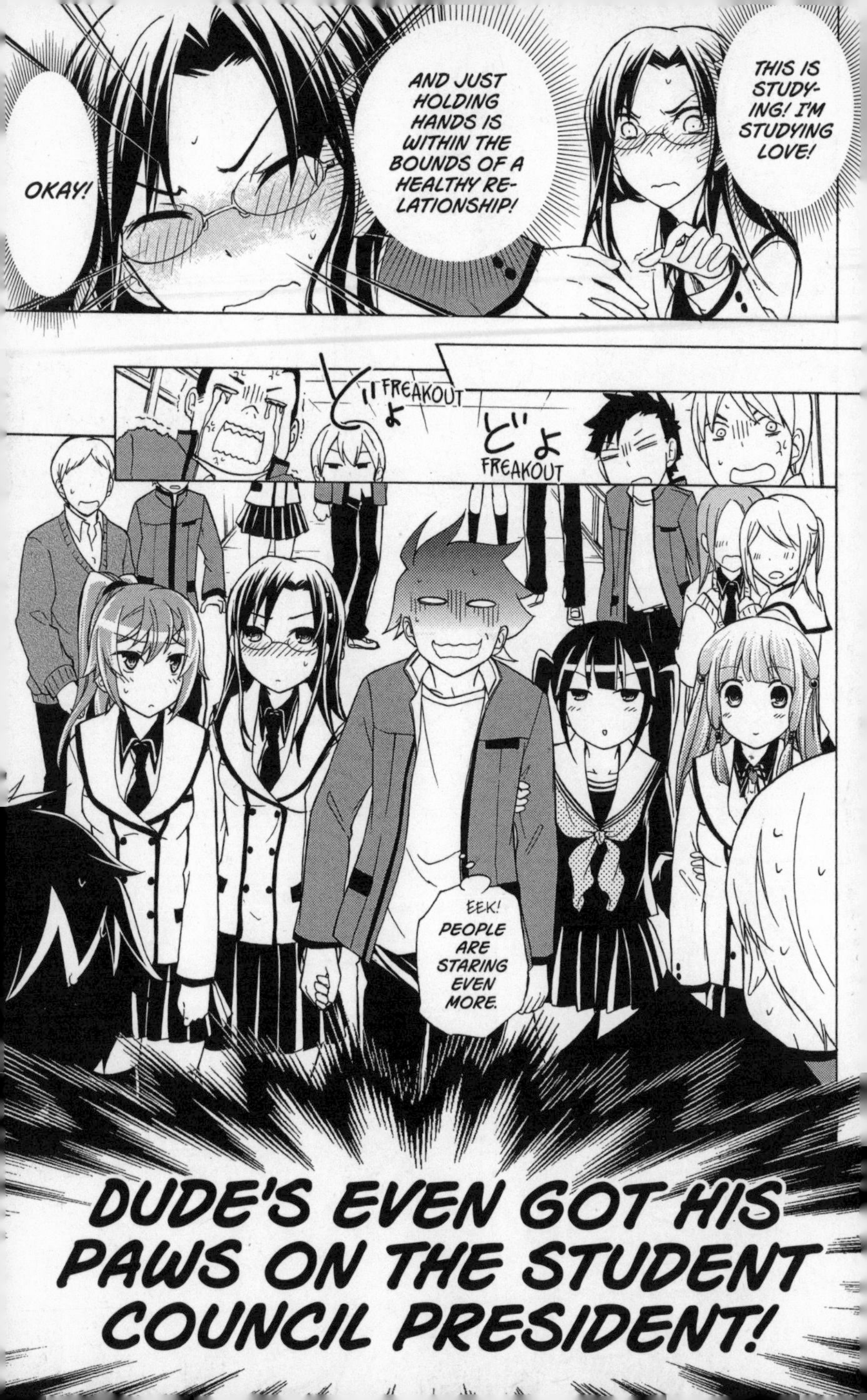
THIS IS STUDYING! I'M STUDYING LOVE!
AND JUST HOLDING HANDS IS WITHIN THE BOUNDS OF A HEALTHY RELATIONSHIP!
OKAY!
どよ
FREAKOUT
どよ
FREAKOUT
EEK! PEOPLE ARE STARING EVEN MORE.
DUDE'S EVEN GOT HIS PAWS ON THE STUDENT COUNCIL PRESIDENT!

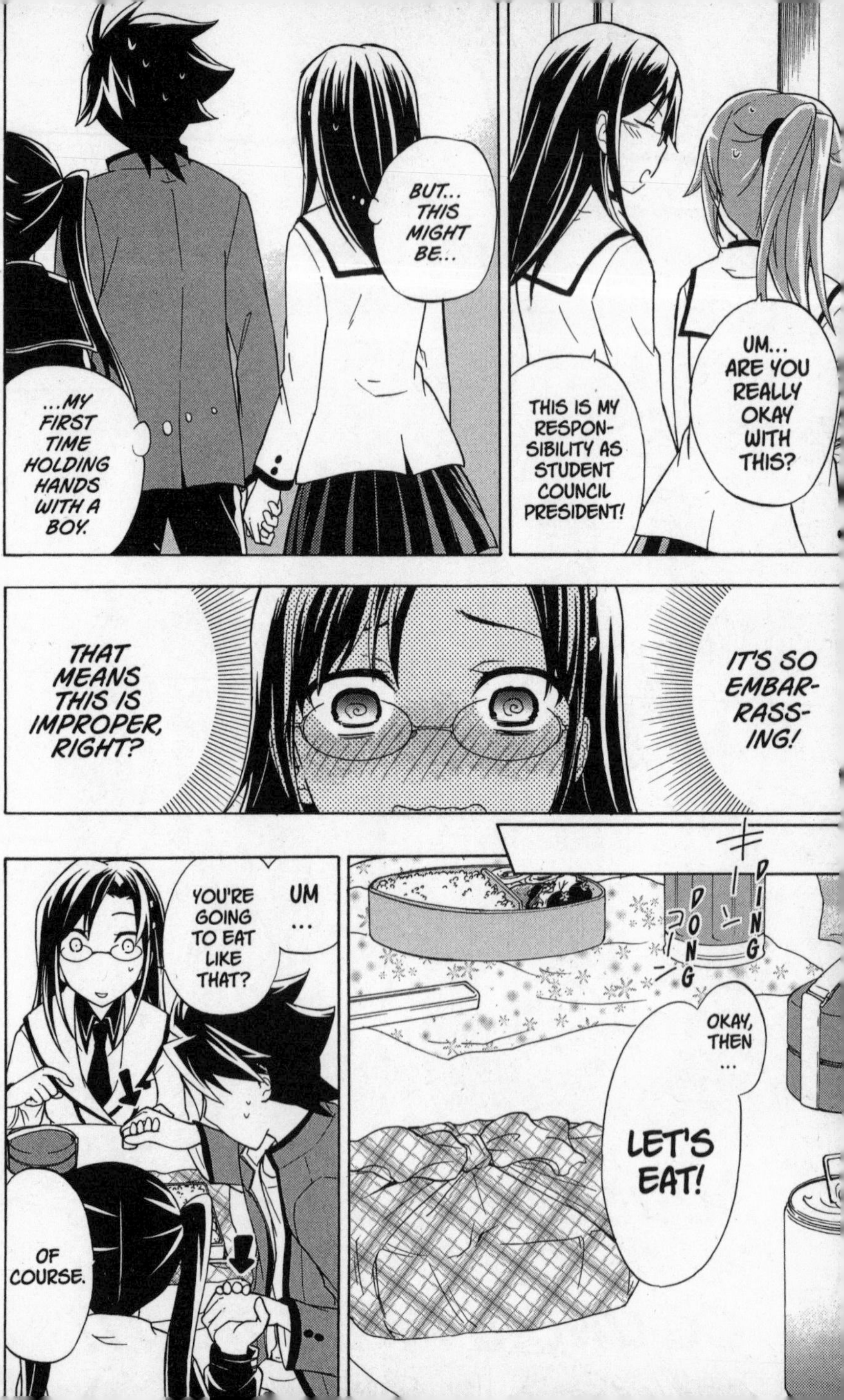
UM... ARE YOU REALLY OKAY WITH THIS?
THIS IS MY RESPONSIBILITY AS STUDENT COUNCIL PRESIDENT!
BUT... THIS MIGHT BE...
...MY FIRST TIME HOLDING HANDS WITH A BOY.
IT'S SO EMBARRASSING!
THAT MEANS THIS IS IMPROPER, RIGHT?
DING
DONG
OKAY, THEN ...
LET'S EAT!
UM ...
YOU'RE GOING TO EAT LIKE THAT?
OF COURSE.

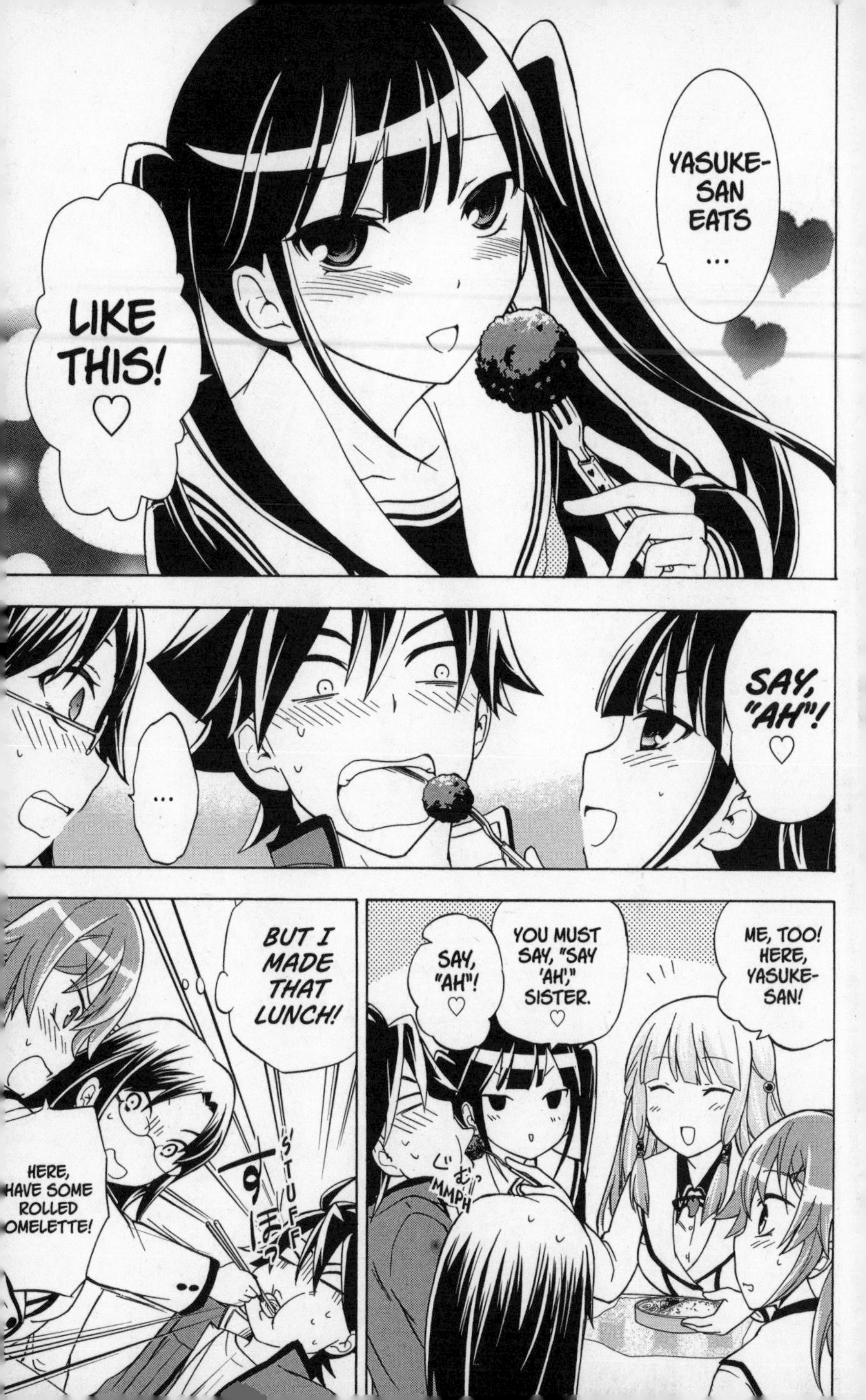
YASUKE-SAN EATS ...
LIKE THIS! ♡
SAY, "AH"! ♡
...
ME, TOO! HERE, YASUKE-SAN!
YOU MUST SAY, "SAY 'AH'," SISTER. ♡
SAY, "AH"! ♡
MMPH
BUT I MADE THAT LUNCH!
STUFF
HERE, HAVE SOME ROLLED OMELETTE!

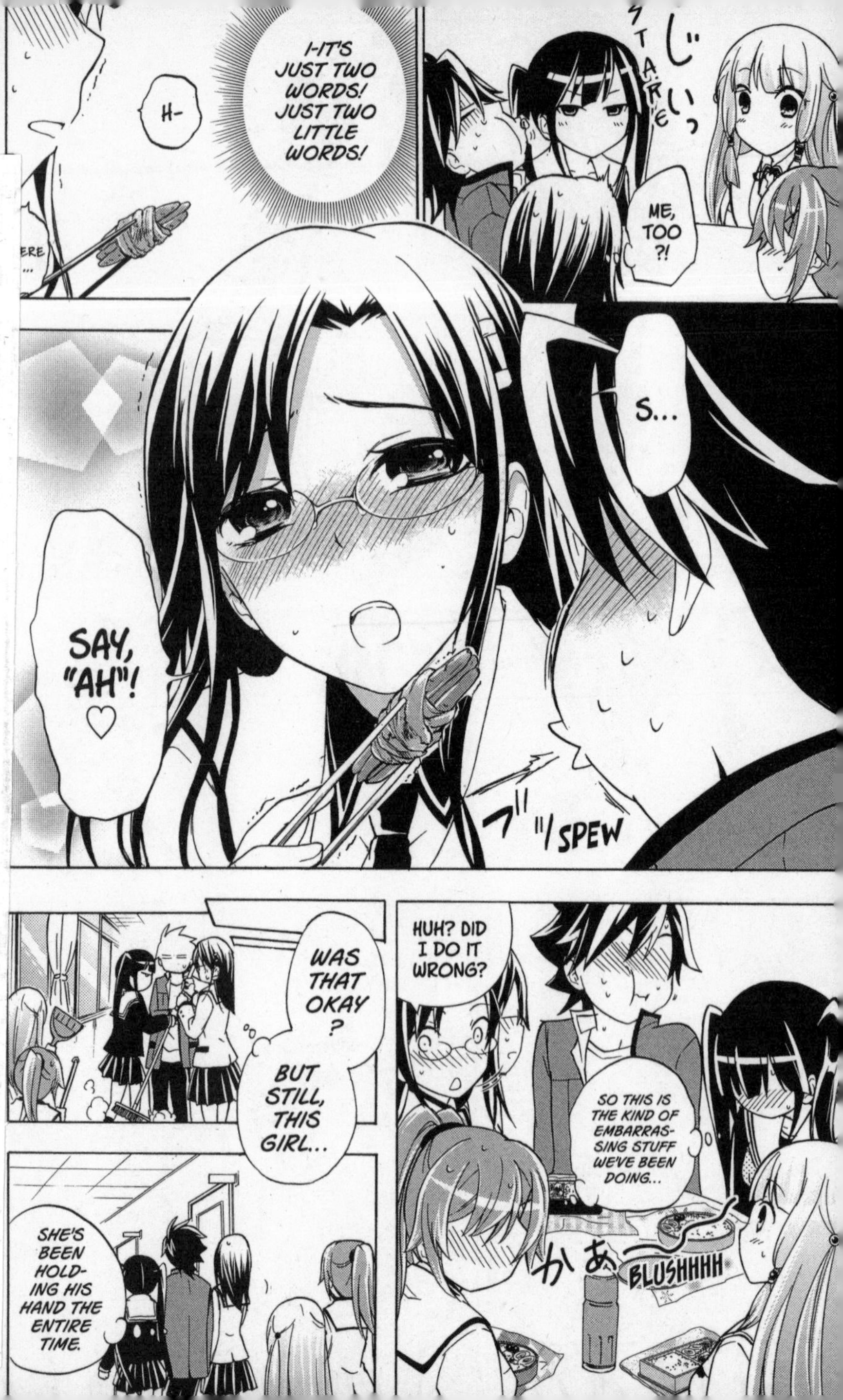
STARE
じいっ
ME, TOO?!
I-IT'S JUST TWO WORDS! JUST TWO LITTLE WORDS!
H-
S...
SAY, "AH"! ♡
SPEW
HUH? DID I DO IT WRONG?
SO THIS IS THE KIND OF EMBARRASSING STUFF WE'VE BEEN DOING...
かあ
BLUSHHHH
WAS THAT OKAY?
BUT STILL, THIS GIRL...
SHE'S BEEN HOLDING HIS HAND THE ENTIRE TIME.

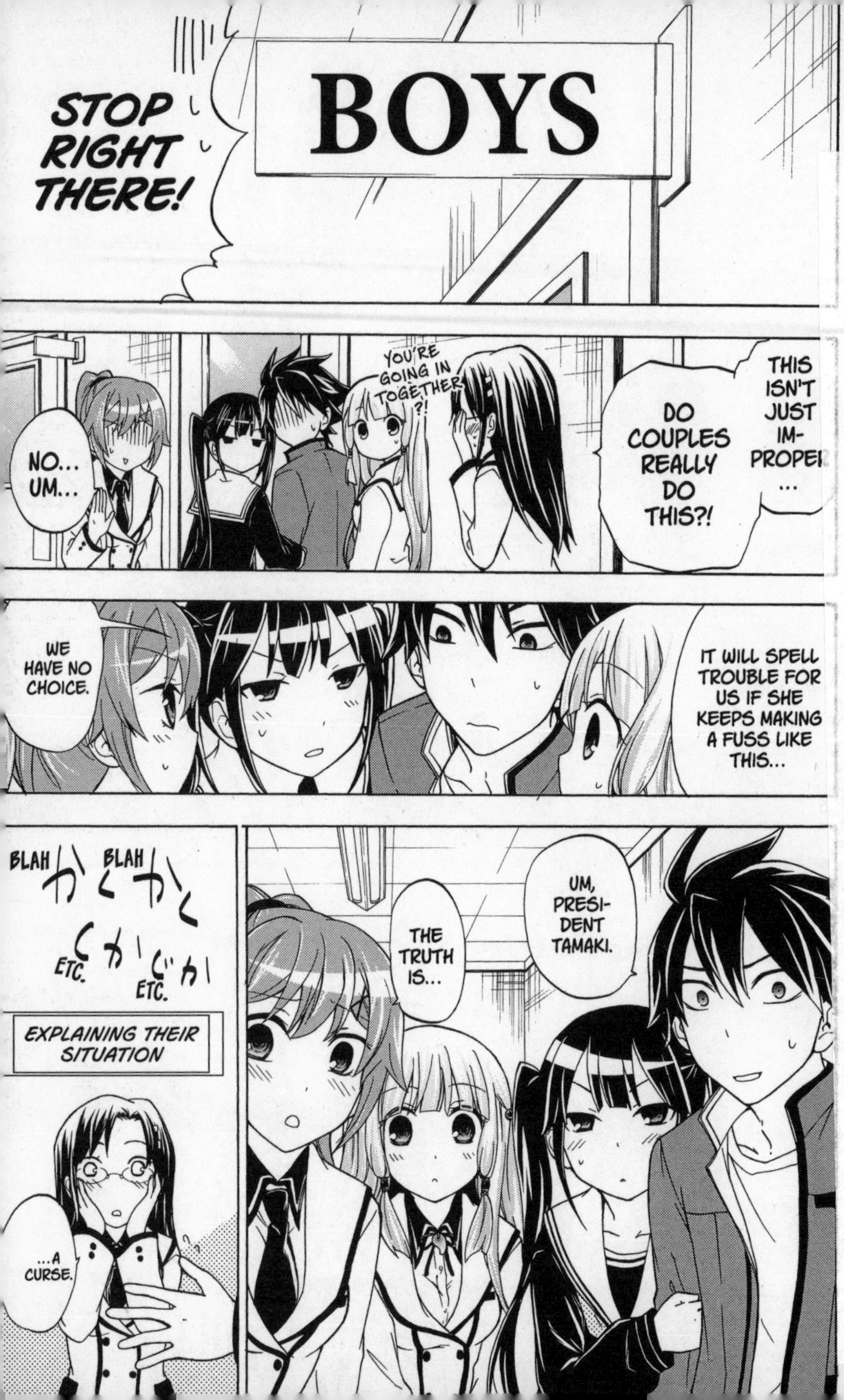
BOYS
STOP RIGHT THERE!
THIS ISN'T JUST IM-PROPER...
DO COUPLES REALLY DO THIS?!
YOU'RE GOING IN TOGETHER?!
NO... UM...
IT WILL SPELL TROUBLE FOR US IF SHE KEEPS MAKING A FUSS LIKE THIS...
WE HAVE NO CHOICE.
UM, PRESI-DENT TAMAKI.
THE TRUTH IS...
BLAH かくかく BLAH
しかじか ETC. ETC.
EXPLAINING THEIR SITUATION
...A CURSE.

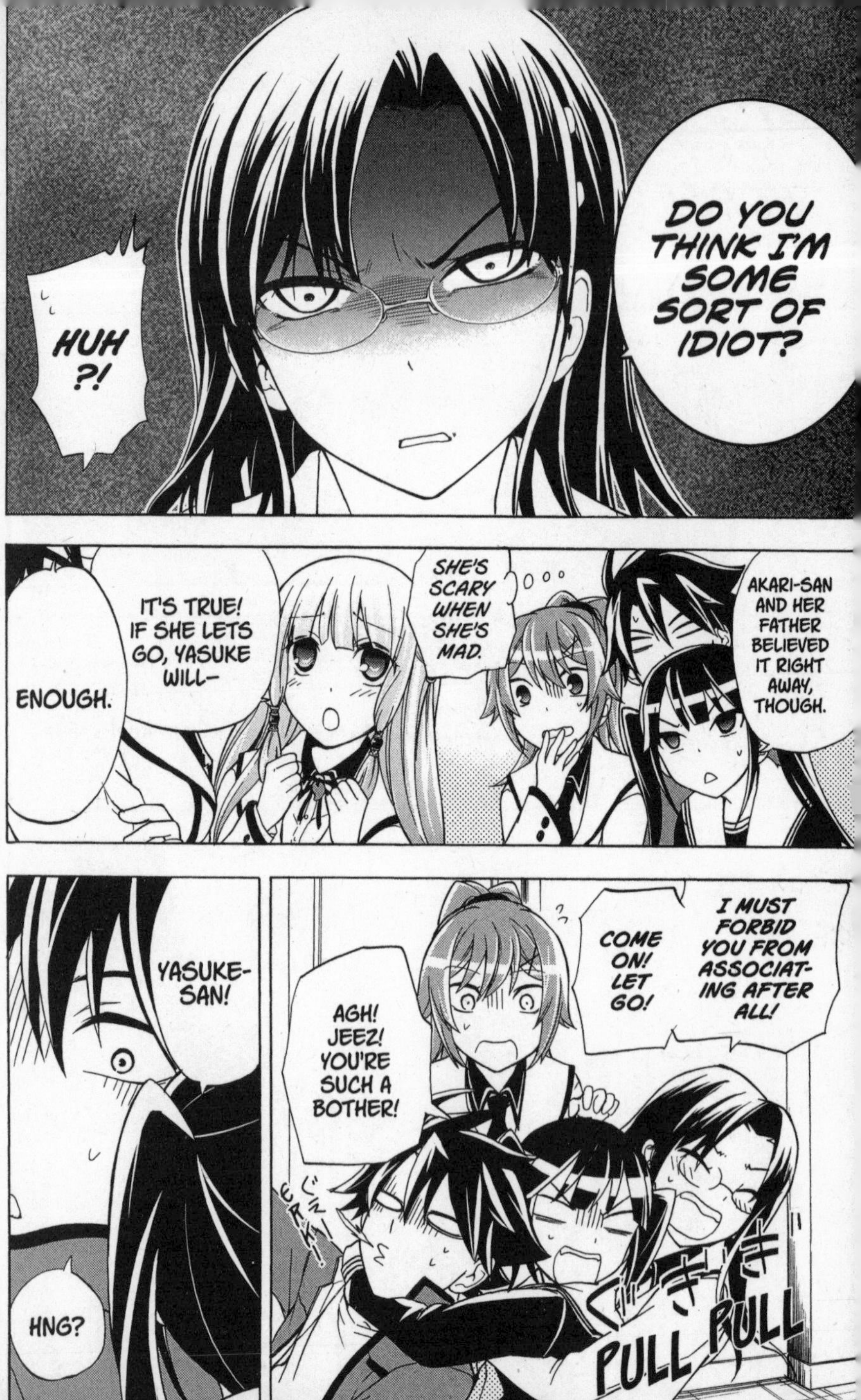
DO YOU THINK I'M SOME SORT OF IDIOT?
HUH ?!
AKARI-SAN AND HER FATHER BELIEVED IT RIGHT AWAY, THOUGH.
SHE'S SCARY WHEN SHE'S MAD.
IT'S TRUE! IF SHE LETS GO, YASUKE WILL–
ENOUGH.
I MUST FORBID YOU FROM ASSOCIATING AFTER ALL!
COME ON! LET GO!
AGH! JEEZ! YOU'RE SUCH A BOTHER!
PULL PULL
YASUKE-SAN!
HNG?

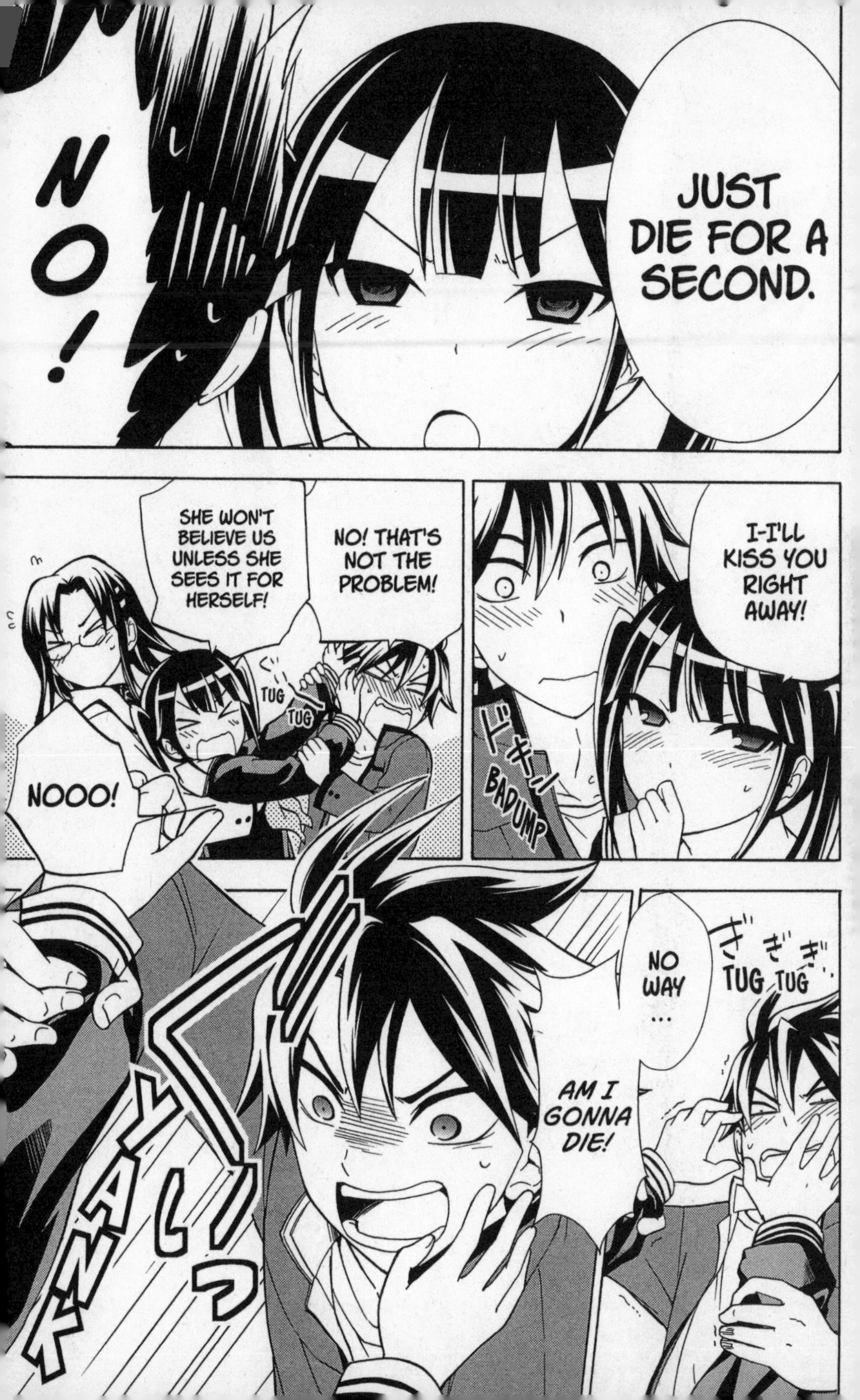
JUST DIE FOR A SECOND.
NO!
I-I'LL KISS YOU RIGHT AWAY!
BADUMP
NO! THAT'S NOT THE PROBLEM!
SHE WON'T BELIEVE US UNLESS SHE SEES IT FOR HERSELF!
TUG
TUG
NOOO!
TUG TUG
NO WAY ...
AM I GONNA DIE!
YANK

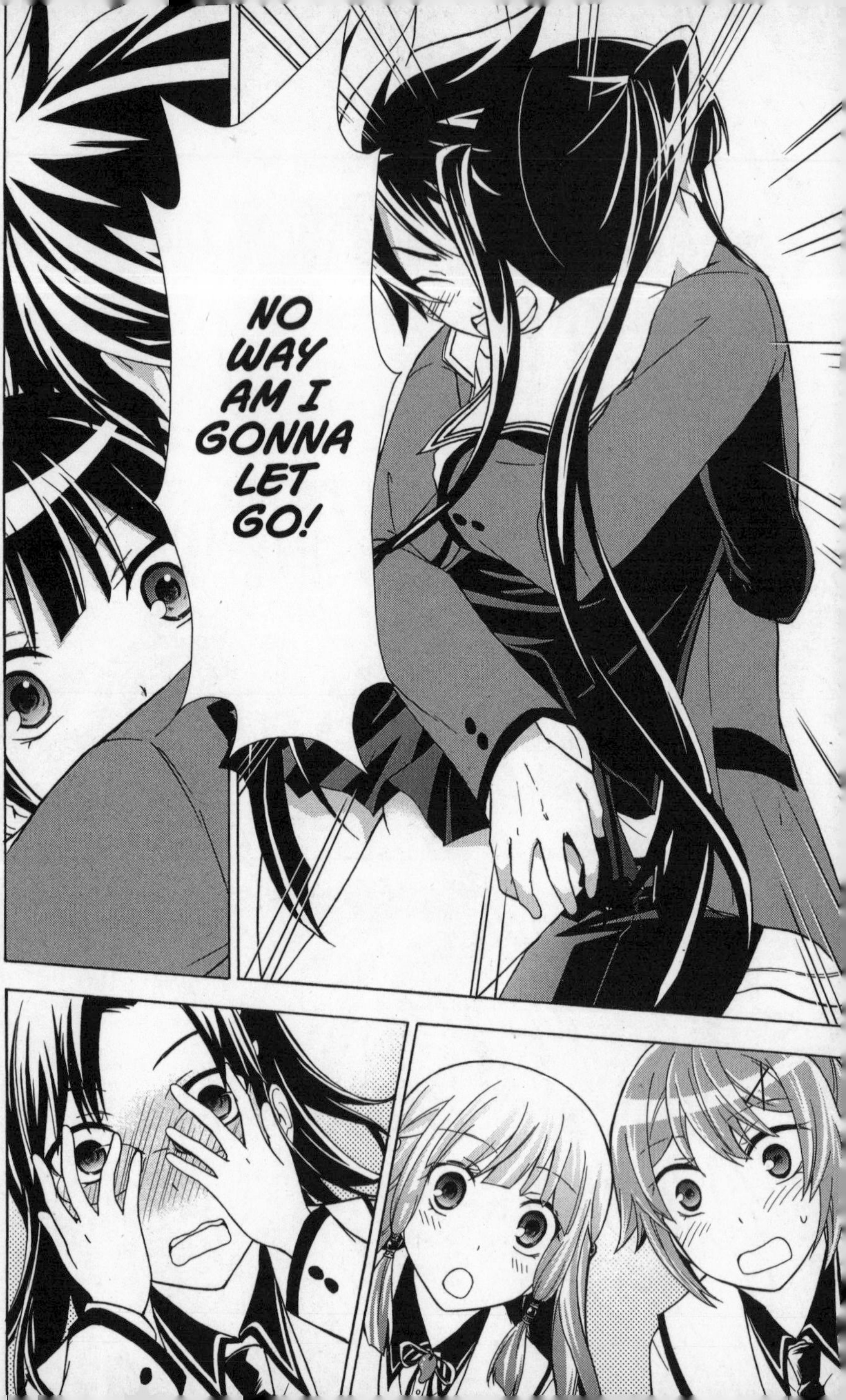
NO WAY AM I GONNA LET GO!

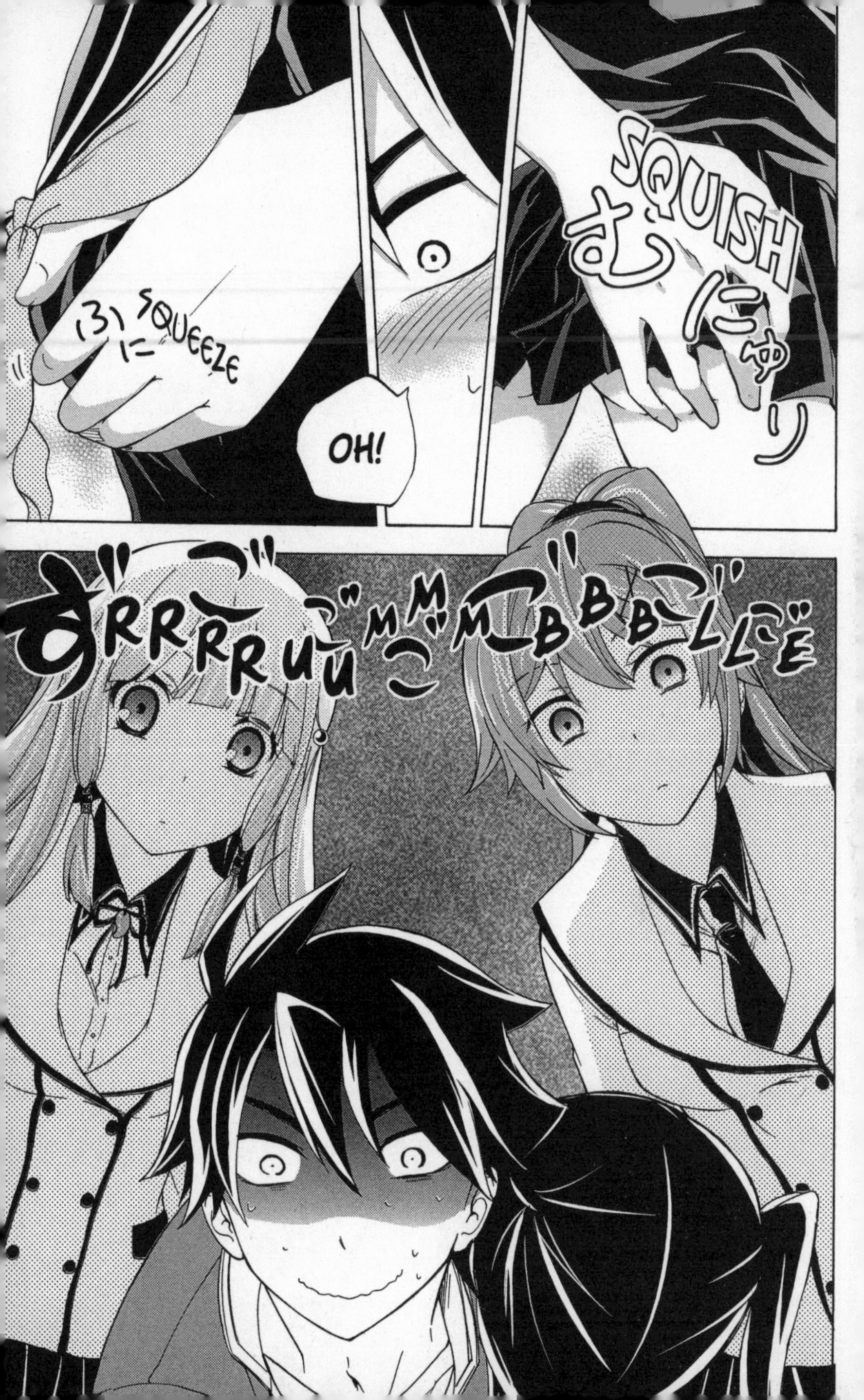
SQUISH
むにゅ
OH!
SQUEEZE
むに
RRRRRUUUMMMMBBBLLLE

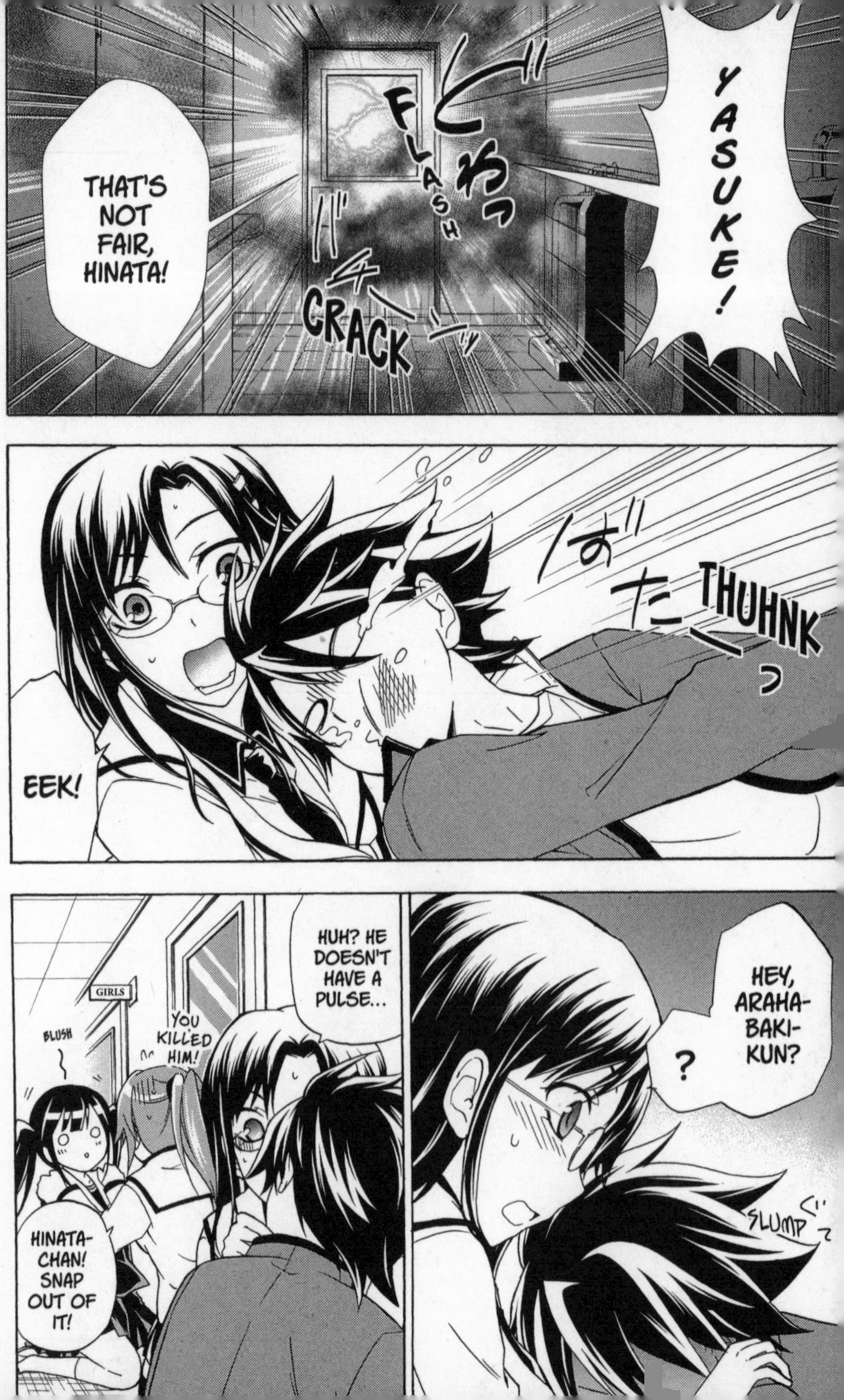
YASUKE!
FLASH
CRACK
THAT'S NOT FAIR, HINATA!
THUHNK
EEK!
HEY, ARAHA-BAKI-KUN?
?
SLUMP
HUH? HE DOESN'T HAVE A PULSE...
YOU KILLED HIM!
GIRLS
BLUSH
HINATA-CHAN! SNAP OUT OF IT!

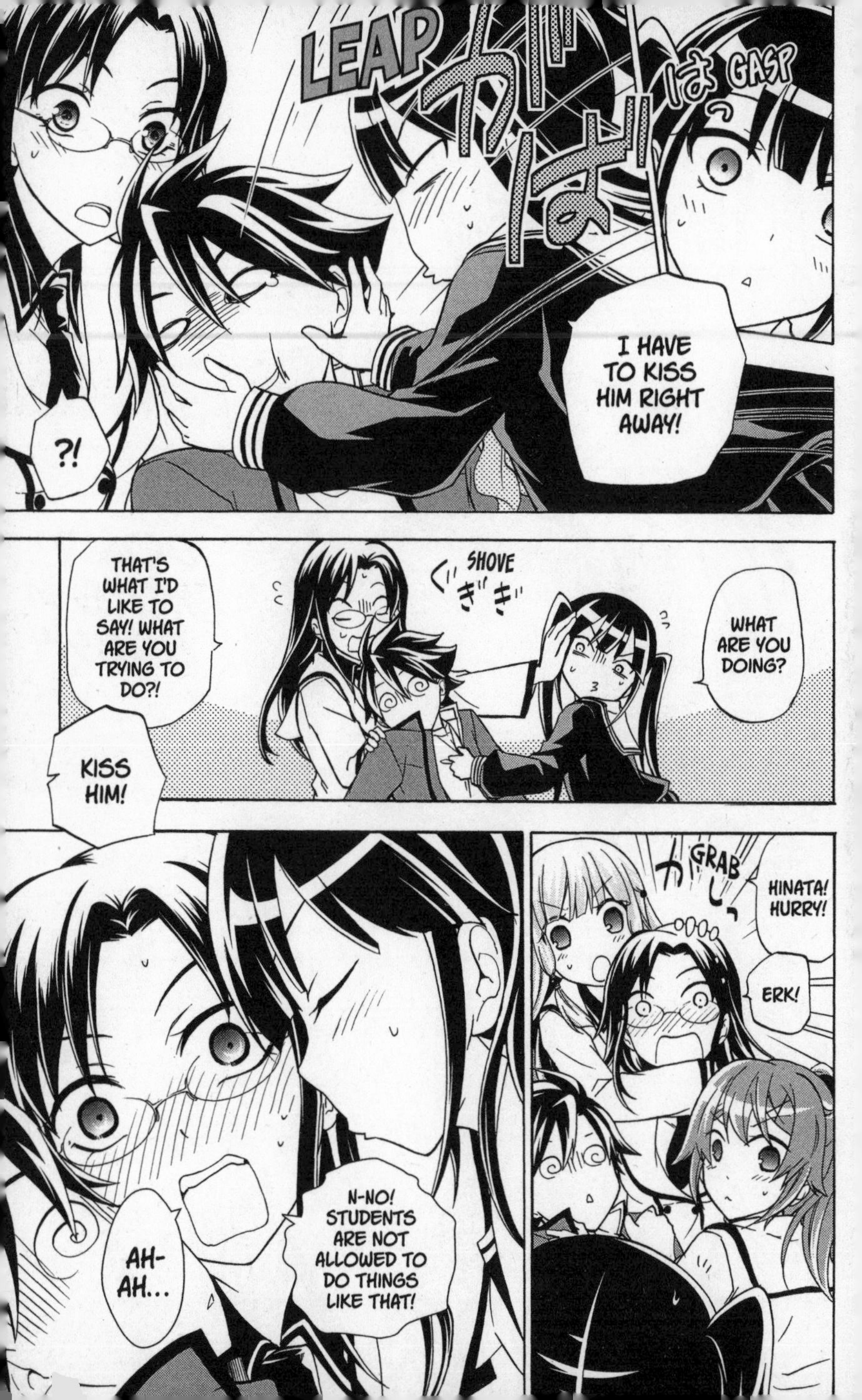
LEAP
はっ GASP
I HAVE TO KISS HIM RIGHT AWAY!
?!
WHAT ARE YOU DOING?
SHOVE
THAT'S WHAT I'D LIKE TO SAY! WHAT ARE YOU TRYING TO DO?!
KISS HIM!
GRAB
HINATA! HURRY!
ERK!
N-NO! STUDENTS ARE NOT ALLOWED TO DO THINGS LIKE THAT!
AH-AH...

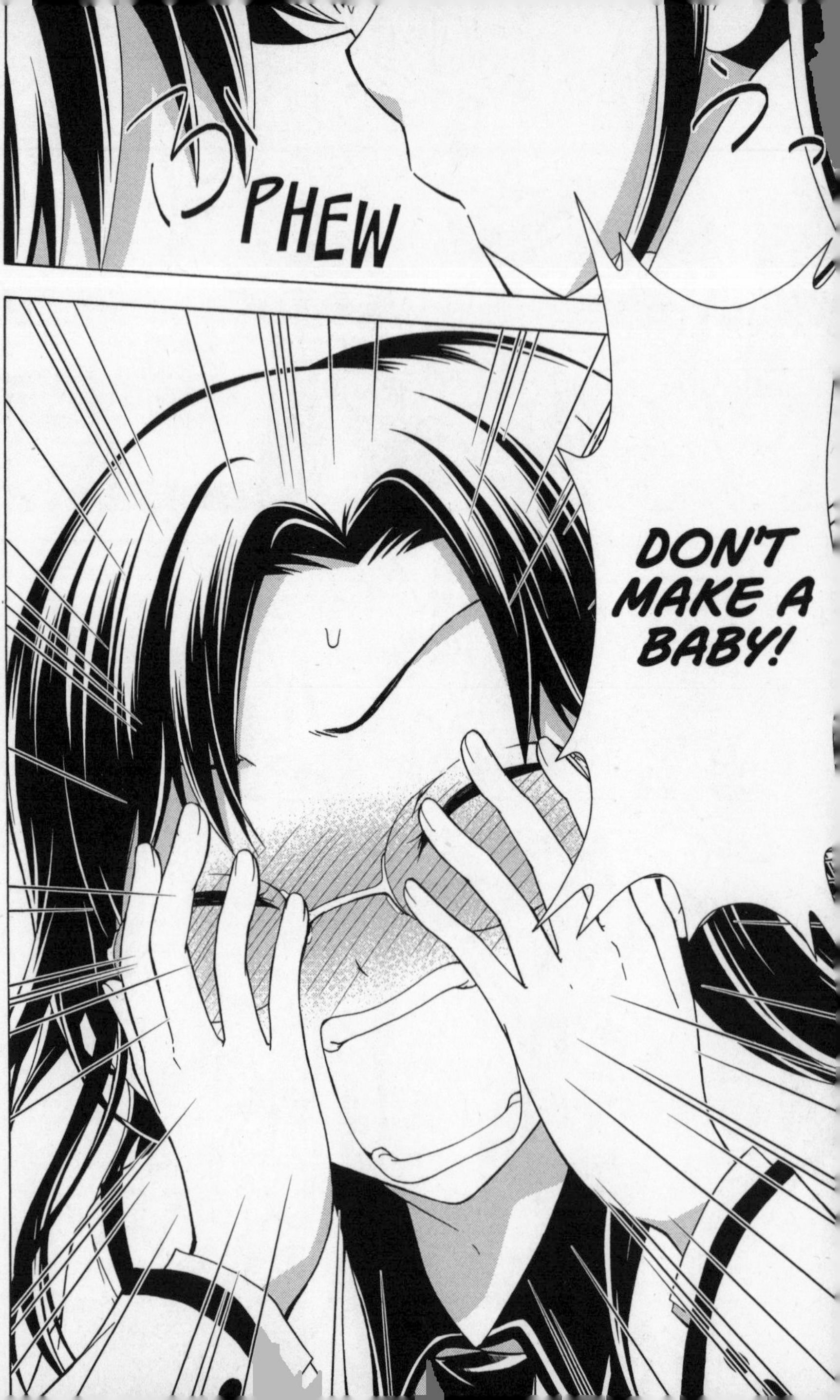
PHEW
DON'T MAKE A BABY!

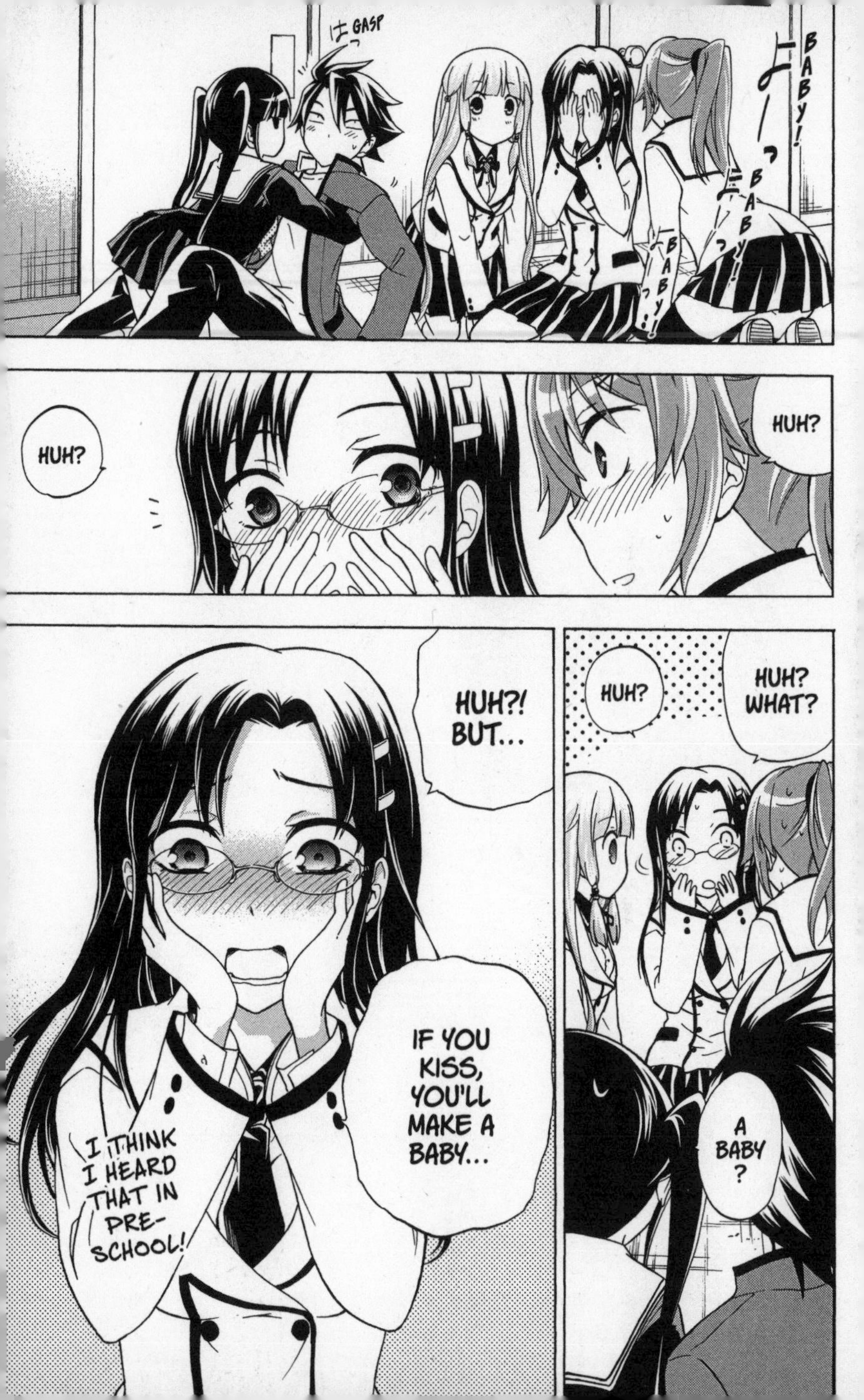
BABY!
BABY!
BABY!
は GASP
HUH?
HUH?
HUH? WHAT?
HUH?
A BABY?
HUH?! BUT...
IF YOU KISS, YOU'LL MAKE A BABY...
I THINK I HEARD THAT IN PRE-SCHOOL!

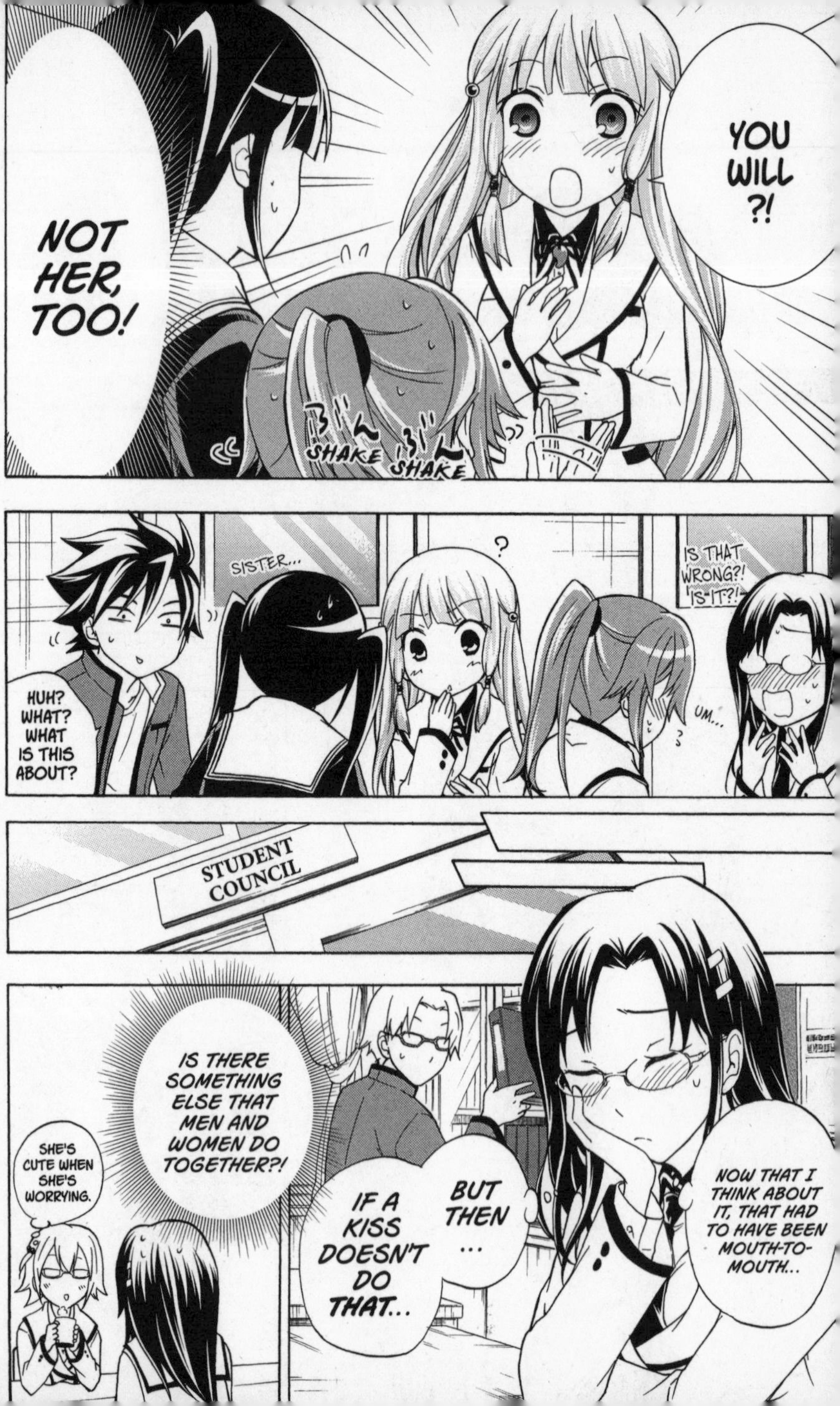
YOU WILL ?!
NOT HER, TOO!
SHAKE SHAKE
IS THAT WRONG?! IS IT?!
UM...
SISTER...
HUH? WHAT? WHAT IS THIS ABOUT?
STUDENT COUNCIL
NOW THAT I THINK ABOUT IT, THAT HAD TO HAVE BEEN MOUTH-TO-MOUTH...
BUT THEN ...
IF A KISS DOESN'T DO THAT...
IS THERE SOMETHING ELSE THAT MEN AND WOMEN DO TOGETHER?!
SHE'S CUTE WHEN SHE'S WORRYING.

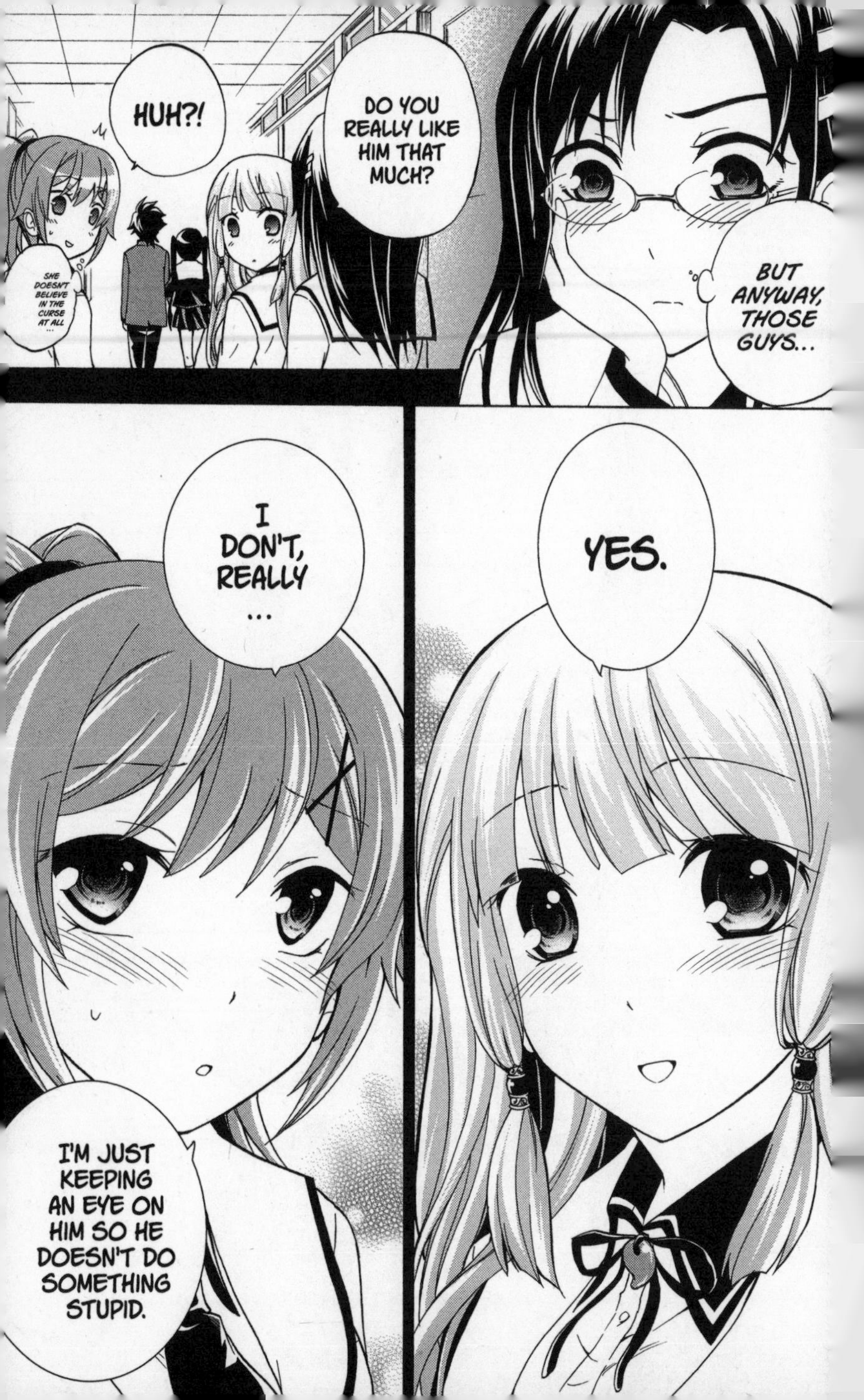
BUT ANYWAY, THOSE GUYS...
DO YOU REALLY LIKE HIM THAT MUCH?
HUH?!
SHE DOESN'T BELIEVE IN THE CURSE AT ALL...
YES.
I DON'T, REALLY...
I'M JUST KEEPING AN EYE ON HIM SO HE DOESN'T DO SOMETHING STUPID.

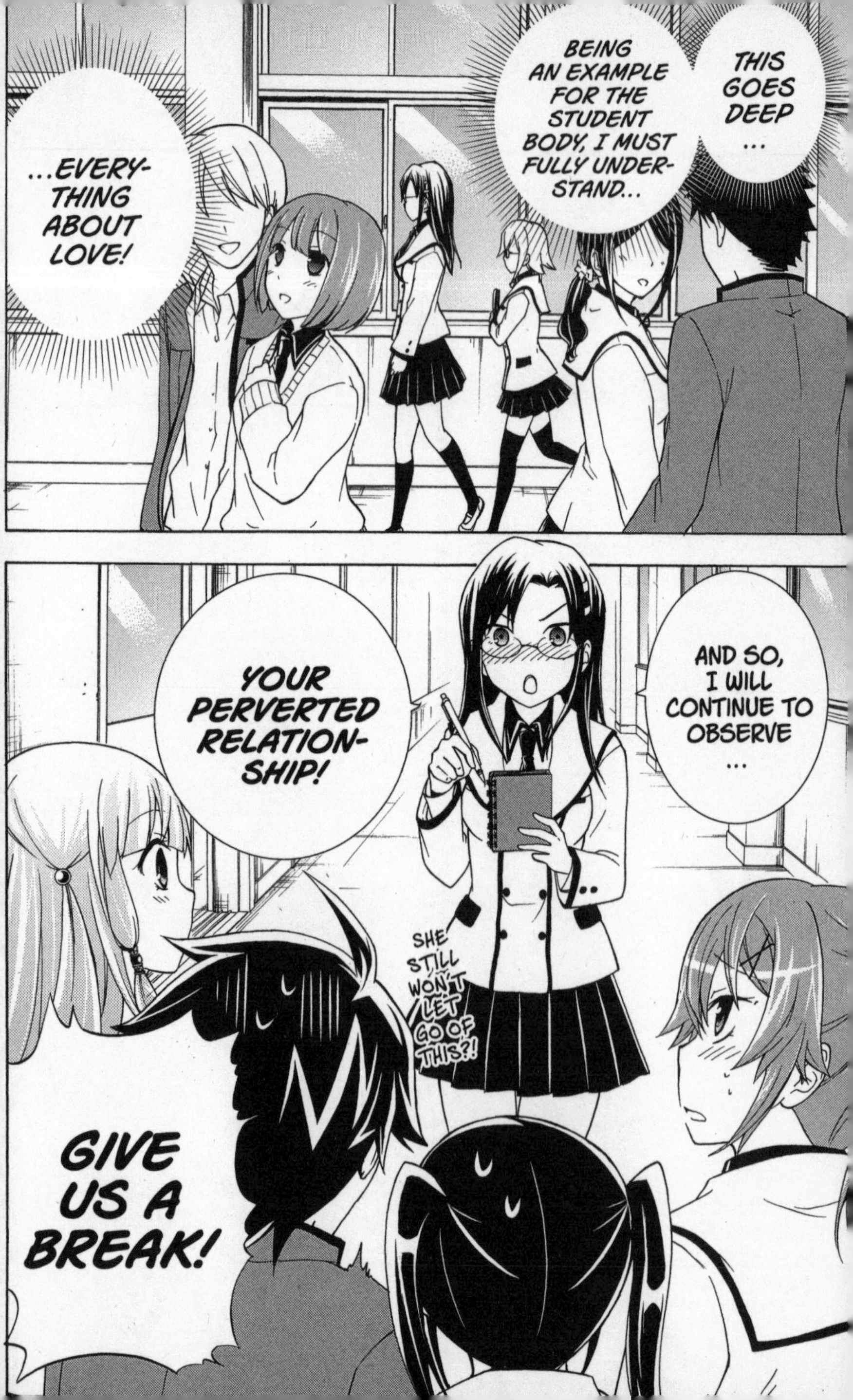
THIS GOES DEEP ...
BEING AN EXAMPLE FOR THE STUDENT BODY, I MUST FULLY UNDER-STAND...
...EVERY-THING ABOUT LOVE!
AND SO, I WILL CONTINUE TO OBSERVE ...
YOUR PERVERTED RELATION-SHIP!
SHE STILL WON'T LET GO OF THIS?!
GIVE US A BREAK!

Maga-Tsuki
Presented by Hoshino Taguchi

*MESSING AROUND AFTER SWITCHING TO A SMARTPHONE.

DON'T PLAY AROUND WITH MEE!

STRETCH

まがつき

Maga-Tsuki
Presented by Hoshino Taguchi

Maga-Tsuki Taguchi Hoshino

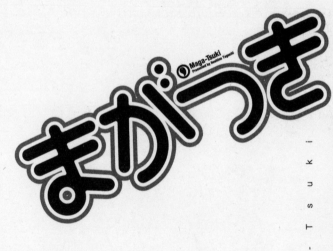

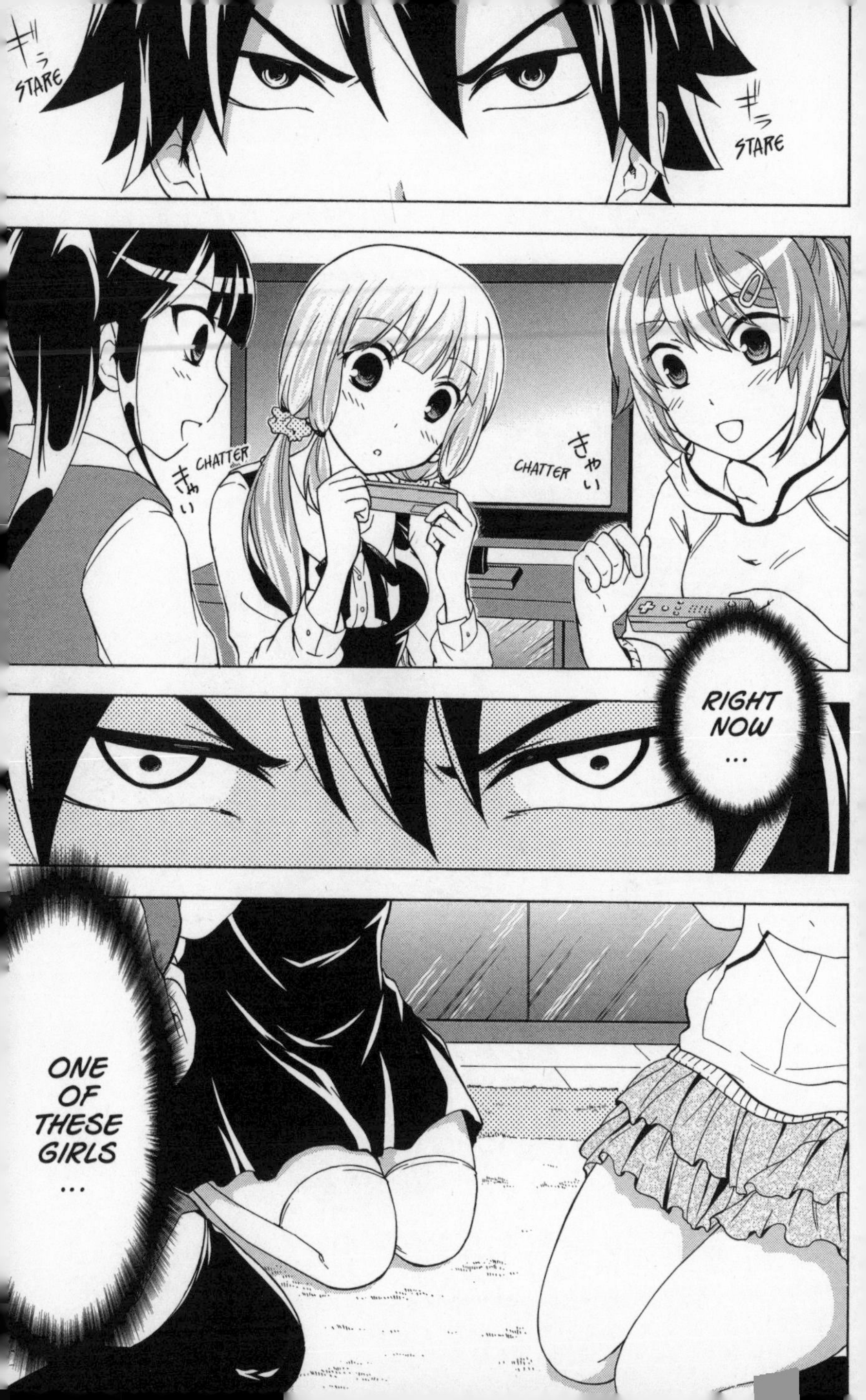
ギラ
STARE
ギラ
STARE
きゃい
CHATTER
きゃい
CHATTER
RIGHT NOW ...
ONE OF THESE GIRLS ...

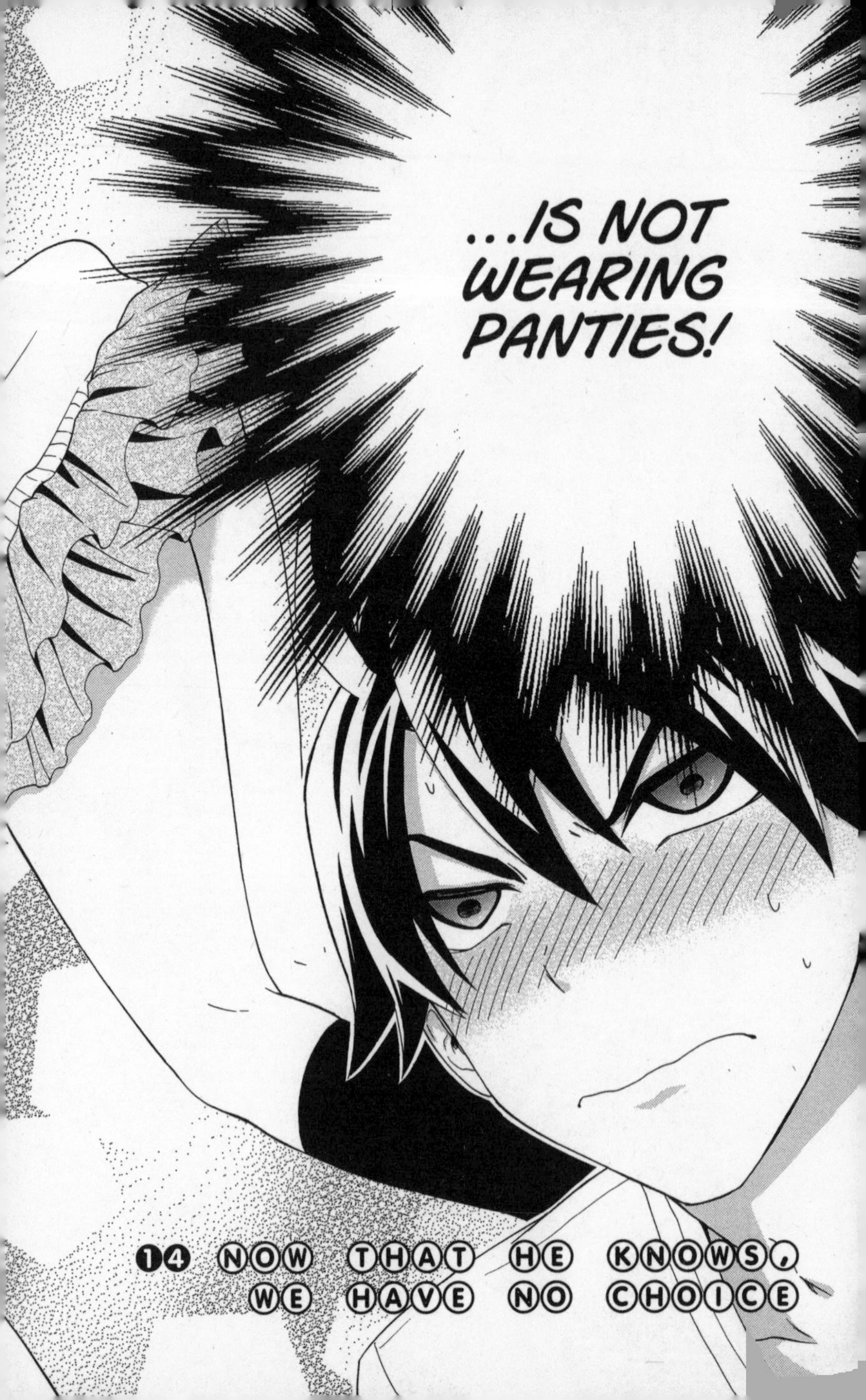
...IS NOT WEARING PANTIES!
14 NOW THAT HE KNOWS, WE HAVE NO CHOICE

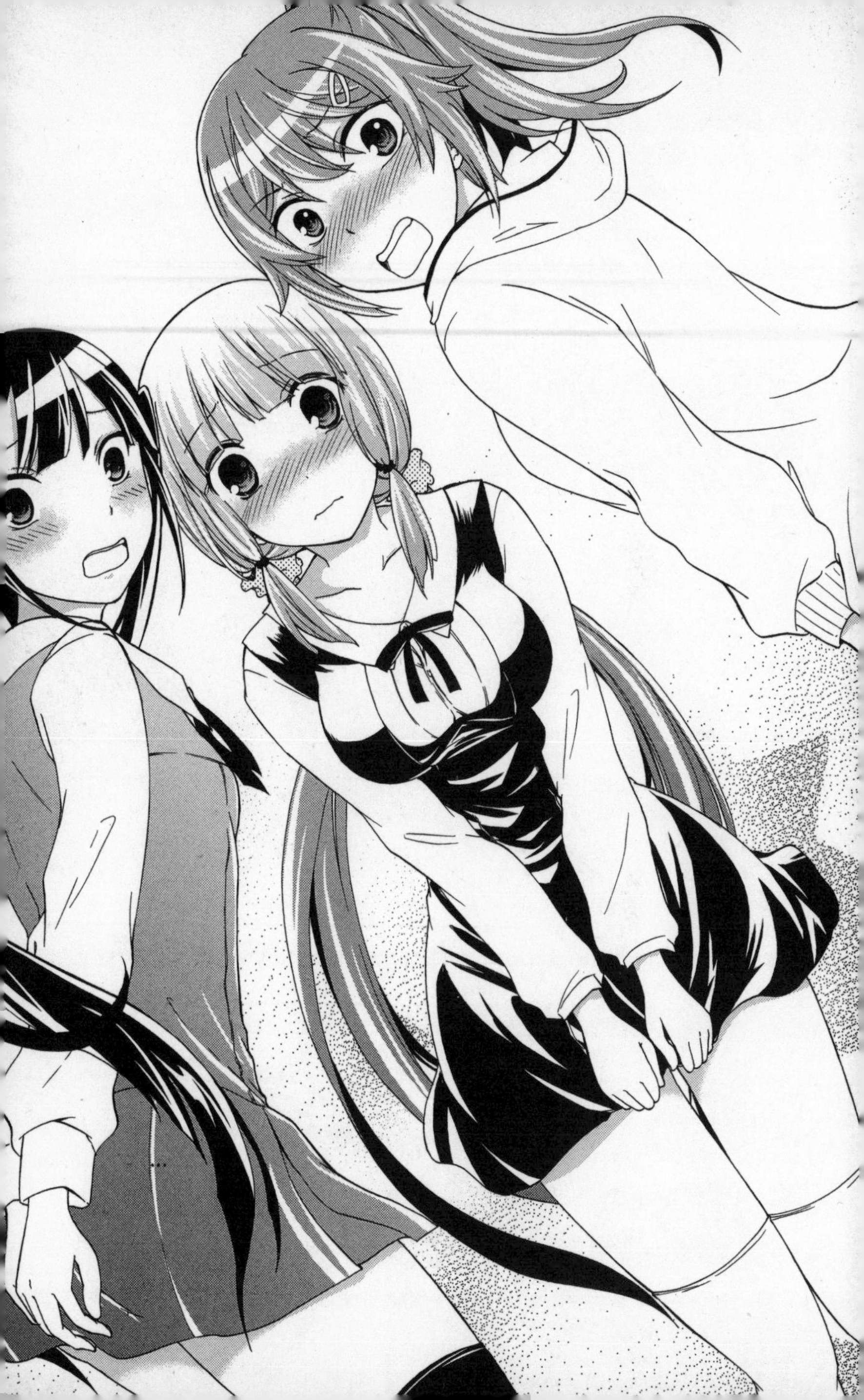

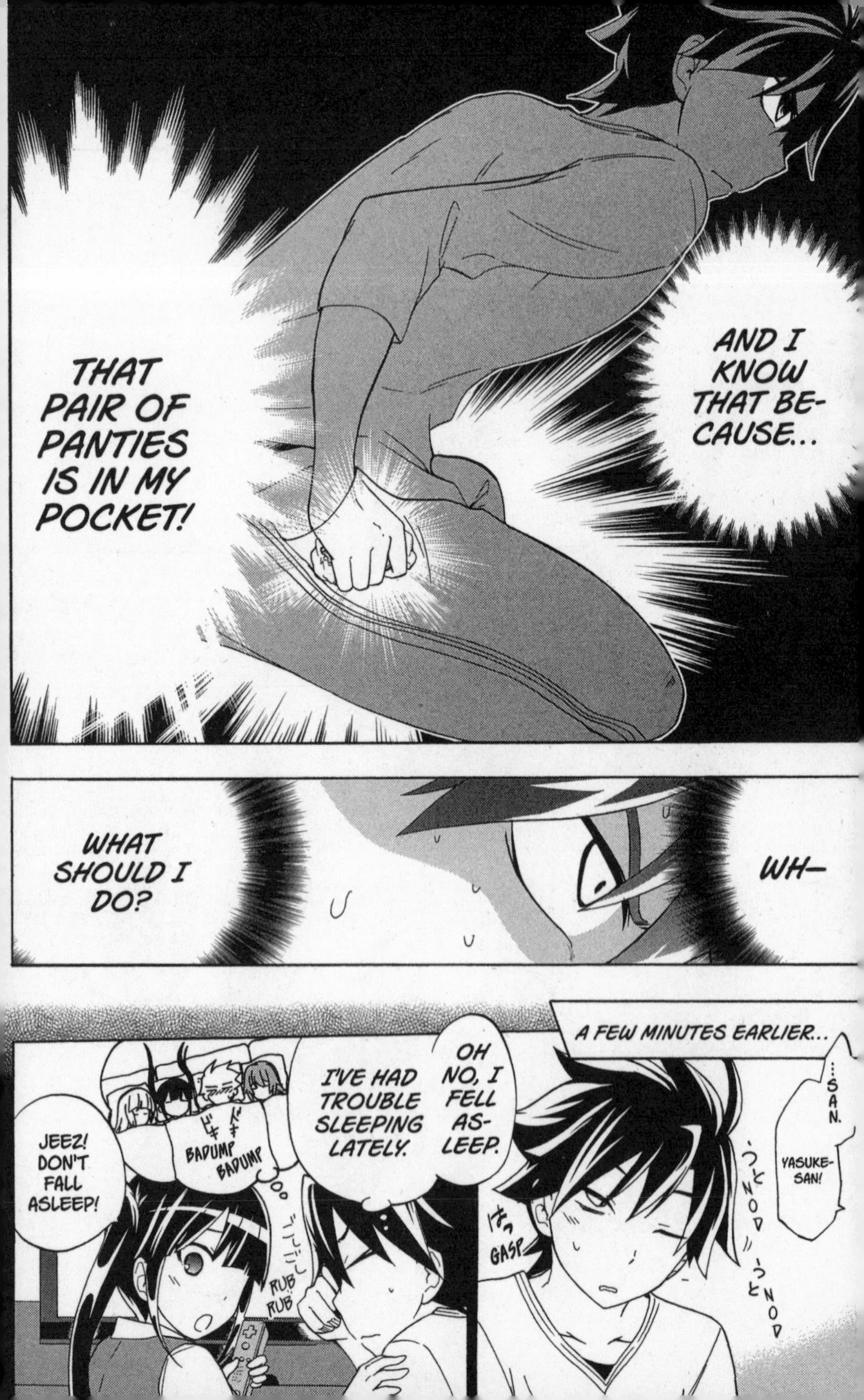
AND I KNOW THAT BECAUSE...
THAT PAIR OF PANTIES IS IN MY POCKET!
WH—
WHAT SHOULD I DO?
A FEW MINUTES EARLIER...
...SAN.
YASUKE-SAN!
NOD NOD
NOD NOD
GASP
OH NO, I FELL ASLEEP.
I'VE HAD TROUBLE SLEEPING LATELY.
BADUMP BADUMP
RUB RUB
JEEZ! DON'T FALL ASLEEP!

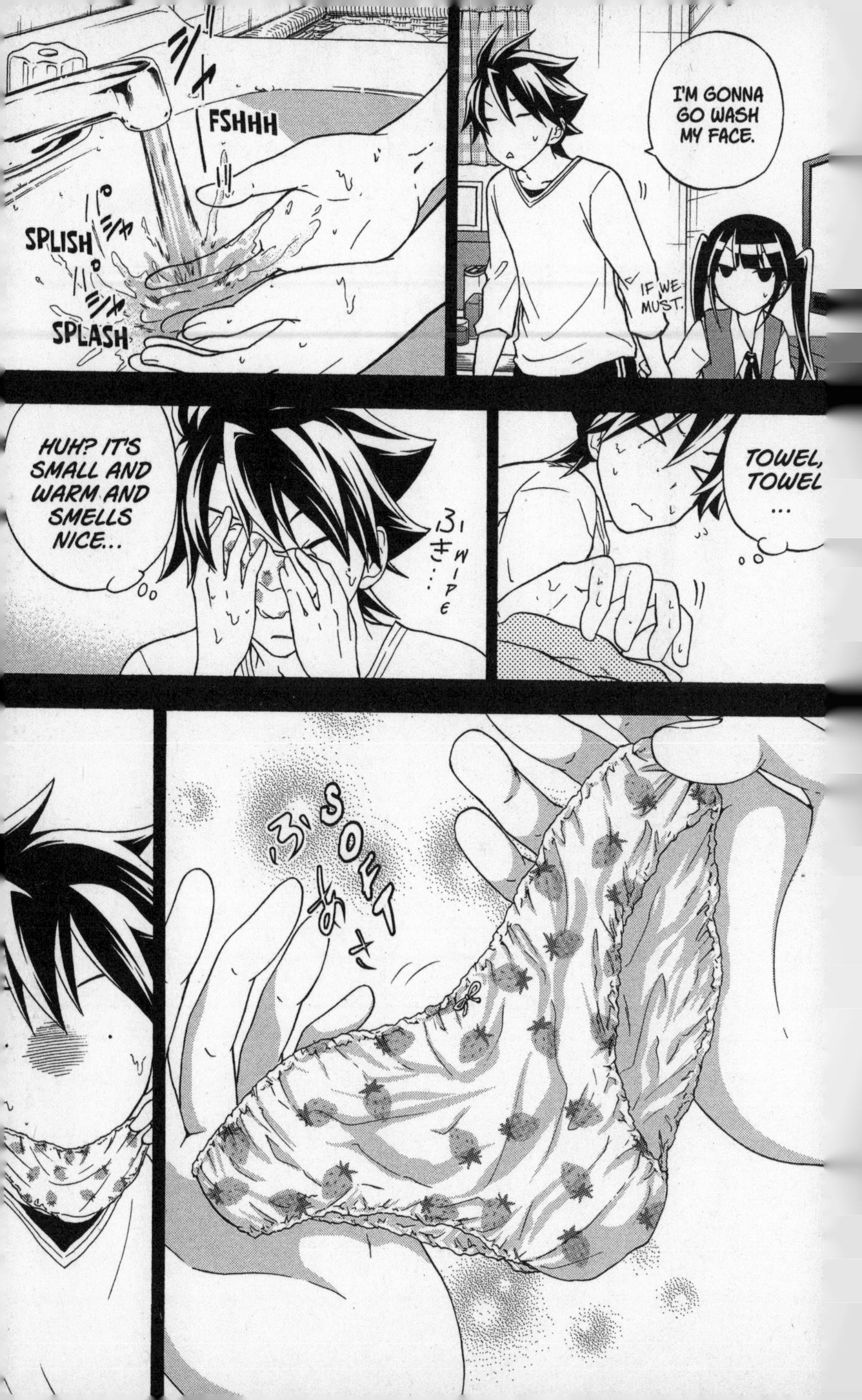
I'M GONNA GO WASH MY FACE.
IF WE MUST.
FSHHH
SPLISH
SPLASH
TOWEL, TOWEL ...
HUH? IT'S SMALL AND WARM AND SMELLS NICE...
ふき…
WIPE
SOFT
ふぁさ

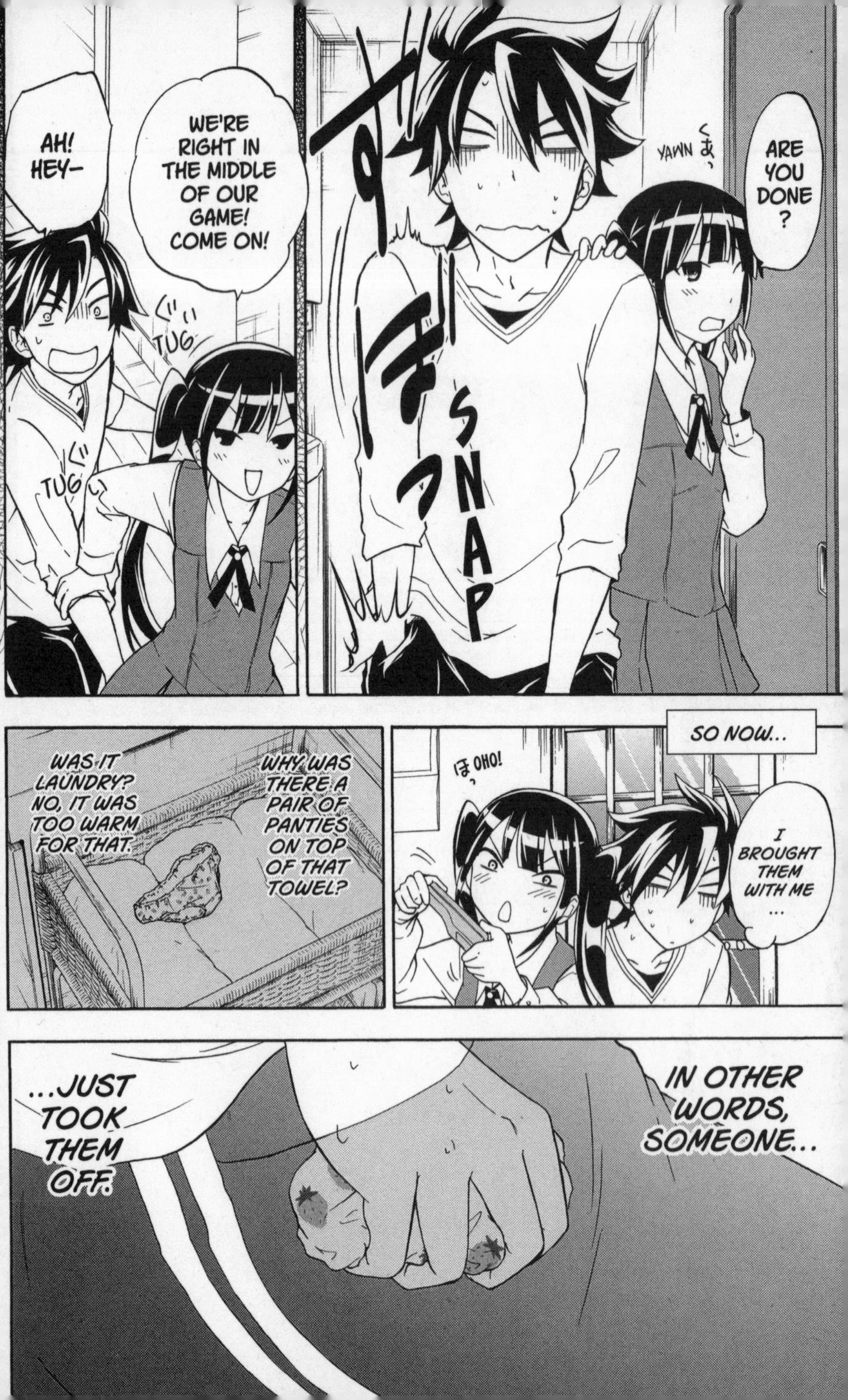
YAWN
ARE YOU DONE?
SNAP
WE'RE RIGHT IN THE MIDDLE OF OUR GAME! COME ON!
AH! HEY-
TUG
TUG
SO NOW...
I BROUGHT THEM WITH ME...
OHO!
WHY WAS THERE A PAIR OF PANTIES ON TOP OF THAT TOWEL?
WAS IT LAUNDRY? NO, IT WAS TOO WARM FOR THAT.
IN OTHER WORDS, SOMEONE...
...JUST TOOK THEM OFF.

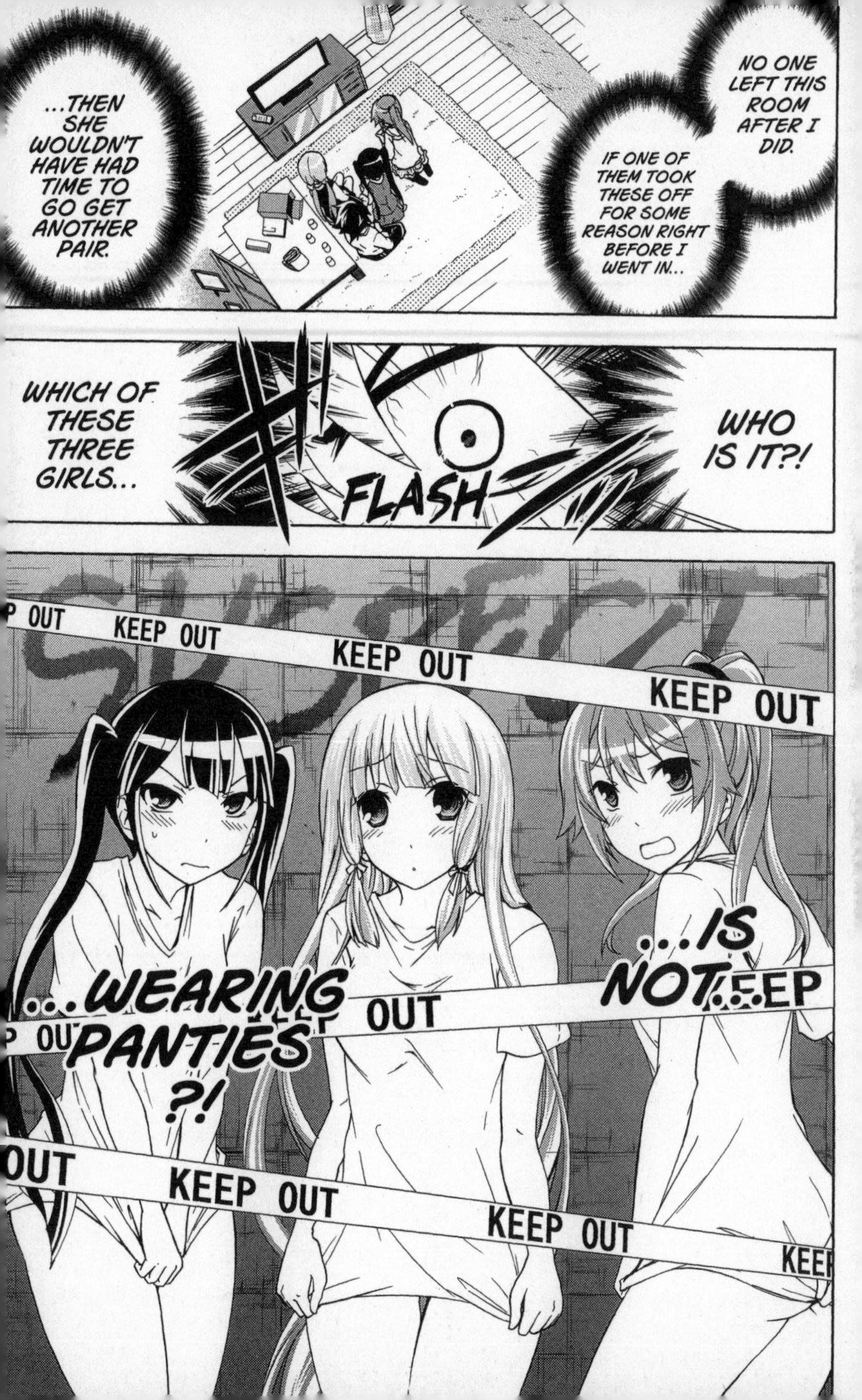
NO ONE LEFT THIS ROOM AFTER I DID.
IF ONE OF THEM TOOK THESE OFF FOR SOME REASON RIGHT BEFORE I WENT IN...
...THEN SHE WOULDN'T HAVE HAD TIME TO GO GET ANOTHER PAIR.
WHO IS IT?!
FLASH
WHICH OF THESE THREE GIRLS...
KEEP OUT
KEEP OUT
KEEP OUT
...IS NOT...
...WEARING PANTIES?!
OUT
KEEP OUT
KEEP OUT

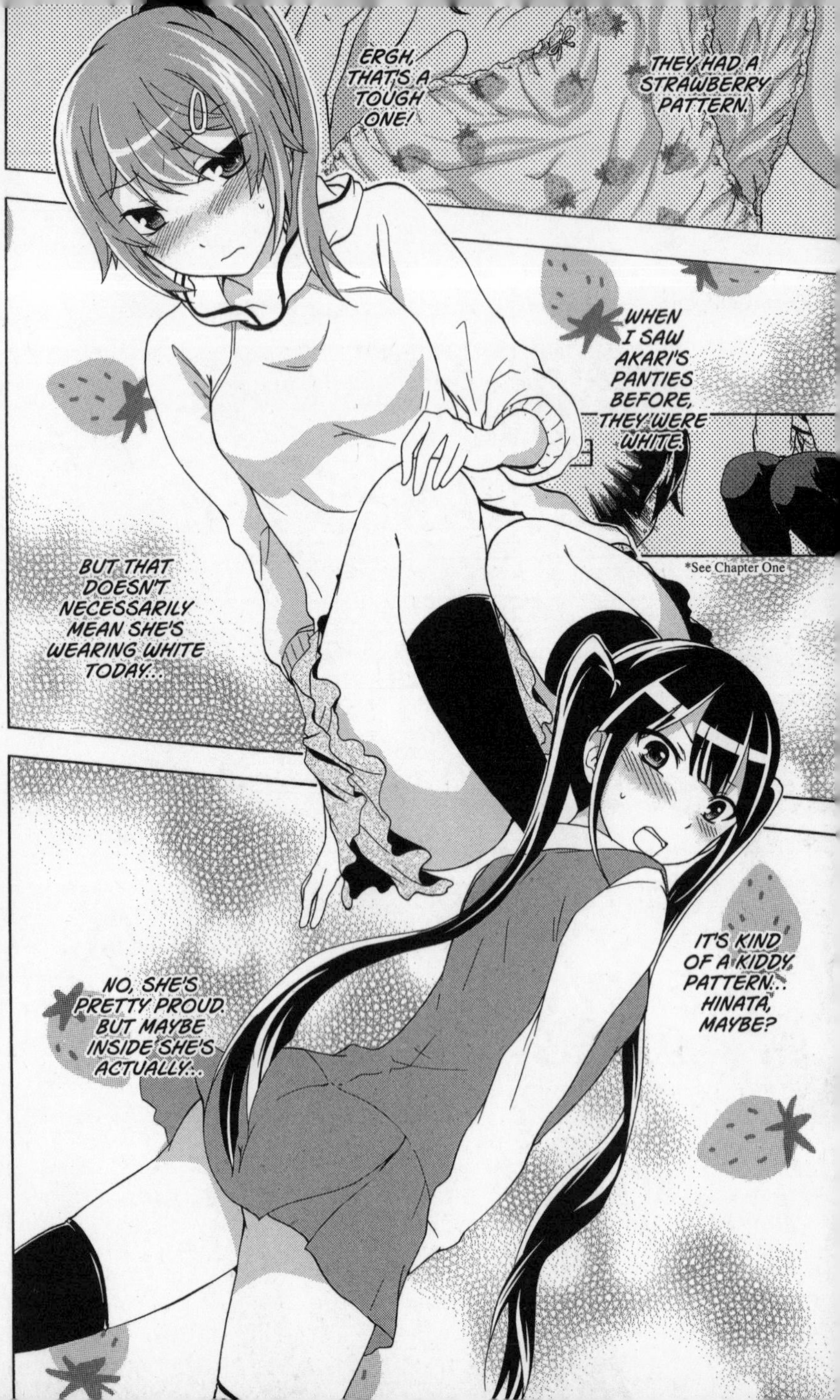
THEY HAD A STRAWBERRY PATTERN.
ERGH, THAT'S A TOUGH ONE!
WHEN I SAW AKARI'S PANTIES BEFORE, THEY WERE WHITE.
*See Chapter One
BUT THAT DOESN'T NECESSARILY MEAN SHE'S WEARING WHITE TODAY...
IT'S KIND OF A KIDDY PATTERN... HINATA, MAYBE?
NO, SHE'S PRETTY PROUD. BUT MAYBE INSIDE SHE'S ACTUALLY...

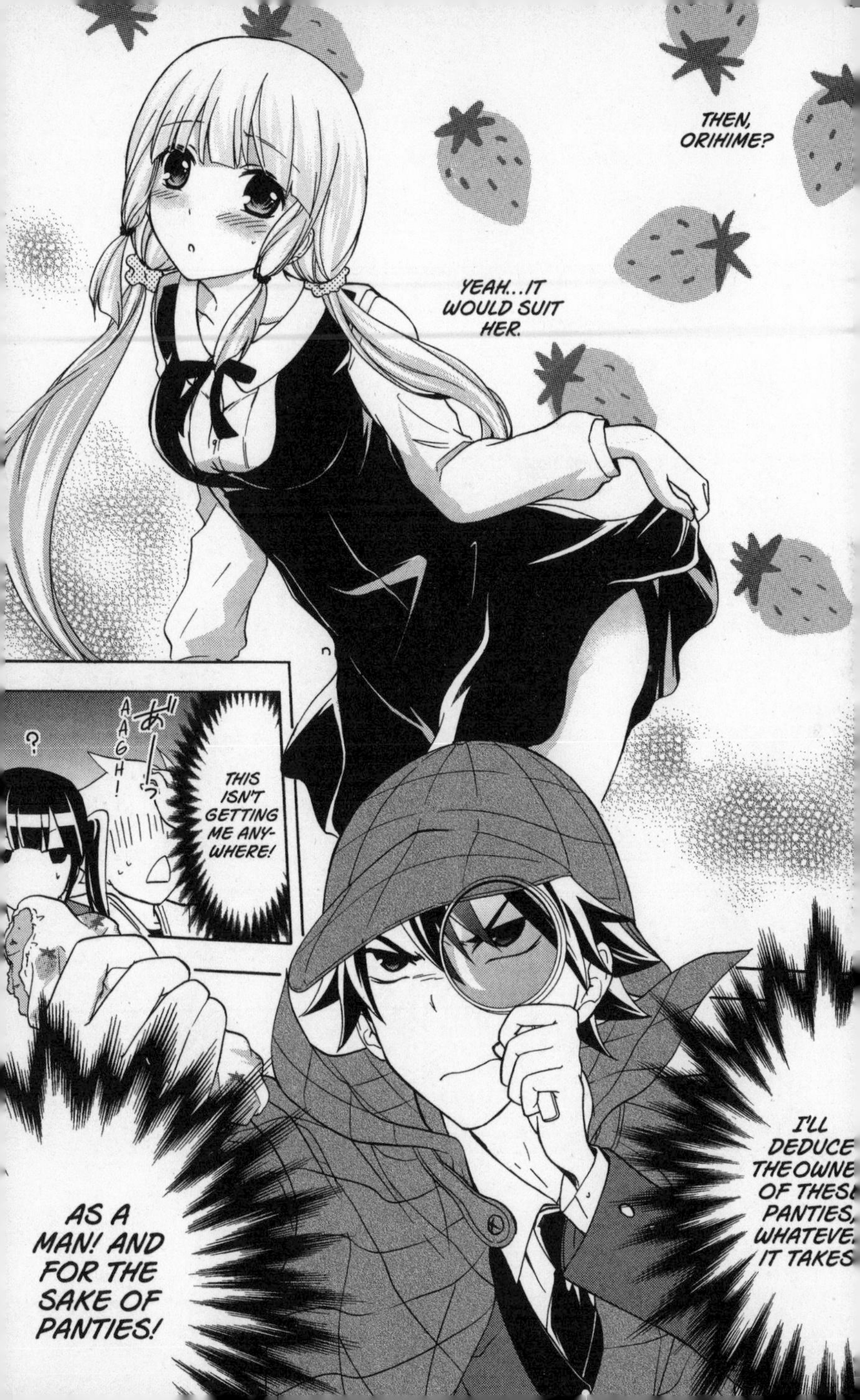
THEN, ORIHIME?
YEAH...IT WOULD SUIT HER.
あ゛ーっ
AAGH!
THIS ISN'T GETTING ME ANY-WHERE!
?
I'LL DEDUCE THEOWNE OF THES PANTIES, WHATEVE IT TAKES
AS A MAN! AND FOR THE SAKE OF PANTIES!

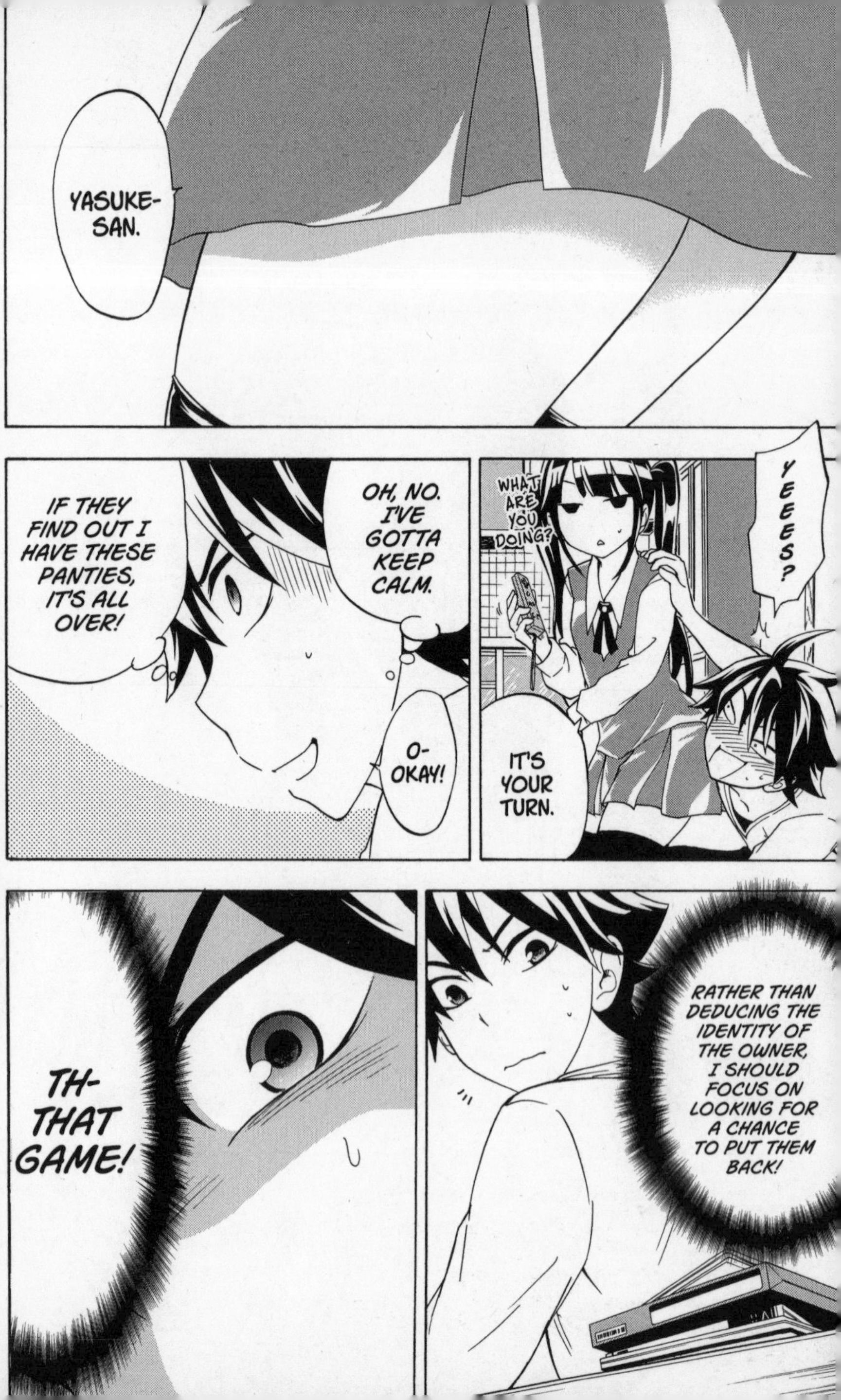
YASUKE-SAN.
YEEES?
WHAT ARE YOU DOING?
IT'S YOUR TURN.
OH, NO. I'VE GOTTA KEEP CALM.
IF THEY FIND OUT I HAVE THESE PANTIES, IT'S ALL OVER!
O-OKAY!
RATHER THAN DEDUCING THE IDENTITY OF THE OWNER, I SHOULD FOCUS ON LOOKING FOR A CHANCE TO PUT THEM BACK!
TH-THAT GAME!

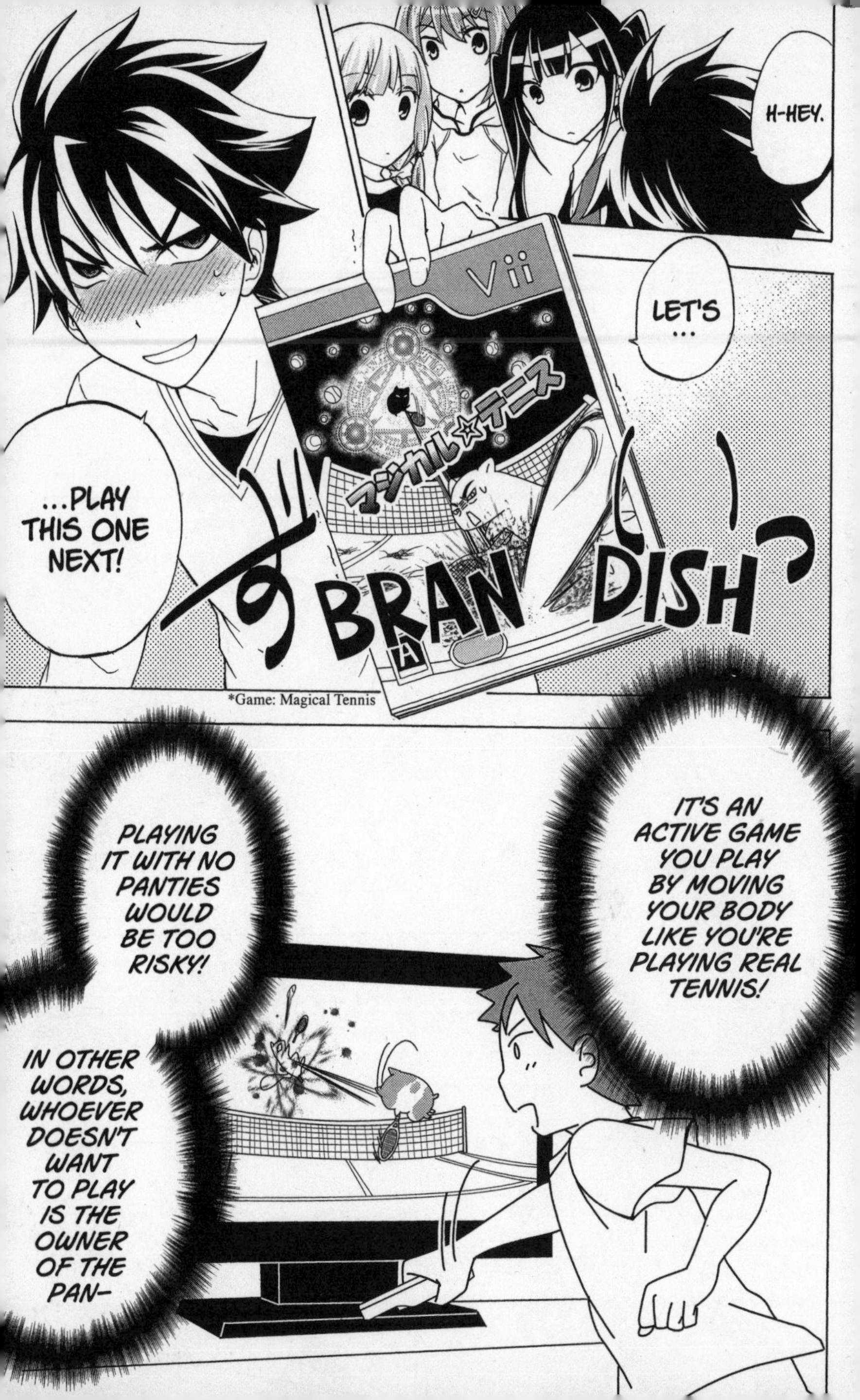
H-HEY.
LET'S...
...PLAY THIS ONE NEXT!
Vii
マジカル☆テニス
BRANDISH
IT'S AN ACTIVE GAME YOU PLAY BY MOVING YOUR BODY LIKE YOU'RE PLAYING REAL TENNIS!
PLAYING IT WITH NO PANTIES WOULD BE TOO RISKY!
IN OTHER WORDS, WHOEVER DOESN'T WANT TO PLAY IS THE OWNER OF THE PAN-
*Game: Magical Tennis

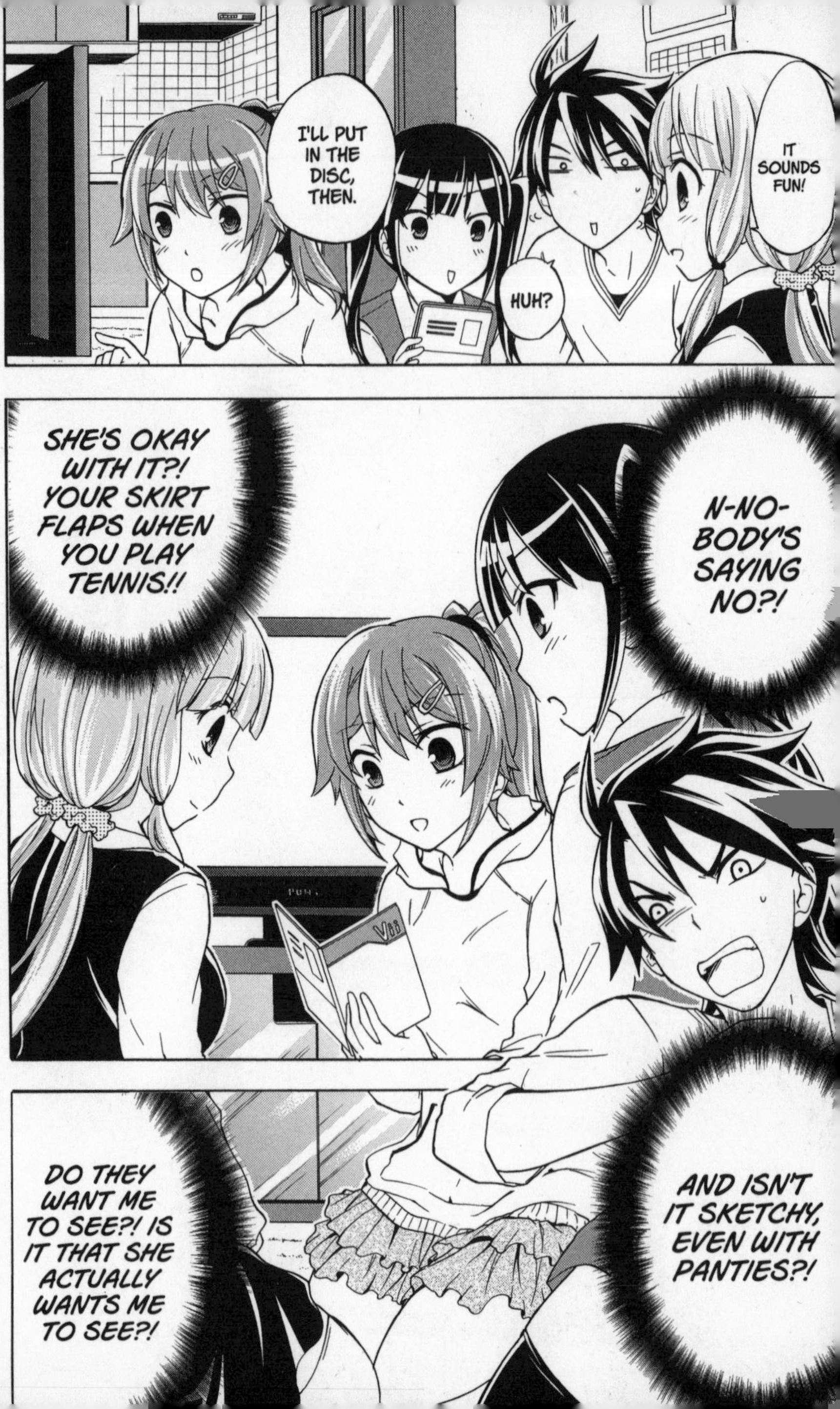
IT SOUNDS FUN!
HUH?
I'LL PUT IN THE DISC, THEN.
N-NO-BODY'S SAYING NO?!
SHE'S OKAY WITH IT?! YOUR SKIRT FLAPS WHEN YOU PLAY TENNIS!!
AND ISN'T IT SKETCHY, EVEN WITH PANTIES?!
DO THEY WANT ME TO SEE?! IS IT THAT SHE ACTUALLY WANTS ME TO SEE?!

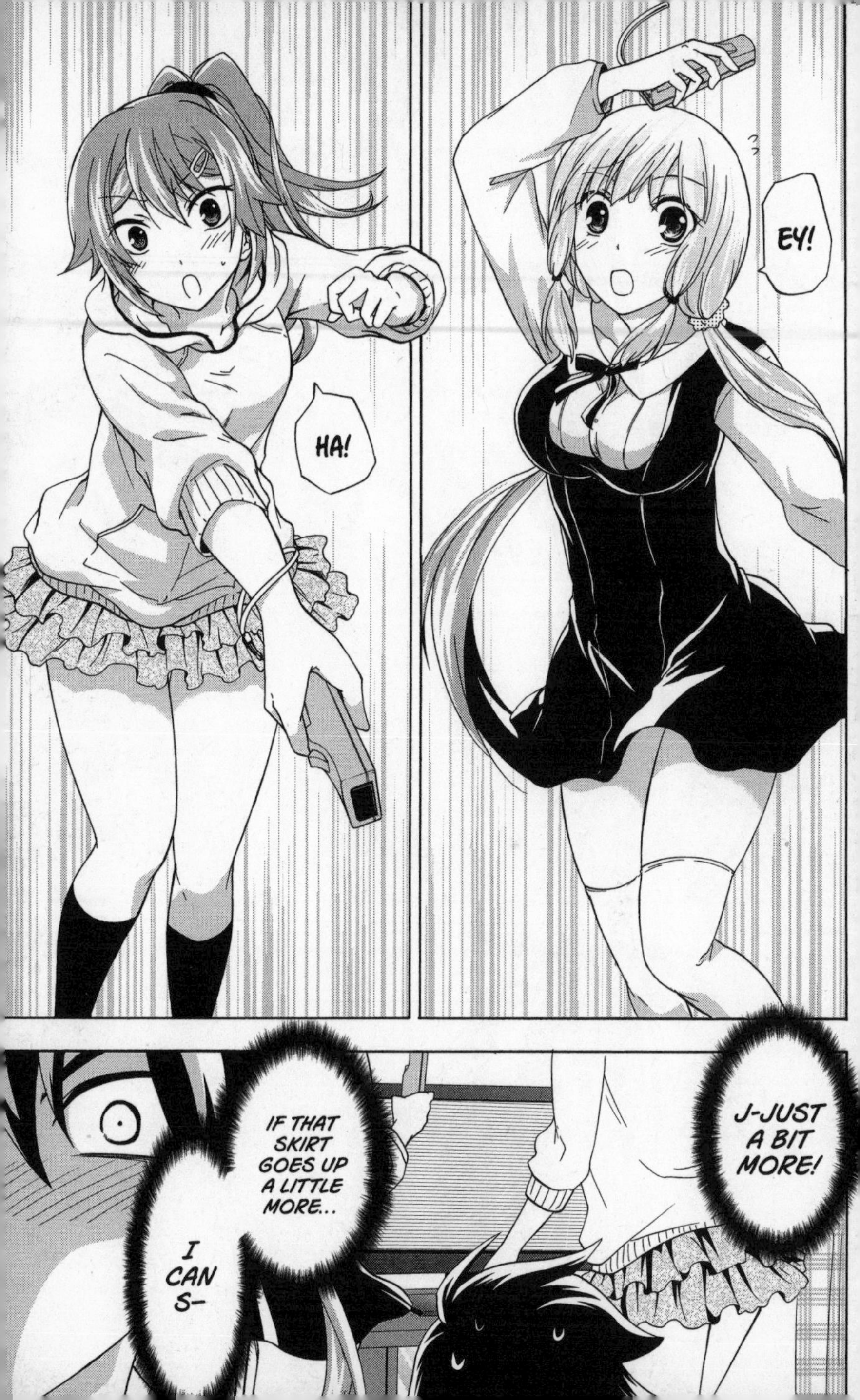
EY!
HA!
J-JUST A BIT MORE!
IF THAT SKIRT GOES UP A LITTLE MORE...
I CAN S-

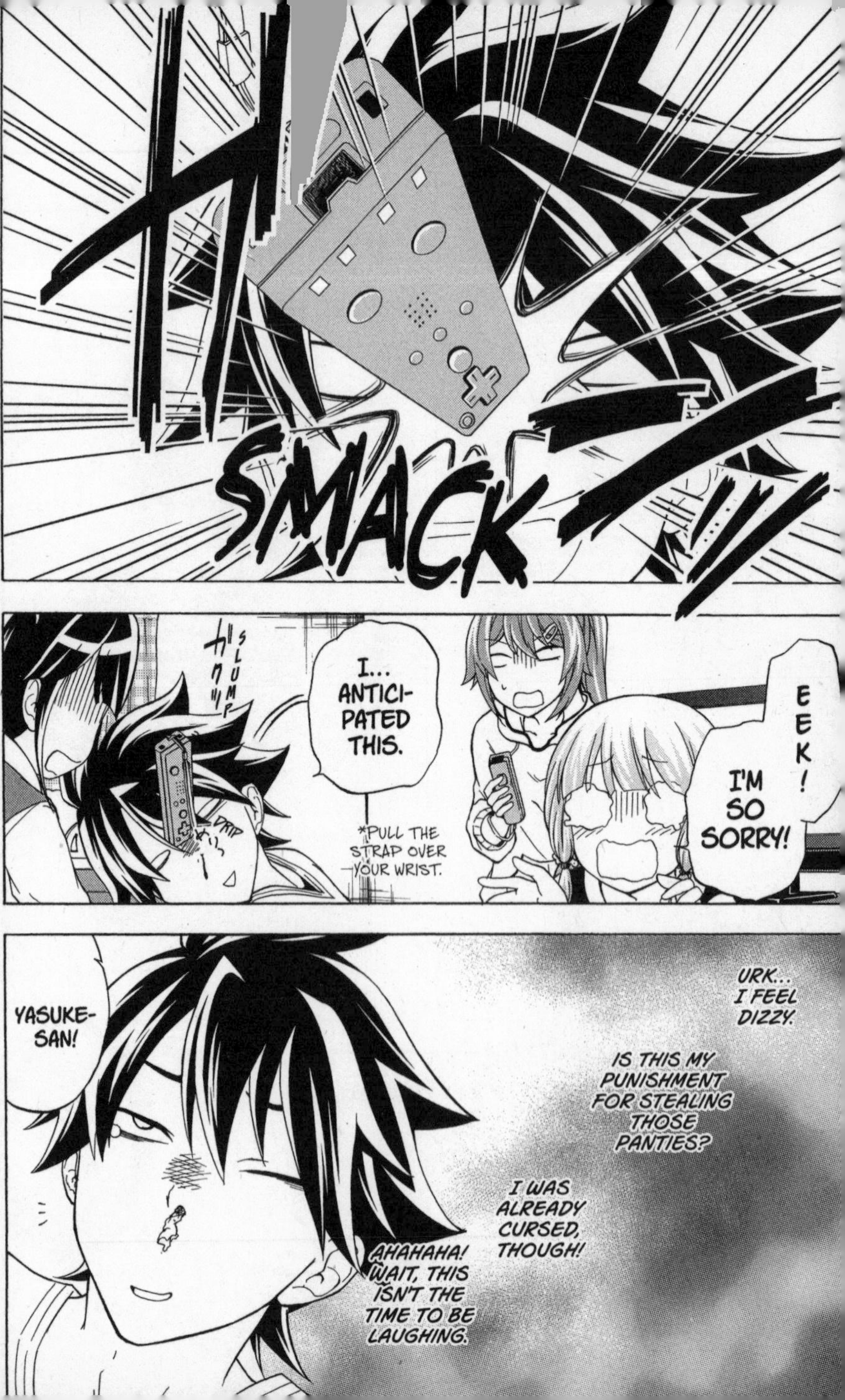
SMACK!!
EEK! I'M SO SORRY!
I... ANTICIPATED THIS.
*PULL THE STRAP OVER YOUR WRIST.
SLUMP
DRIP
URK... I FEEL DIZZY.
IS THIS MY PUNISHMENT FOR STEALING THOSE PANTIES?
I WAS ALREADY CURSED, THOUGH!
AHAHAHA! WAIT, THIS ISN'T THE TIME TO BE LAUGHING.
YASUKE-SAN!

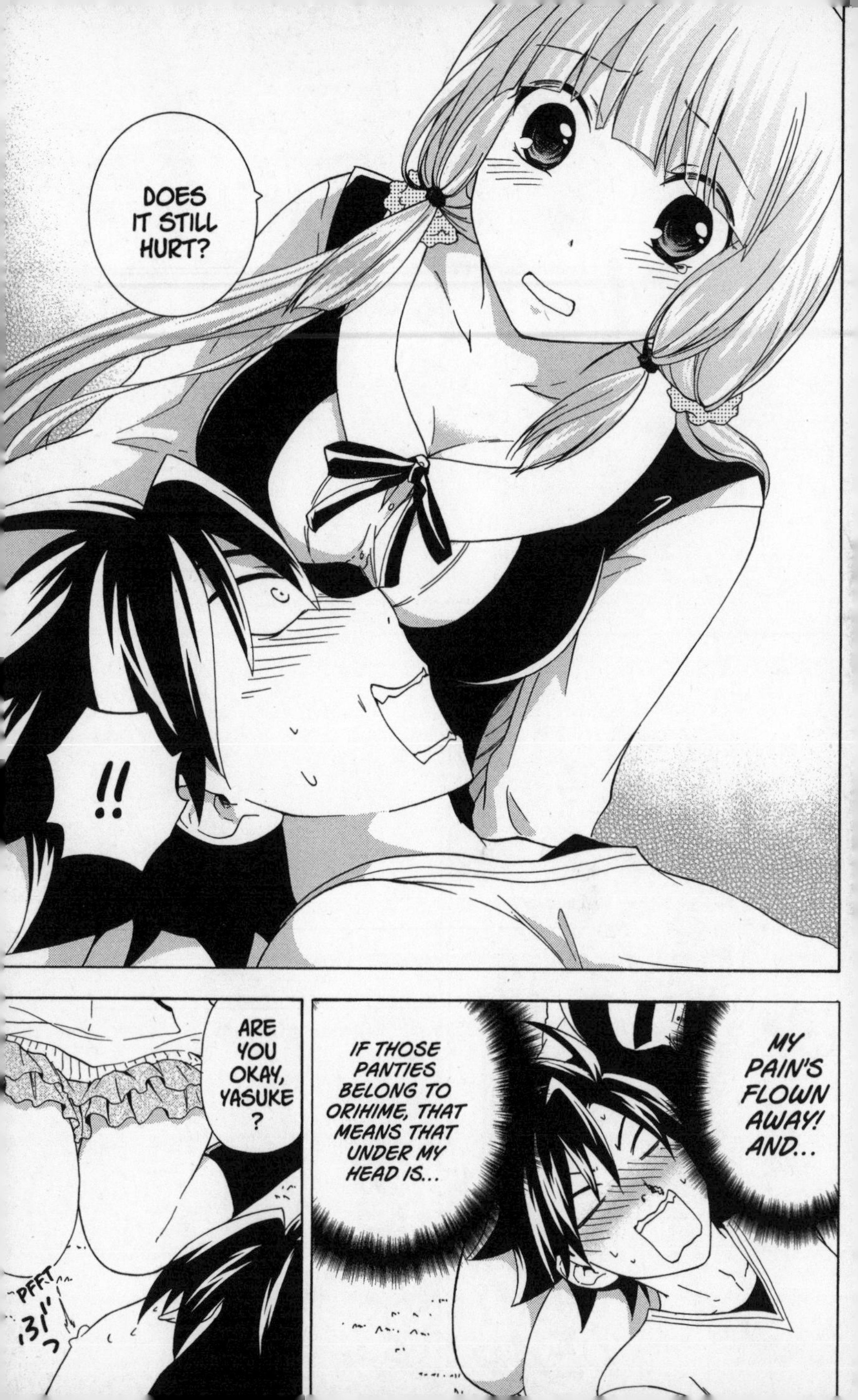
DOES IT STILL HURT?
!!
MY PAIN'S FLOWN AWAY! AND...
IF THOSE PANTIES BELONG TO ORIHIME, THAT MEANS THAT UNDER MY HEAD IS...
ARE YOU OKAY, YASUKE?
PFFT

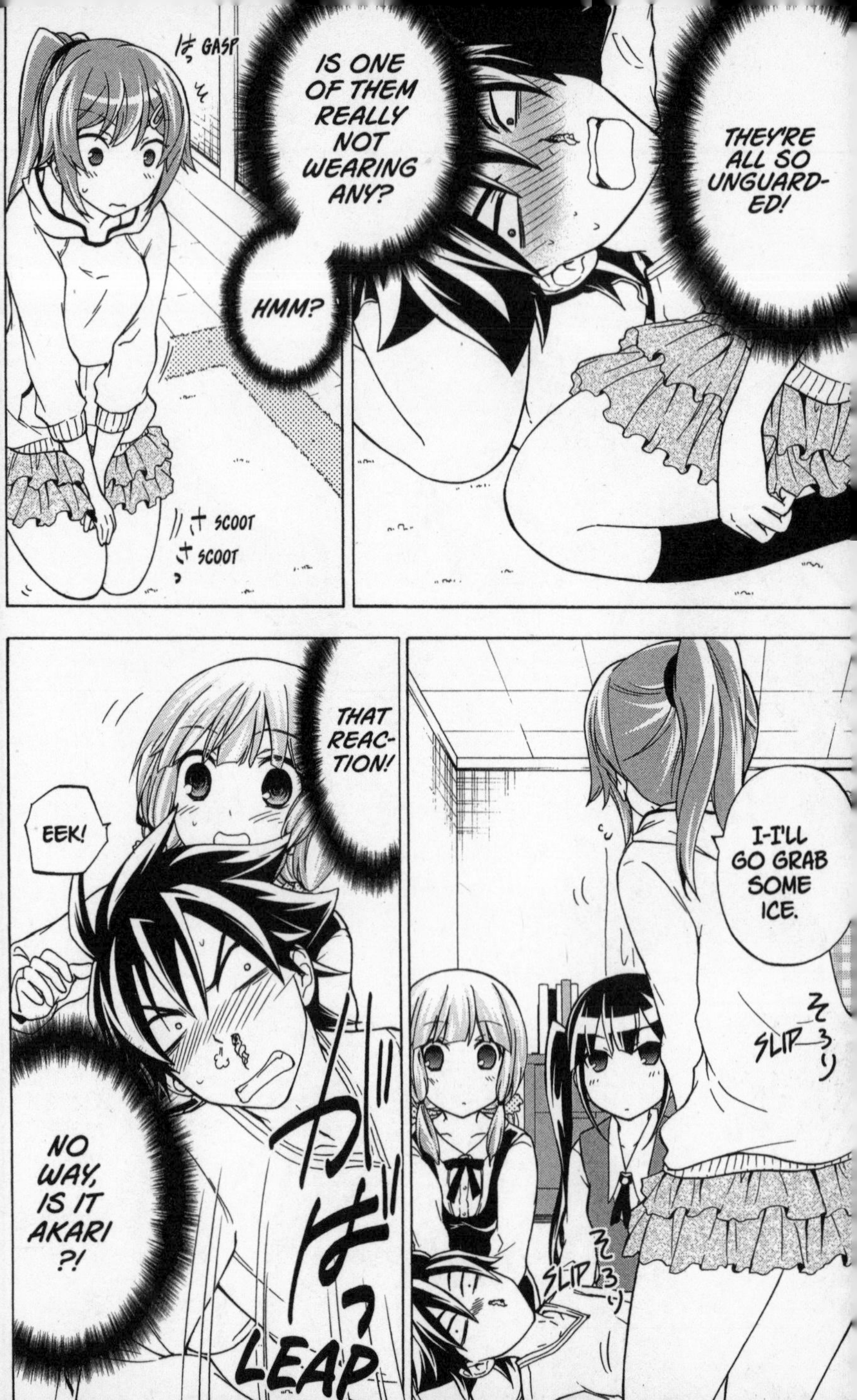
THEY'RE ALL SO UNGUARD-ED!
IS ONE OF THEM REALLY NOT WEARING ANY?
HMM?
GASP
SCOOT
SCOOT
I-I'LL GO GRAB SOME ICE.
SLIP
SLIP
THAT REAC-TION!
EEK!
NO WAY, IS IT AKARI ?!
LEAP

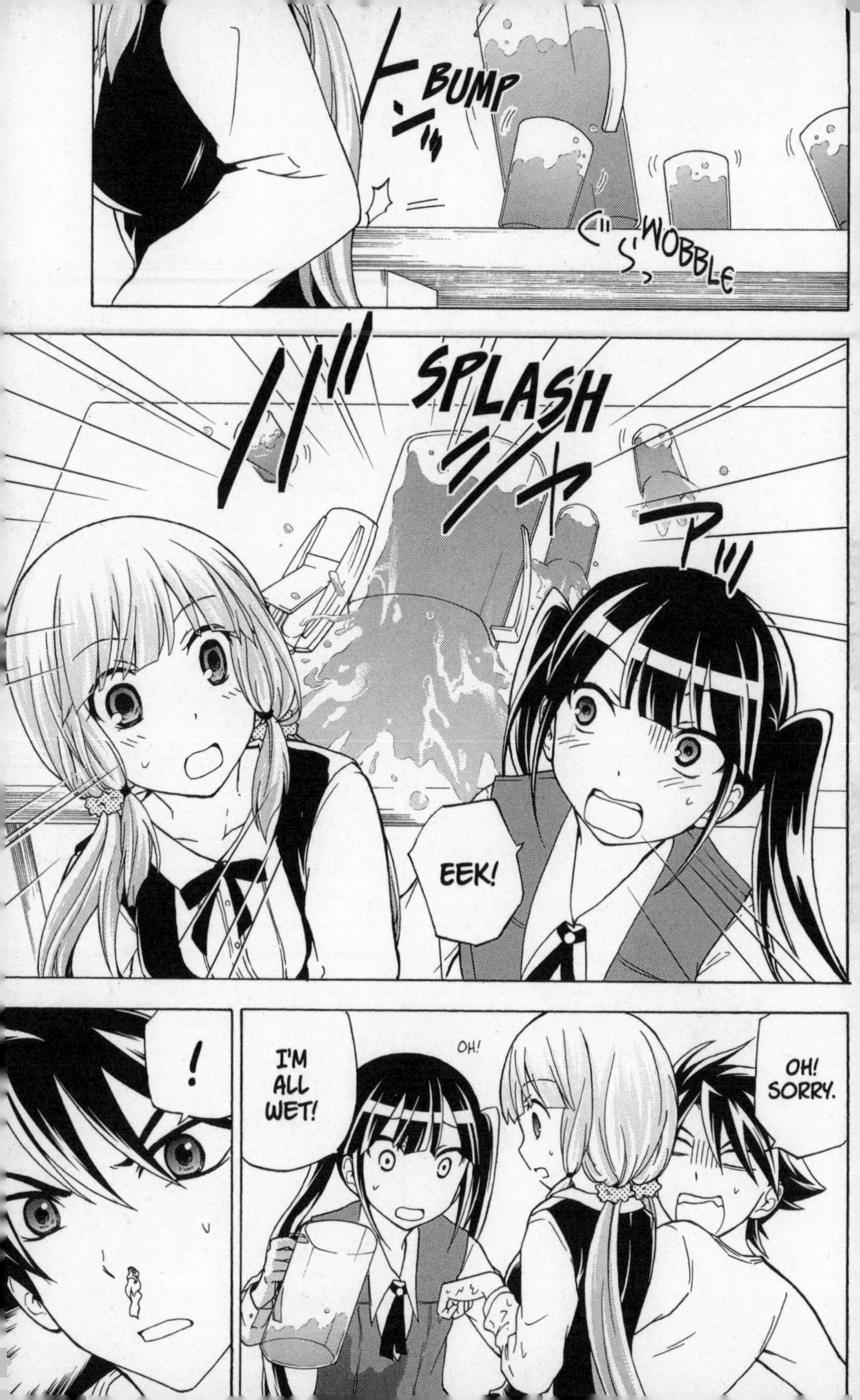
BUMP
WOBBLE
SPLASH
EEK!
OH! SORRY.
OH!
I'M ALL WET!
!

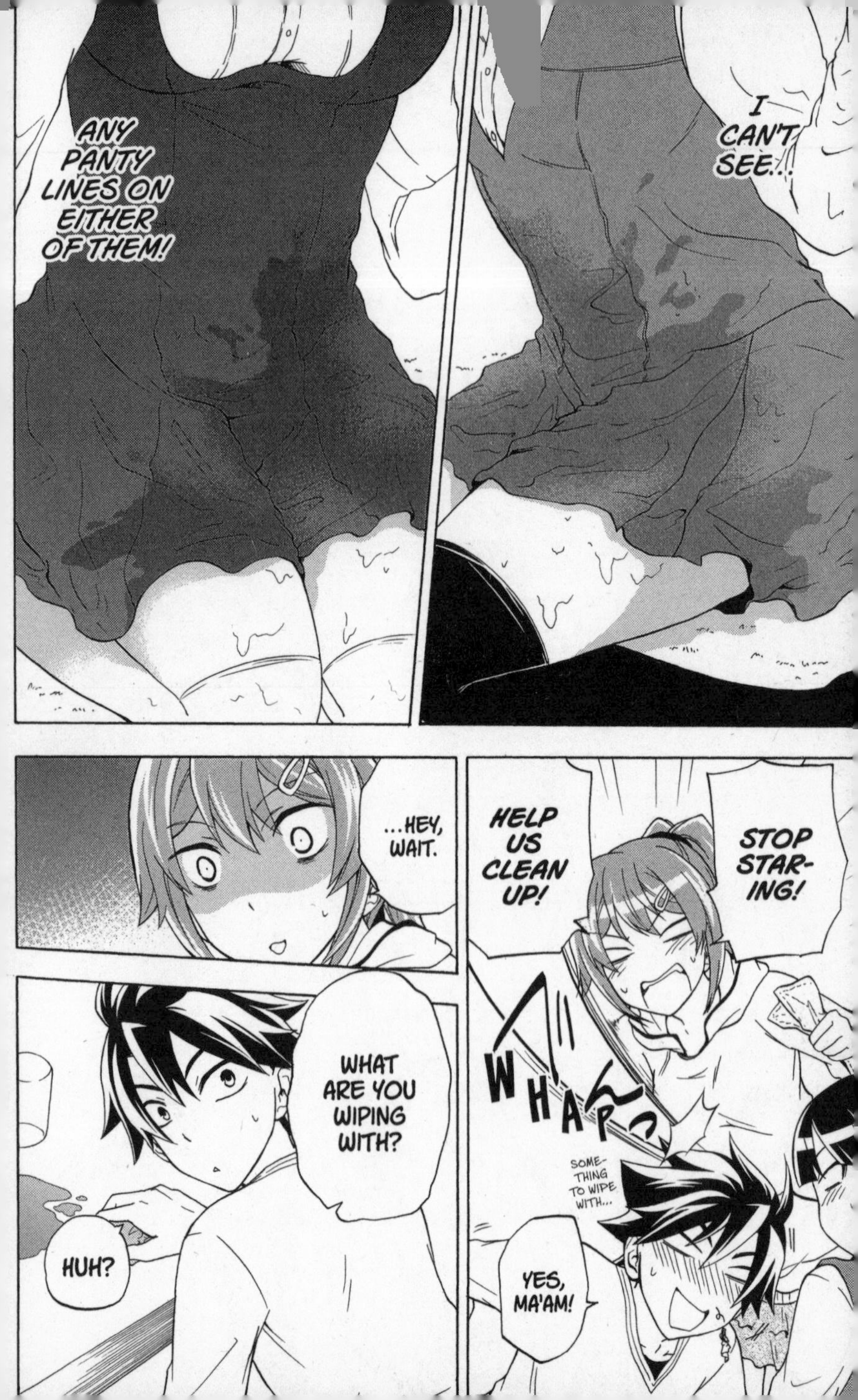
I CAN'T SEE...
ANY PANTY LINES ON EITHER OF THEM!
STOP STAR-ING!
HELP US CLEAN UP!
WHAP
SOME-THING TO WIPE WITH...
YES, MA'AM!
...HEY, WAIT.
WHAT ARE YOU WIPING WITH?
HUH?

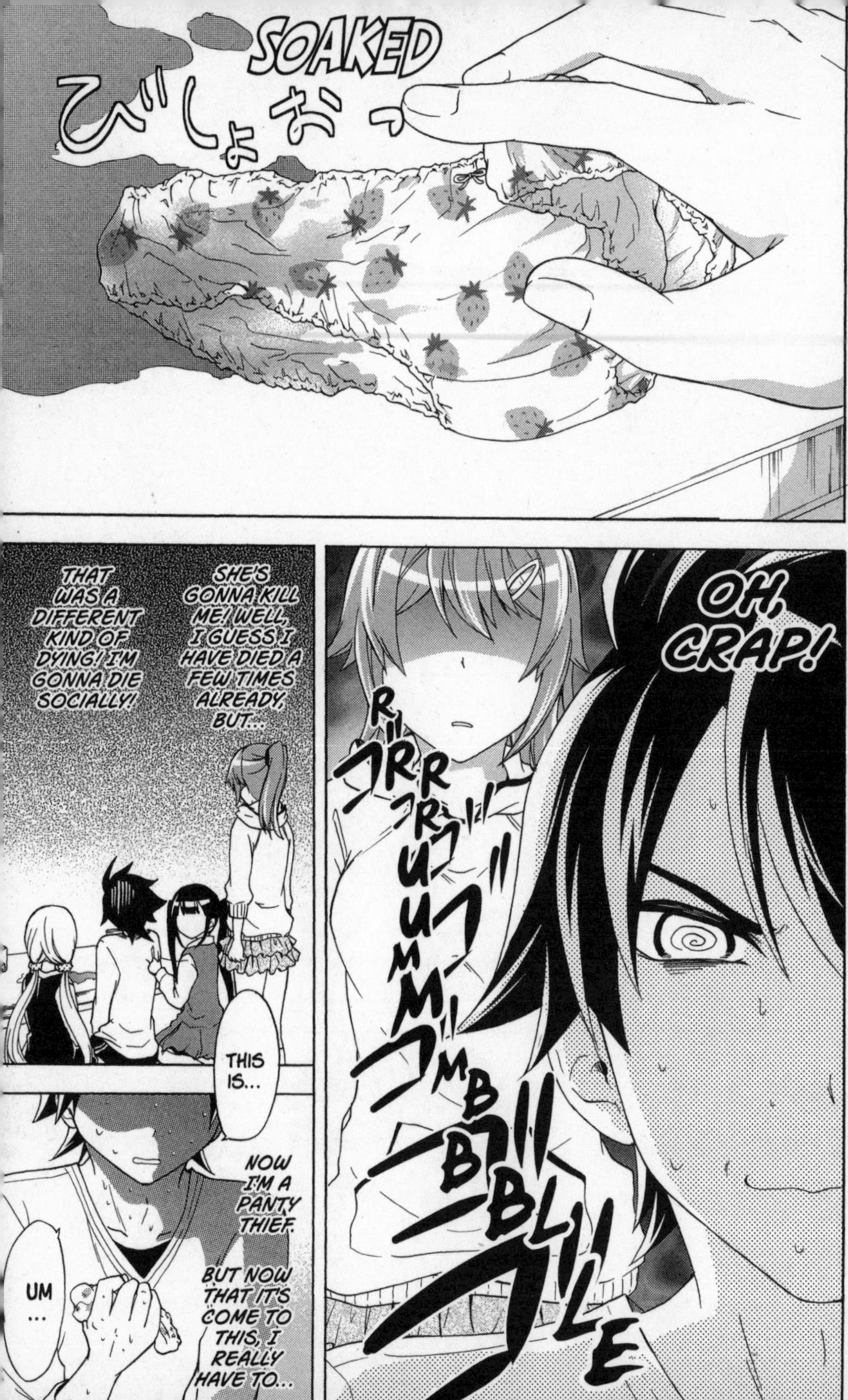
SOAKED
びしょおっ
OH, CRAP!
RRRUMMMBBBLE
SHE'S GONNA KILL ME! WELL, I GUESS I HAVE DIED A FEW TIMES ALREADY, BUT...
THAT WAS A DIFFERENT KIND OF DYING! I'M GONNA DIE SOCIALLY!
THIS IS...
NOW I'M A PANTY THIEF.
BUT NOW THAT IT'S COME TO THIS, I REALLY HAVE TO...
UM...

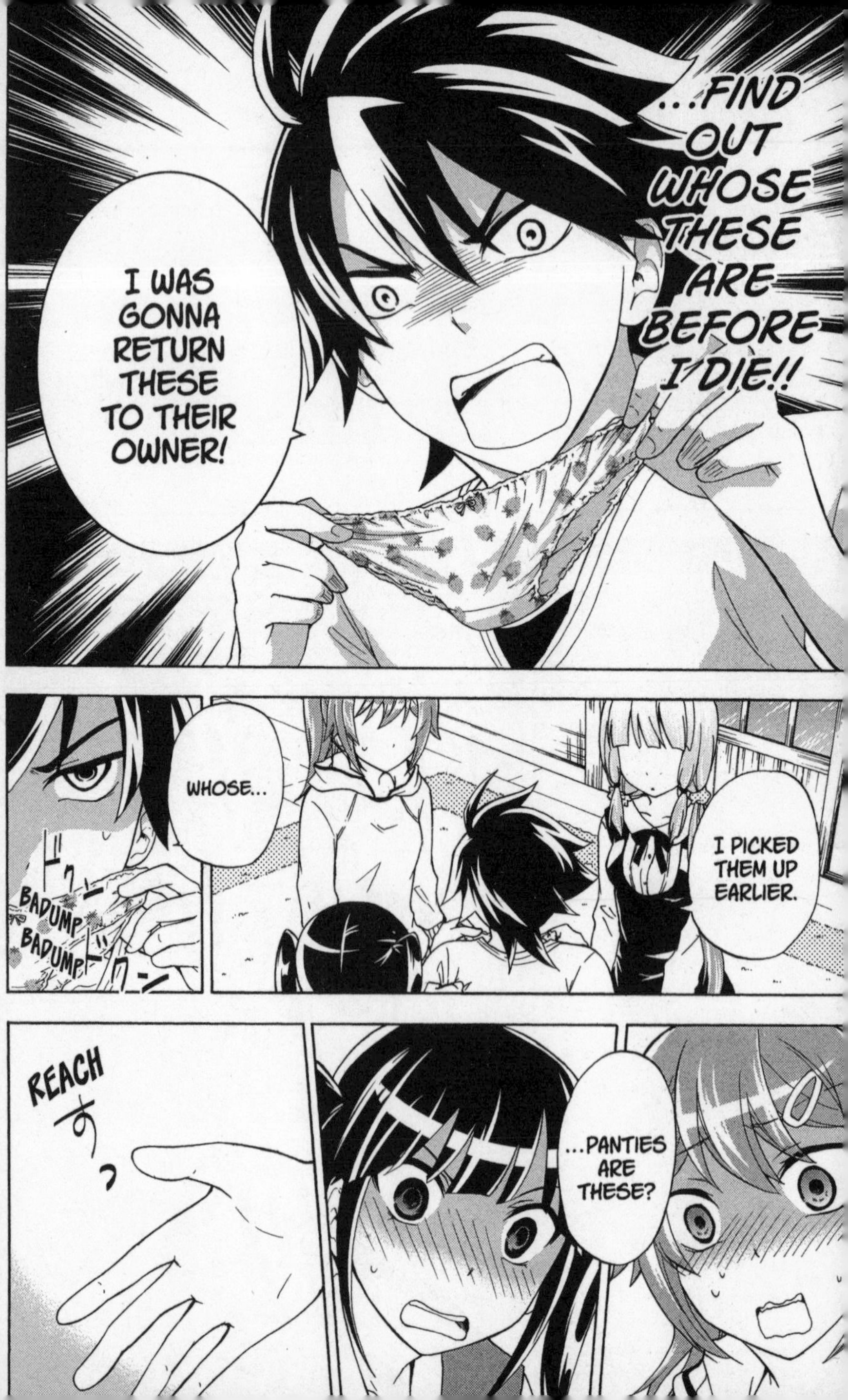
...FIND OUT WHOSE THESE ARE BEFORE I DIE!!
I WAS GONNA RETURN THESE TO THEIR OWNER!
I PICKED THEM UP EARLIER.
WHOSE...
BADUMP BADUMP
...PANTIES ARE THESE?
REACH
すっ

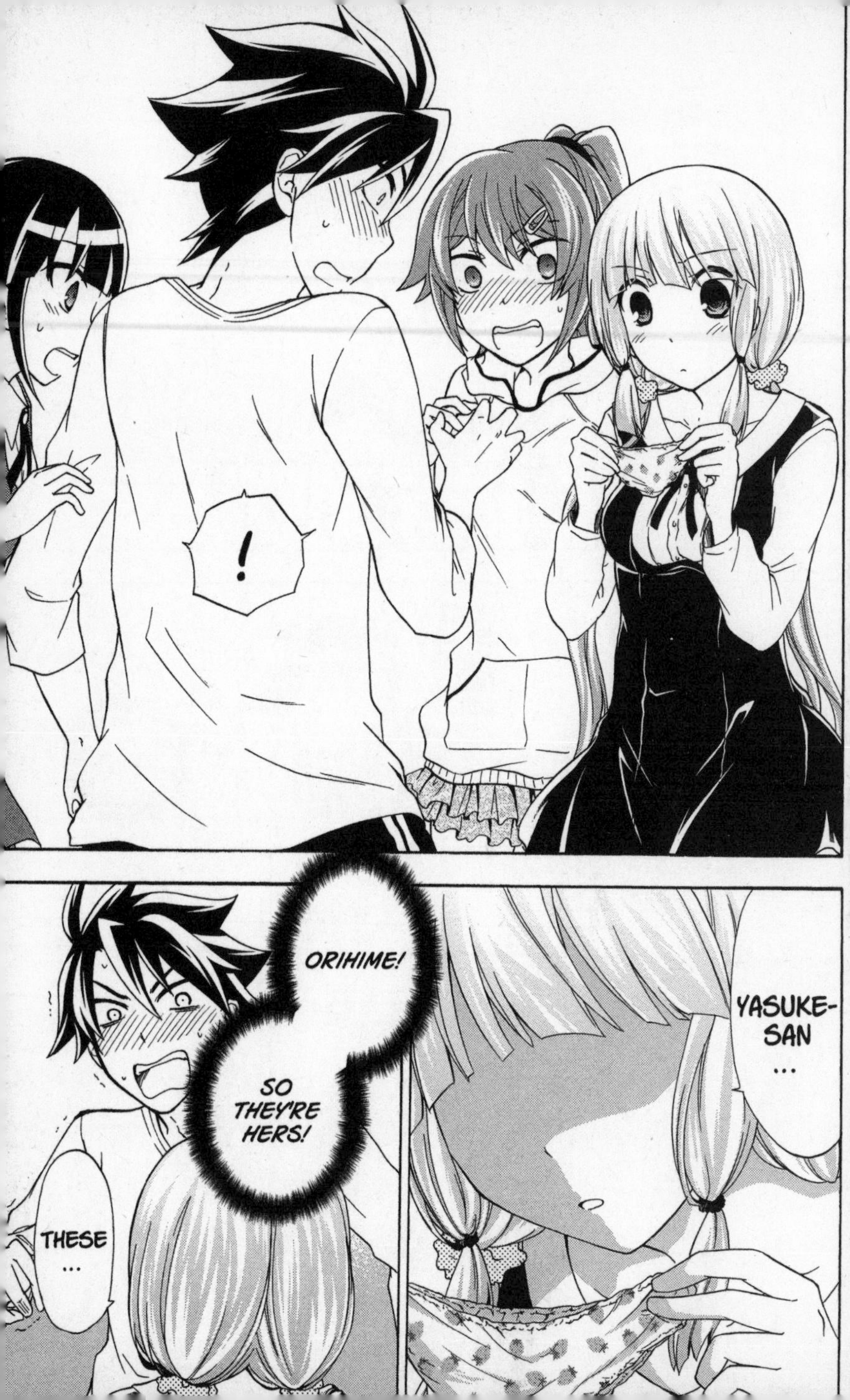
!
YASUKE-SAN ...
ORIHIME!
SO THEY'RE HERS!
THESE ...

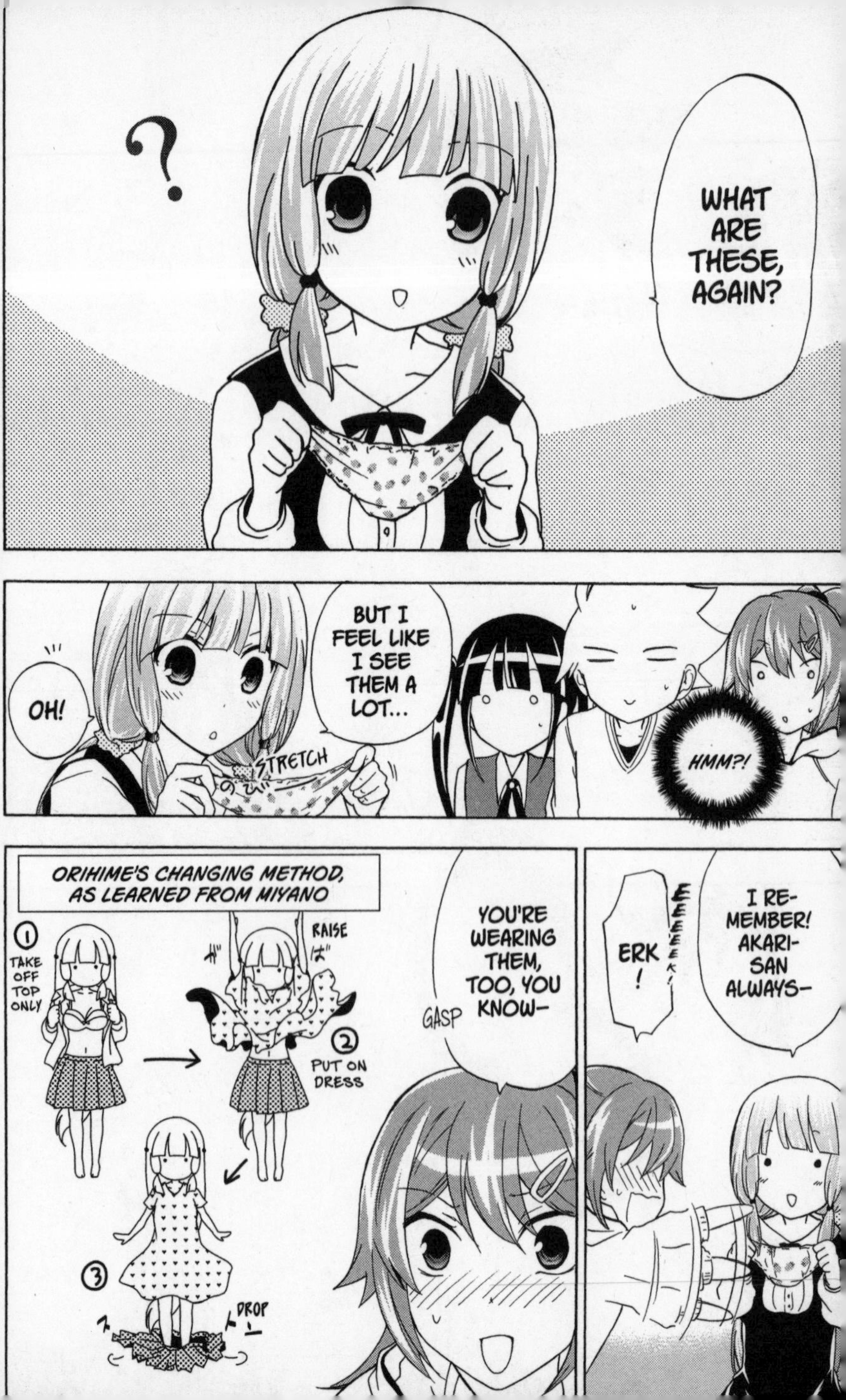
WHAT ARE THESE, AGAIN?
?
OH!
BUT I FEEL LIKE I SEE THEM A LOT...
STRETCH
HMM?!
I RE-MEMBER! AKARI-SAN ALWAYS-
EEEEEK!
ERK!
YOU'RE WEARING THEM, TOO, YOU KNOW-
GASP
ORIHIME'S CHANGING METHOD, AS LEARNED FROM MIYANO
① TAKE OFF TOP ONLY
RAISE
② PUT ON DRESS
③
DROP

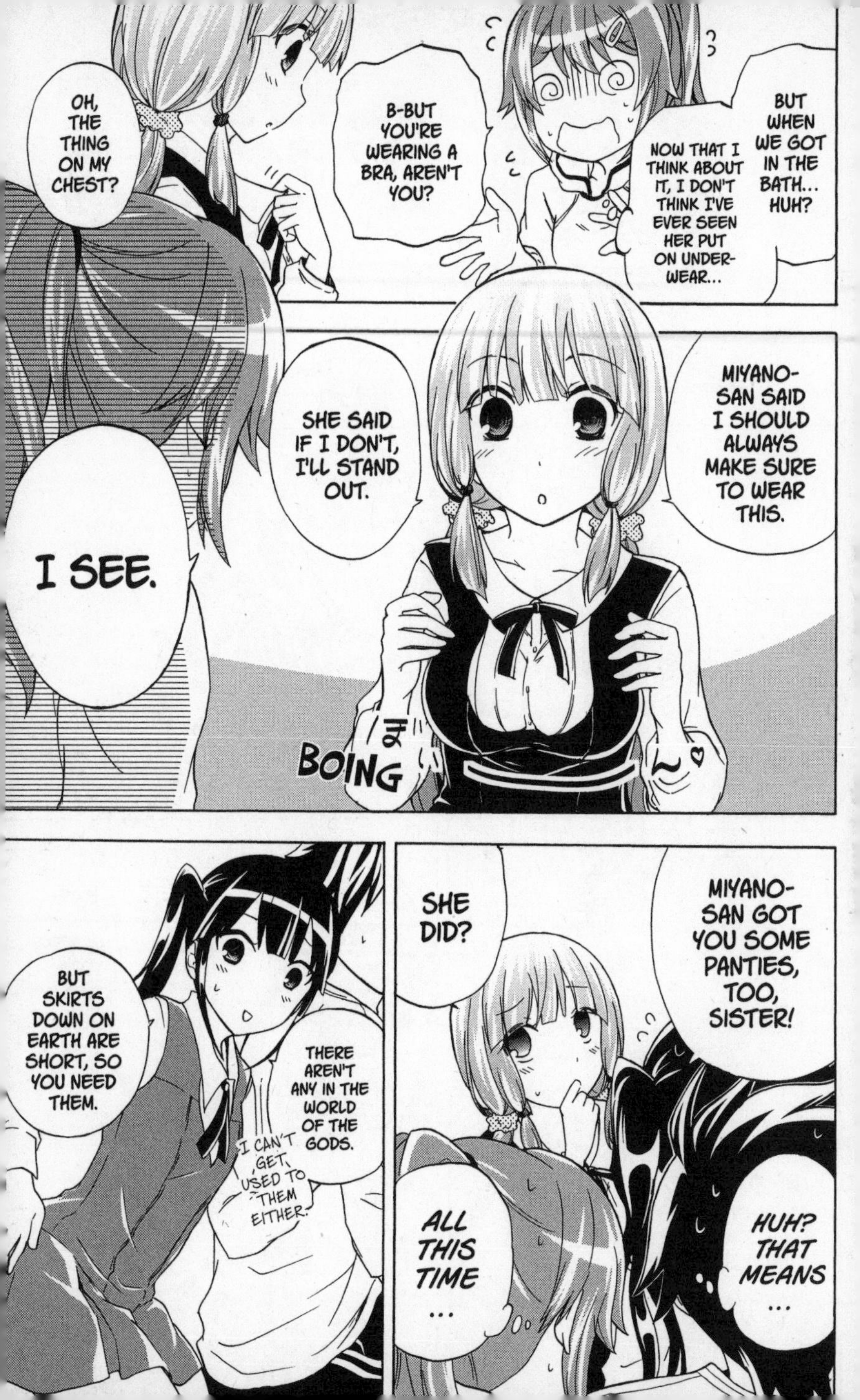
BUT WHEN WE GOT IN THE BATH... HUH?
NOW THAT I THINK ABOUT IT, I DON'T THINK I'VE EVER SEEN HER PUT ON UNDER-WEAR...
B-BUT YOU'RE WEARING A BRA, AREN'T YOU?
OH, THE THING ON MY CHEST?
MIYANO-SAN SAID I SHOULD ALWAYS MAKE SURE TO WEAR THIS.
SHE SAID IF I DON'T, I'LL STAND OUT.
BOING
I SEE.
MIYANO-SAN GOT YOU SOME PANTIES, TOO, SISTER!
SHE DID?
HUH? THAT MEANS...
ALL THIS TIME...
THERE AREN'T ANY IN THE WORLD OF THE GODS.
BUT SKIRTS DOWN ON EARTH ARE SHORT, SO YOU NEED THEM.
I CAN'T GET USED TO THEM EITHER.

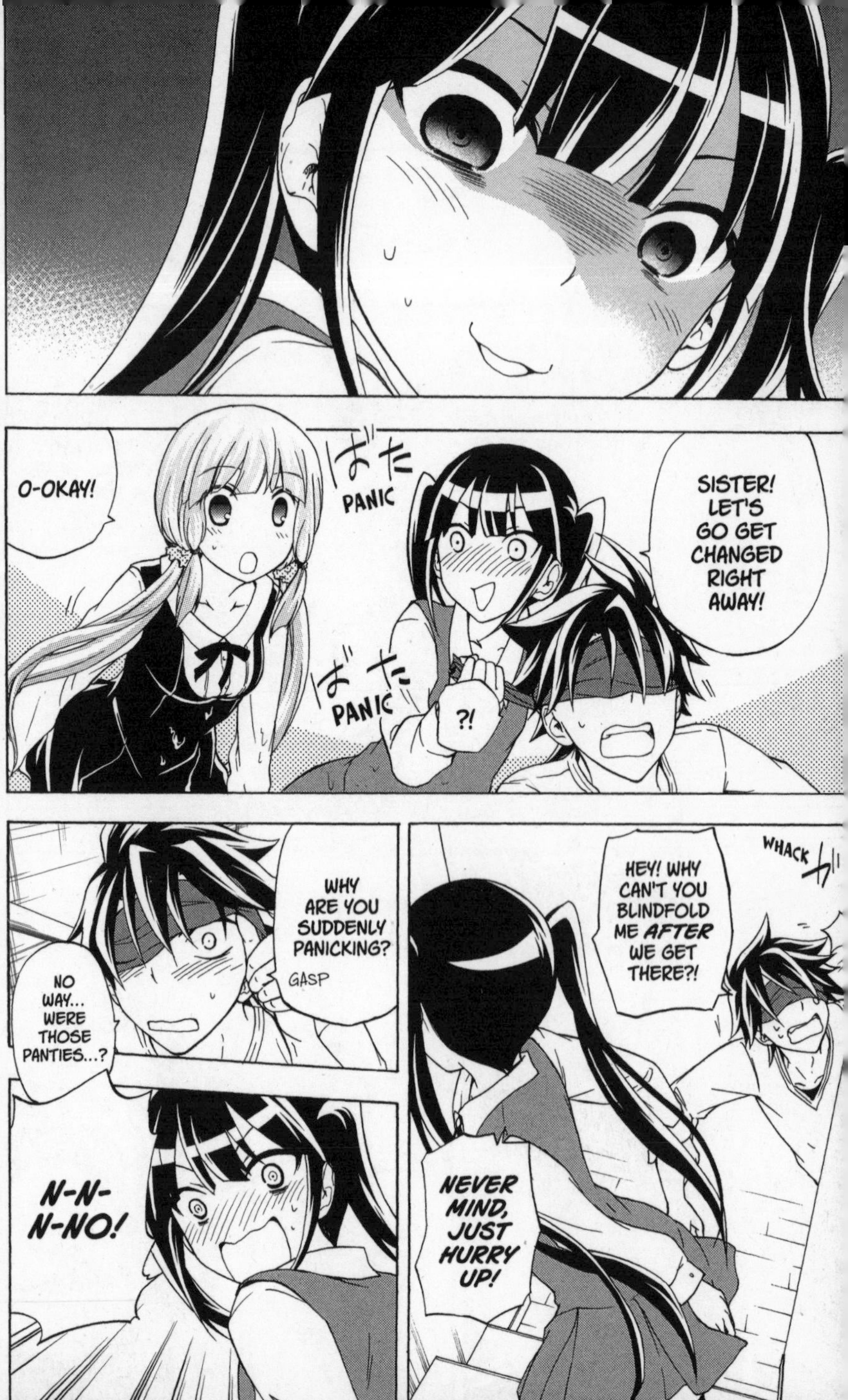
SISTER! LET'S GO GET CHANGED RIGHT AWAY!
ばた PANIC
O-OKAY!
ばた PANIC
?!
WHACK ガ
HEY! WHY CAN'T YOU BLINDFOLD ME *AFTER* WE GET THERE?!
NEVER MIND, JUST HURRY UP!
WHY ARE YOU SUDDENLY PANICKING?
GASP
NO WAY... WERE THOSE PANTIES...?
N-N-N-NO!

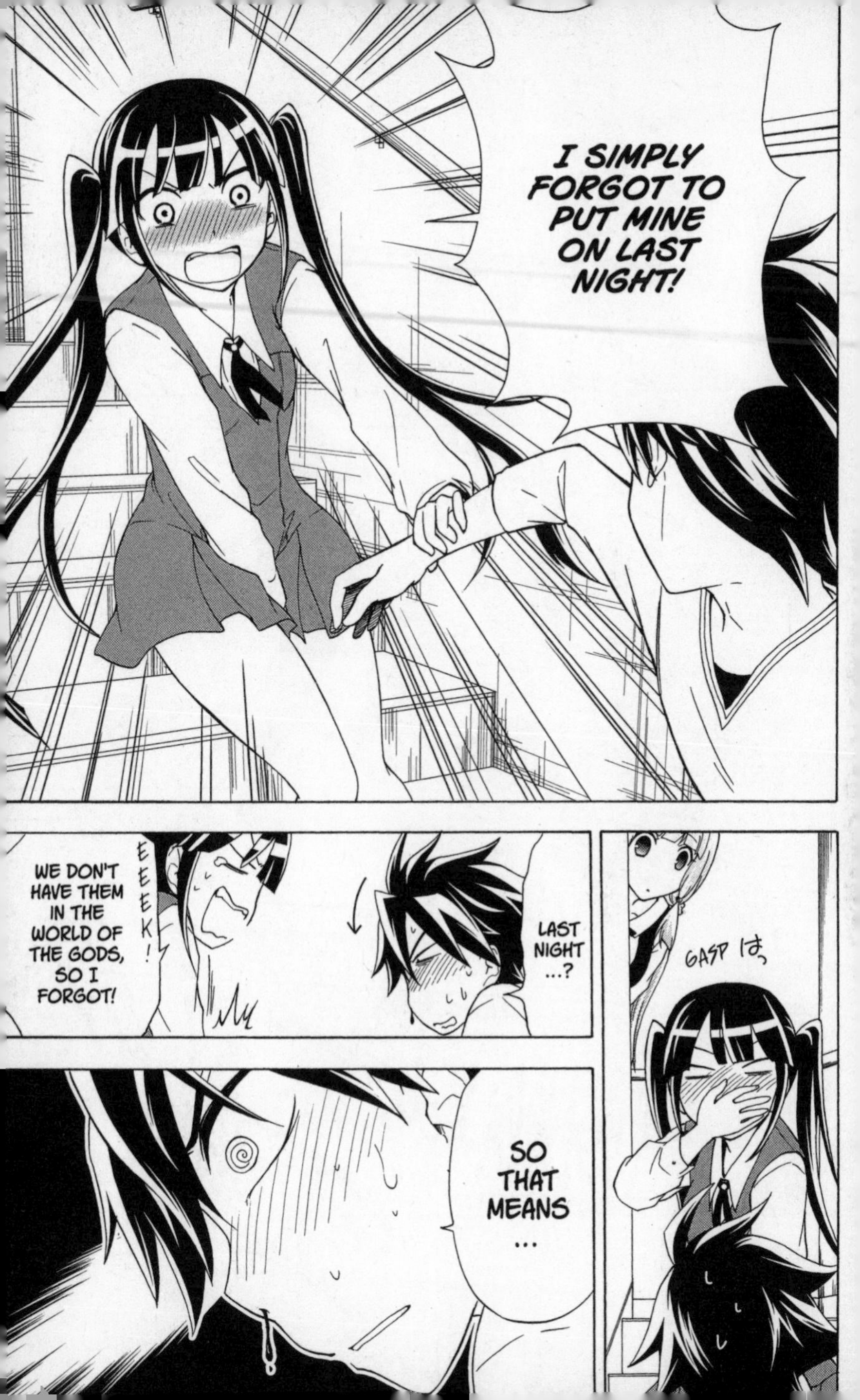
I SIMPLY FORGOT TO PUT MINE ON LAST NIGHT!
GASP はっ
EEEEK!
WE DON'T HAVE THEM IN THE WORLD OF THE GODS, SO I FORGOT!
LAST NIGHT ...?
SO THAT MEANS ...

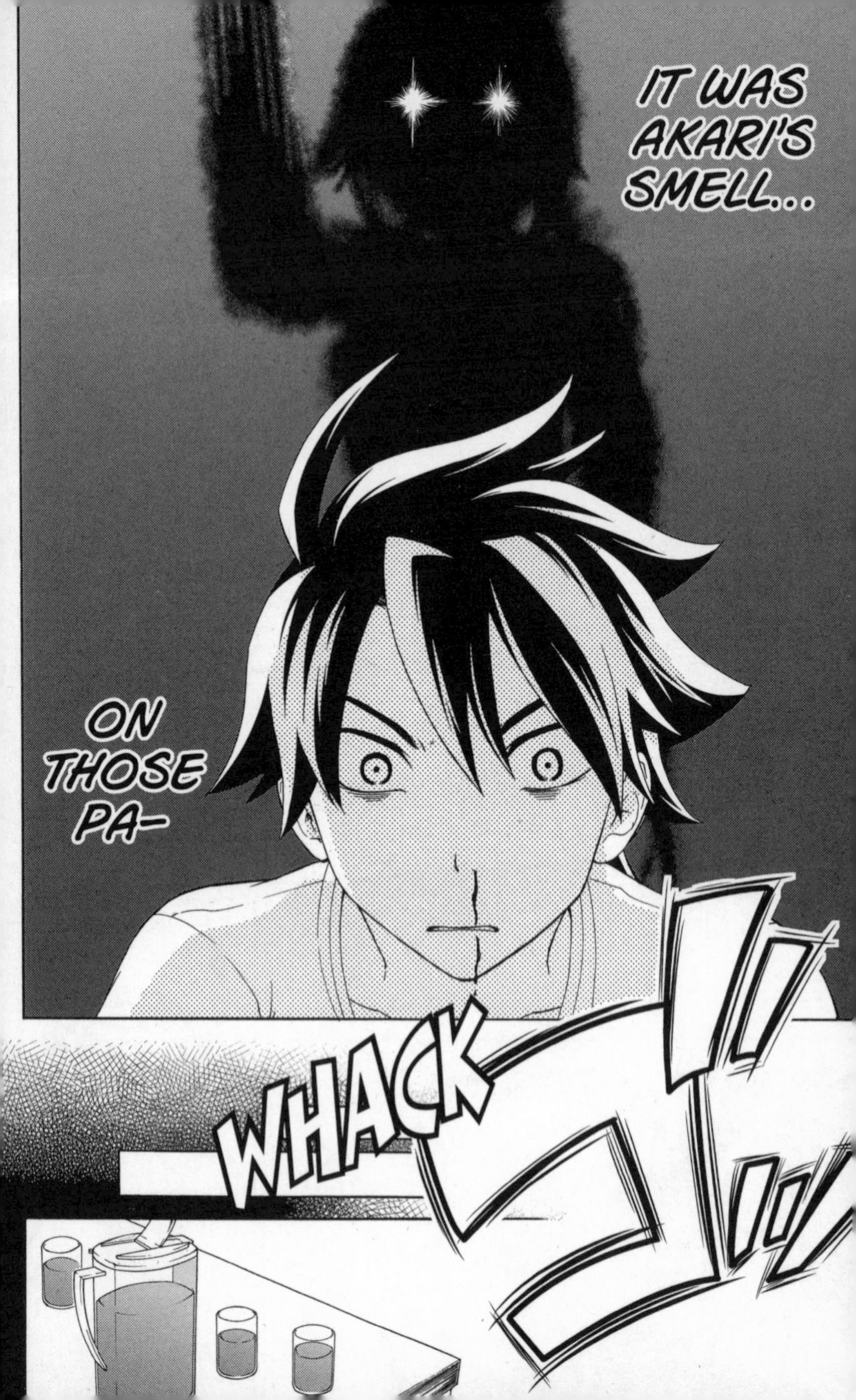
IT WAS AKARI'S SMELL...
ON THOSE PA-
WHACK

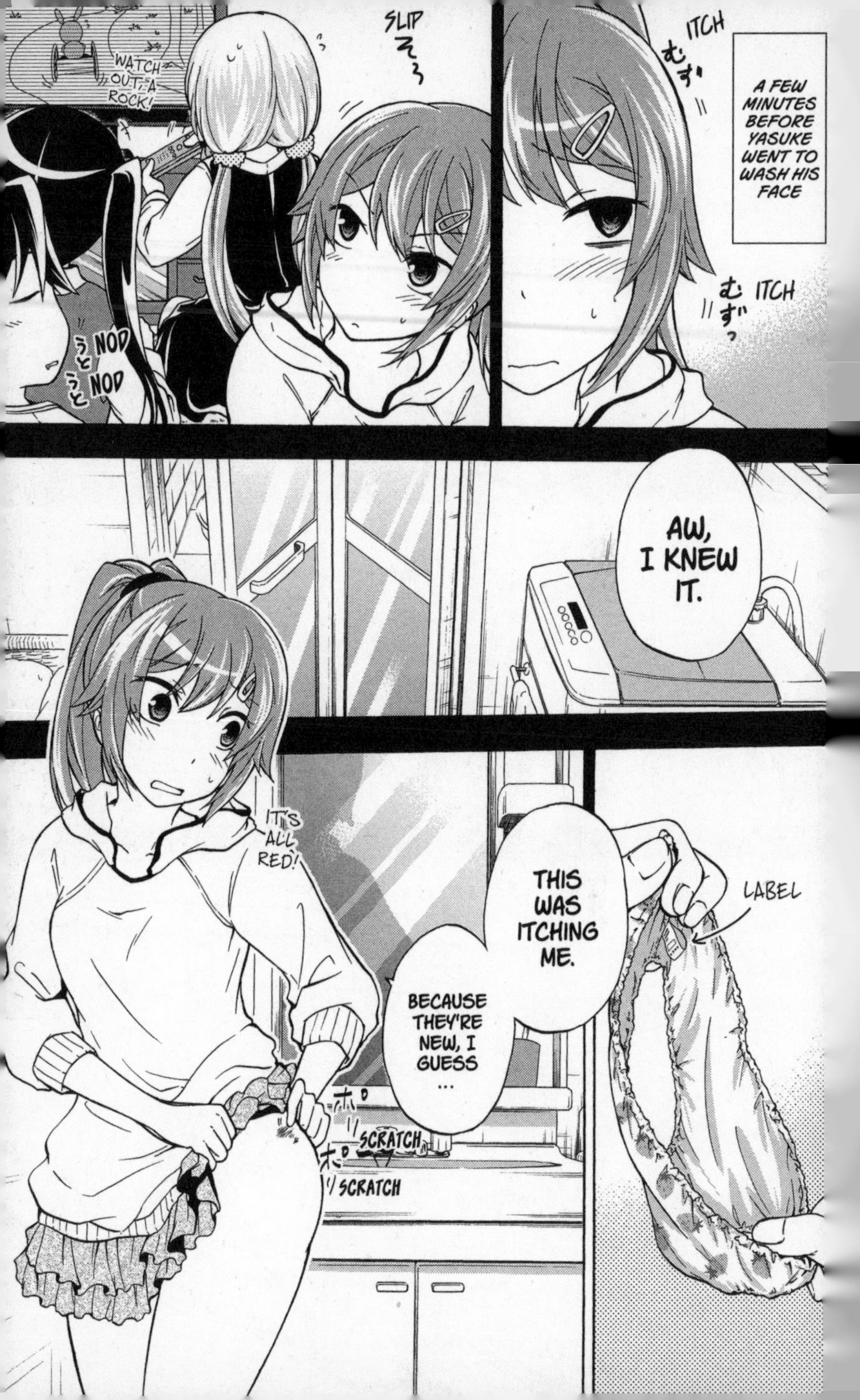
A FEW MINUTES BEFORE YASUKE WENT TO WASH HIS FACE
ITCH むず
ITCH むずっ
SLIP
WATCH OUT A ROCK!
NOD NOD うとうと
AW, I KNEW IT.
THIS WAS ITCHING ME.
LABEL
BECAUSE THEY'RE NEW, I GUESS ...
IT'S ALL RED!
SCRATCH ポリ
SCRATCH ポリ

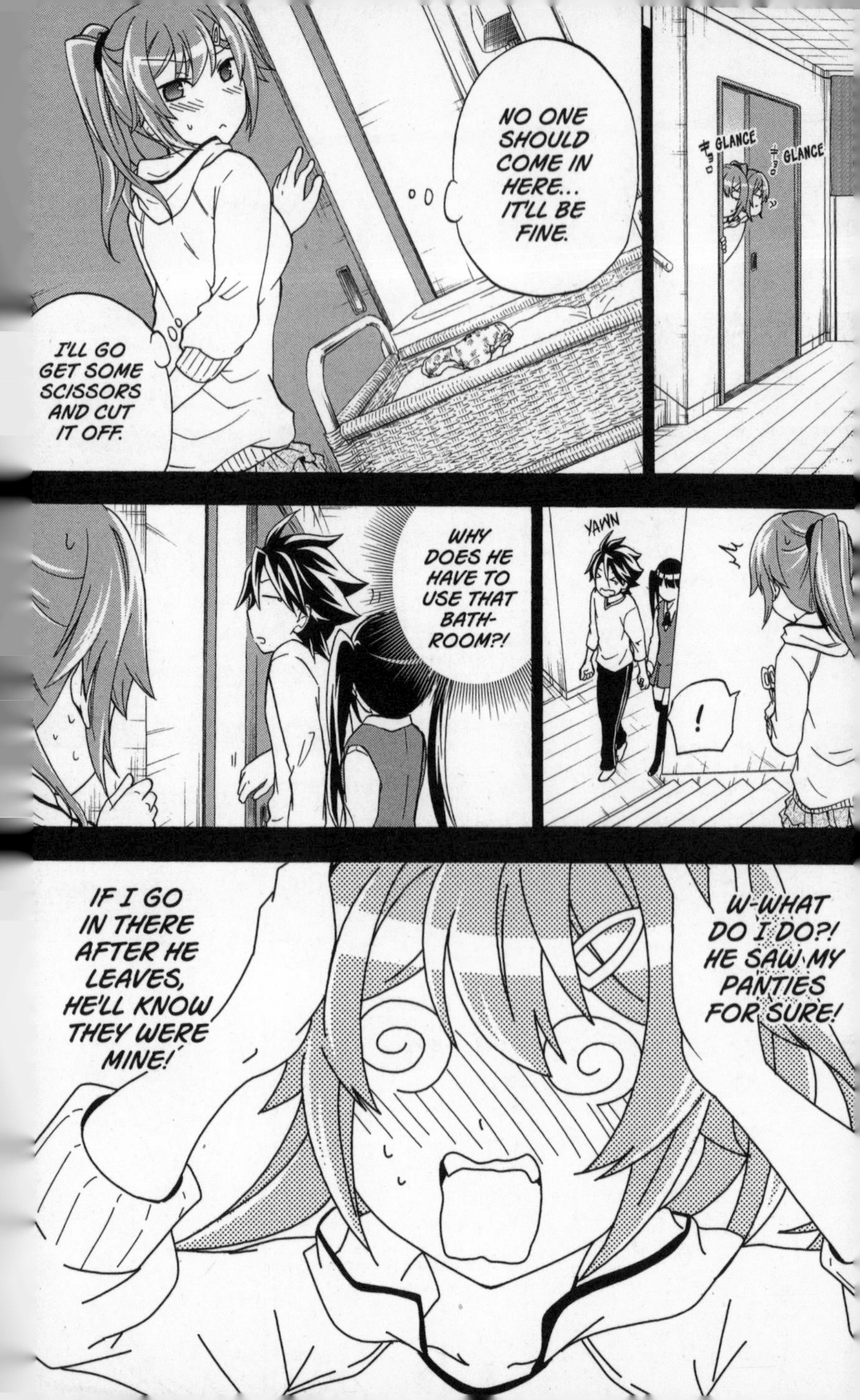
GLANCE
GLANCE
NO ONE SHOULD COME IN HERE... IT'LL BE FINE.
I'LL GO GET SOME SCISSORS AND CUT IT OFF.
YAWN
!
WHY DOES HE HAVE TO USE THAT BATH-ROOM?!
W-WHAT DO I DO?! HE SAW MY PANTIES FOR SURE!
IF I GO IN THERE AFTER HE LEAVES, HE'LL KNOW THEY WERE MINE!

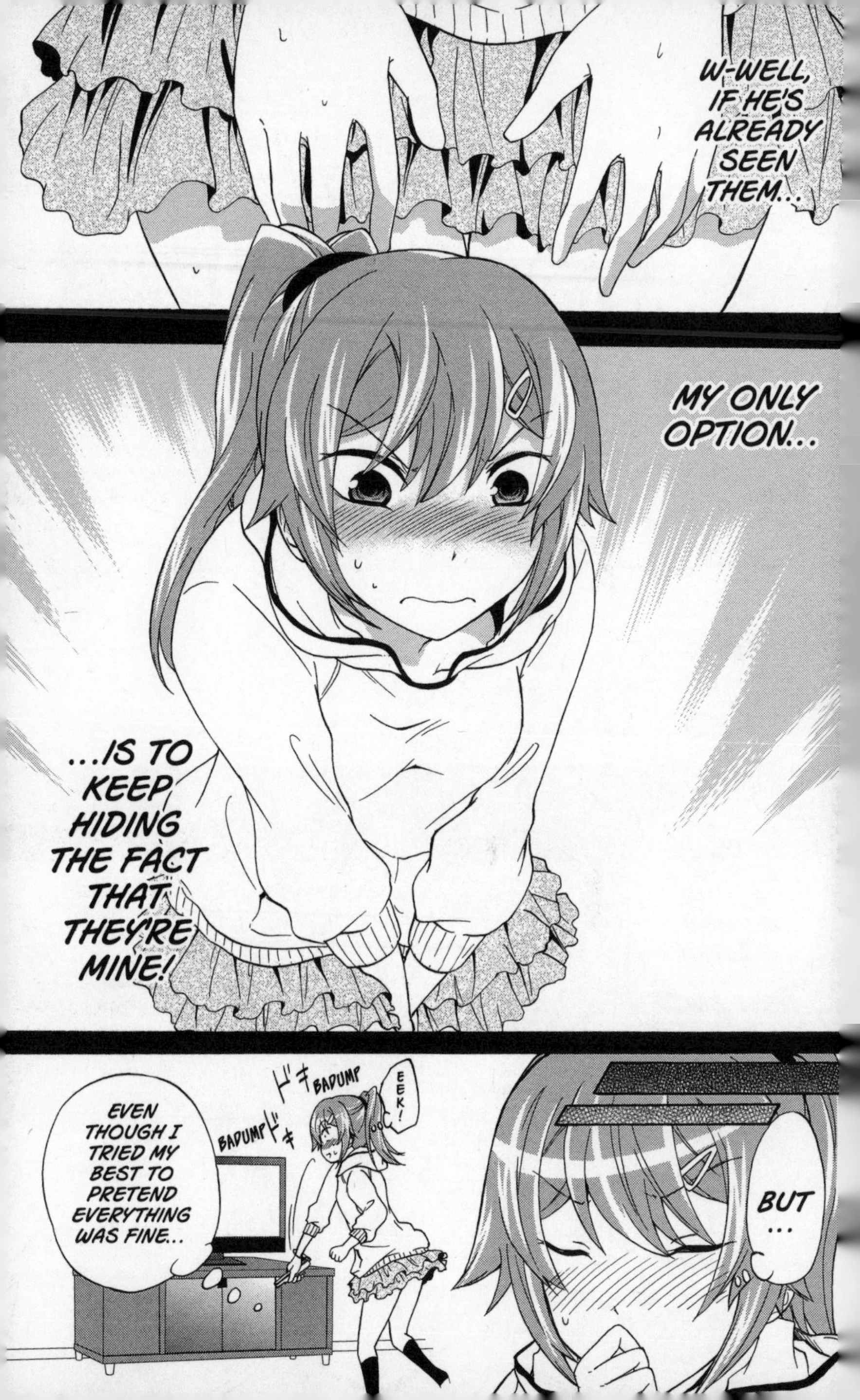
W-WELL, IF HE'S ALREADY SEEN THEM...
MY ONLY OPTION...
...IS TO KEEP HIDING THE FACT THAT THEY'RE MINE!
BUT...
ドキ BADUMP
EEK!
BADUMP ドキ
EVEN THOUGH I TRIED MY BEST TO PRETEND EVERYTHING WAS FINE...

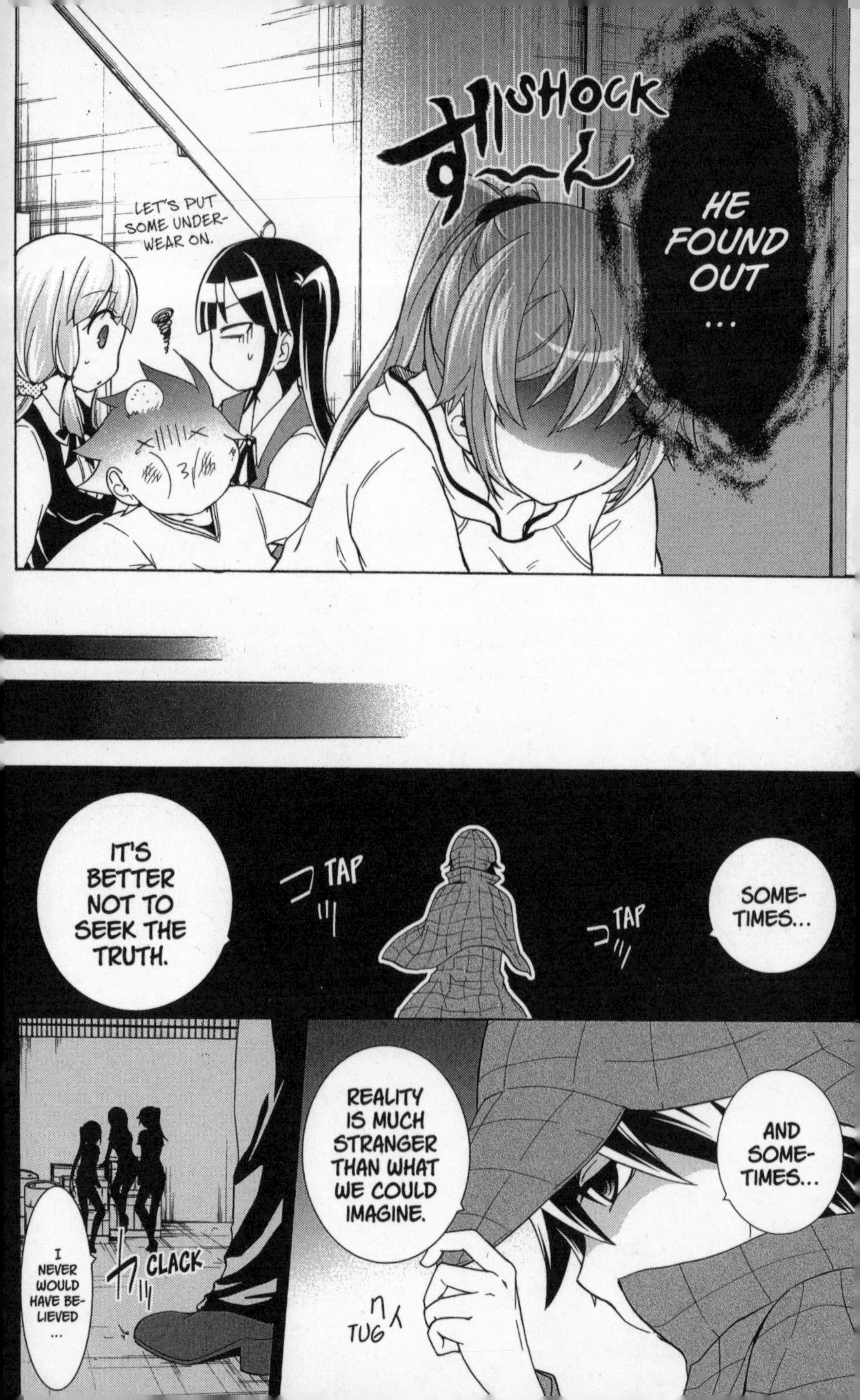
SHOCK
HE FOUND OUT ...
LET'S PUT SOME UNDER-WEAR ON.
SOME-TIMES...
TAP
TAP
IT'S BETTER NOT TO SEEK THE TRUTH.
AND SOME-TIMES...
REALITY IS MUCH STRANGER THAN WHAT WE COULD IMAGINE.
TUG
CLACK
I NEVER WOULD HAVE BE-LIEVED ...

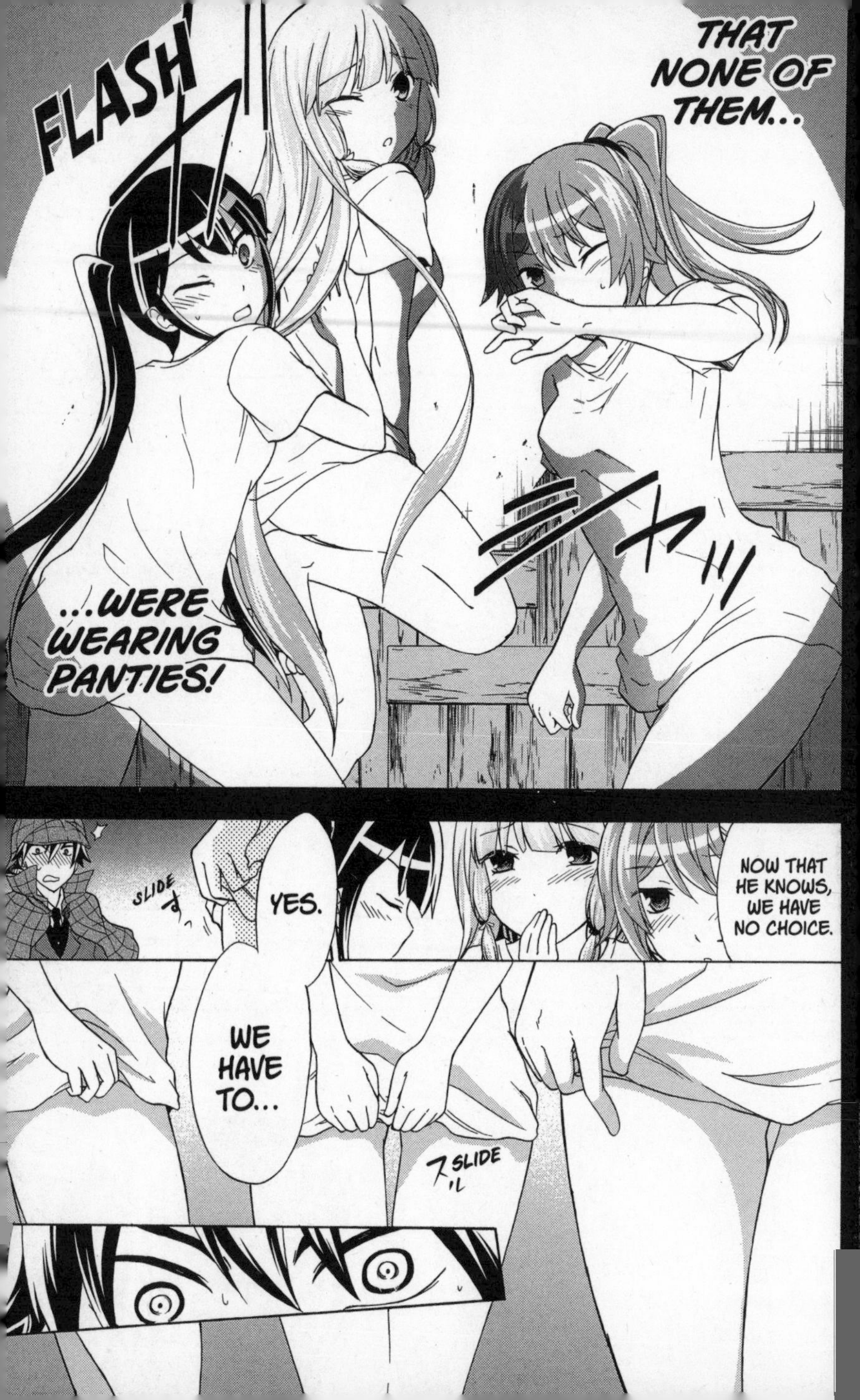
THAT NONE OF THEM...
FLASH
...WERE WEARING PANTIES!
NOW THAT HE KNOWS, WE HAVE NO CHOICE.
YES.
SLIDE す
WE HAVE TO...
SLIDE スル

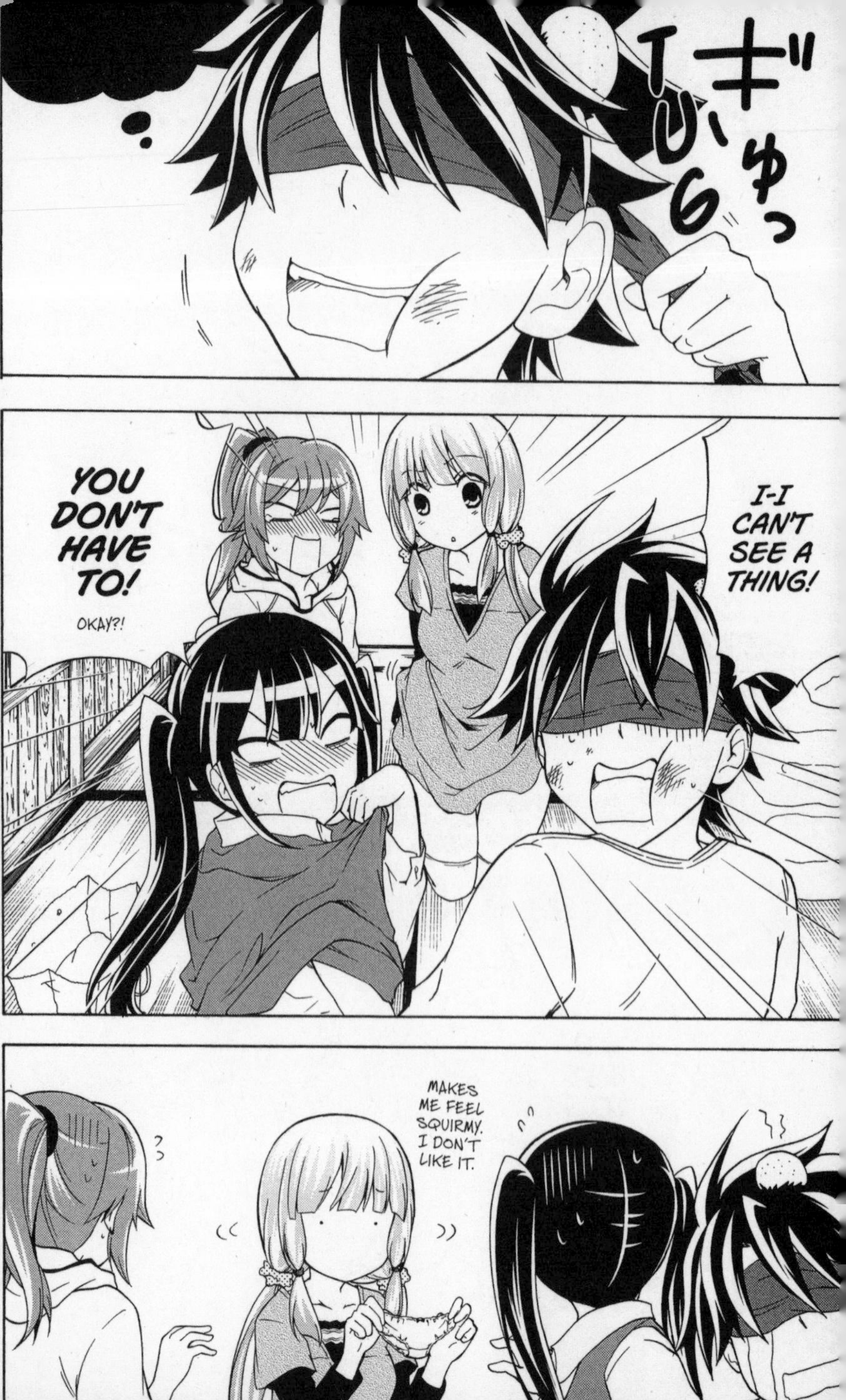
ギゅっ
TUG
I-I CAN'T SEE A THING!
YOU DON'T HAVE TO!
OKAY?!
MAKES ME FEEL SQUIRMY. I DON'T LIKE IT.

Maga-Tsuki
Presented by Hoshino Taguchi

YOU SHOULDA BROUGHT THOSE PANTIES.

HERE!

まがつき

Maga-Tsuki
Presented by Hoshino Taguchi

Maga-Tsuki Taguchi Hoshino

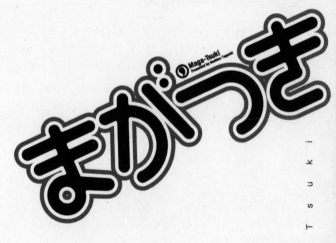

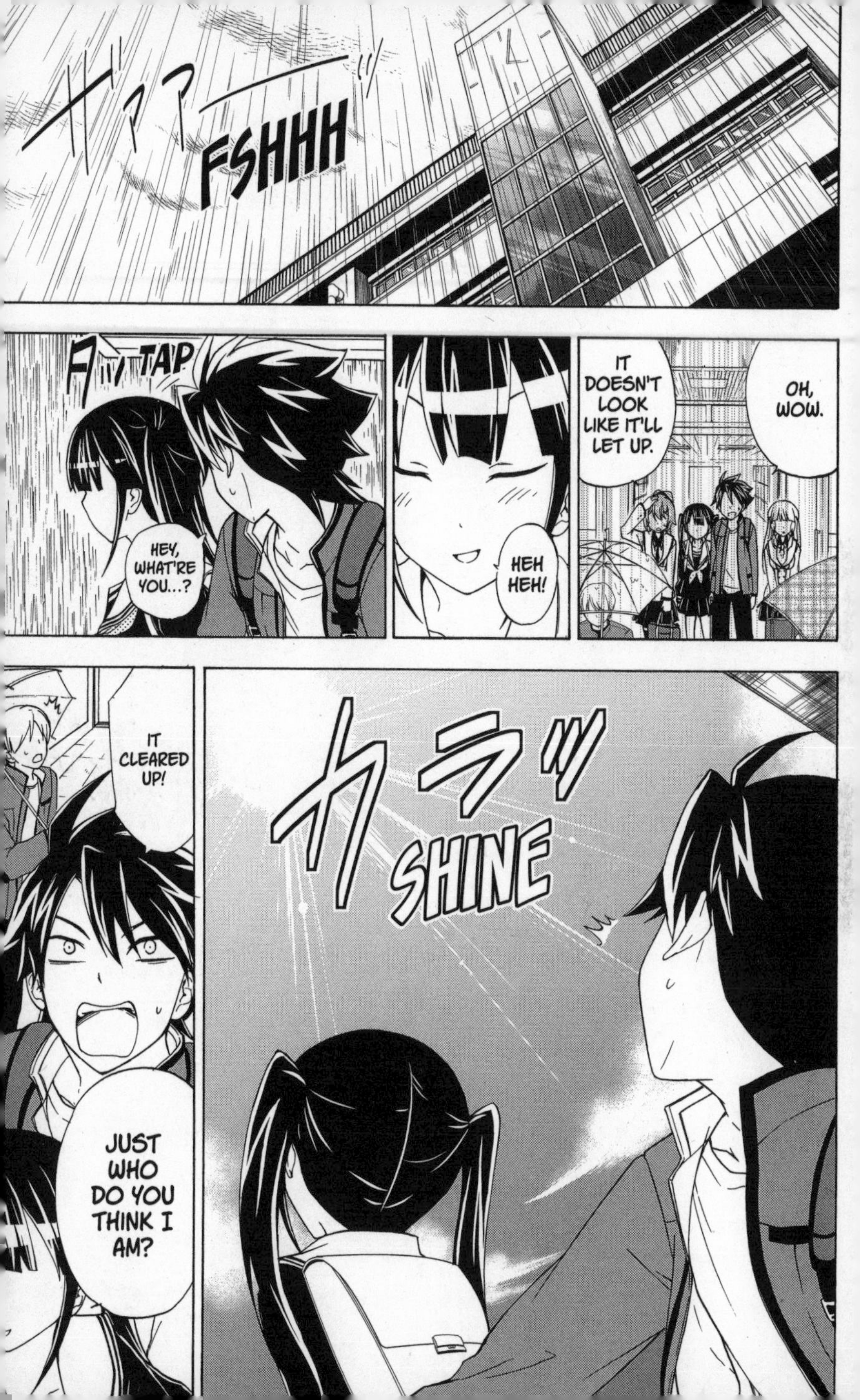
FSHHH
OH, WOW.
IT DOESN'T LOOK LIKE IT'LL LET UP.
HEH HEH!
TAP
HEY, WHAT'RE YOU...?
SHINE
IT CLEARED UP!
JUST WHO DO YOU THINK I AM?

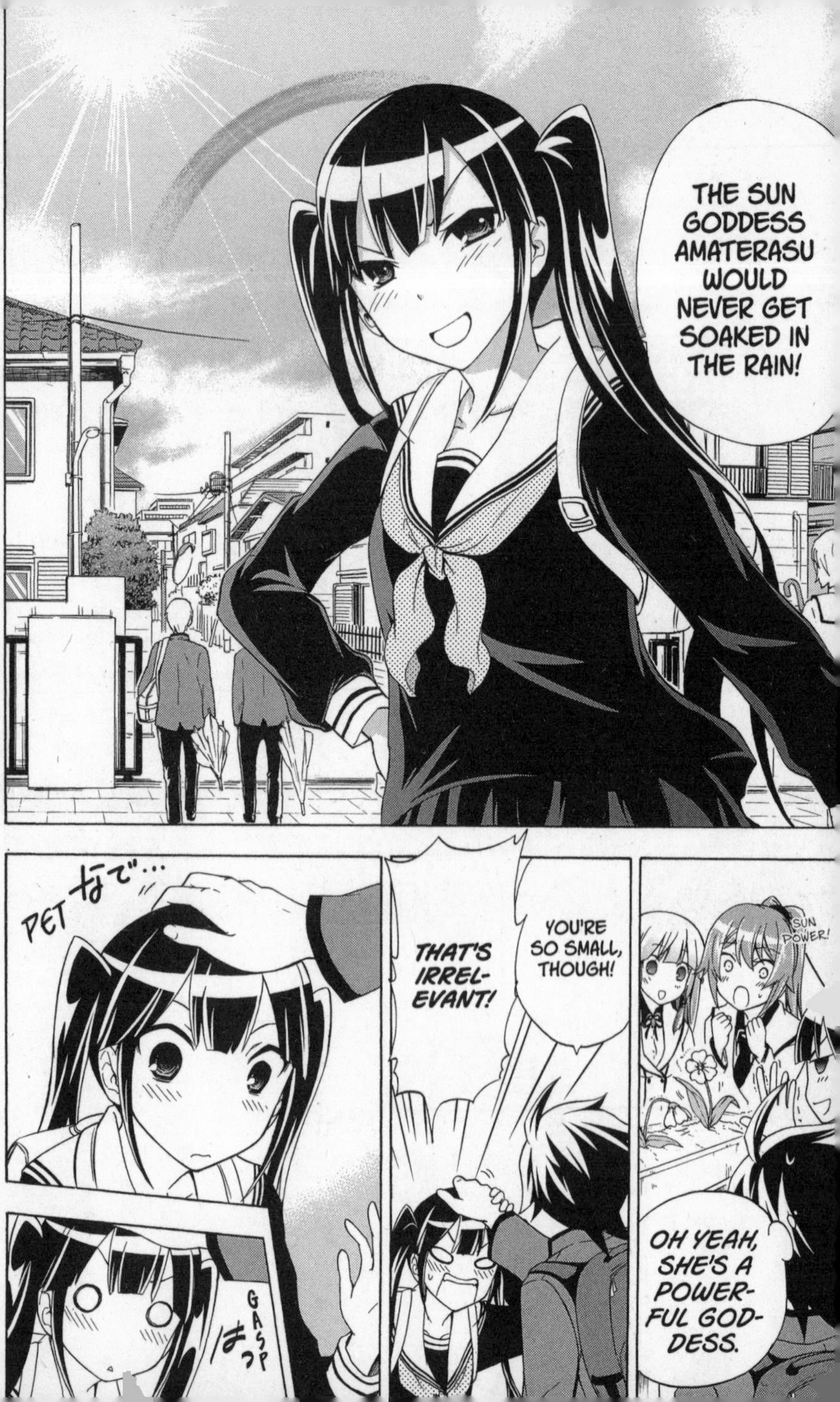
THE SUN GODDESS AMATERASU WOULD NEVER GET SOAKED IN THE RAIN!
SUN POWER!
OH YEAH, SHE'S A POWER-FUL GOD-DESS.
YOU'RE SO SMALL, THOUGH!
THAT'S IRREL-EVANT!
PET なで…
GASP
はっ

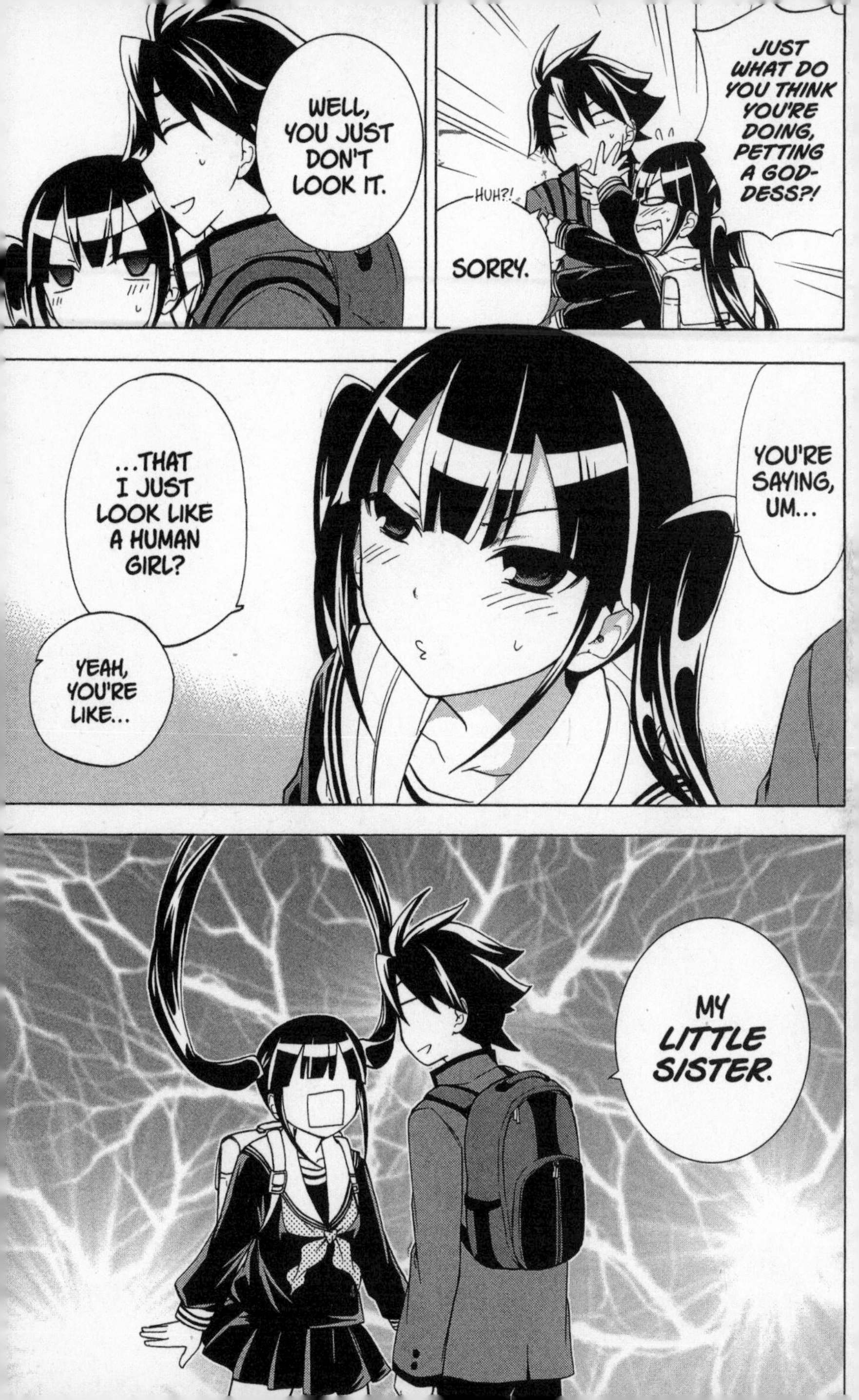
JUST WHAT DO YOU THINK YOU'RE DOING, PETTING A GOD-DESS?!
HUH?!
SORRY.
WELL, YOU JUST DON'T LOOK IT.
YOU'RE SAYING, UM...
...THAT I JUST LOOK LIKE A HUMAN GIRL?
YEAH, YOU'RE LIKE...
MY *LITTLE SISTER.*

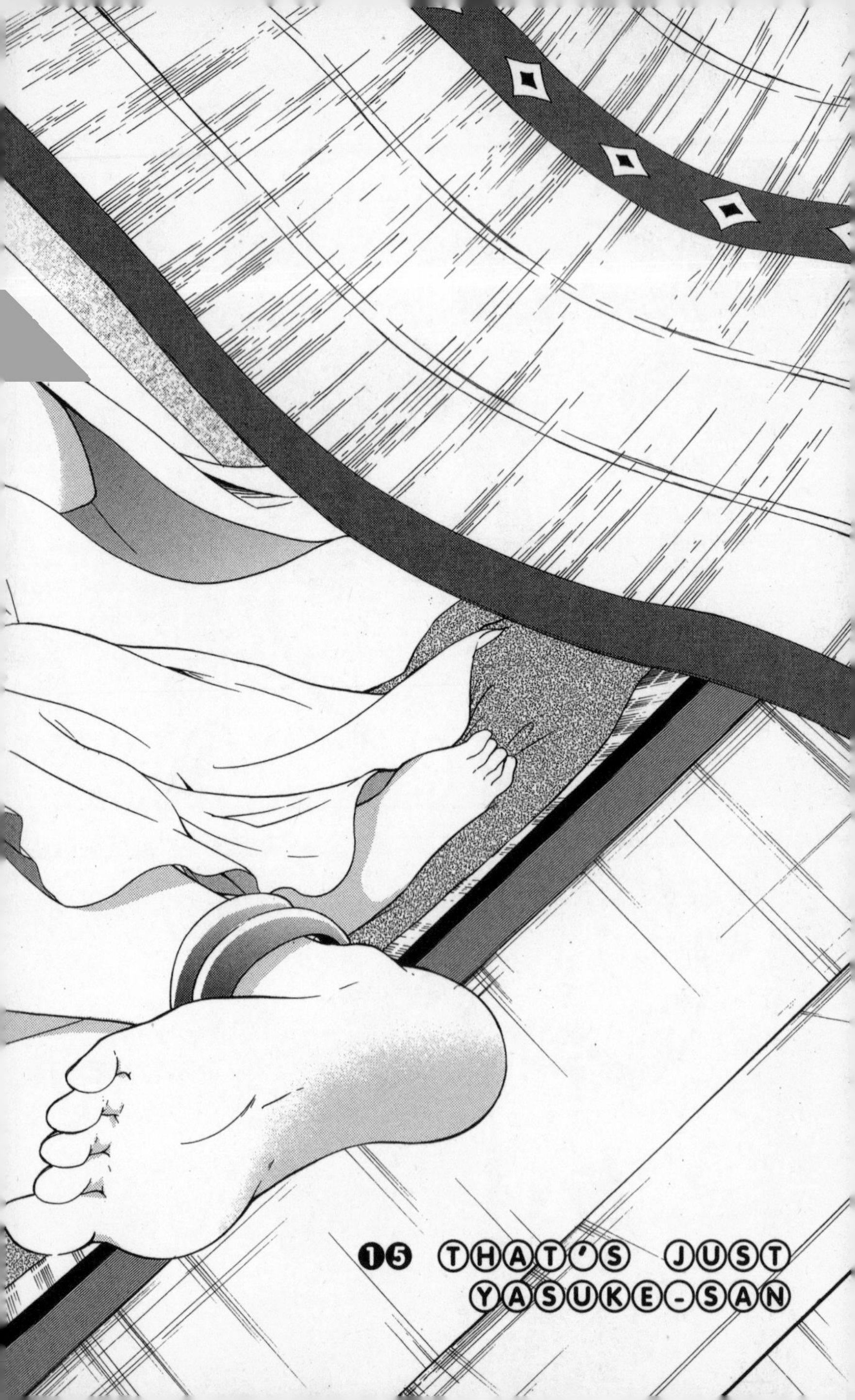
15 THAT'S JUST YASUKE-SAN

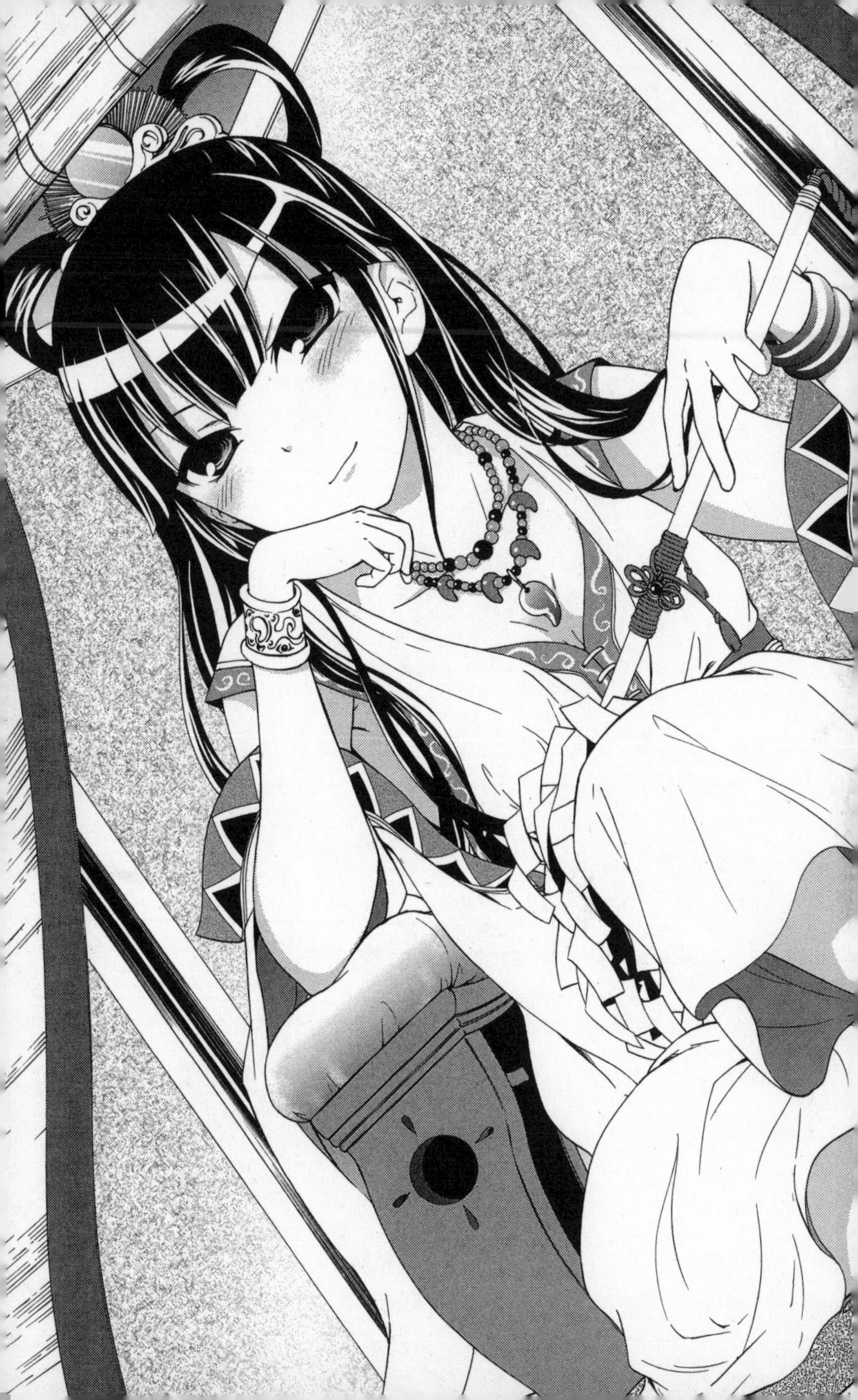

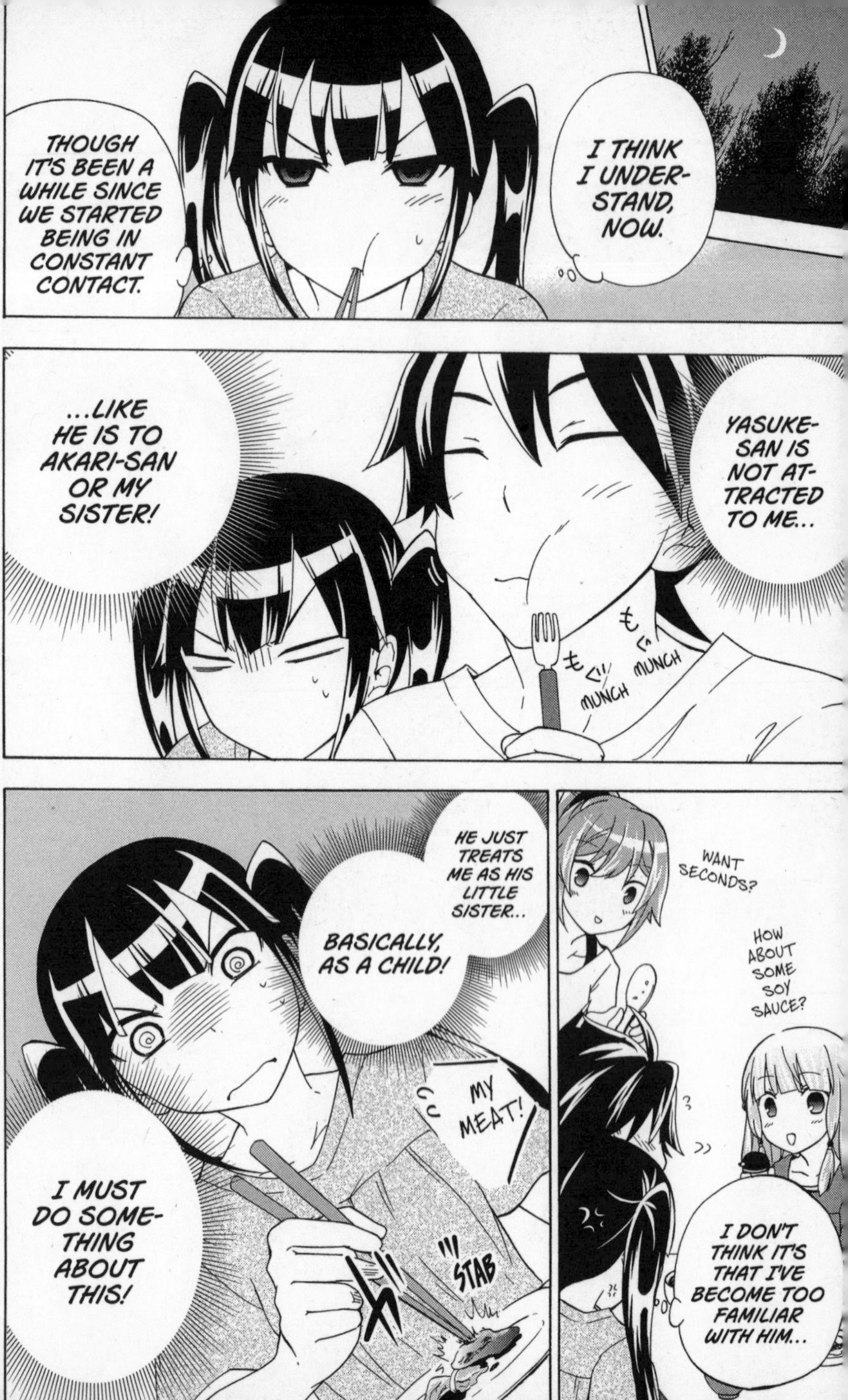
I THINK I UNDER-STAND, NOW.
THOUGH IT'S BEEN A WHILE SINCE WE STARTED BEING IN CONSTANT CONTACT.
YASUKE-SAN IS NOT AT-TRACTED TO ME...
もぐ MUNCH
もぐ MUNCH
...LIKE HE IS TO AKARI-SAN OR MY SISTER!
WANT SECONDS?
HOW ABOUT SOME SOY SAUCE?
I DON'T THINK IT'S THAT I'VE BECOME TOO FAMILIAR WITH HIM...
HE JUST TREATS ME AS HIS LITTLE SISTER...
BASICALLY, AS A CHILD!
MY MEAT!
I MUST DO SOME-THING ABOUT THIS!
STAB

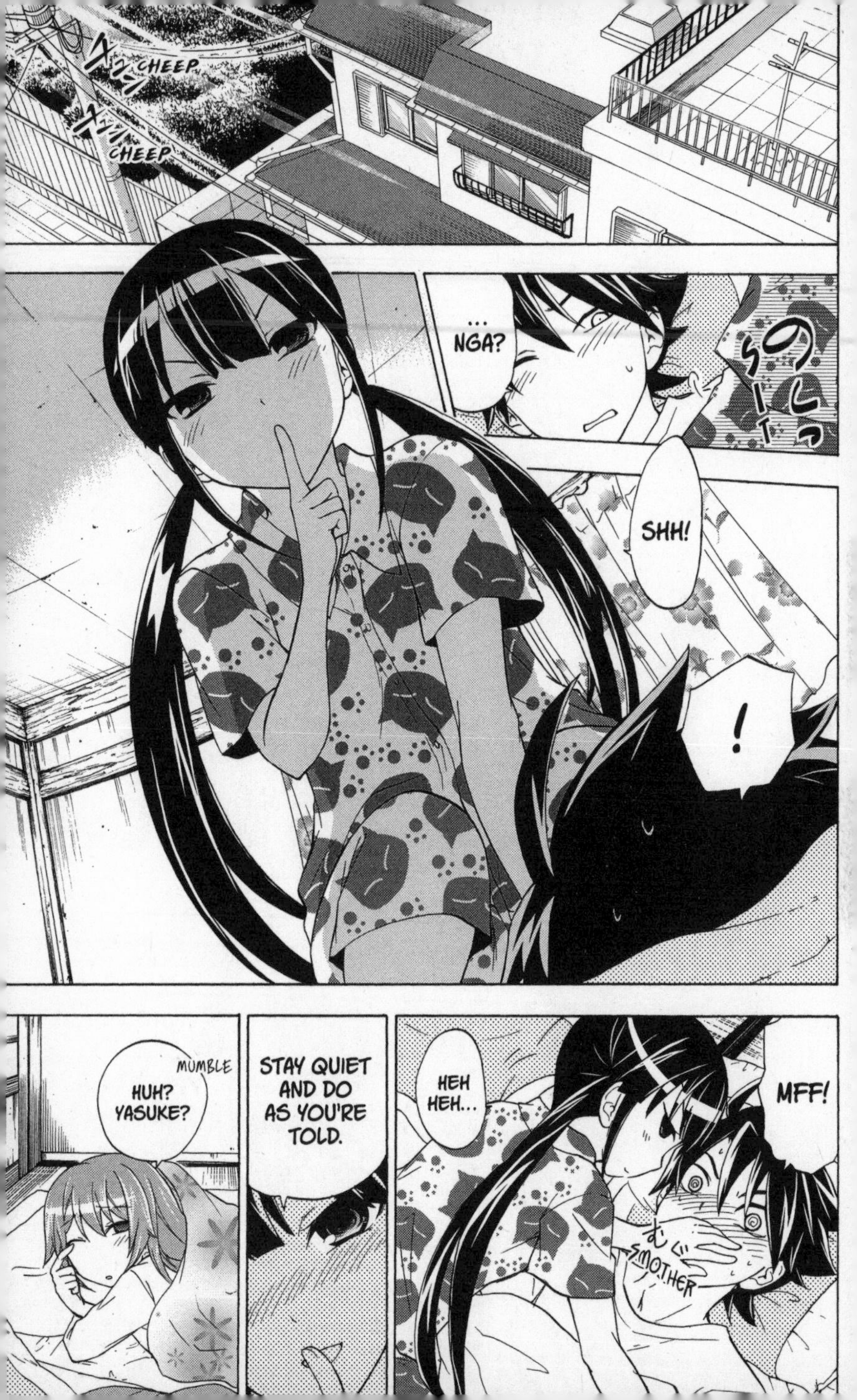
CHEEP
CHEEP
... NGA?
SHH!
!
MFF!
HEH HEH...
SMOTHER
STAY QUIET AND DO AS YOU'RE TOLD.
MUMBLE
HUH? YASUKE?

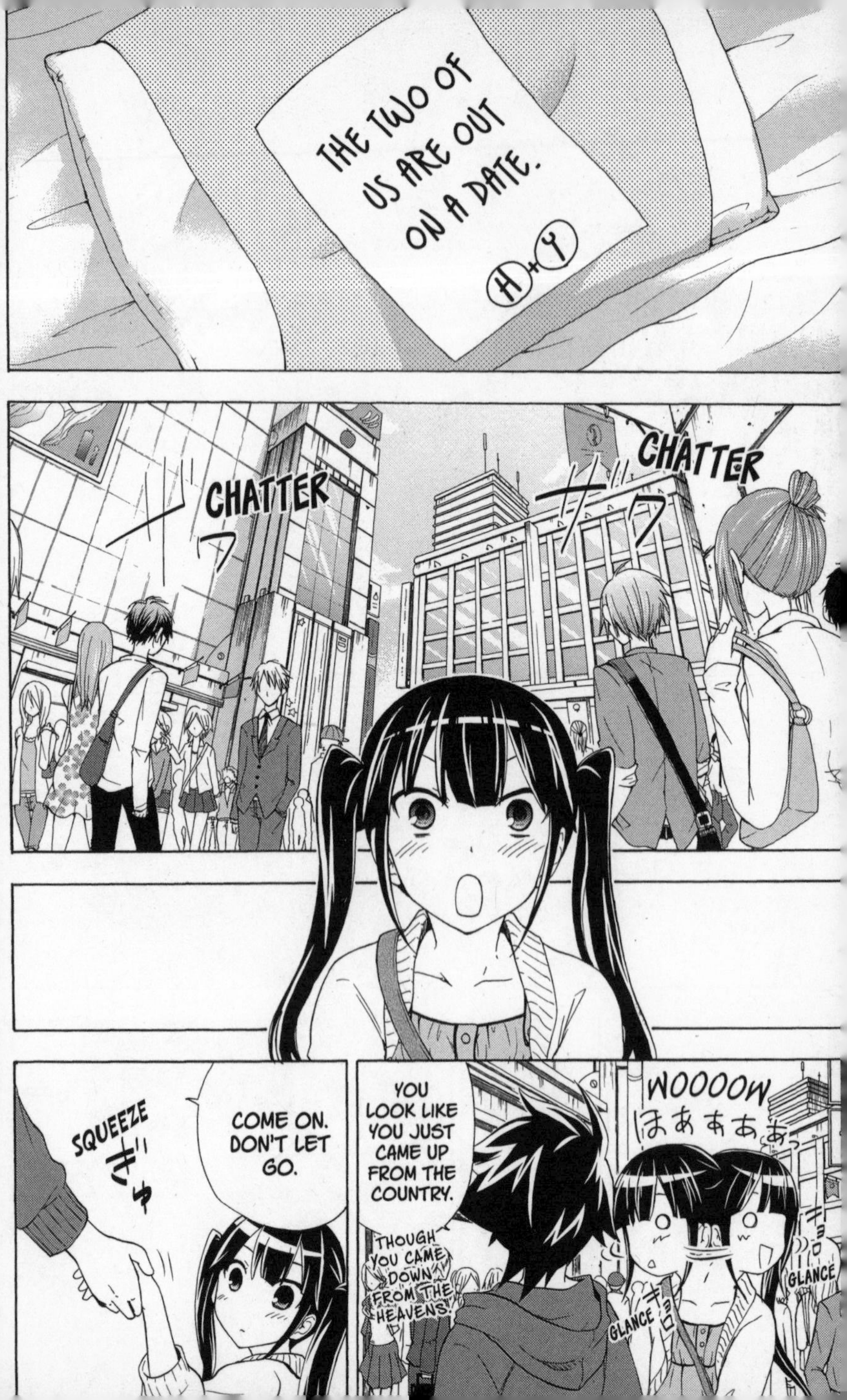
THE TWO OF US ARE OUT ON A DATE.
H+Y
CHATTER
ザワ
CHATTER
ザワ
WOOOOW
はあああああっ
キョロ
GLANCE
YOU LOOK LIKE YOU JUST CAME UP FROM THE COUNTRY.
THOUGH YOU CAME DOWN FROM THE HEAVENS.
キョロ
GLANCE
COME ON. DON'T LET GO.
SQUEEZE
ぎゅ

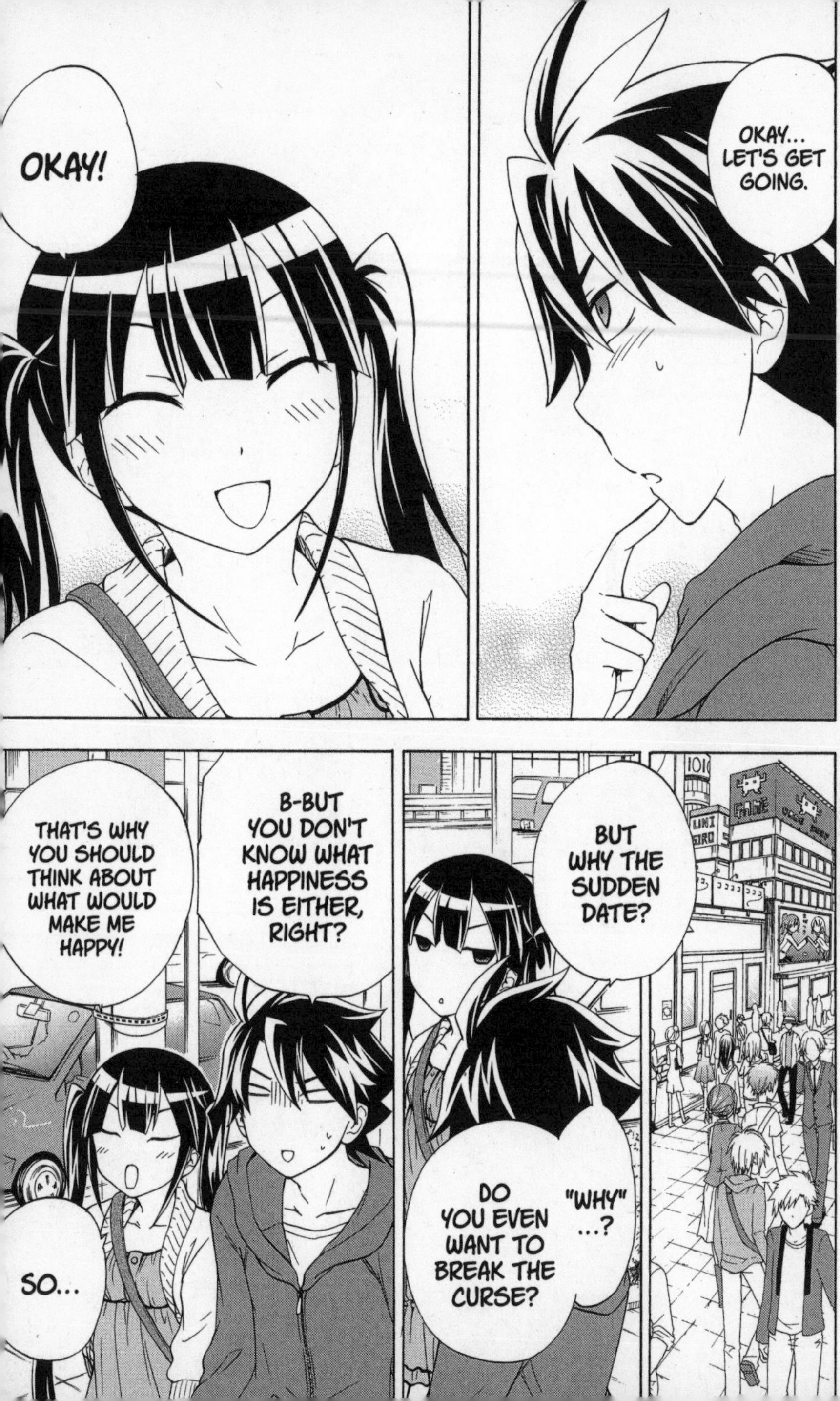
OKAY... LET'S GET GOING.
OKAY!
BUT WHY THE SUDDEN DATE?
"WHY" ...?
DO YOU EVEN WANT TO BREAK THE CURSE?
B-BUT YOU DON'T KNOW WHAT HAPPINESS IS EITHER, RIGHT?
THAT'S WHY YOU SHOULD THINK ABOUT WHAT WOULD MAKE ME HAPPY!
SO...

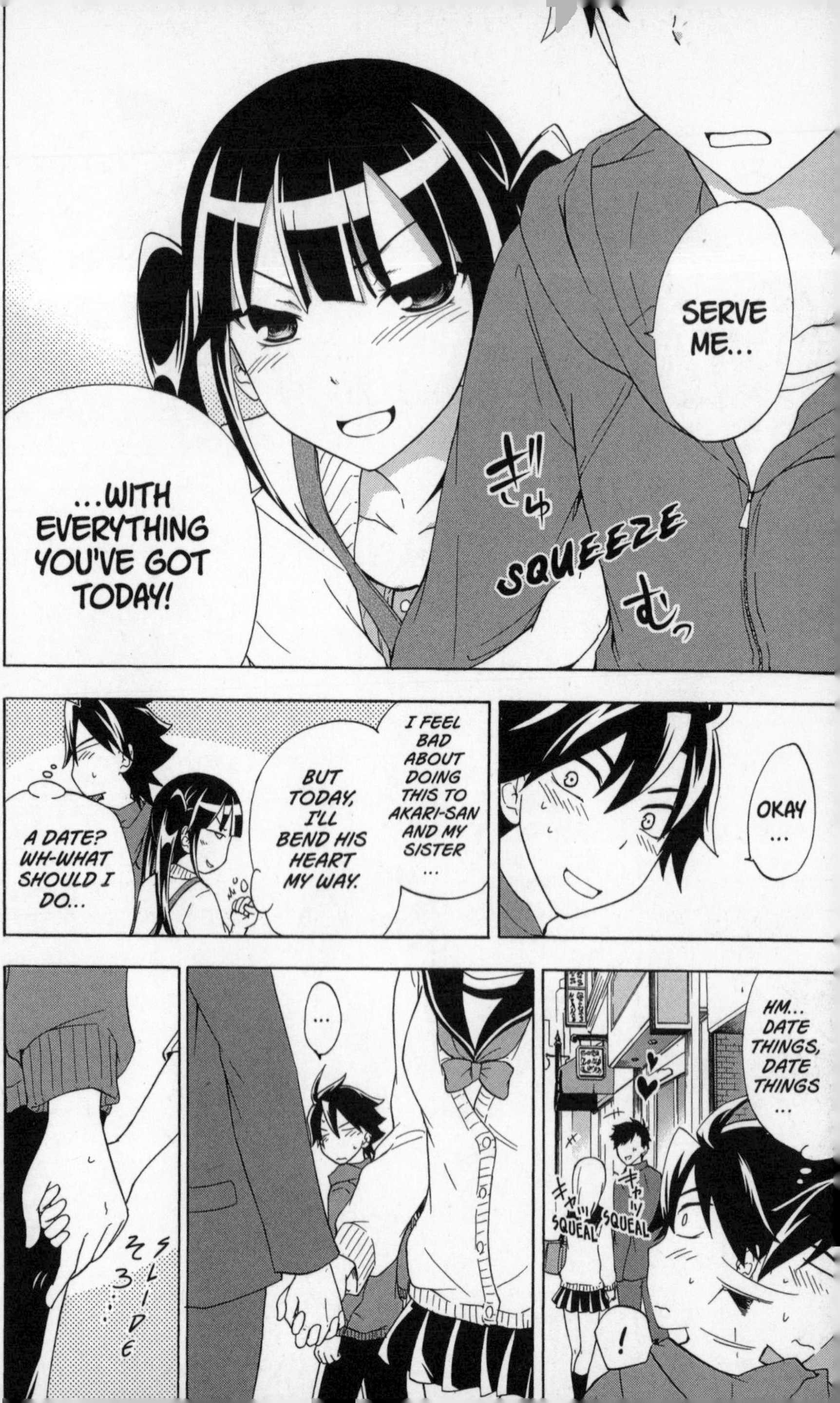
SERVE ME...
ぎゅ
SQUEEZE
むっ
...WITH EVERYTHING YOU'VE GOT TODAY!
OKAY ...
I FEEL BAD ABOUT DOING THIS TO AKARI-SAN AND MY SISTER ...
BUT TODAY, I'LL BEND HIS HEART MY WAY.
A DATE? WH-WHAT SHOULD I DO...
HM... DATE THINGS, DATE THINGS ...
キャッ
SQUEAL
キャッ
SQUEAL
!
...
SLIDE

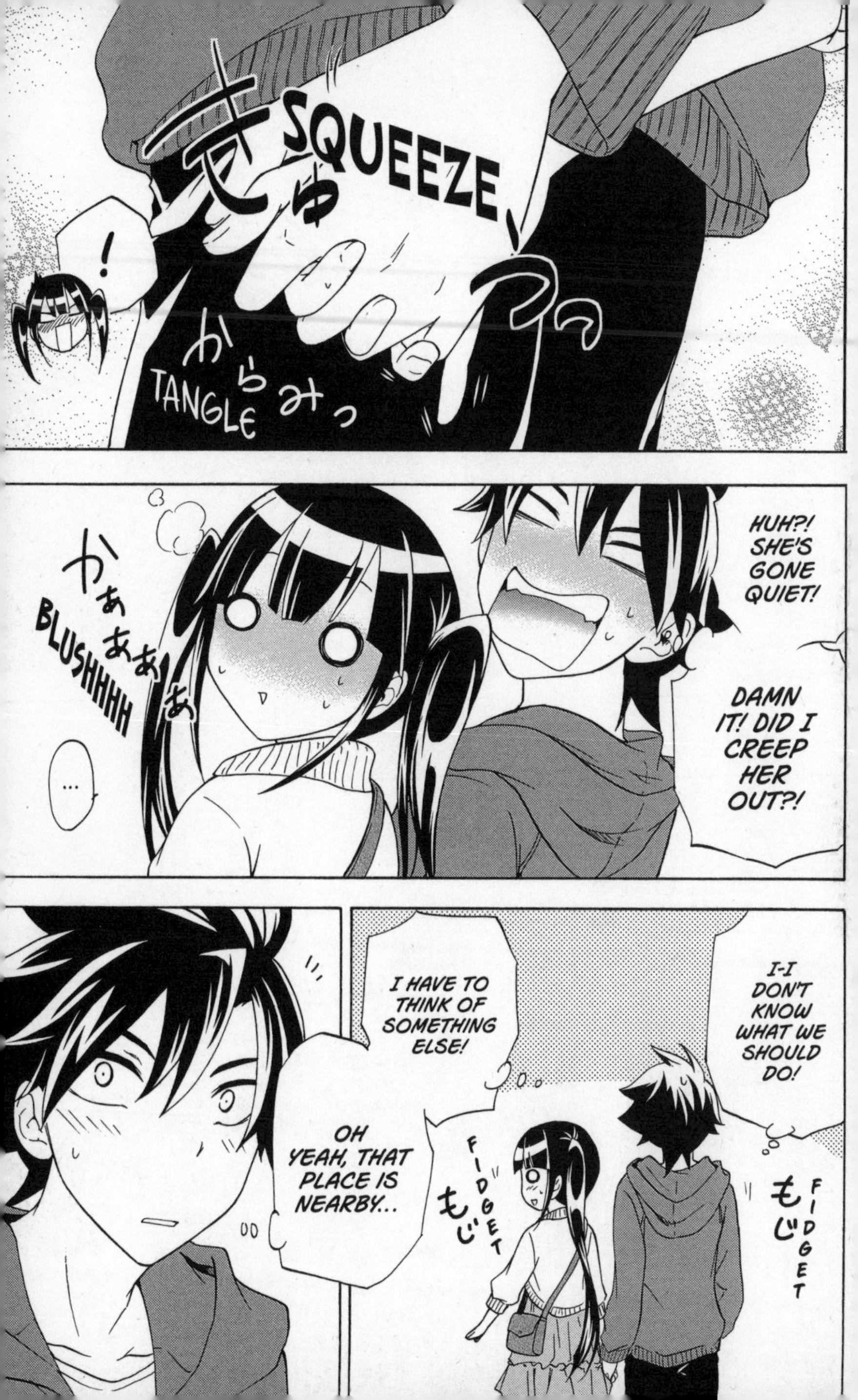
きゅっ
SQUEEZE
!
からみっ
TANGLE
HUH?! SHE'S GONE QUIET!
DAMN IT! DID I CREEP HER OUT?!
かぁぁぁぁ
BLUSHHHH
...
I-I DON'T KNOW WHAT WE SHOULD DO!
I HAVE TO THINK OF SOMETHING ELSE!
もじ
FIDGET
もじ
FIDGET
OH YEAH, THAT PLACE IS NEARBY...

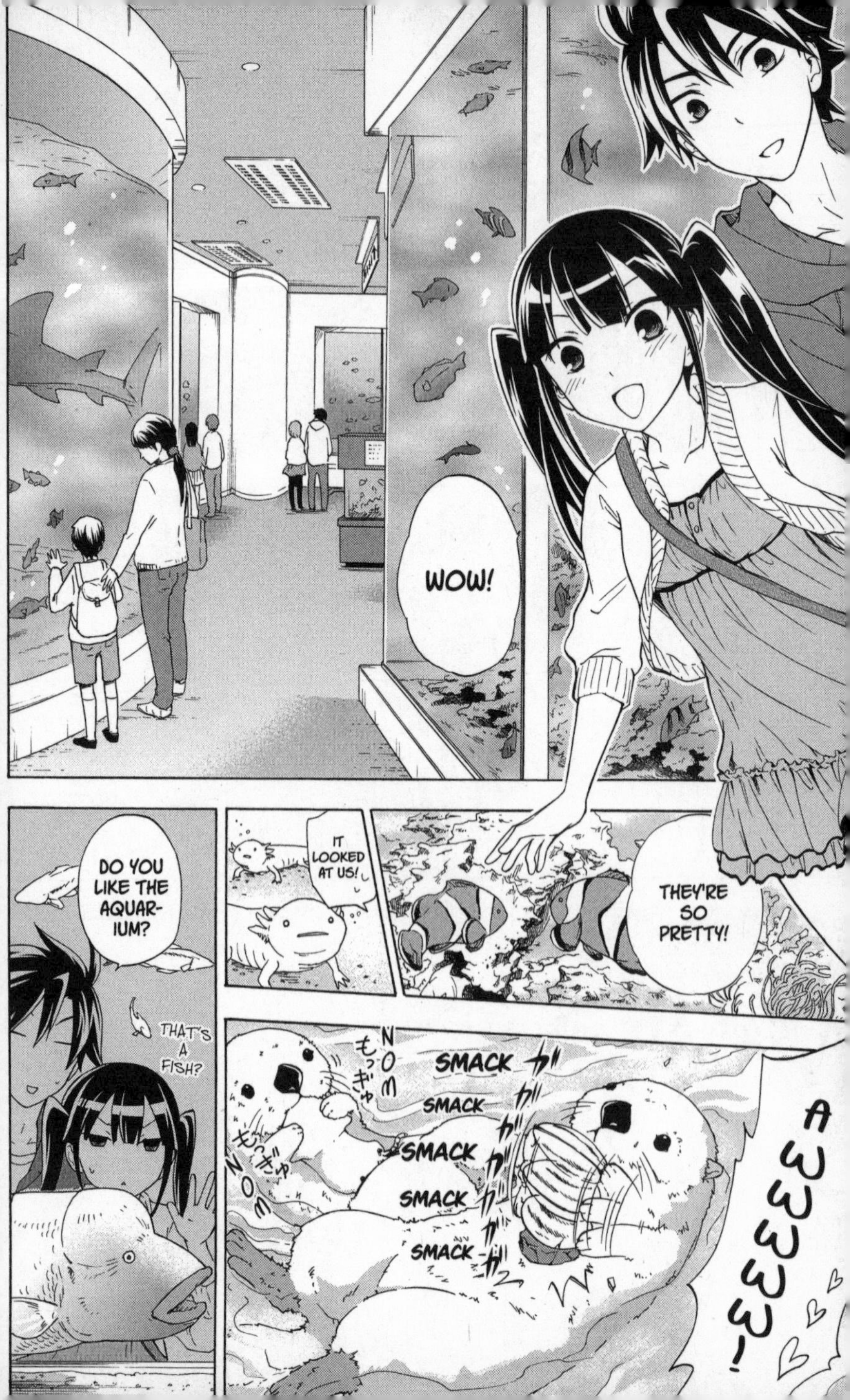
WOW!
THEY'RE SO PRETTY!
IT LOOKED AT US!
AWWWWW!
SMACK
SMACK
SMACK
SMACK
SMACK
NOM もっぎゅ
NOM もっぎゅ
DO YOU LIKE THE AQUAR-IUM?
THAT'S A FISH?

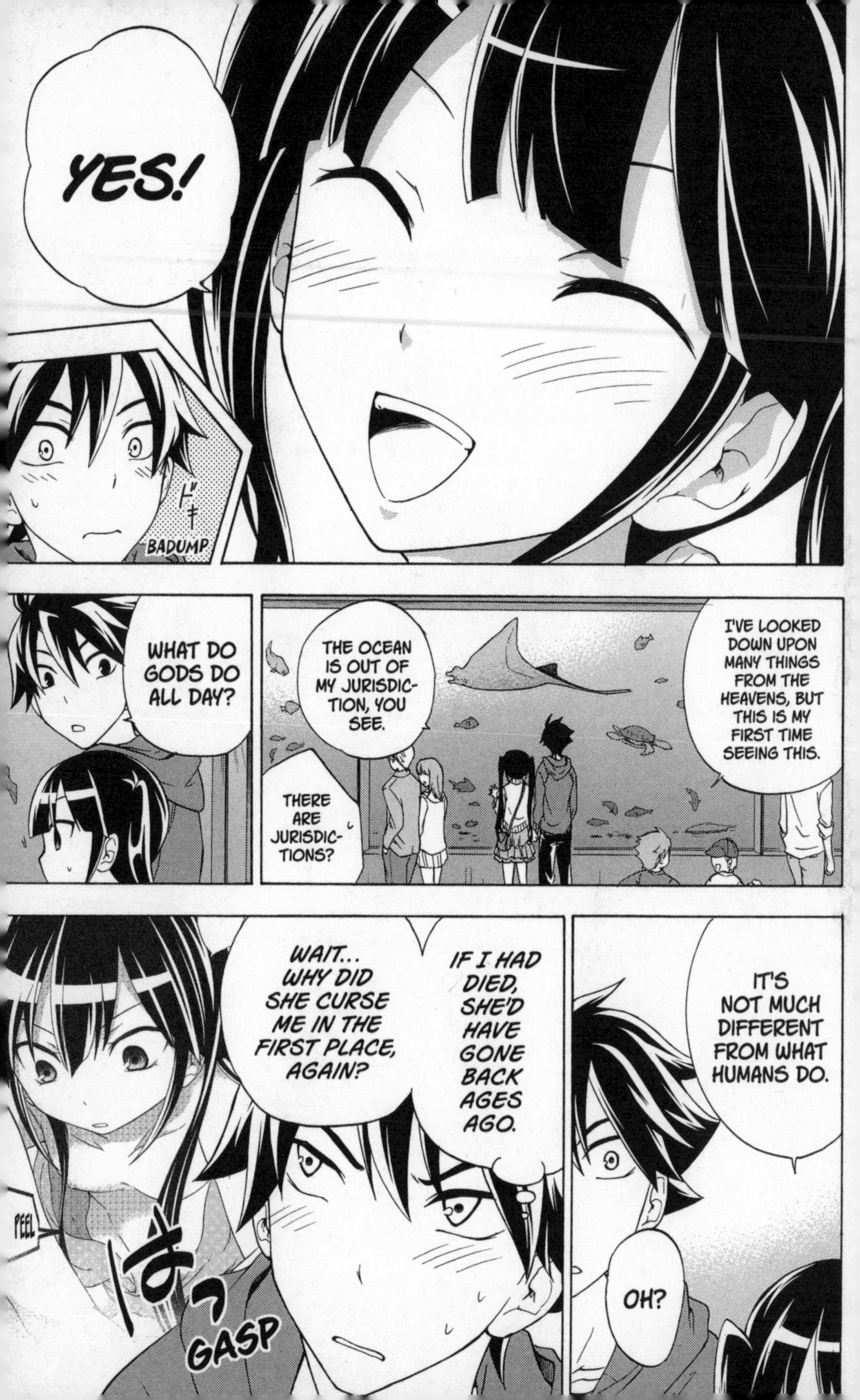
YES!
ドキ
BADUMP
I'VE LOOKED DOWN UPON MANY THINGS FROM THE HEAVENS, BUT THIS IS MY FIRST TIME SEEING THIS.
THE OCEAN IS OUT OF MY JURISDICTION, YOU SEE.
THERE ARE JURISDICTIONS?
WHAT DO GODS DO ALL DAY?
IT'S NOT MUCH DIFFERENT FROM WHAT HUMANS DO.
OH?
IF I HAD DIED, SHE'D HAVE GONE BACK AGES AGO.
WAIT... WHY DID SHE CURSE ME IN THE FIRST PLACE, AGAIN?
PEEL
GASP

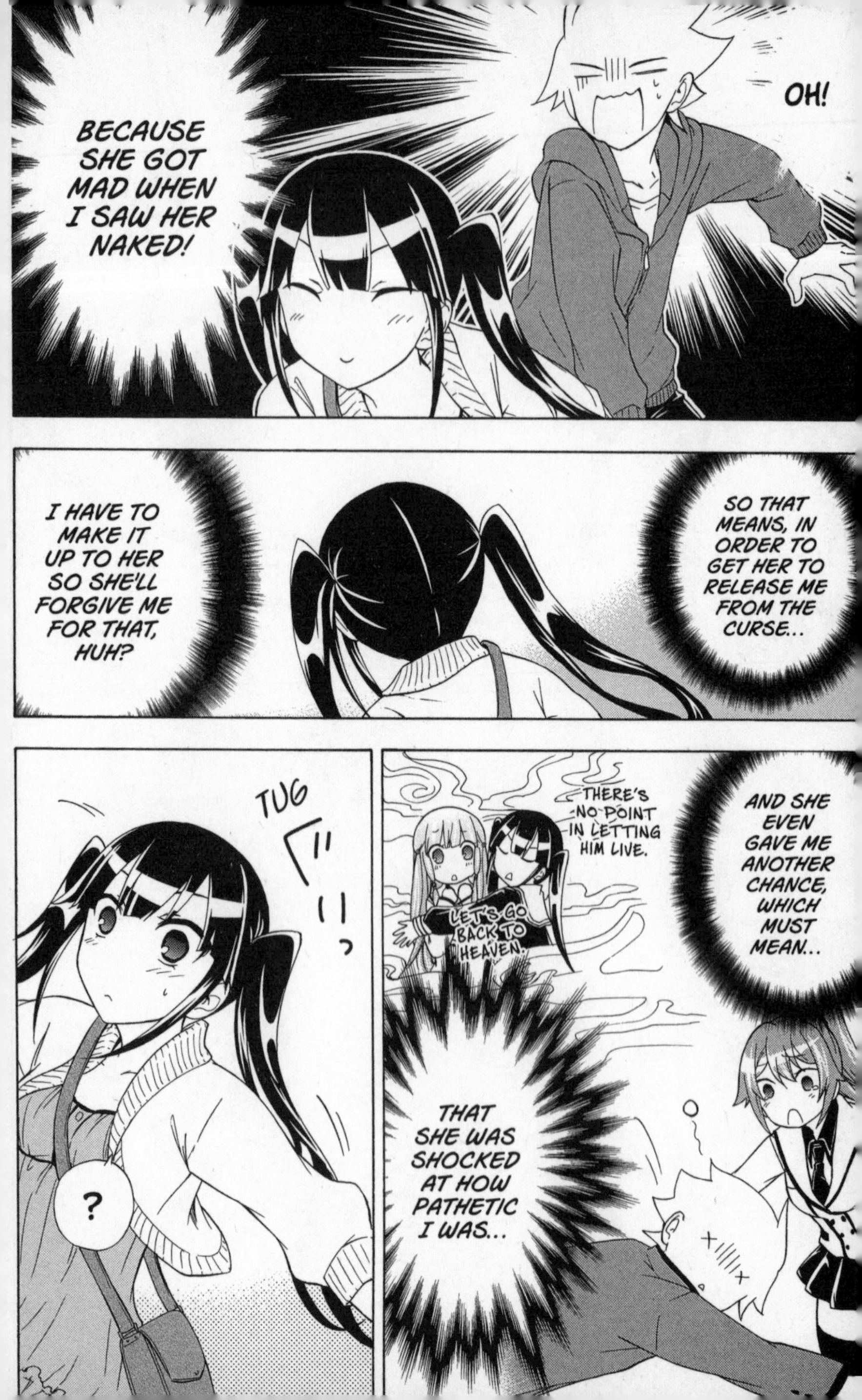
OH!
BECAUSE SHE GOT MAD WHEN I SAW HER NAKED!
SO THAT MEANS, IN ORDER TO GET HER TO RELEASE ME FROM THE CURSE...
I HAVE TO MAKE IT UP TO HER SO SHE'LL FORGIVE ME FOR THAT, HUH?
AND SHE EVEN GAVE ME ANOTHER CHANCE, WHICH MUST MEAN...
THERE'S NO POINT IN LETTING HIM LIVE.
LET'S GO BACK TO HEAVEN.
THAT SHE WAS SHOCKED AT HOW PATHETIC I WAS...
TUG
?

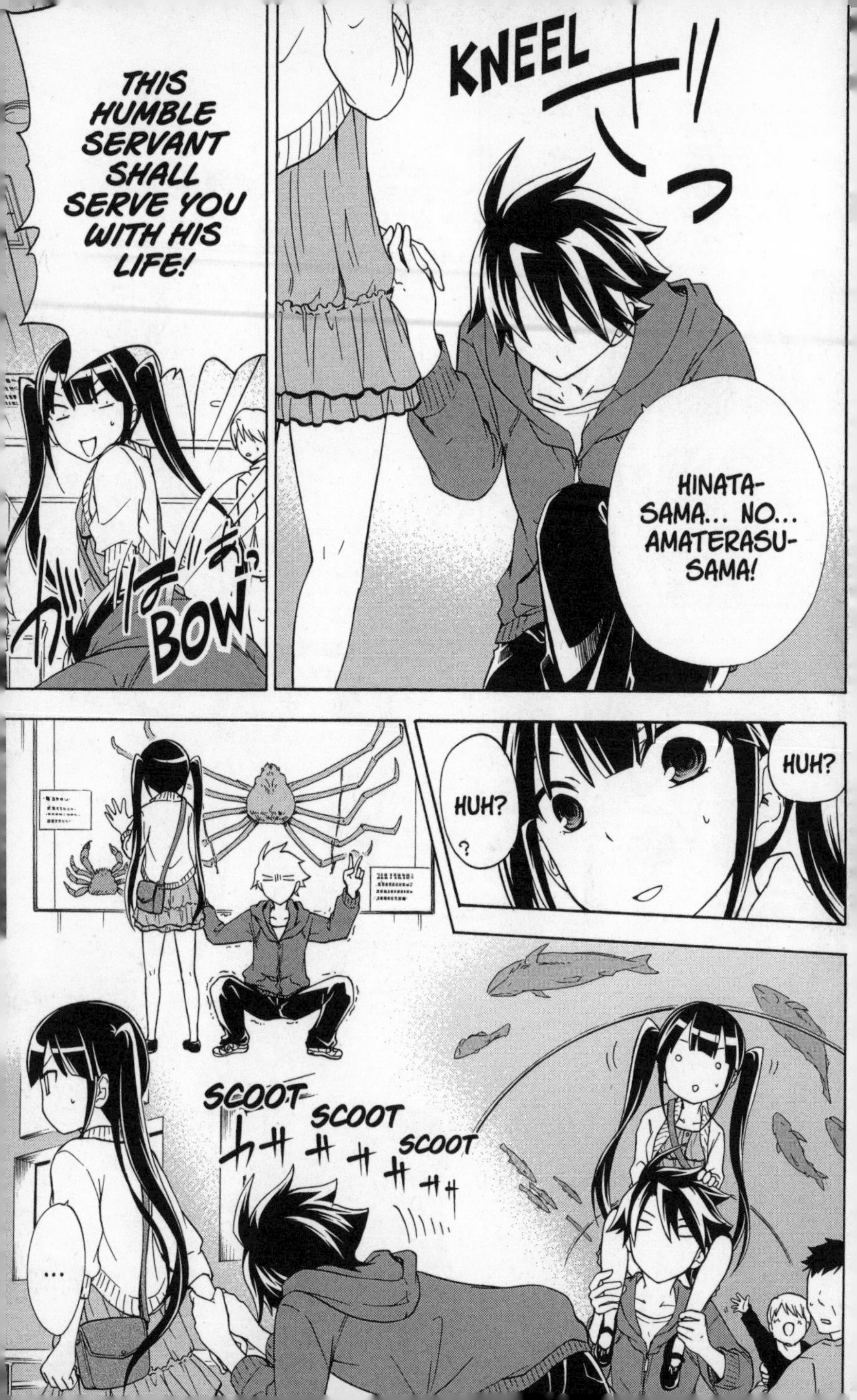
KNEEL
HINATA-SAMA... NO... AMATERASU-SAMA!
THIS HUMBLE SERVANT SHALL SERVE YOU WITH HIS LIFE!
BOW
HUH?
HUH?
?
SCOOT
SCOOT
SCOOT
...

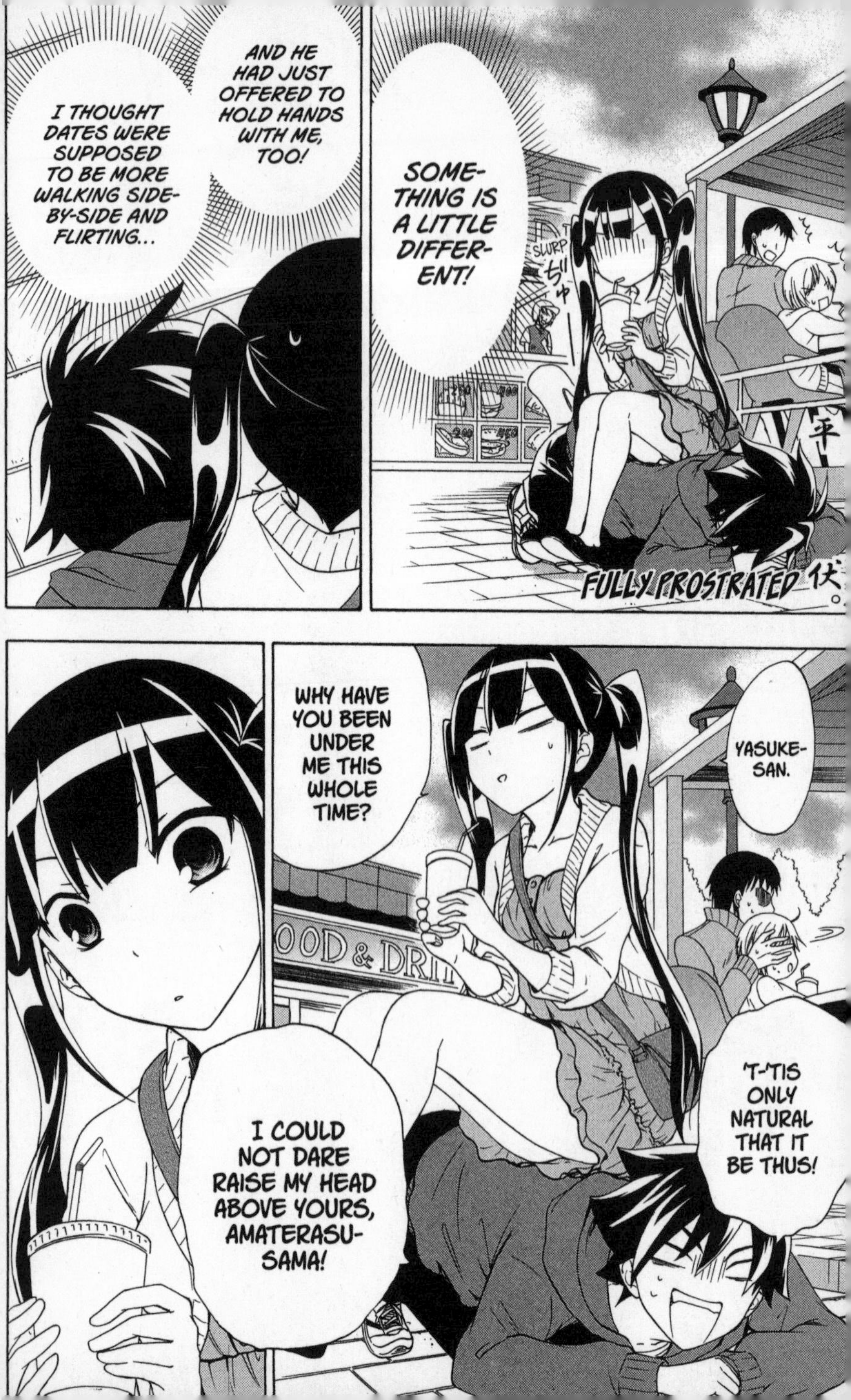
SOME-THING IS A LITTLE DIFFER-ENT!
SLURP ぢゅ
平
FULLY PROSTRATED 伏。
AND HE HAD JUST OFFERED TO HOLD HANDS WITH ME, TOO!
I THOUGHT DATES WERE SUPPOSED TO BE MORE WALKING SIDE-BY-SIDE AND FLIRTING...
YASUKE-SAN.
WHY HAVE YOU BEEN UNDER ME THIS WHOLE TIME?
'T-'TIS ONLY NATURAL THAT IT BE THUS!
I COULD NOT DARE RAISE MY HEAD ABOVE YOURS, AMATERASU-SAMA!

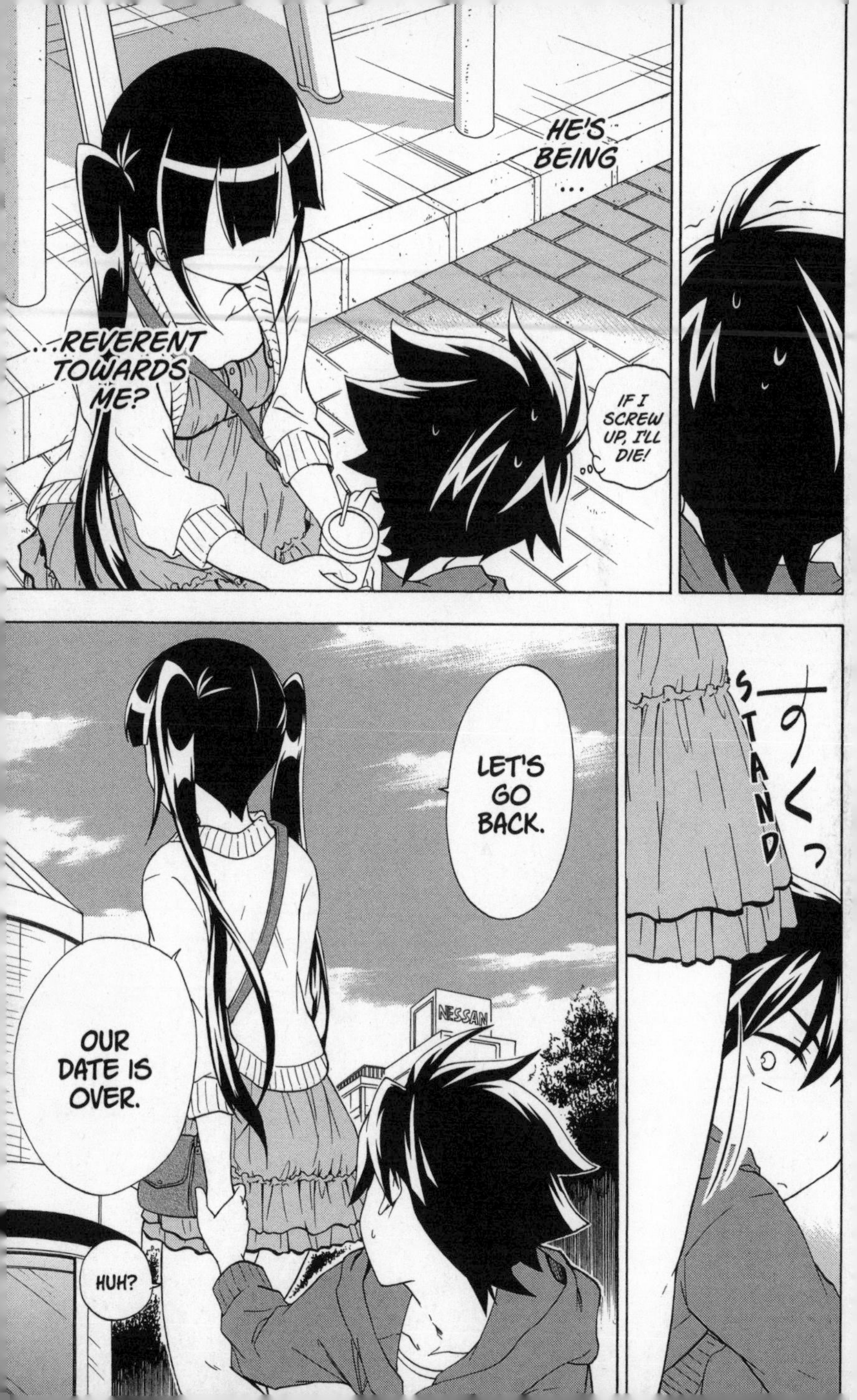
HE'S BEING...
...REVERENT TOWARDS ME?
IF I SCREW UP, I'LL DIE!
STAND
LET'S GO BACK.
OUR DATE IS OVER.
NESSAN
HUH?

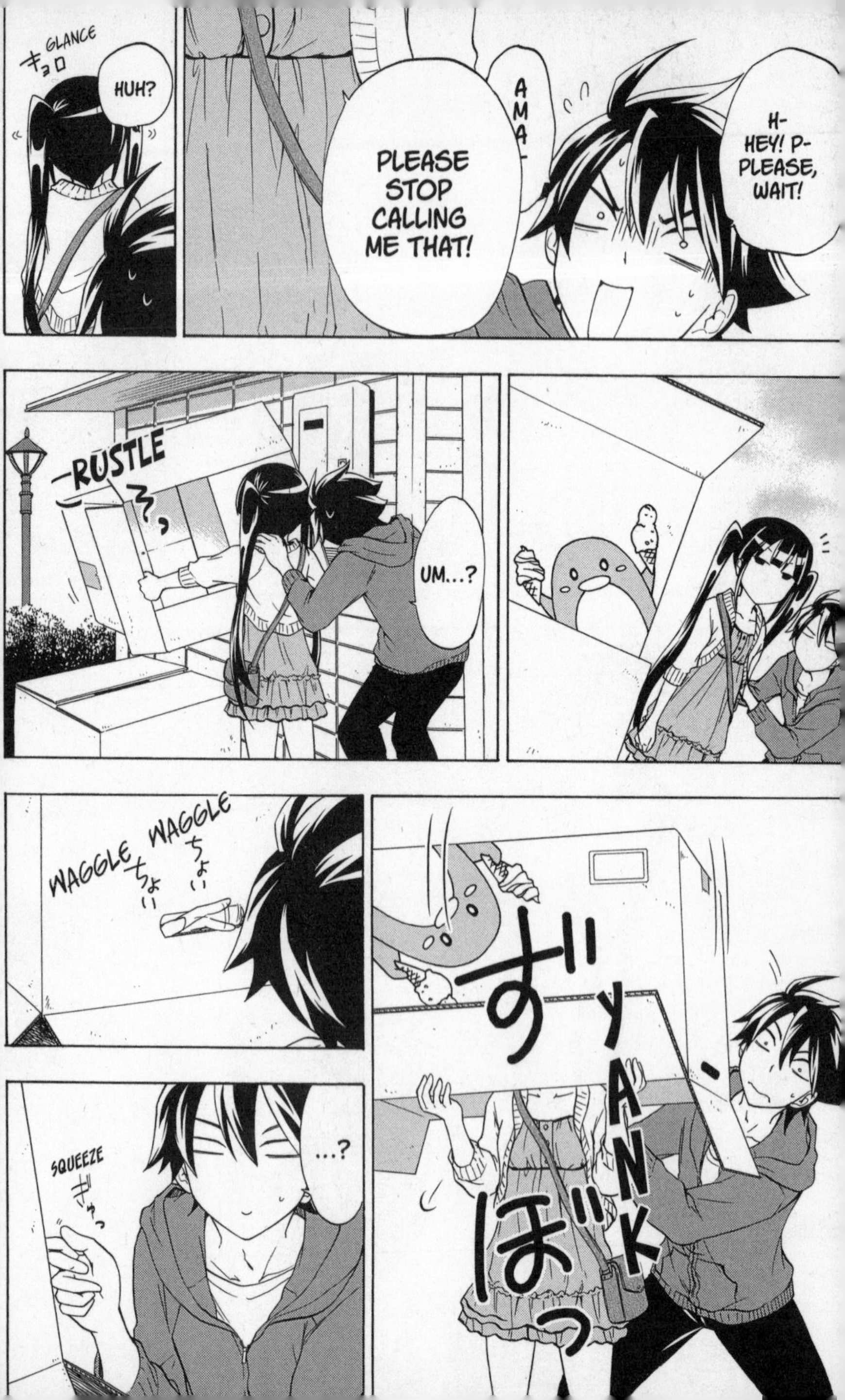
H-HEY! P-PLEASE, WAIT!
AMA—
PLEASE STOP CALLING ME THAT!
GLANCE
キョロ
HUH?
RUSTLE
UM...?
ず
YANK
ぼっ
WAGGLE
ちょい
WAGGLE
ちょい
SQUEEZE
ぎゅっ
...?

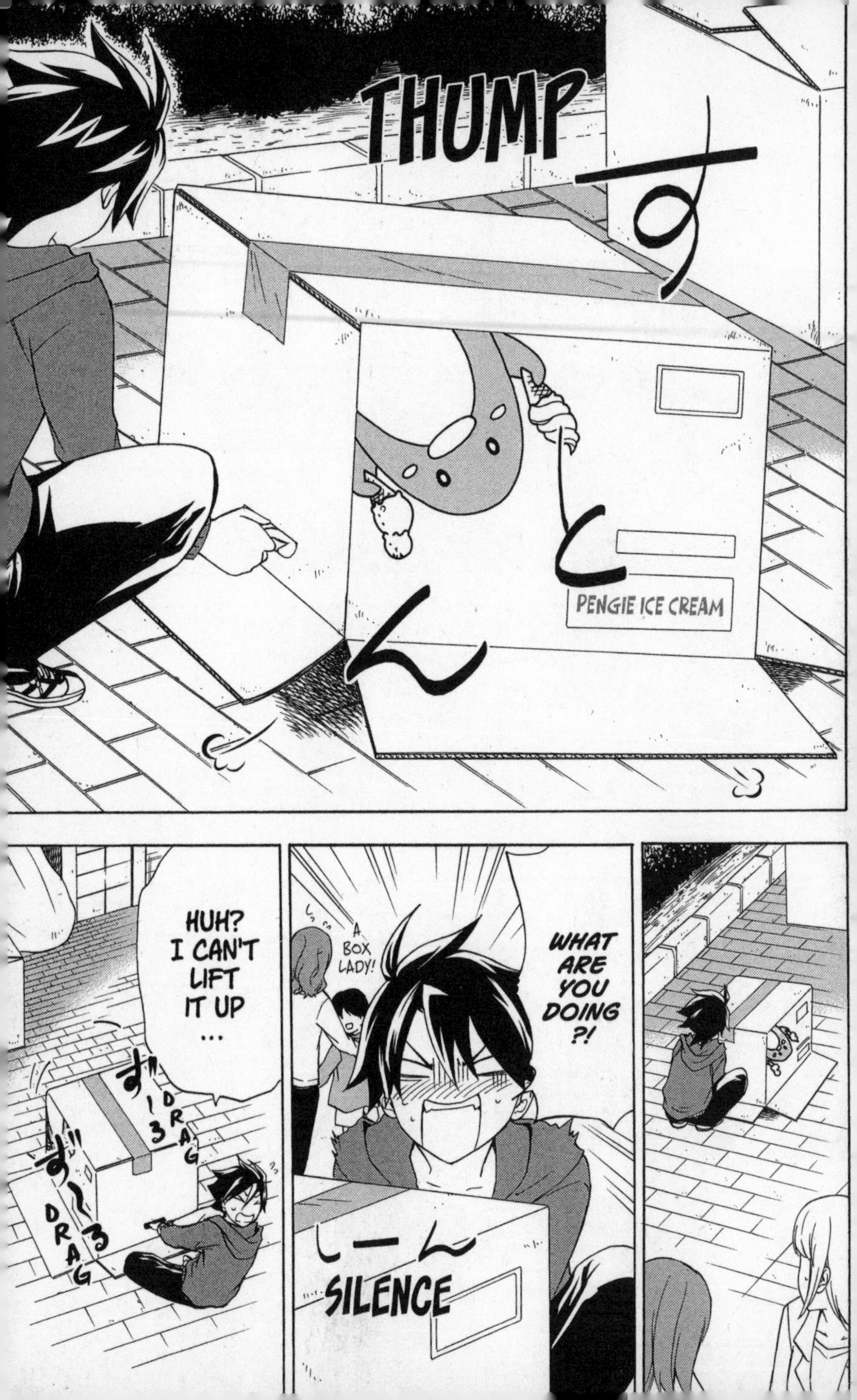
THUMP
すとん
PENGIE ICE CREAM
A BOX LADY!
WHAT ARE YOU DOING?!
しーん
SILENCE
HUH? I CAN'T LIFT IT UP...
DRAG
DRAG

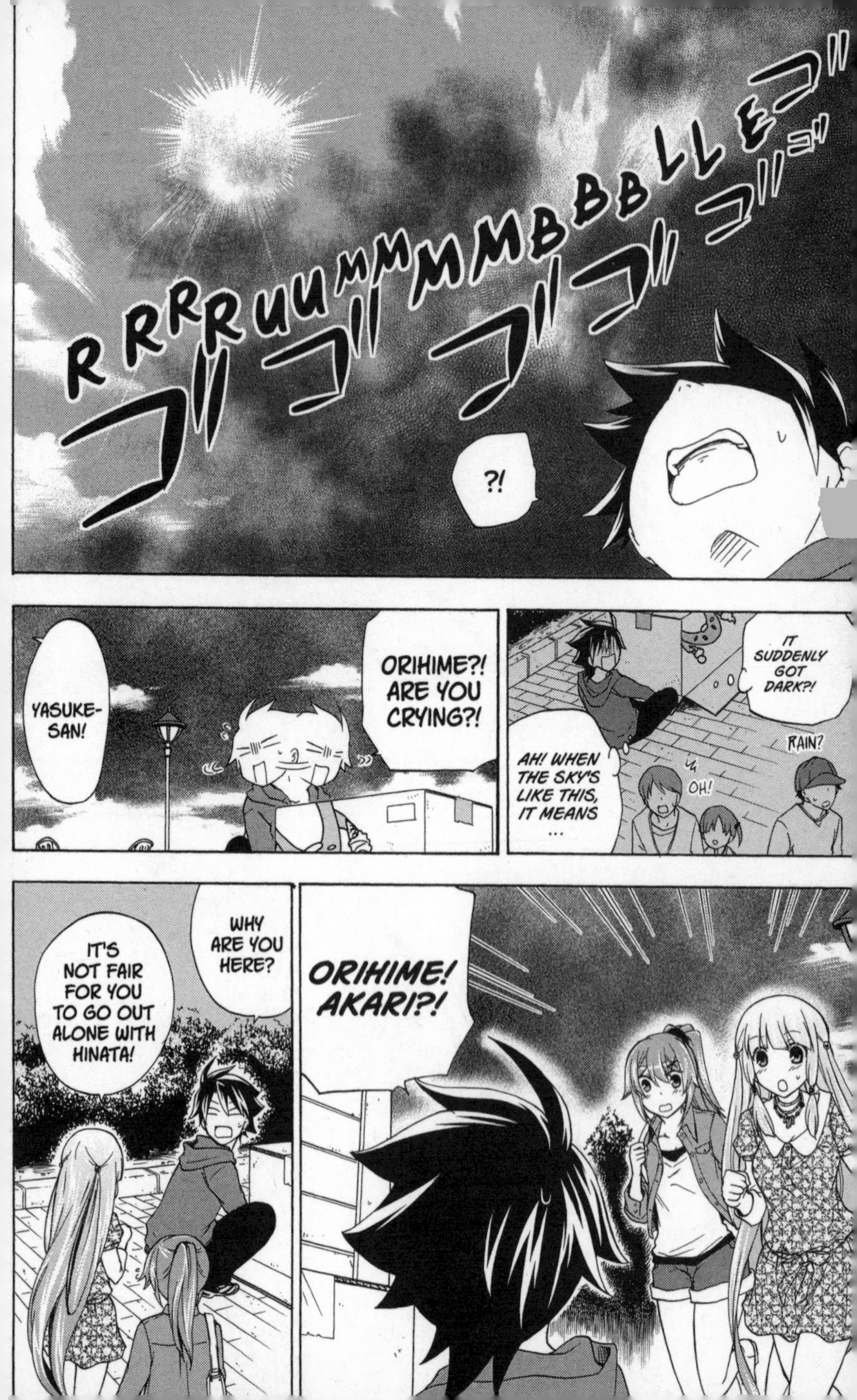
RRRRUUMMMMMBBBLLE
?!
IT SUDDENLY GOT DARK?!
RAIN?
OH!
AH! WHEN THE SKY'S LIKE THIS, IT MEANS ...
ORIHIME?! ARE YOU CRYING?!
YASUKE-SAN!
ORIHIME! AKARI?!
WHY ARE YOU HERE?
IT'S NOT FAIR FOR YOU TO GO OUT ALONE WITH HINATA!

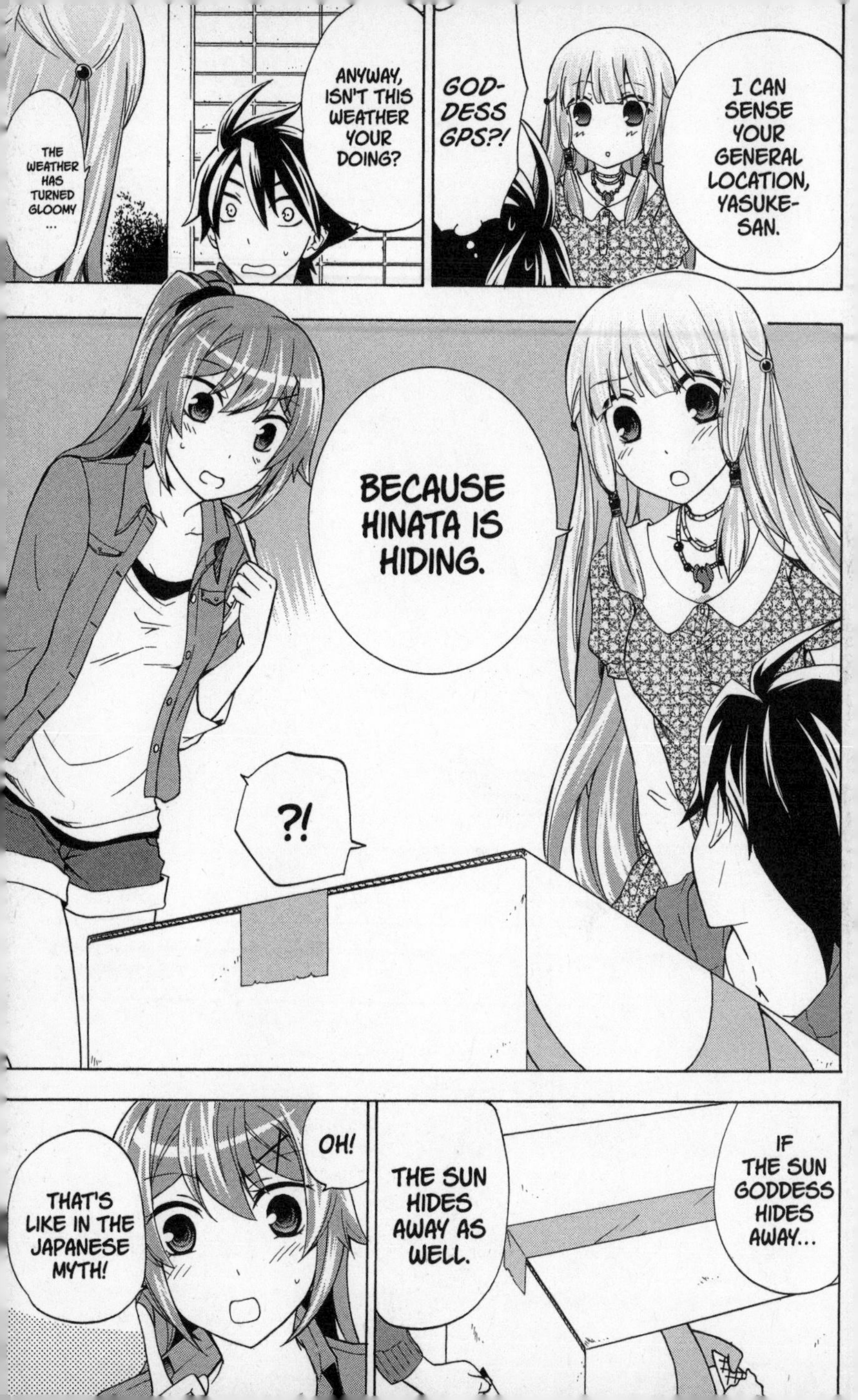
I CAN SENSE YOUR GENERAL LOCATION, YASUKE-SAN.
GOD-DESS GPS?!
ANYWAY, ISN'T THIS WEATHER YOUR DOING?
THE WEATHER HAS TURNED GLOOMY ...
BECAUSE HINATA IS HIDING.
?!
IF THE SUN GODDESS HIDES AWAY...
THE SUN HIDES AWAY AS WELL.
OH!
THAT'S LIKE IN THE JAPANESE MYTH!

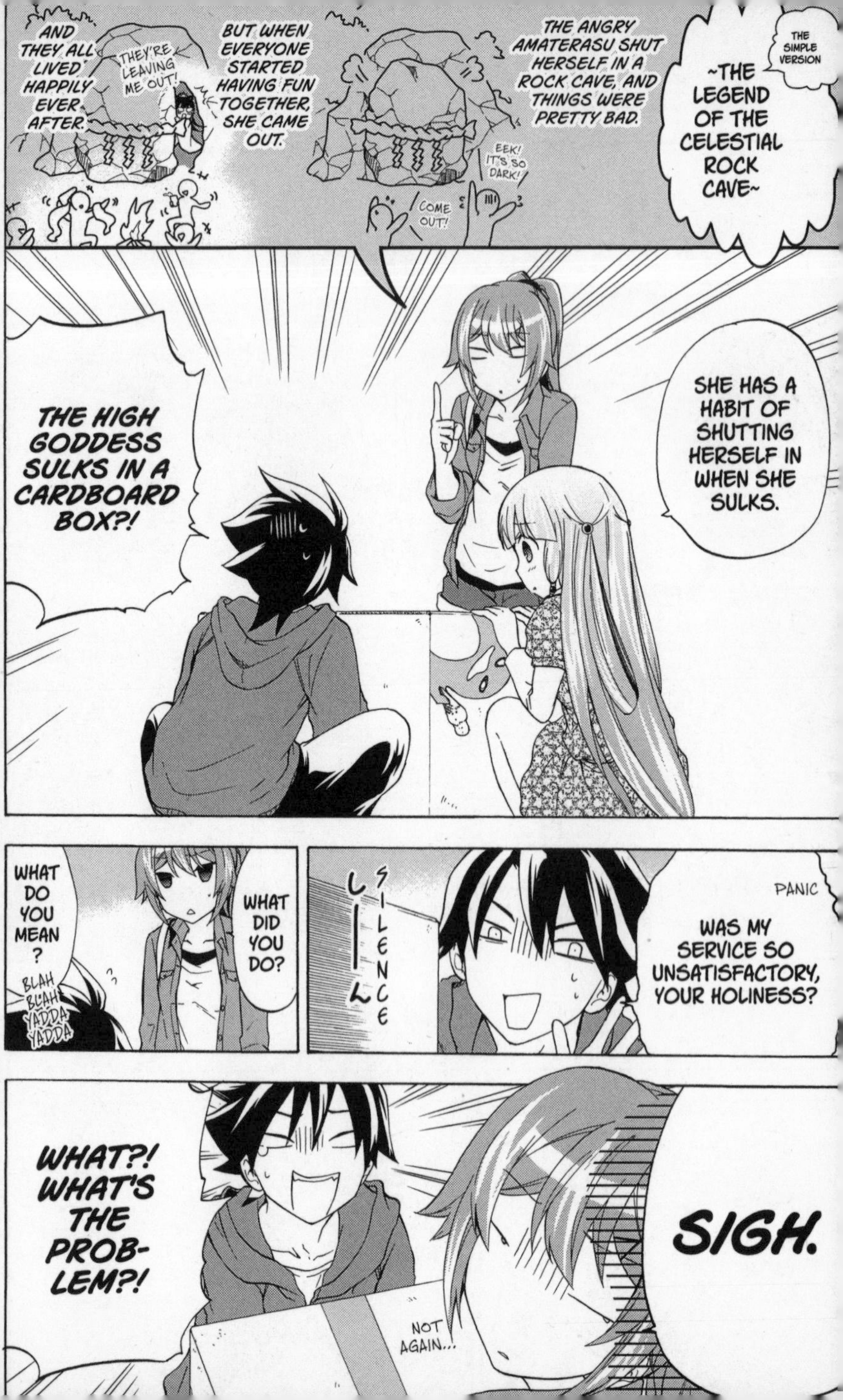
THE SIMPLE VERSION
~THE LEGEND OF THE CELESTIAL ROCK CAVE~
THE ANGRY AMATERASU SHUT HERSELF IN A ROCK CAVE, AND THINGS WERE PRETTY BAD.
EEK! IT'S SO DARK!
COME OUT!
BUT WHEN EVERYONE STARTED HAVING FUN TOGETHER, SHE CAME OUT.
THEY'RE LEAVING ME OUT!
AND THEY ALL LIVED HAPPILY EVER AFTER.
SHE HAS A HABIT OF SHUTTING HERSELF IN WHEN SHE SULKS.
THE HIGH GODDESS SULKS IN A CARDBOARD BOX?!
PANIC
WAS MY SERVICE SO UNSATISFACTORY, YOUR HOLINESS?
SILENCE
WHAT DID YOU DO?
WHAT DO YOU MEAN?
BLAH BLAH YADDA YADDA
SIGH.
NOT AGAIN...
WHAT?! WHAT'S THE PROB-LEM?!

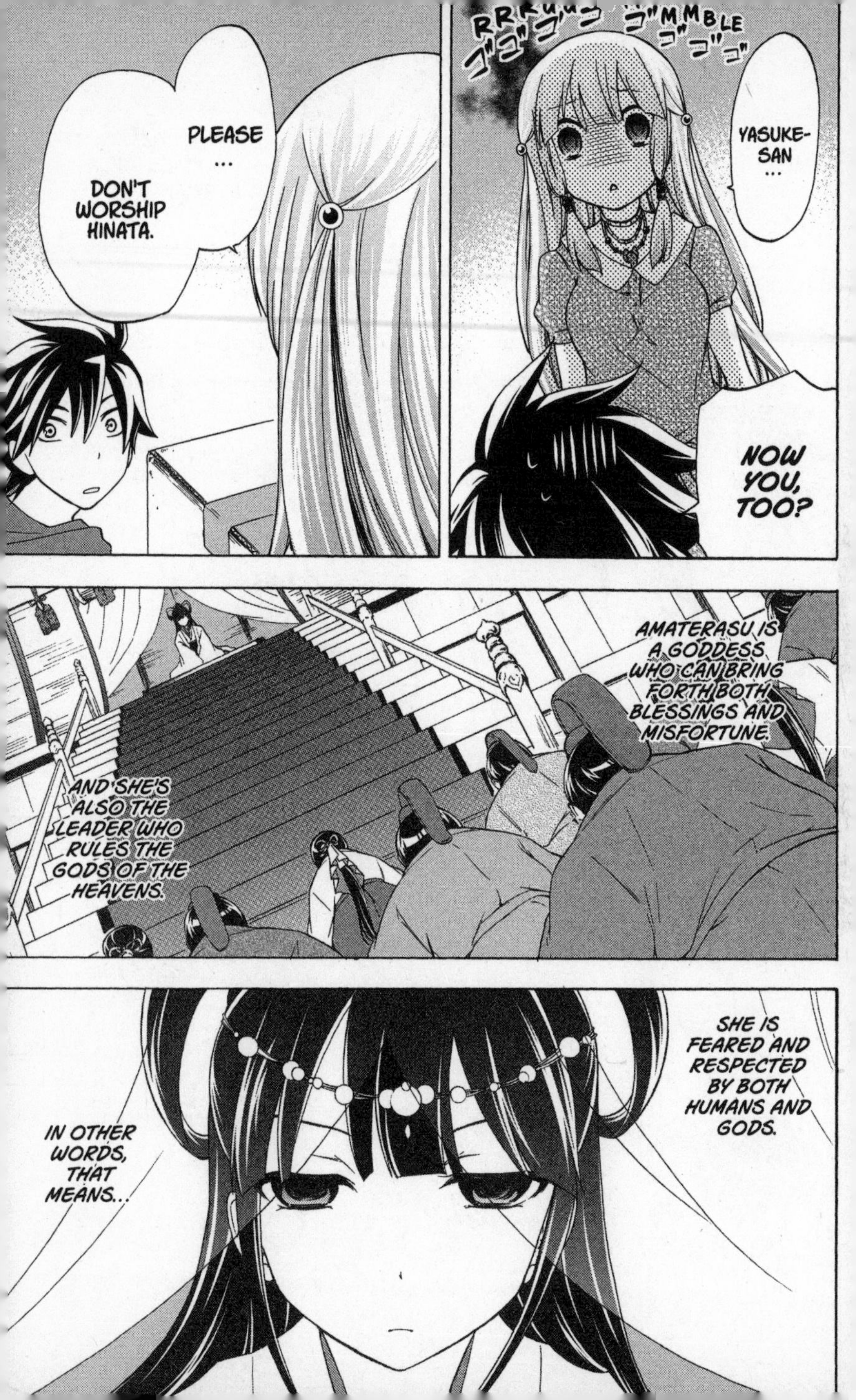
RRRU MMBLE
YASUKE-SAN ...
NOW YOU, TOO?
PLEASE ...
DON'T WORSHIP HINATA.
AMATERASU IS A GODDESS WHO CAN BRING FORTH BOTH BLESSINGS AND MISFORTUNE.
AND SHE'S ALSO THE LEADER WHO RULES THE GODS OF THE HEAVENS.
SHE IS FEARED AND RESPECTED BY BOTH HUMANS AND GODS.
IN OTHER WORDS, THAT MEANS...

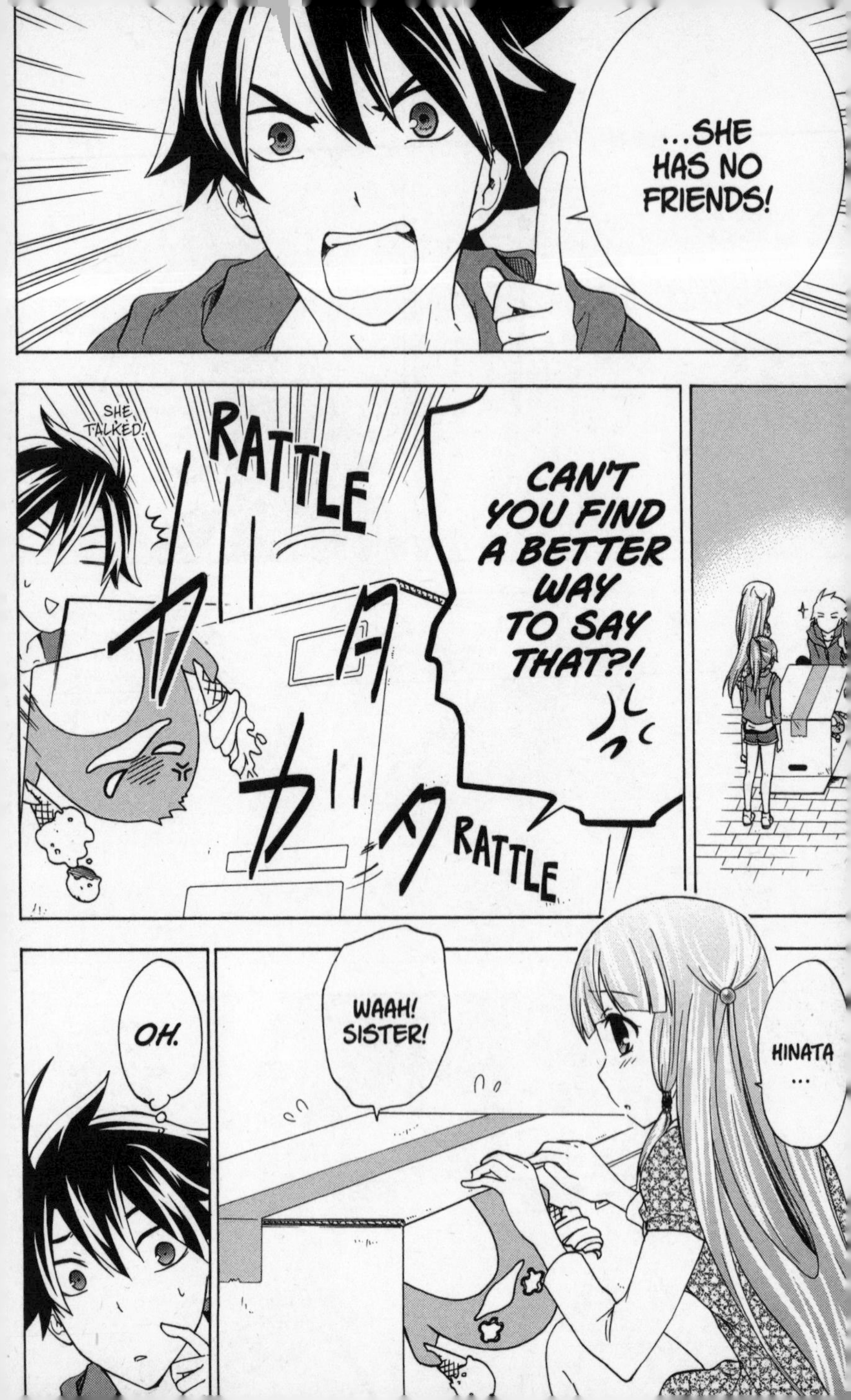
...SHE HAS NO FRIENDS!
CAN'T YOU FIND A BETTER WAY TO SAY THAT?!
RATTLE
SHE TALKED!
RATTLE
HINATA ...
WAAH! SISTER!
OH.

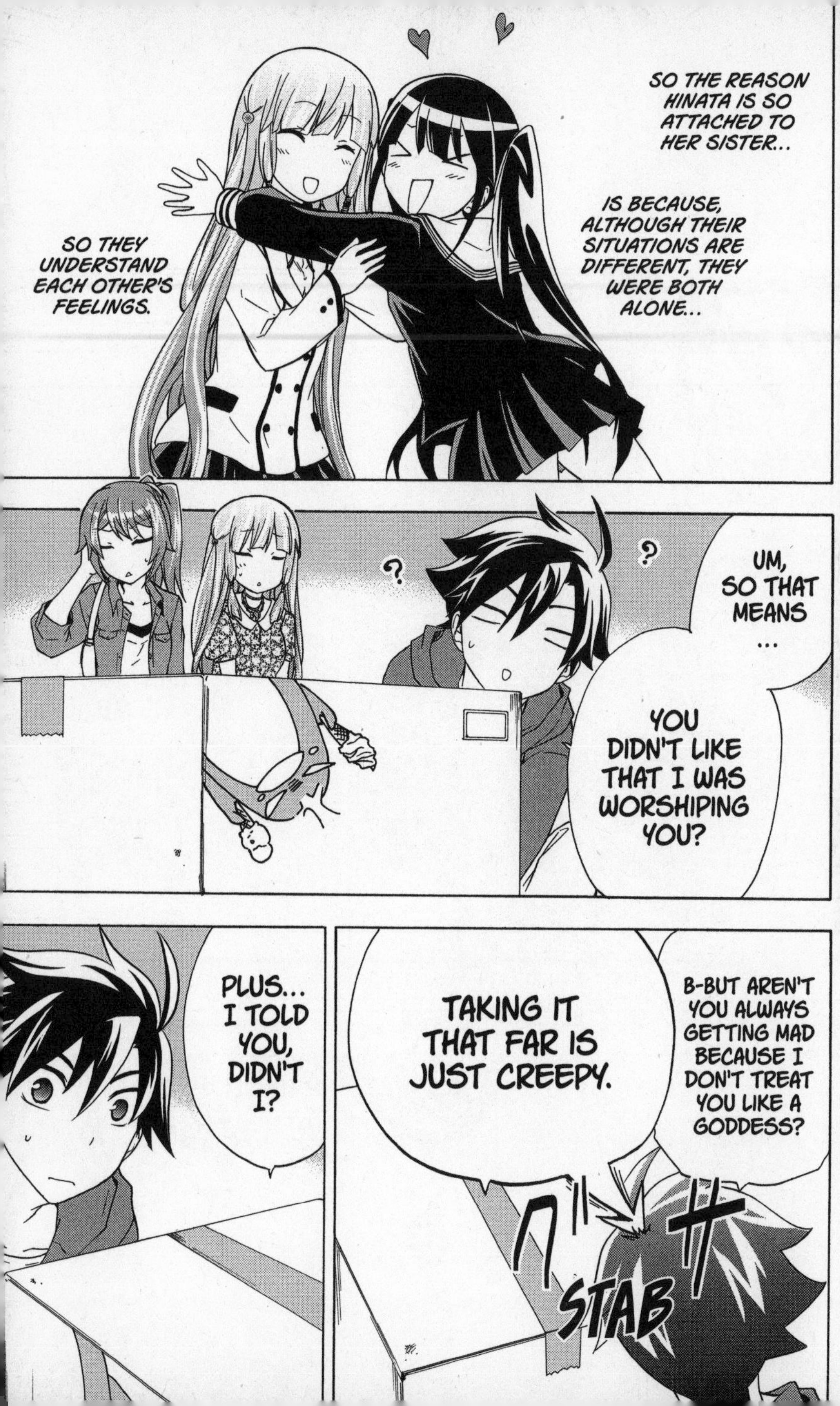
SO THE REASON HINATA IS SO ATTACHED TO HER SISTER...
IS BECAUSE, ALTHOUGH THEIR SITUATIONS ARE DIFFERENT, THEY WERE BOTH ALONE...
SO THEY UNDERSTAND EACH OTHER'S FEELINGS.
UM, SO THAT MEANS... YOU DIDN'T LIKE THAT I WAS WORSHIPING YOU?
B-BUT AREN'T YOU ALWAYS GETTING MAD BECAUSE I DON'T TREAT YOU LIKE A GODDESS?
TAKING IT THAT FAR IS JUST CREEPY.
STAB
PLUS... I TOLD YOU, DIDN'T I?

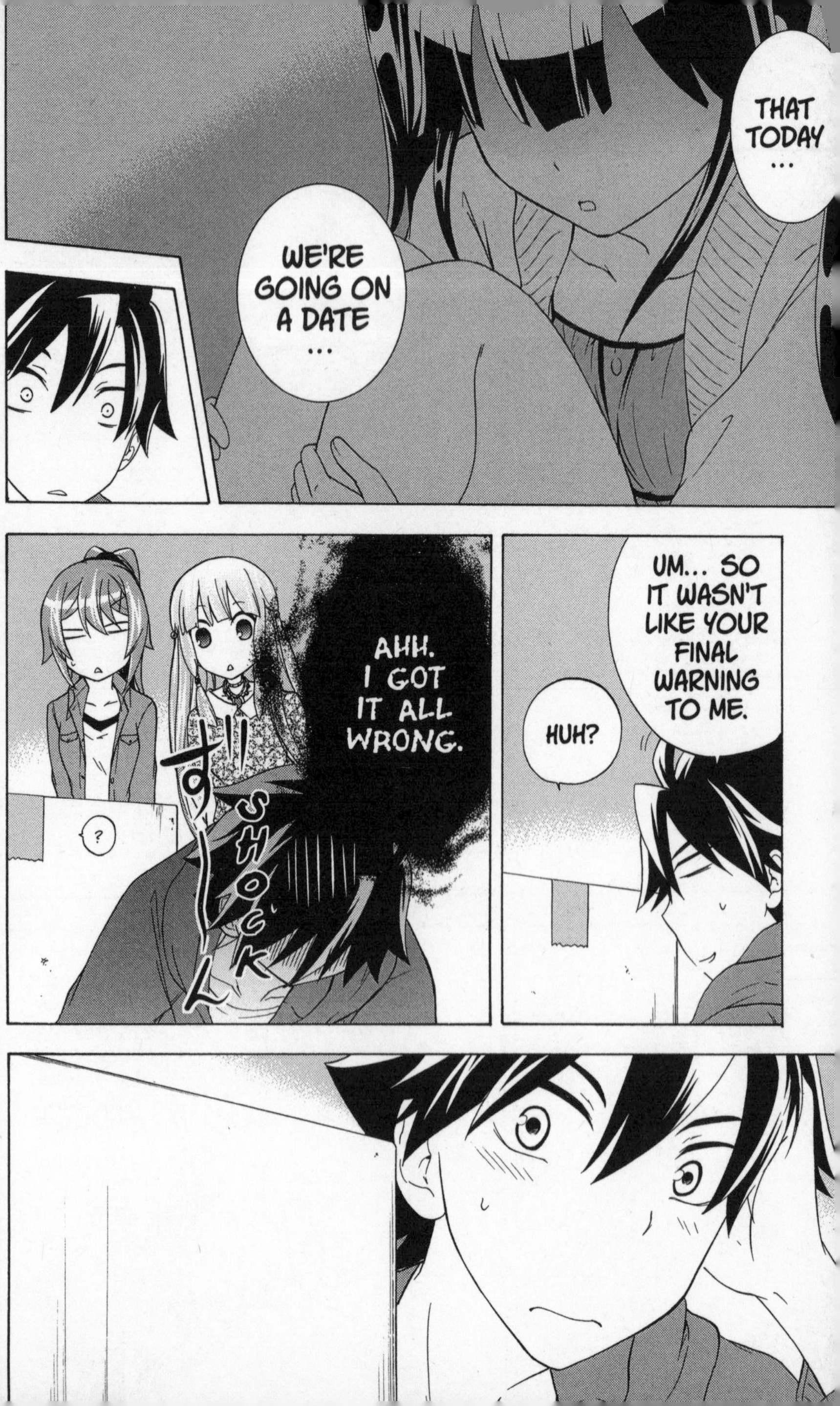
THAT TODAY...
WE'RE GOING ON A DATE...
UM... SO IT WASN'T LIKE YOUR FINAL WARNING TO ME.
HUH?
AHH. I GOT IT ALL WRONG.
?
SHOCK

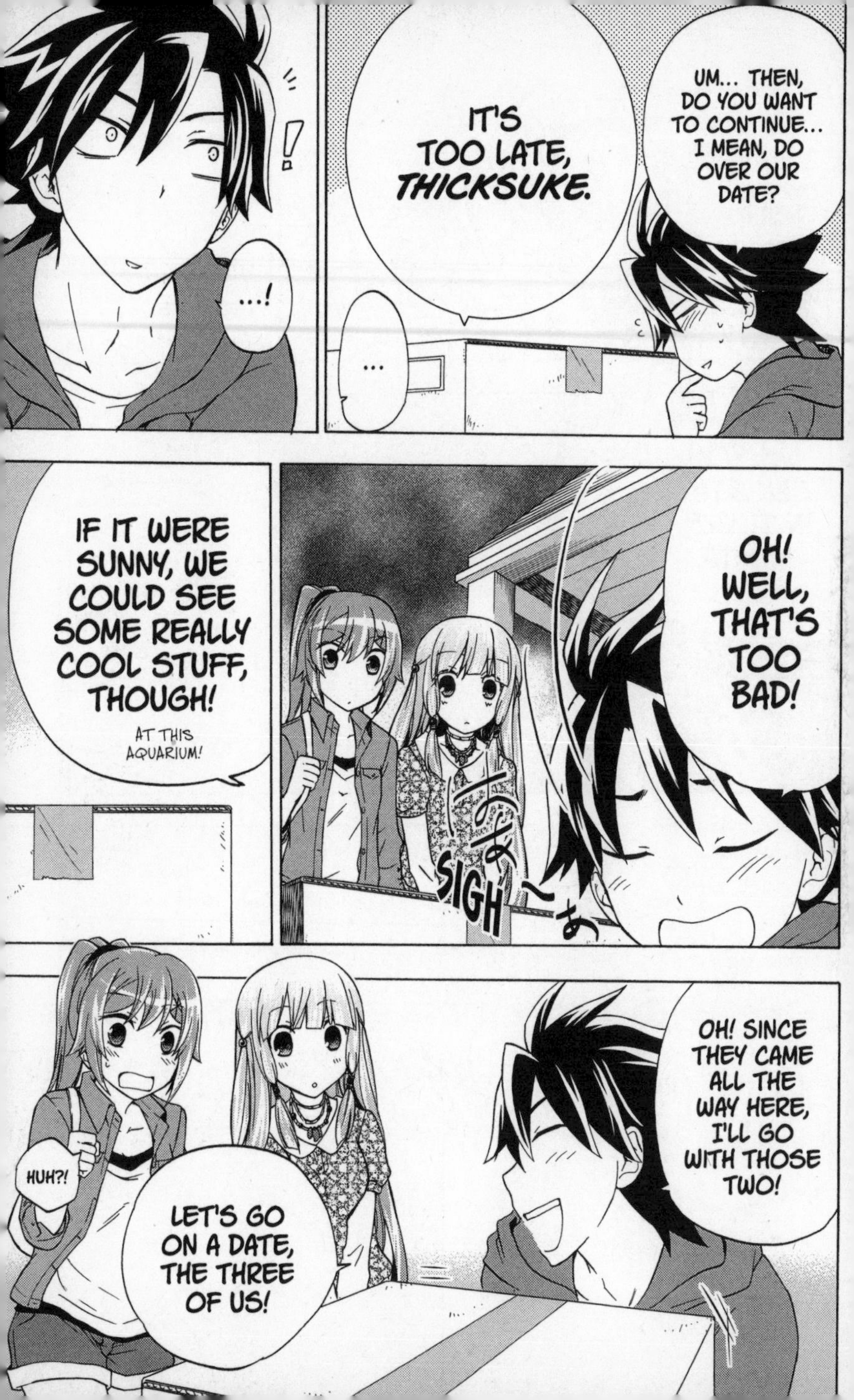
UM... THEN, DO YOU WANT TO CONTINUE... I MEAN, DO OVER OUR DATE?
IT'S TOO LATE, *THICKSUKE.*
...
!
...!
OH! WELL, THAT'S TOO BAD!
SIGH
IF IT WERE SUNNY, WE COULD SEE SOME REALLY COOL STUFF, THOUGH!
AT THIS AQUARIUM!
OH! SINCE THEY CAME ALL THE WAY HERE, I'LL GO WITH THOSE TWO!
LET'S GO ON A DATE, THE THREE OF US!
HUH?!

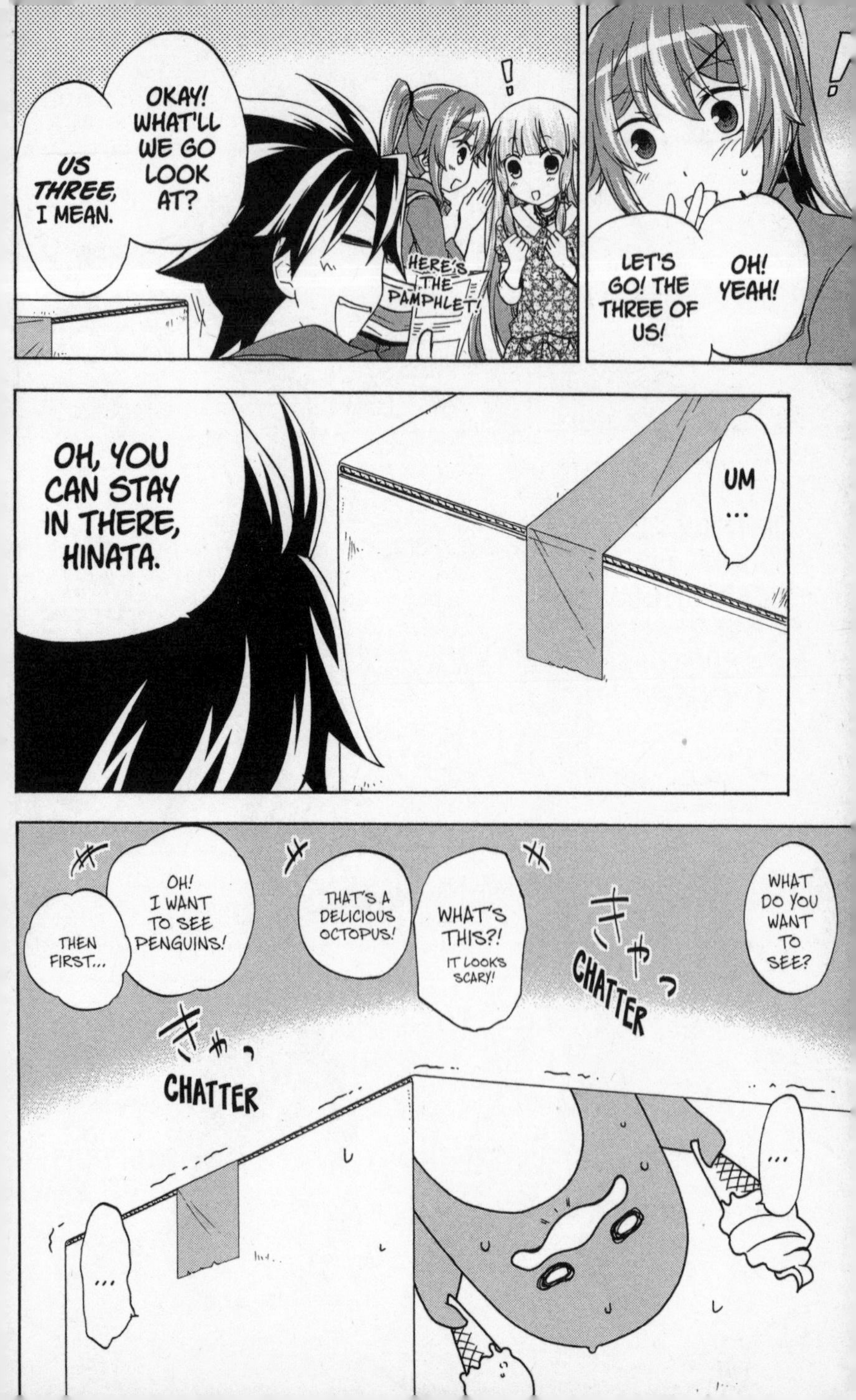
OH! YEAH!
LET'S GO! THE THREE OF US!
!
OKAY! WHAT'LL WE GO LOOK AT?
US THREE, I MEAN.
HERE'S THE PAMPHLET!
UM ...
OH, YOU CAN STAY IN THERE, HINATA.
WHAT DO YOU WANT TO SEE?
CHATTER
WHAT'S THIS?! IT LOOKS SCARY!
THAT'S A DELICIOUS OCTOPUS!
OH! I WANT TO SEE PENGUINS!
THEN FIRST...
CHATTER
...
...

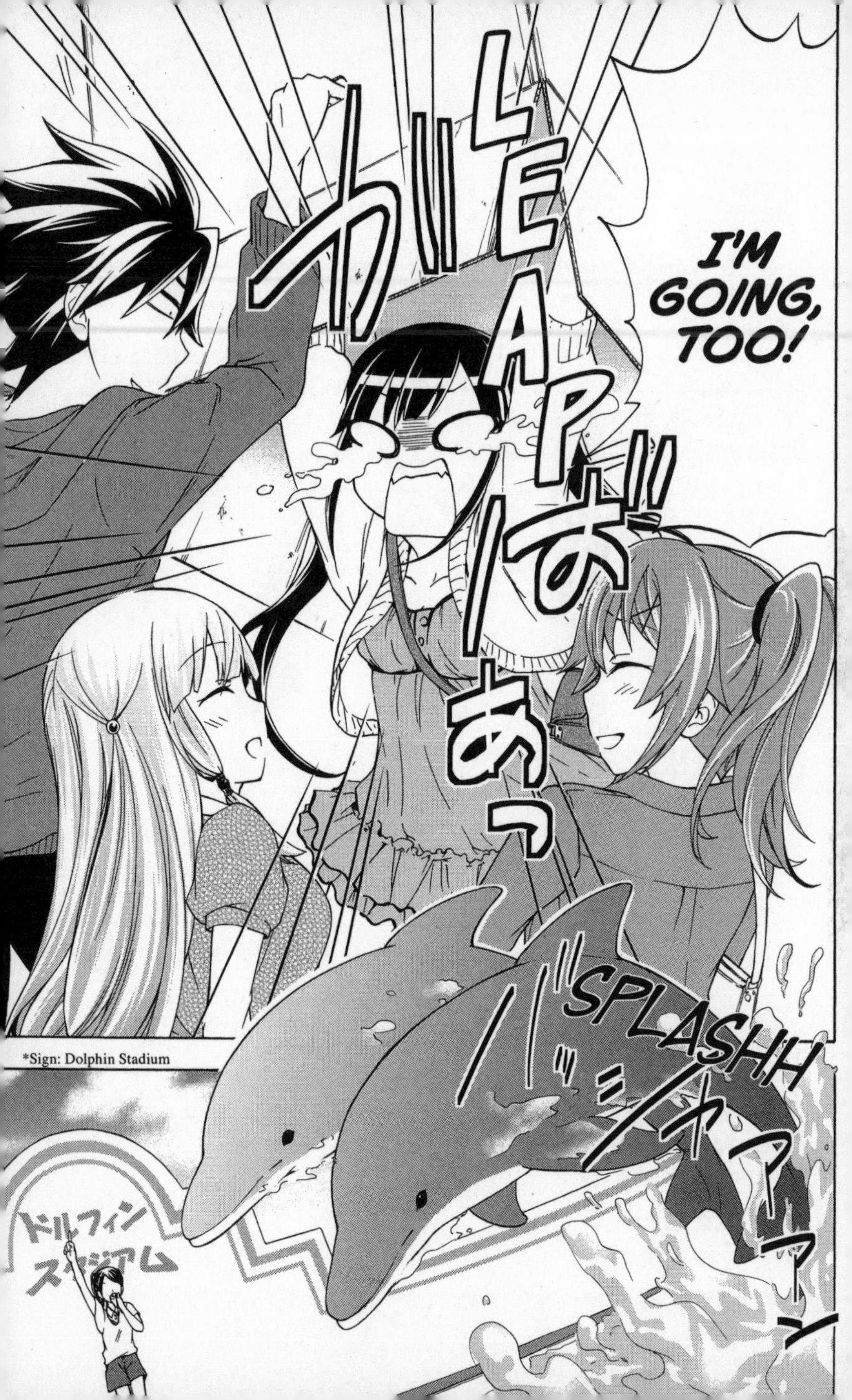
I'M GOING, TOO!
LEAP
*Sign: Dolphin Stadium
SPLASHH
ドルフィンスタジアム

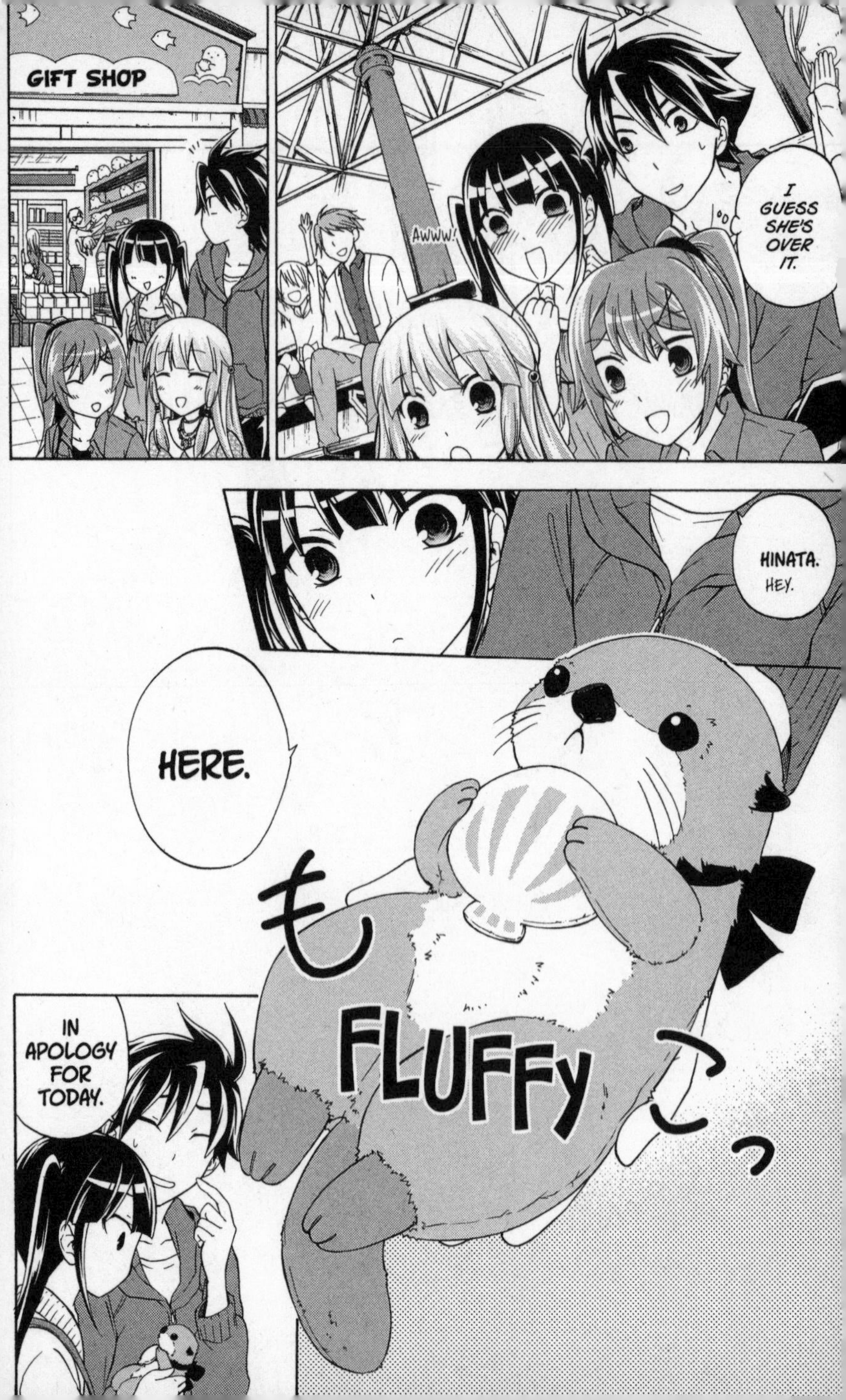
I GUESS SHE'S OVER IT.
AWWW!
GIFT SHOP
HINATA. HEY.
HERE.
も
FLUFFY
っ
IN APOLOGY FOR TODAY.

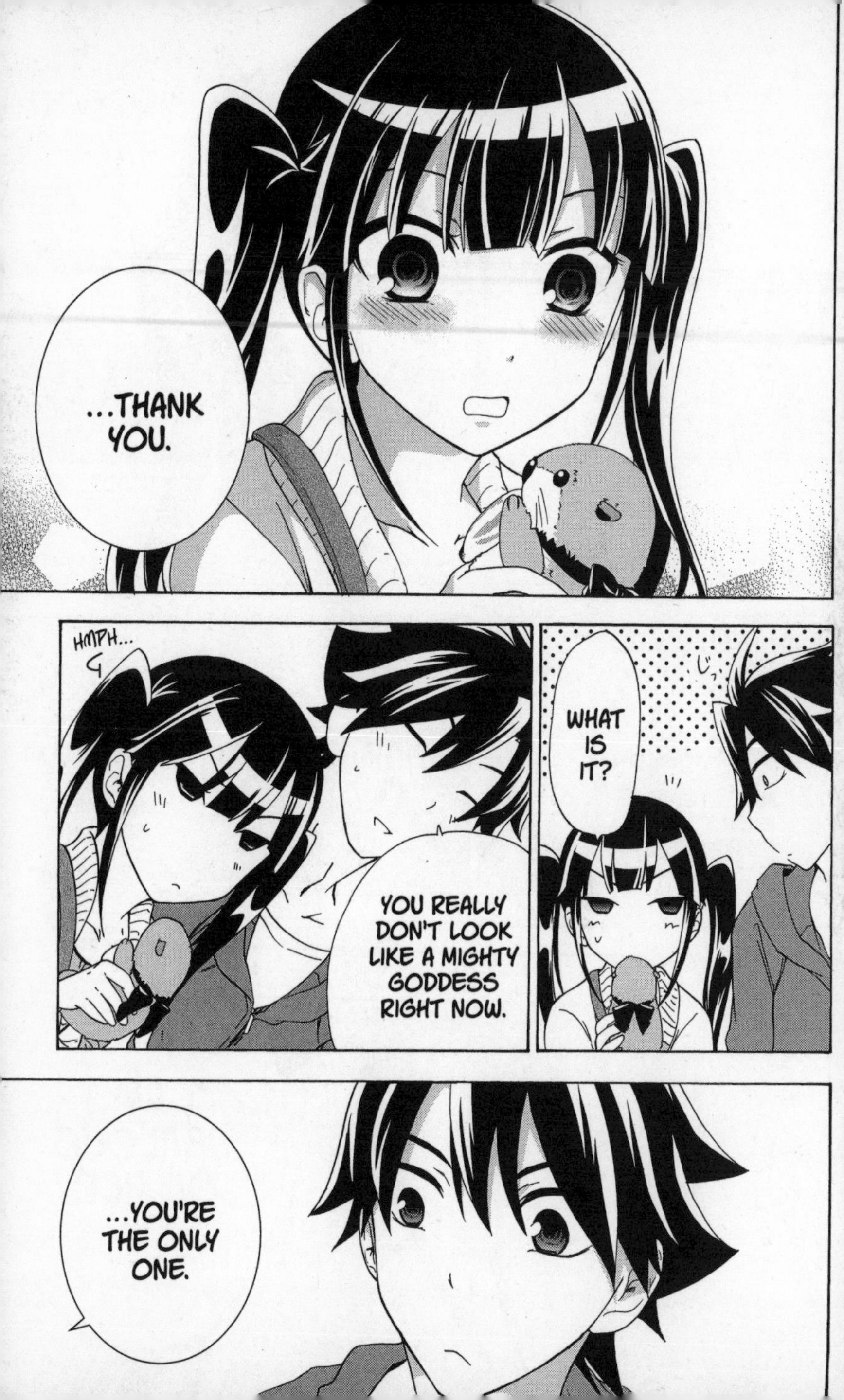
...THANK YOU.
WHAT IS IT?
じっ
HMPH...
YOU REALLY DON'T LOOK LIKE A MIGHTY GODDESS RIGHT NOW.
...YOU'RE THE ONLY ONE.

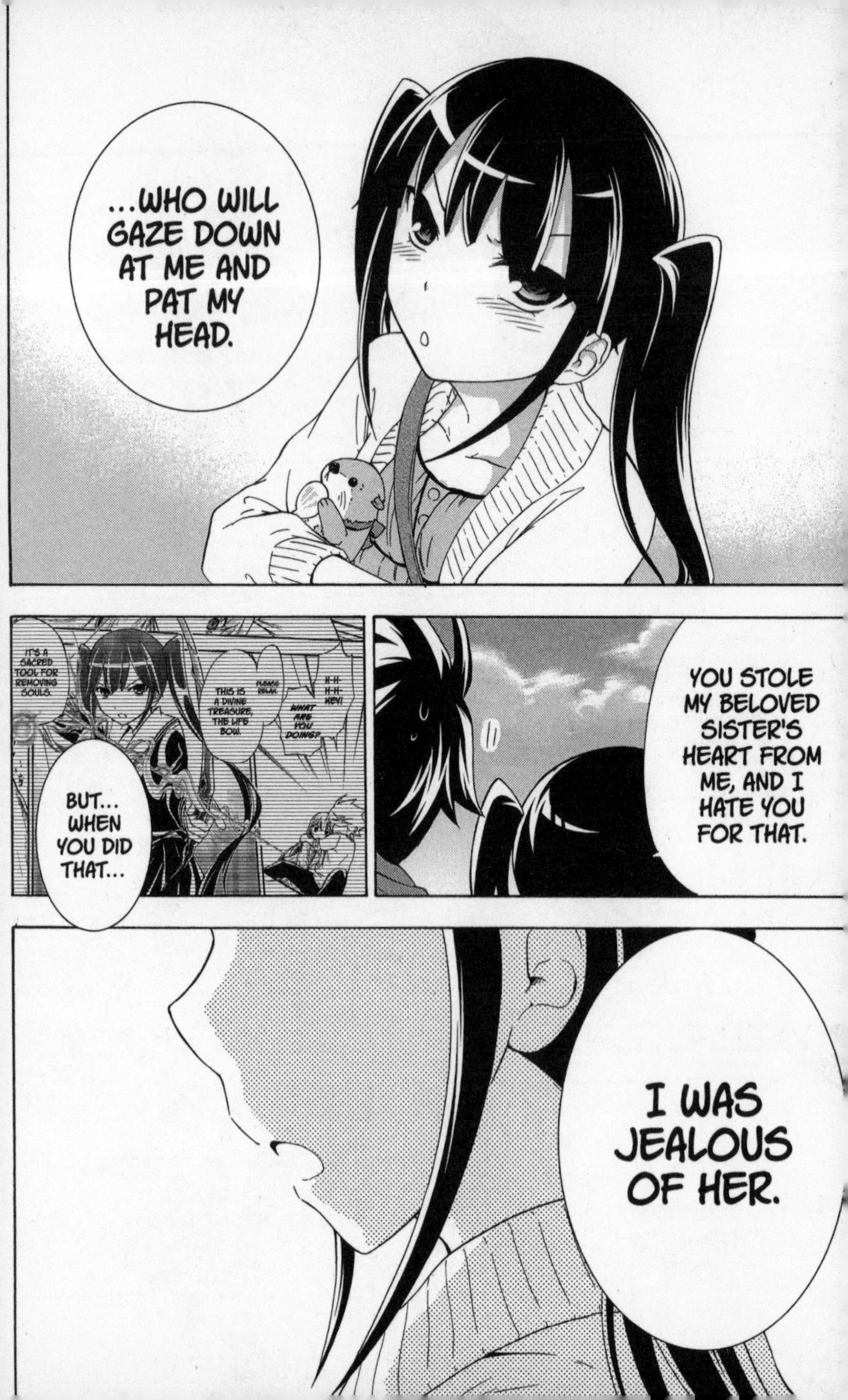
...WHO WILL GAZE DOWN AT ME AND PAT MY HEAD.
YOU STOLE MY BELOVED SISTER'S HEART FROM ME, AND I HATE YOU FOR THAT.
H-H-H-H-HEY!
WHAT ARE YOU DOING?
PLEASE RELAX.
THIS IS A DIVINE TREASURE, THE LIFE BOW.
IT'S A SACRED TOOL FOR REMOVING SOULS.
BUT... WHEN YOU DID THAT...
I WAS JEALOUS OF HER.

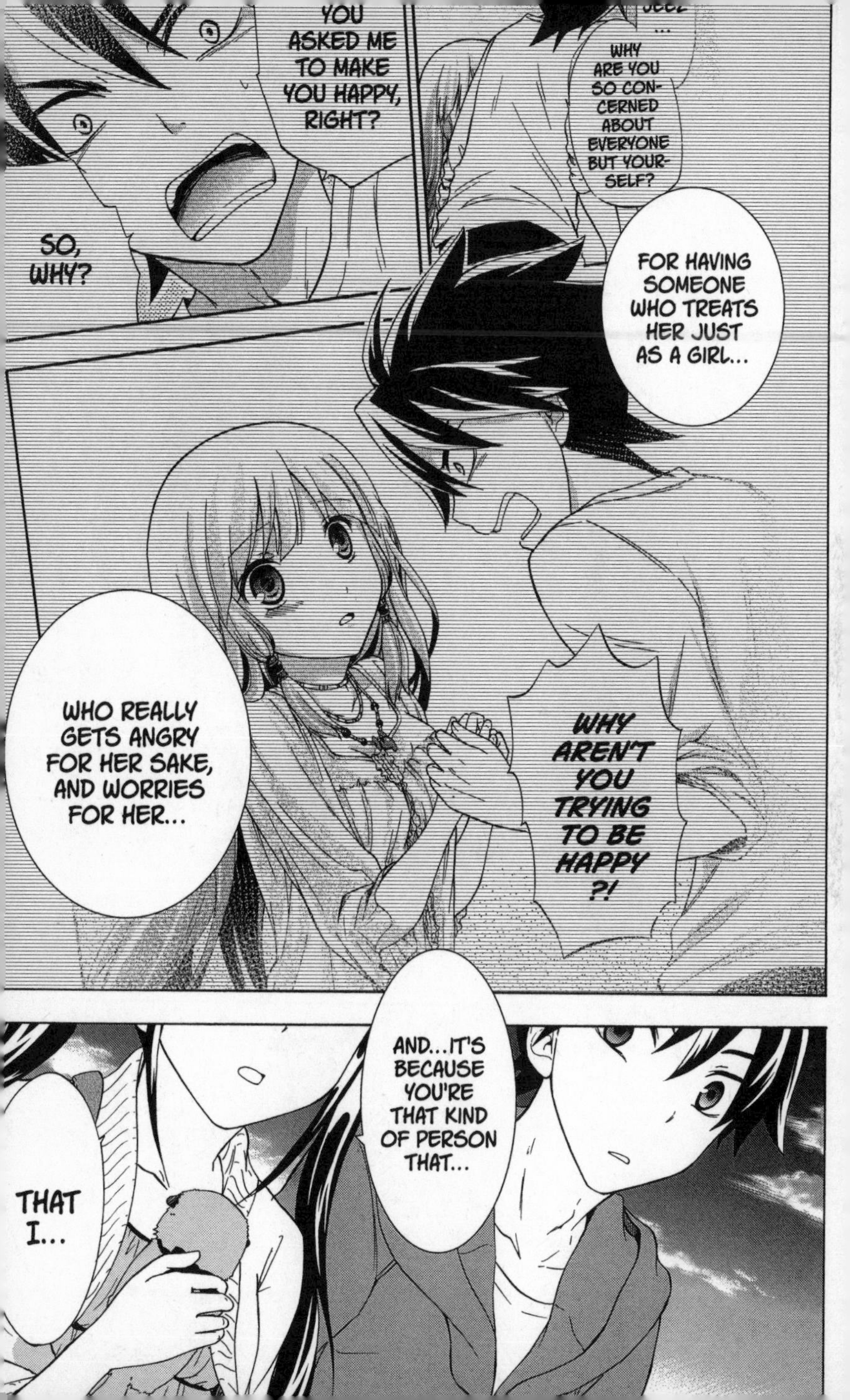
WHY ARE YOU SO CON-CERNED ABOUT EVERYONE BUT YOUR-SELF?
YOU ASKED ME TO MAKE YOU HAPPY, RIGHT?
SO, WHY?
WHY AREN'T YOU TRYING TO BE HAPPY?!
FOR HAVING SOMEONE WHO TREATS HER JUST AS A GIRL...
WHO REALLY GETS ANGRY FOR HER SAKE, AND WORRIES FOR HER...
AND...IT'S BECAUSE YOU'RE THAT KIND OF PERSON THAT...
THAT I...

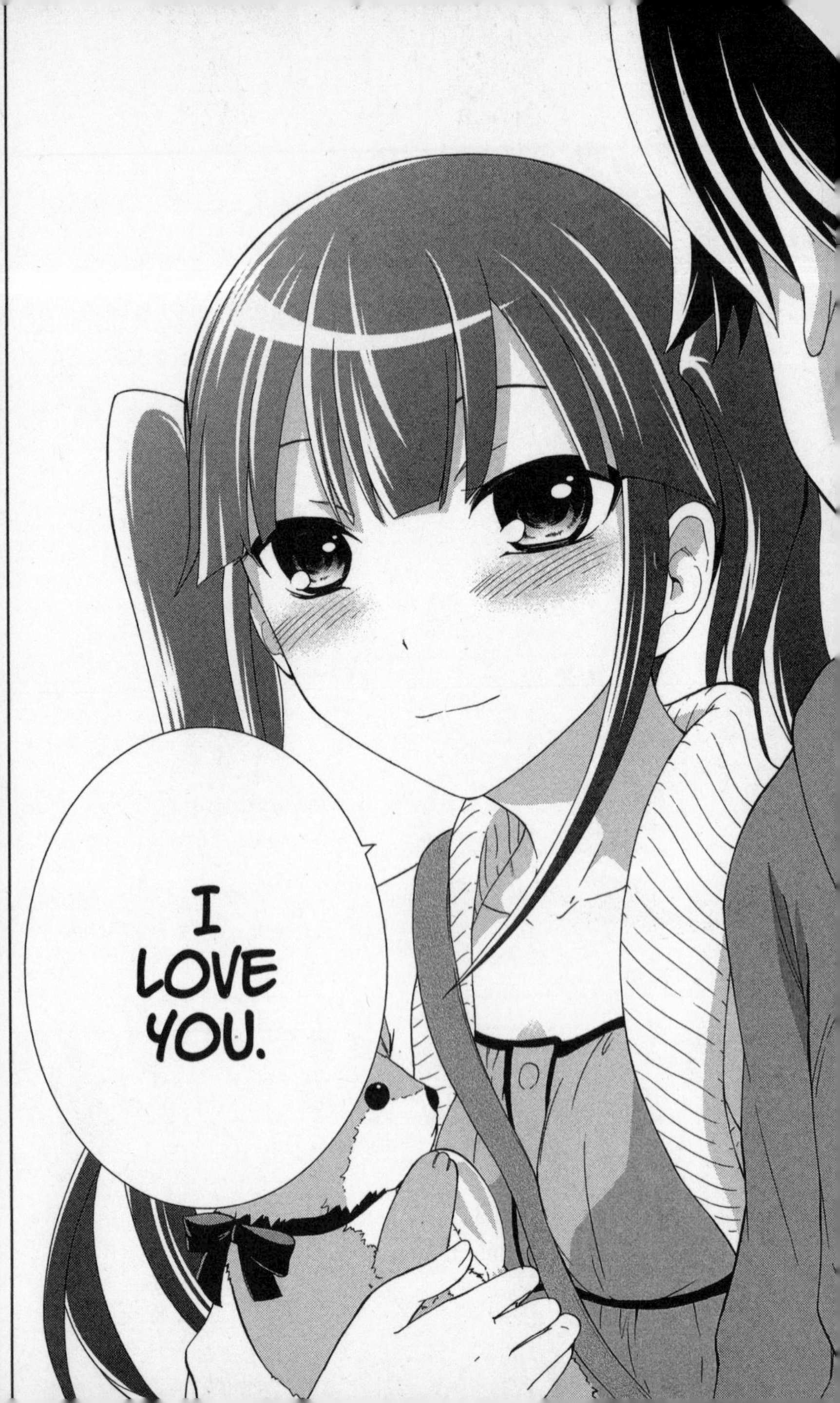
I LOVE YOU.

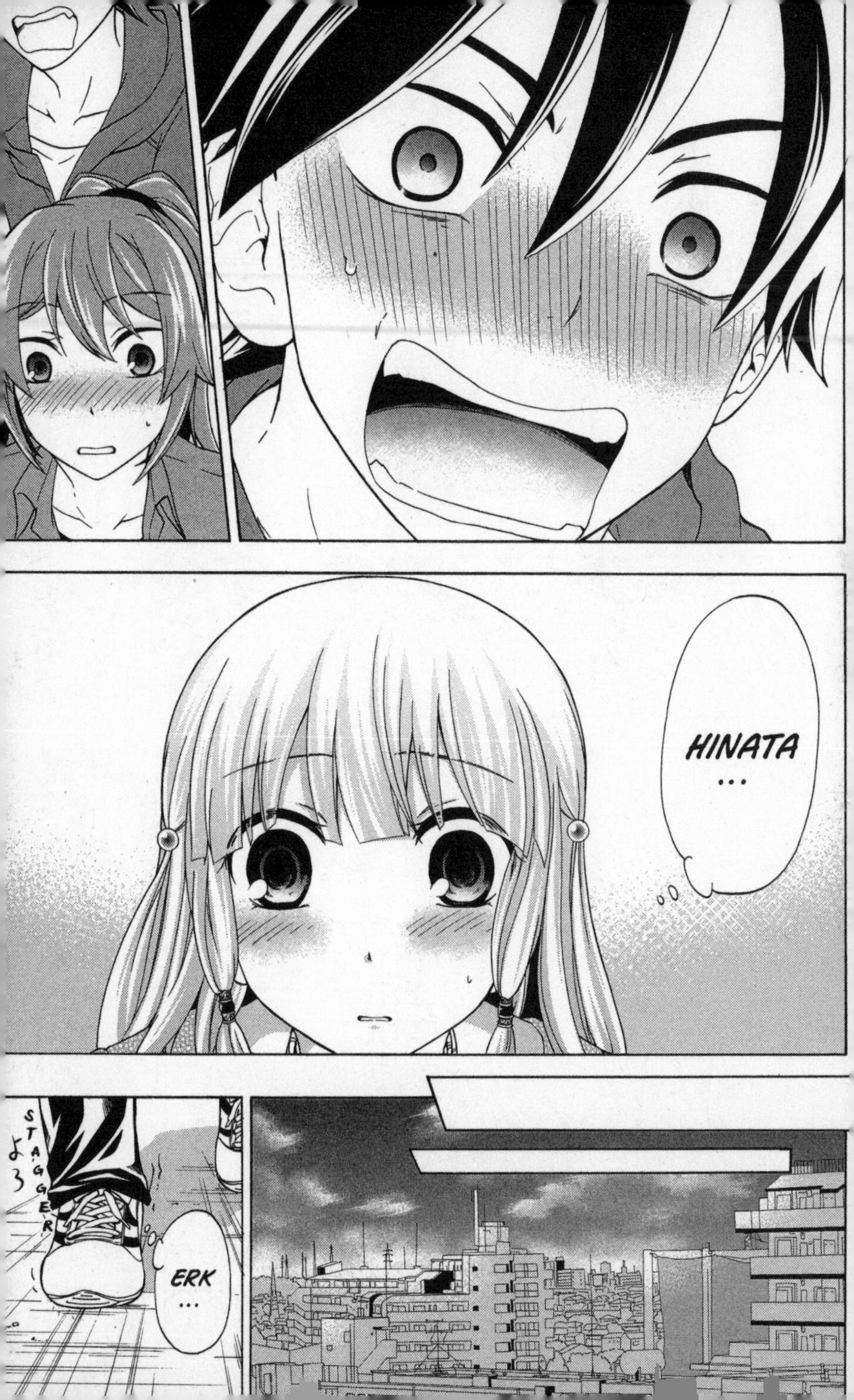
HINATA
...
STAGGER
よろ
ERK
...

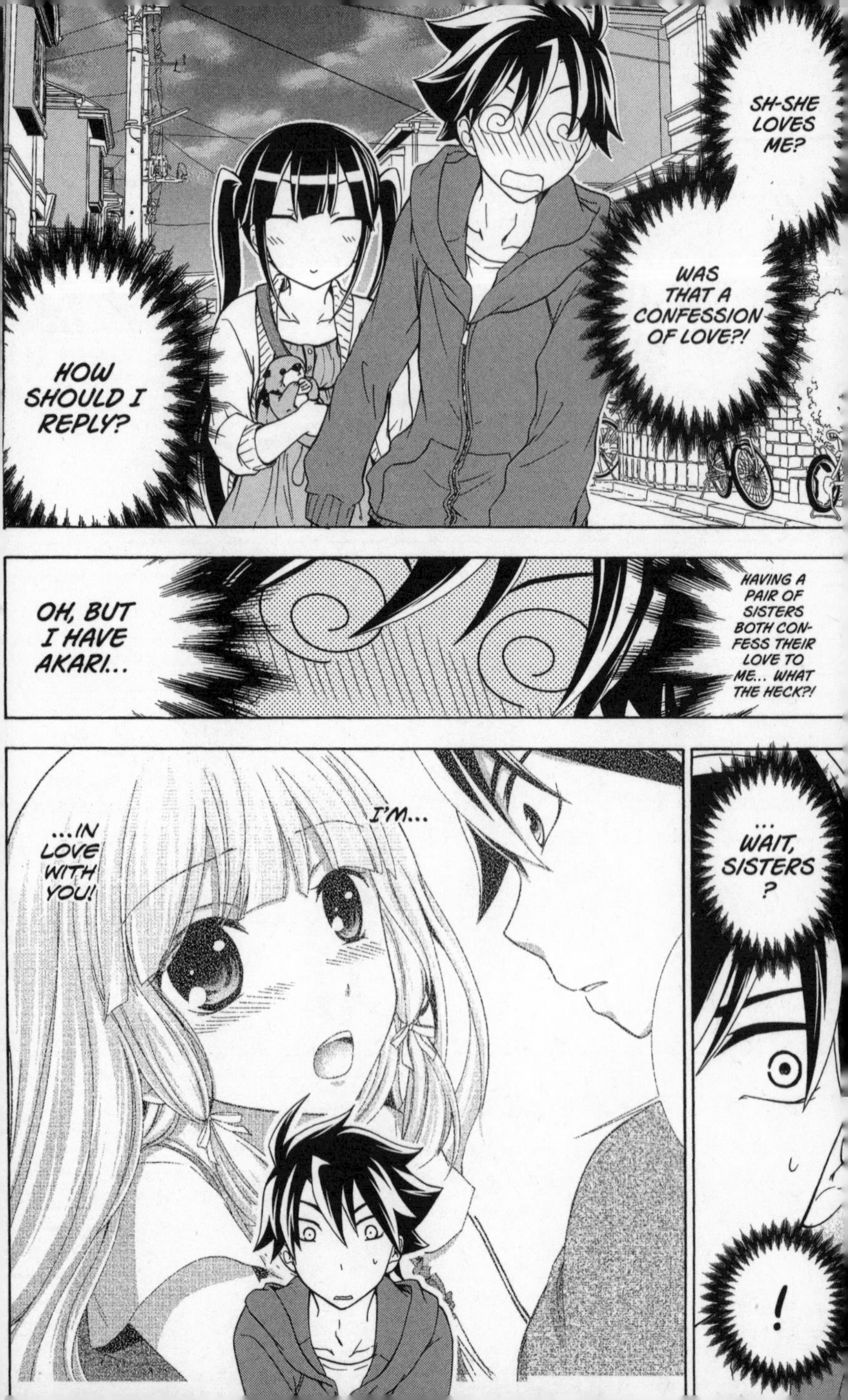
SH-SHE LOVES ME?
WAS THAT A CONFESSION OF LOVE?!
HOW SHOULD I REPLY?
HAVING A PAIR OF SISTERS BOTH CONFESS THEIR LOVE TO ME... WHAT THE HECK?!
OH, BUT I HAVE AKARI...
...WAIT, SISTERS?
!
I'M...
...IN LOVE WITH YOU!

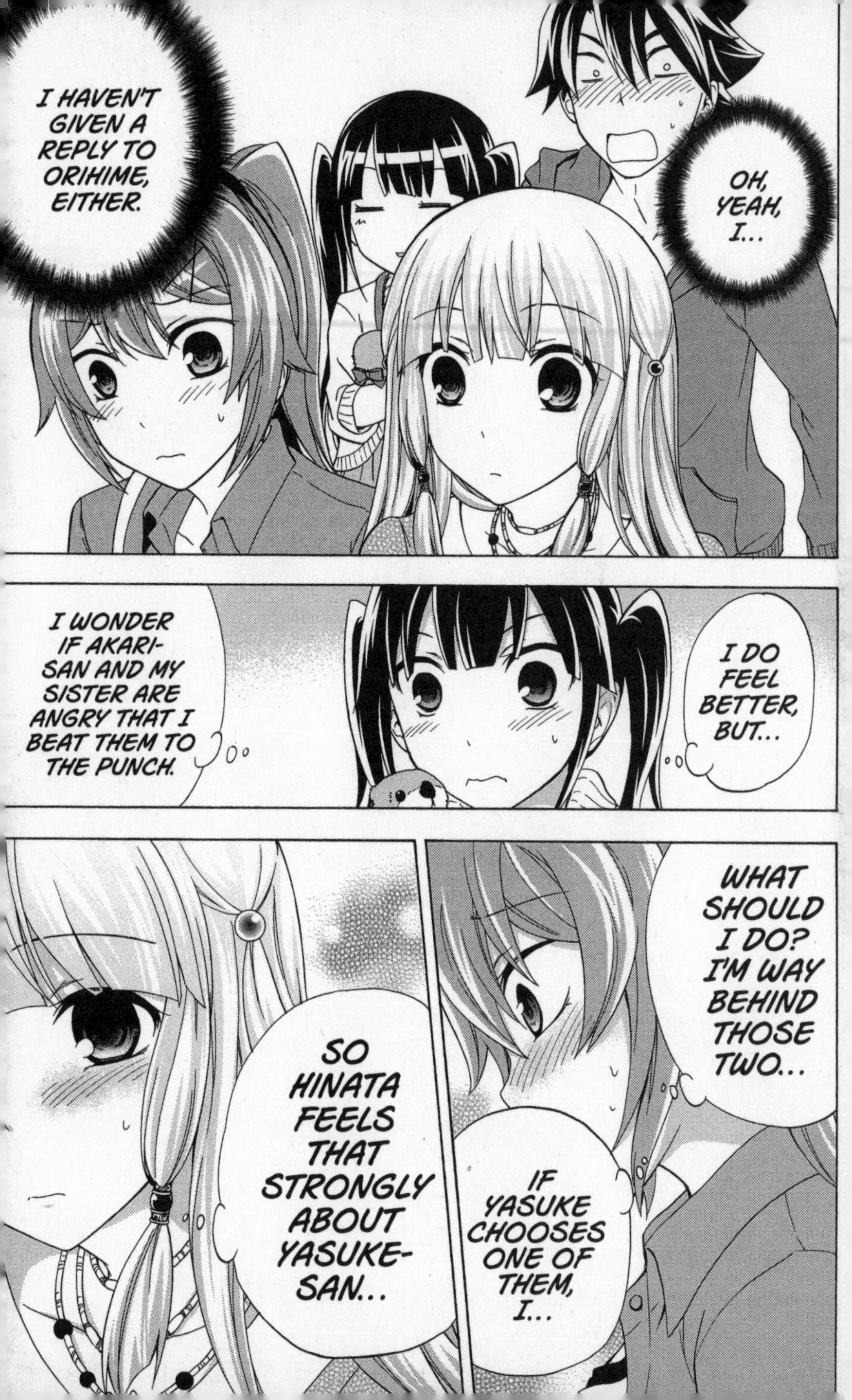
OH, YEAH, I...
I HAVEN'T GIVEN A REPLY TO ORIHIME, EITHER.
I DO FEEL BETTER, BUT...
I WONDER IF AKARI-SAN AND MY SISTER ARE ANGRY THAT I BEAT THEM TO THE PUNCH.
WHAT SHOULD I DO? I'M WAY BEHIND THOSE TWO...
IF YASUKE CHOOSES ONE OF THEM, I...
SO HINATA FEELS THAT STRONGLY ABOUT YASUKE-SAN...

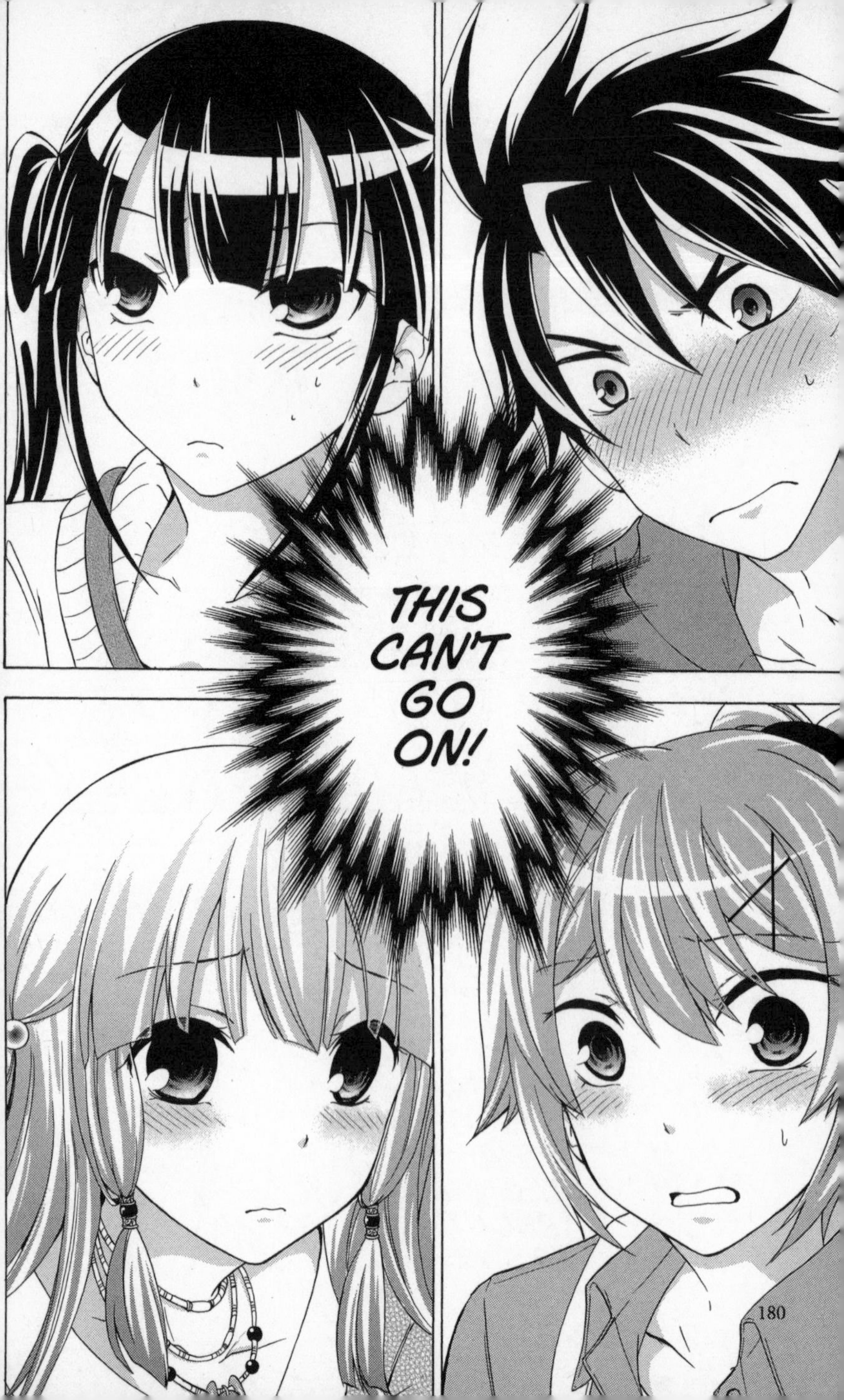
THIS CAN'T GO ON!

Maga-Tsuki

Presented by Hoshino Taguchi

PEOPLE SOMETIMES TALK ABOUT GIRLS RUNNING ROUGHSHOD OVER THEM, RIGHT?
THAT
HUH? ER...
DOES MOM RUN ROUGH-SHOD OVER YOU, DAD?
...YEAH.
CONTIN-MEWED IN VOLUME 4!

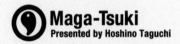

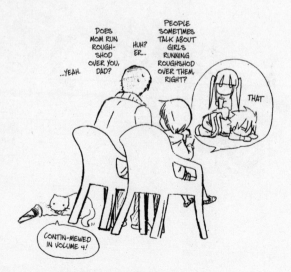

まがつき

Maga-Tsuki

Presented by Hoshino Taguchi

Maga-Tsuki Taguchi Hoshino

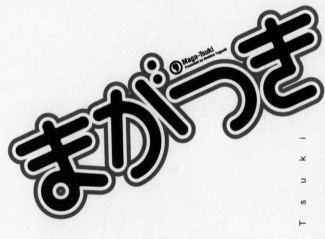

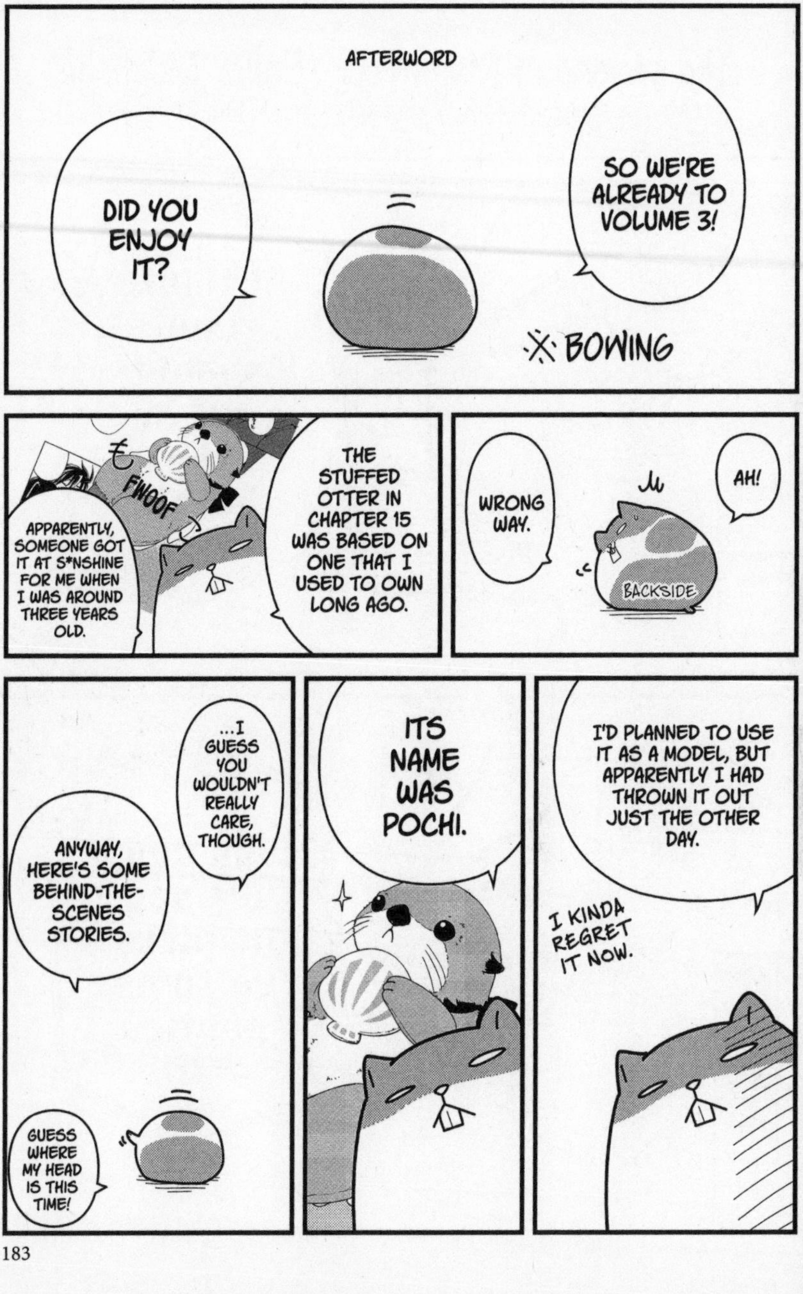
AFTERWORD
SO WE'RE ALREADY TO VOLUME 3!
※BOWING
DID YOU ENJOY IT?
AH!
WRONG WAY.
BACKSIDE
THE STUFFED OTTER IN CHAPTER 15 WAS BASED ON ONE THAT I USED TO OWN LONG AGO.
FWOOF
APPARENTLY, SOMEONE GOT IT AT S*NSHINE FOR ME WHEN I WAS AROUND THREE YEARS OLD.
I'D PLANNED TO USE IT AS A MODEL, BUT APPARENTLY I HAD THROWN IT OUT JUST THE OTHER DAY.
I KINDA REGRET IT NOW.
ITS NAME WAS POCHI.
...I GUESS YOU WOULDN'T REALLY CARE, THOUGH.
ANYWAY, HERE'S SOME BEHIND-THE-SCENES STORIES.
GUESS WHERE MY HEAD IS THIS TIME!

The Making of Maga-Tsuki: Editor Meetings

*Editor Meetings: Talking to an assigned editor about the upcoming chapter before it's drawn.

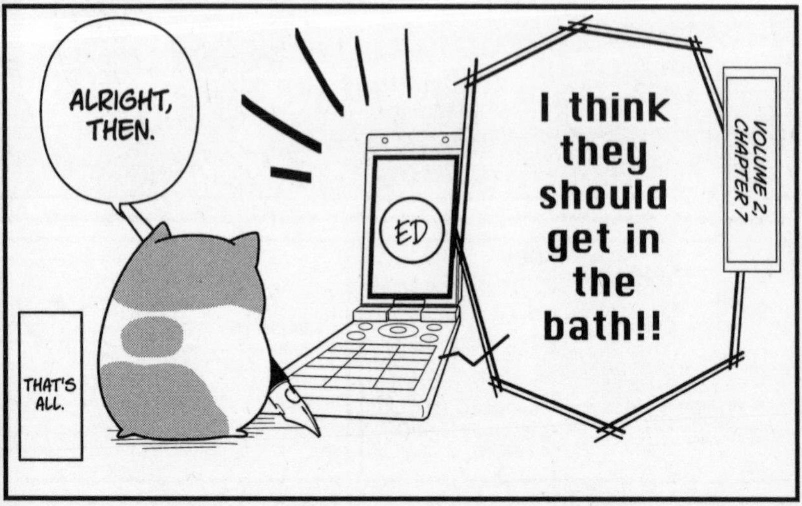
VOLUME 2, CHAPTER 7
I think they should get in the bath!!
ED
ALRIGHT, THEN.
THAT'S ALL.

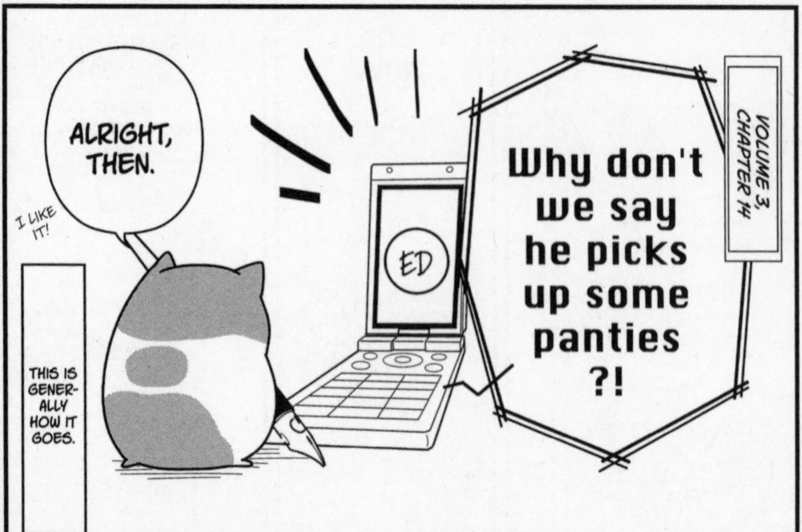
VOLUME 3, CHAPTER 14
Why don't we say he picks up some panties?!
ED
ALRIGHT, THEN.
I LIKE IT!
THIS IS GENERALLY HOW IT GOES.

MISTER SHAKY, CLASS 1-A'S TEACHER! CHAPTER 2

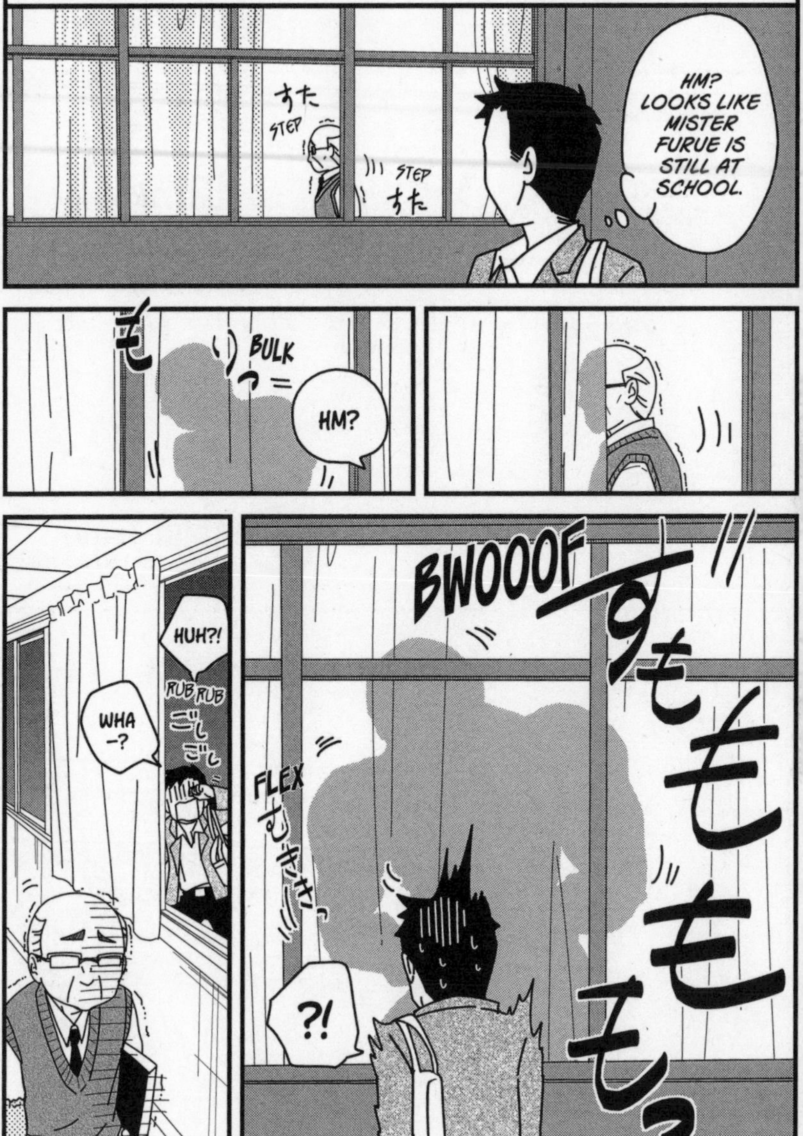

HM? LOOKS LIKE MISTER FURUE IS STILL AT SCHOOL.
STEP すた
すた STEP
も BULK つ
HM?
BWOOOF すもももも
FLEX むききっ
?!
HUH?!
RUB RUB ごしごし
WHA-?

Maga-Tsuki
Presented by Hoshino Taguchi

...THERE ARE STILL SOME BONUSES LEFT...

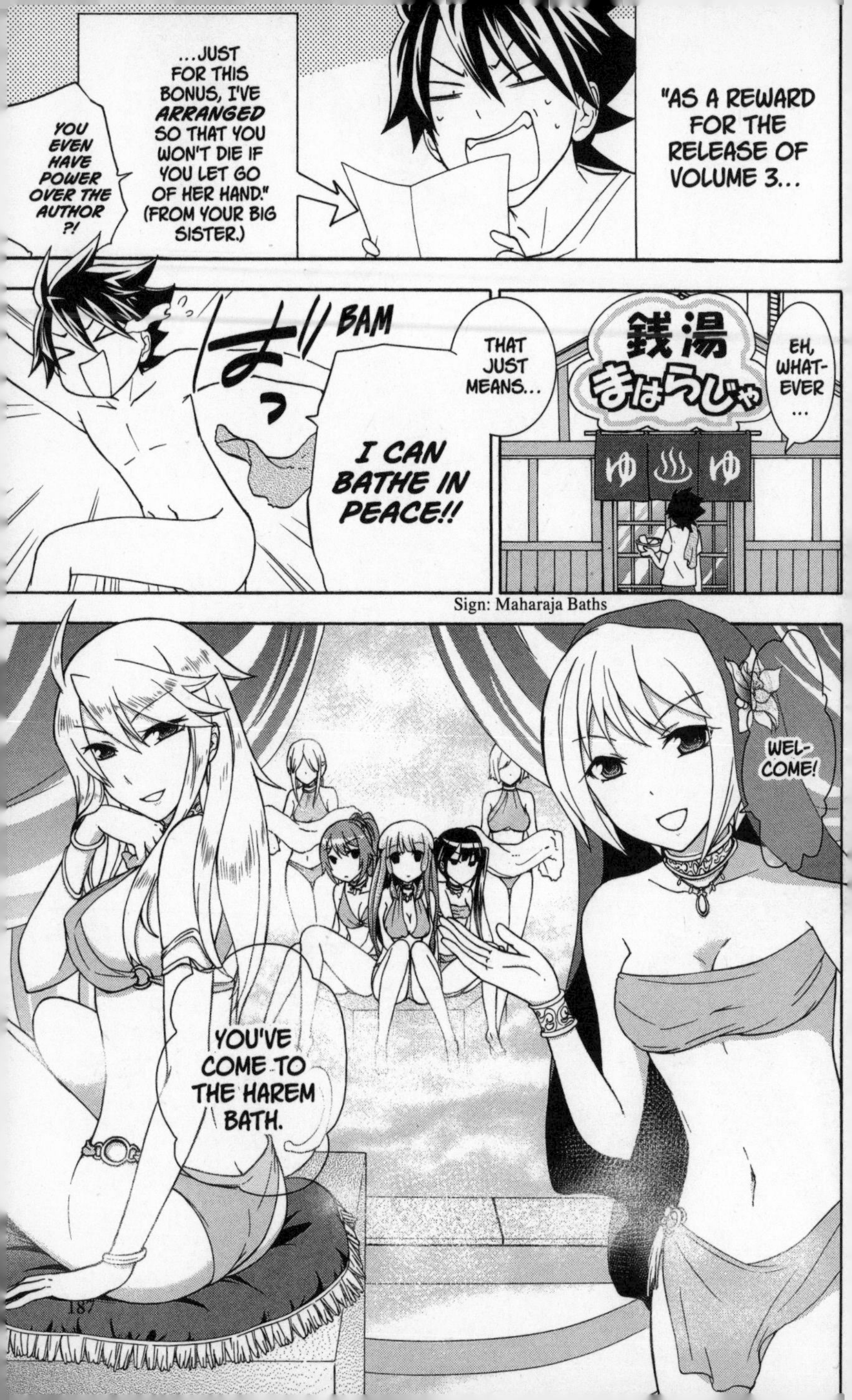
"AS A REWARD FOR THE RELEASE OF VOLUME 3...
...JUST FOR THIS BONUS, I'VE ARRANGED SO THAT YOU WON'T DIE IF YOU LET GO OF HER HAND." (FROM YOUR BIG SISTER.)
YOU EVEN HAVE POWER OVER THE AUTHOR ?!
銭湯
まはらじゃ
ゆ
ゆ
EH, WHATEVER ...
THAT JUST MEANS...
BAM
I CAN BATHE IN PEACE!!
WEL-COME!
YOU'VE COME TO THE HAREM BATH.

Sign: Maharaja Baths

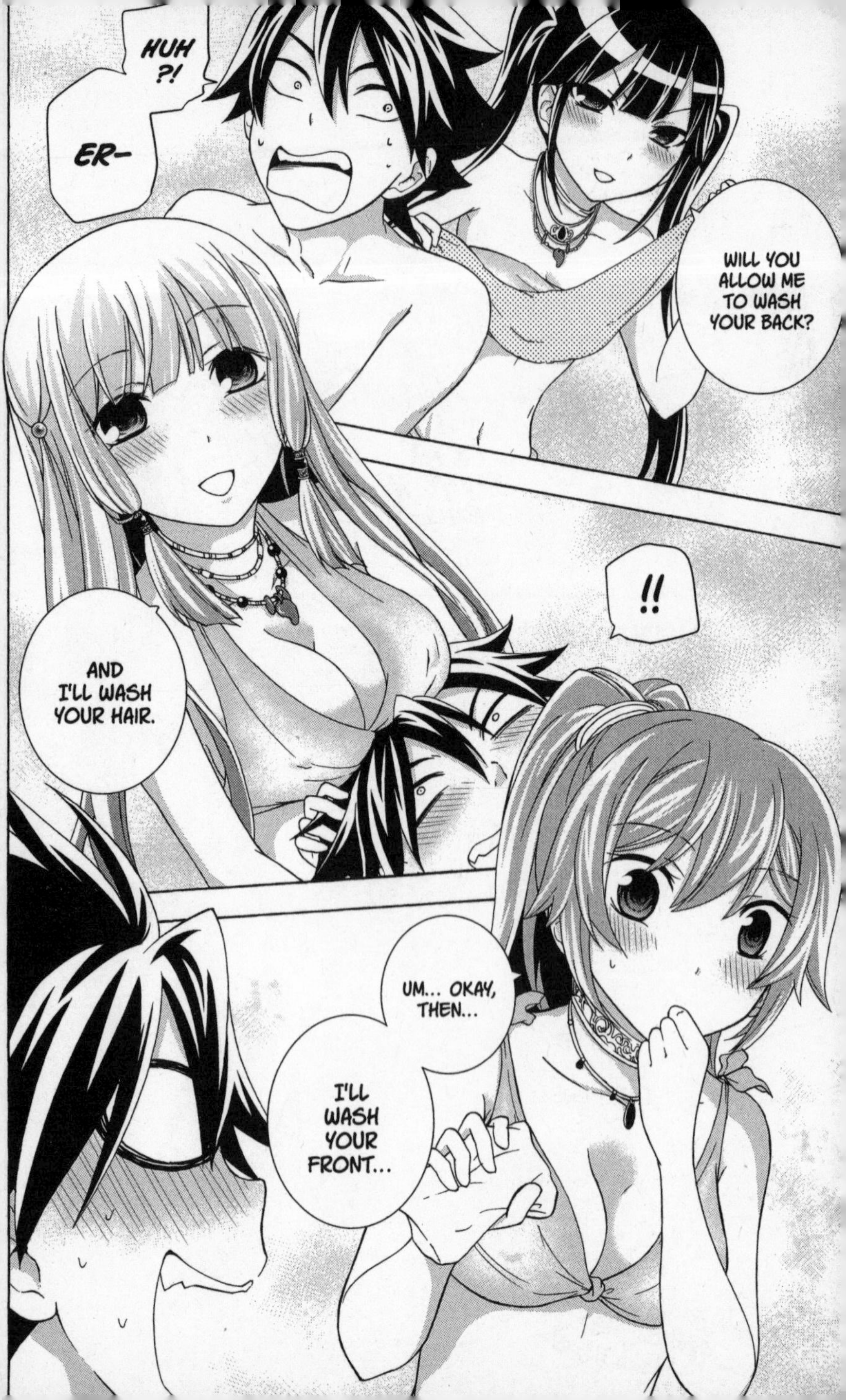
WILL YOU ALLOW ME TO WASH YOUR BACK?
HUH ?!
ER-
!!
AND I'LL WASH YOUR HAIR.
UM... OKAY, THEN...
I'LL WASH YOUR FRONT...

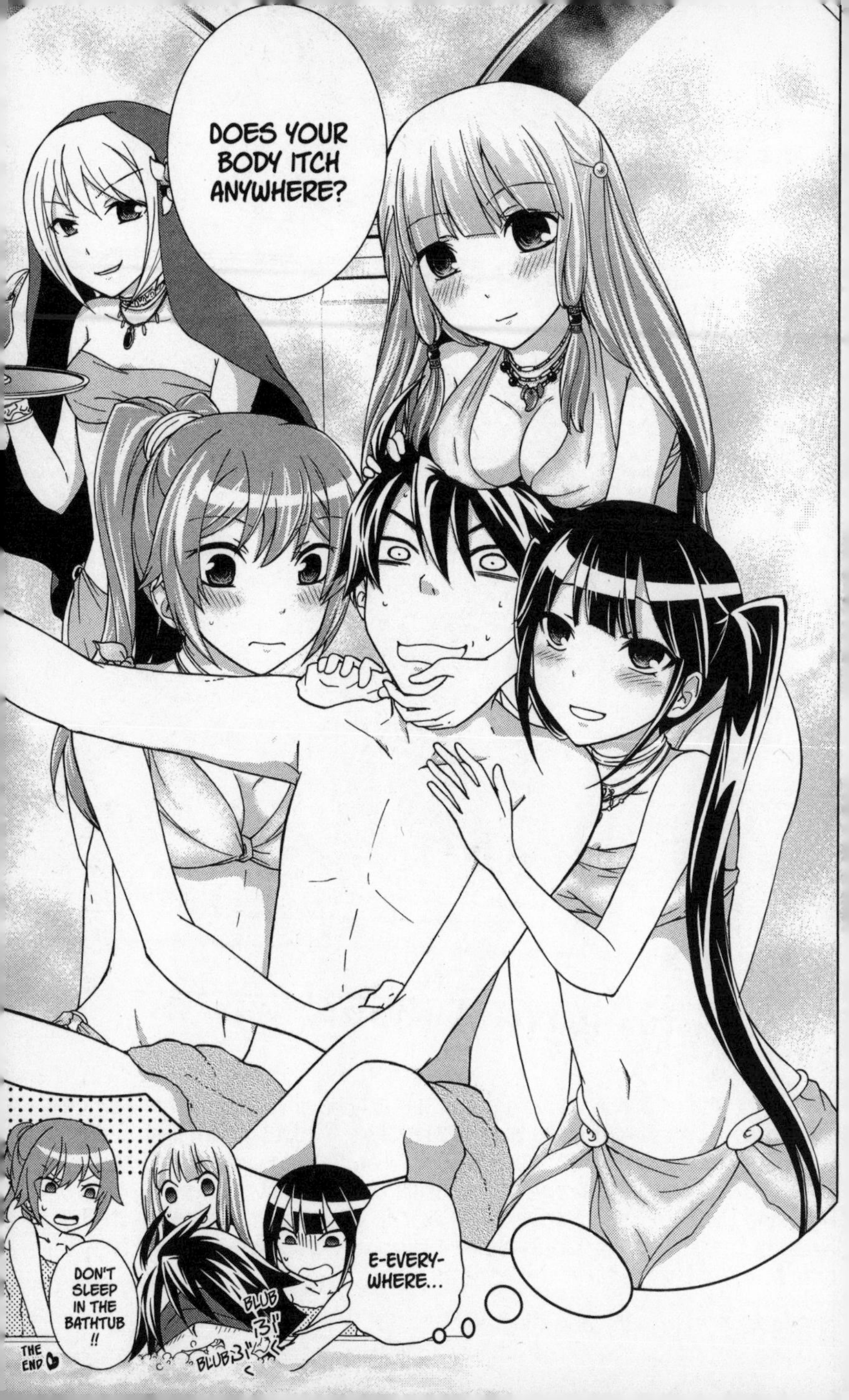
DOES YOUR BODY ITCH ANYWHERE?
E-EVERY-WHERE...
BLUB
BLUB
DON'T SLEEP IN THE BATHTUB !!
THE END

SWAPPED WITH A KISS?!

Class troublemaker Ryu Yamada is already having a bad day when he stumbles down a staircase along with star student Urara Shiraishi. When he wakes up, he realizes they have switched bodies—and that Ryu has the power to trade places with anyone just by kissing them! Ryu and Urara take full advantage of the situation to improve their lives, but with such an oddly amazing power, just how long will they be able to keep their secret under wraps?

Available now in print and digitally!

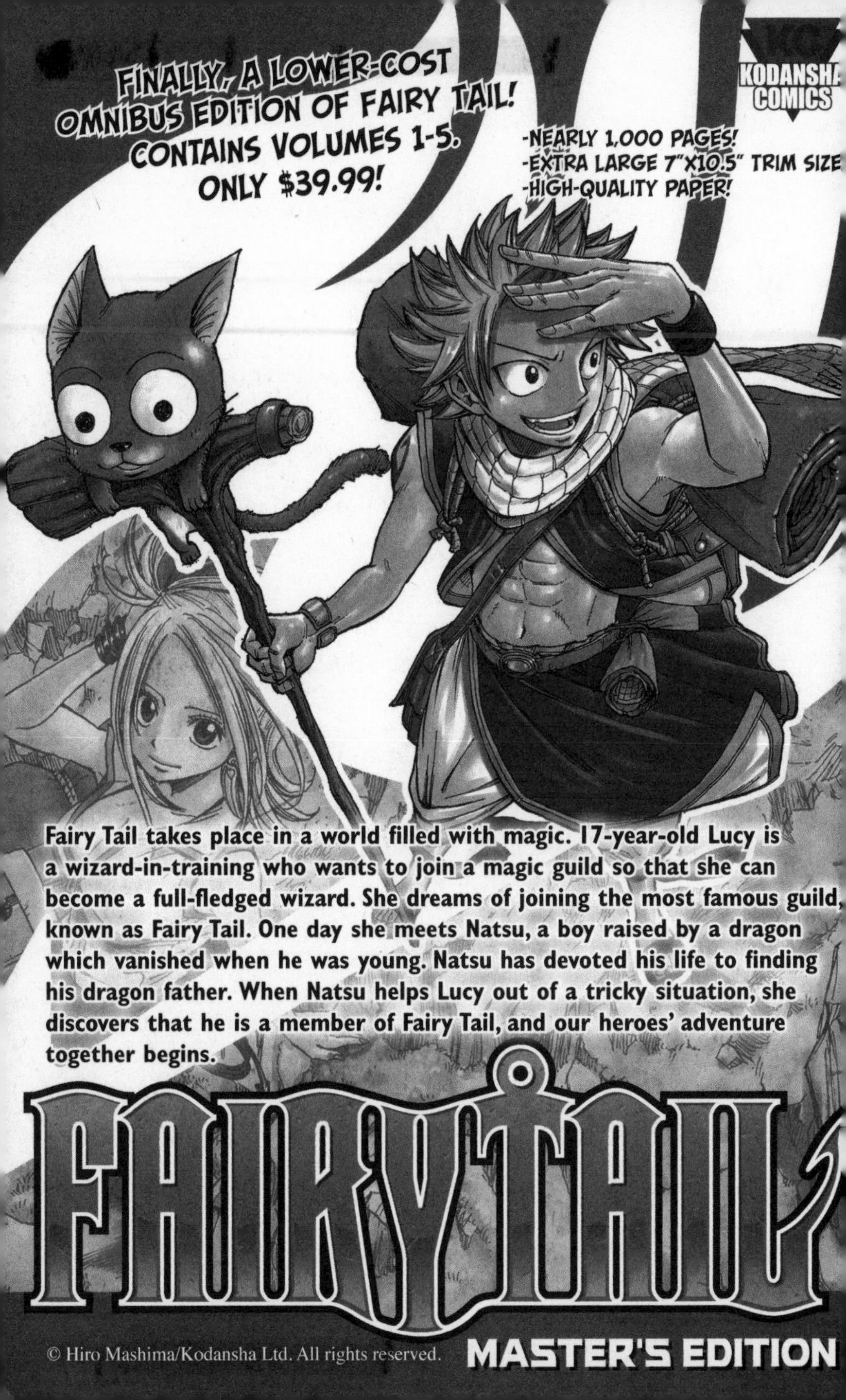
KODANSHA COMICS
FINALLY, A LOWER-COST OMNIBUS EDITION OF FAIRY TAIL! CONTAINS VOLUMES 1-5. ONLY $39.99!
-NEARLY 1,000 PAGES!
-EXTRA LARGE 7"X10.5" TRIM SIZE
-HIGH-QUALITY PAPER!
Fairy Tail takes place in a world filled with magic. 17-year-old Lucy is a wizard-in-training who wants to join a magic guild so that she can become a full-fledged wizard. She dreams of joining the most famous guild, known as Fairy Tail. One day she meets Natsu, a boy raised by a dragon which vanished when he was young. Natsu has devoted his life to finding his dragon father. When Natsu helps Lucy out of a tricky situation, she discovers that he is a member of Fairy Tail, and our heroes' adventure together begins.
FAIRY TAIL
MASTER'S EDITION
© Hiro Mashima/Kodansha Ltd. All rights reserved.

A Kodansha Comics Trade Paperback Original.

Magatsuki volume 3 copyright © 2012 Hoshino Taguchi
English translation copyright © 2016 Hoshino Taguchi

All rights reserved.

Published in the United States by Kodansha Comics, an imprint of Kodansha USA Publishing, LLC, New York.

Publication rights for this English edition arranged through Kodansha Ltd., Tokyo.

First published in Japan in 2012 by Kodansha Ltd., Tokyo.

ISBN 978-1-63236-241-4

Printed in the United States of America.

www.kodanshacomics.com

9 8 7 6 5 4 3 2 1

Translation: Ko Ransom
Lettering: AndWorld Design
Editing: Lauren Scanlan
Kodansha Comics edition cover design: Phil Balsman